Cambridge Lower Secondary

Maths

STAGE 7: STUDENT'S BOOK

Michele Conway, Sarah Sharratt and Deborah McCarthy
Series Editors: Michele Conway and Sarah Sharratt

Collins

William Collins' dream of knowledge for all began with the publication of his first book in 1819.

A self-educated mill worker, he not only enriched millions of lives, but also founded a flourishing publishing house. Today, staying true to this spirit, Collins books are packed with inspiration, innovation and practical expertise. They place you at the centre of a world of possibility and give you exactly what you need to explore it.

Collins. Freedom to teach.

Published by Collins
An imprint of HarperCollins*Publishers*
The News Building
1 London Bridge Street
London
SE1 9GF

Browse the complete Collins catalogue at
www.collins.co.uk

© HarperCollins*Publishers* Limited 2018

10 9 8 7 6 5 4 3 2

ISBN 978-0-00-821349-7

All rights reserved. No part of this publication may be reproduced, stored in a retrieval system, or transmitted in any form by any means, electronic, mechanical, photocopying, recording or otherwise, without the prior written permission of the Publisher or a licence permitting restricted copying in the United Kingdom issued by the Copyright Licensing Agency Ltd., Barnard's Inn, 86 Fetter Lane, London, EC4A 1EN.

MIX
Paper from responsible sources
FSC
www.fsc.org
FSC C007454

This book is produced from independently certified FSC paper to ensure responsible forest management.

For more information visit:
www.harpercollins.co.uk/green

British Library Cataloguing in Publication Data
A catalogue record for this publication is available from the British Library.

Authors: Michele Conway, Sarah Sharratt and Deborah McCarthy
Series editors: Michele Conway and Sarah Sharratt
Contributors: Matt Nixon and Gill Hewlett
Advisors: Caroline Fawcus and Steve Lomax
Publisher: Celia Wigley
Commissioning editor: Karen Jamieson
In-house project editor: Amanda Redstone/Isabelle Sinclair
Editorial manager: Wendy Alderton
Project manager: Maheswari Pon Saravanan at Jouve
Copyeditor: Alison Bewsher
Proofreaders: Tim Jackson and Anna Cox
Answer checker: Steven Matchett
Cover designer: Gordon MacGilp
Cover illustrator: Maria Herbert-Liew
Typesetter: Jouve India Private Limited
Production controller: Tina Paul
Printed and bound by: Grafica Veneta SpA in Italy

Acknowledgements

The publishers gratefully acknowledge the permission granted to reproduce the copyright material in this book. Every effort has been made to trace copyright holders and to obtain their permission for the use of copyright material. The publishers will gladly receive any information enabling them to rectify any error or omission at the first opportunity.

p1 BALANCE PICTURES/Shutterstock, p32 Christopher Elwell/Shutterstock, p57 Vladitto/Shutterstock, p88 VTT Studio/Shutterstock, p100 Ken Hawkins/Alamy Stock Photo, p137 shinobi/Shutterstock, p168 ESB Professional/Shutterstock, p210(l) Samot/Shutterstock, p210(r) Vixit/Shutterstock, p219 Lorna Roberts/Shutterstock, p255 Ekaterina Iatcenko/Shutterstock, p269 Jne Valokuvaus/Shutterstock.

All exam-style questions and sample answers have been written by the authors.

Introduction

The *Collins Lower Secondary Maths* Stage 7 Student's Book covers the Cambridge Lower Secondary curriculum framework through 9 topic-based units, broken down into 34 chapters. The series is designed to illustrate concepts and provide practice questions at a range of difficulties to allow you to build confidence on a topic.

The authors have included plenty of worked examples in every chapter. These worked examples will lead you, step-by-step, through the new concepts, with clear and detailed explanations. Where possible, links have been made between topics, encouraging you to build on what you know already, and to practise mathematical concepts in a different context. You will learn to develop mental maths strategies, spot patterns and improve your ability to solve mathematical problems.

Every chapter has these helpful features:
- 'Starting point': to remind you of what you know already and why this will be helpful in the new chapter
- 'This will also be helpful when …': to let you know where you will use this mathematics in the future
- 'Hook': to get you interested in the new topic through an activity or game
- 'Key terms' boxes: to identify new mathematical words you need to know in that chapter, and provide a definition
- Worked examples: to show you how to address questions with both formal and informal (diagrammatic) explanations provided
- Clear topic headings: so that you can see what you are going to be learning in each section of the chapter
- 'Tip' boxes: to give you guidance on the possible methods and common errors
- 'Develop' questions (shown as a red question number): to encourage you to think more deeply about the ideas you have been learning in this chapter and practising in this exercise
- 'Challenge' questions (shown as a blue question number): to help you to think beyond the ideas covered in this chapter, and stretch you to apply the concepts in a different context
- 'Think about' boxes: to suggest areas of the mathematics that you might want to consider in more detail
- 'Discuss' boxes: to encourage you to talk about mathematical ideas with a partner or in class
- 'End of chapter reflection': to help you think about how well you have understood the ideas in the chapter, so that you can monitor your own progress.

We hope that you find this approach enjoyable and engaging as you progress through your mathematical journey.

The series editors

Contents

Unit 1A • Number and calculation

Chapter 1 Place value and rounding 2
Place value
Multiplication and division by powers of 10
Ordering decimals and measurements
Rounding

Chapter 2 Multiplying and dividing 12
Consolidation of number facts
Mental multiplication and division
Divisibility tests
Multiplying decimals by integers

Chapter 3 Equivalent fractions 19
Equivalent fractions, decimals and percentages
Equivalent fractions
Mixed numbers
Changing decimals to fractions

Chapter 4 Negative numbers 27
Using negative numbers
Adding and subtracting positive and negative integers in context

Unit 1B • Algebra and measures

Chapter 5 Units of measurement 33

Chapter 6 Algebra 38
Letters for numbers
Order of algebraic operations
Forming expressions
Simplifying expressions
Multiplying a constant over a bracket

Chapter 7 Sequences 49
Generating sequences
Spatial patterns

Unit 1C • Handling data and geometry

Chapter 8 2D shapes 58
Drawing and describing 2D shapes
Geometrical conventions
Properties of special shapes

Chapter 9 Estimating angles 69

Chapter 10 Data collection 74
Collecting data
Data collection sheets and questionnaires

Chapter 11 Probability 1 80
Probability words
Calculating probabilities

Unit 2A • Number and calculation

Chapter 12 Time and scales 89
Units of time and the 24-hour clock
Time intervals and timetables
Reading scales

Chapter 13 Numbers 100
Multiples, factors and primes
Common multiples and the sieve of Eratosthenes
Squares and square roots

Chapter 14 Fractions 110
Adding and subtracting fractions
Finding fractions of numbers
Multiplying fractions by integers

Chapter 15 Percentages and fractions 120
Percentages and fractions
Mental methods

Chapter 16 Calculations 129
Simplifying calculations
Interpreting results of calculations

Unit 2B • Algebra and measures

Chapter 17   Area and perimeter   138
Converting between metric units
Perimeter and area of shapes made from rectangles

Chapter 18   Formulae   146
Constructing and using formulae
Substitution

Chapter 19   Coordinates, functions, graphs and equations   151
Coordinates
Mappings
Linear equations and their graphs
Solving equations

Unit 2C • Handling data and geometry

Chapter 20   Angles   169
Angles and parallel lines
Calculating angles

Chapter 21   Symmetry   180
Line and rotational symmetry

Chapter 22   Averages   186
Mode, median and range
The mean

Chapter 23   Displaying data   196
Pictograms, bar charts and bar-line graphs
Frequency diagrams for grouped discrete data
Simple pie charts

Chapter 24   Probability 2   210
Identifying outcomes
Estimating probabilities
Comparing probabilities

Unit 3A • Number and calculation

Chapter 25   Calculation   220
Order of operations
Addition and subtraction
Multiplication and division
Remainders

Chapter 26   Percentages   232
Finding a percentage of an amount
Writing one amount as a percentage of another
Comparing using percentages

Chapter 27   Ratio and proportion   240
Ratio
Sharing in a ratio
Ratio and proportion
Direct proportion

Chapter 28   Fractions and decimals   249
Comparing fractions using diagrams
Comparing fractions using decimals

Unit 3B • Algebra and measures

Chapter 29   Volumes of cuboids   256
Volume of cuboids
Surface area of cubes and cuboids

Chapter 30   Graphs in real-life contexts   264
Drawing and interpreting graphs

Unit 3C • Handling data and geometry

Chapter 31   Statistics   270
Frequency tables
Drawing conclusions from graphs
Comparing sets of data using averages and the range

Chapter 32   Transformations   284

Chapter 33   Geometrical reasoning and 3D shapes   291
3D shapes
Geometrical reasoning

Chapter 34   Construction   299
Measuring and constructing lines and angles
Construction of parallel and perpendicular lines and triangles
Constructing squares, rectangles and simple polygons

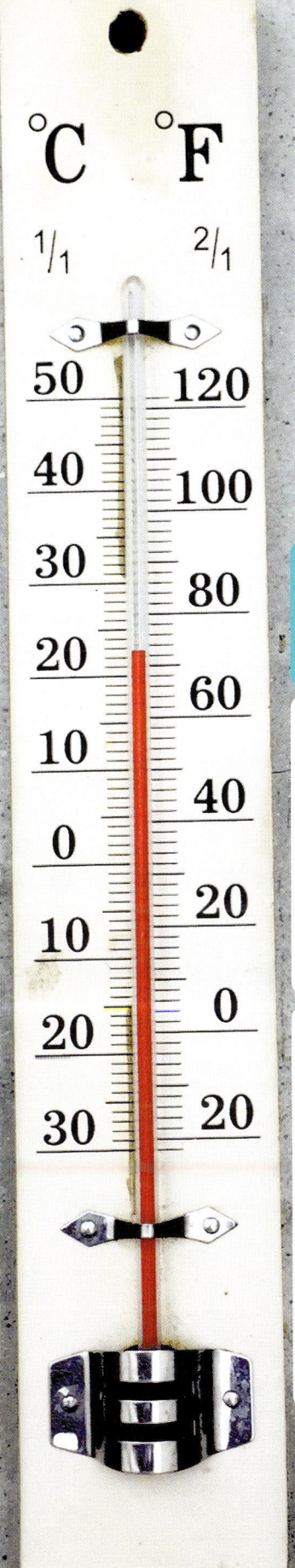

Unit 1A
Number and calculation

What's it all about?

- The importance of place value and ordering numbers
- Identifying equivalent fractions, decimals and percentages
- Improving mental strategies for multiplication and division
- Working with negative numbers

You will learn about:

- Ordering positive and negative numbers
- Recognising and using place value
- How to use multiplication tables
- Divisibility tests
- How to recognise equivalent fractions, decimals and percentages
- Comparing fractions

You will build your skills in:

- Mental maths
- Understanding the use of numbers in real life such as measurements

Unit 1A • Chapter 1

Place value and rounding

You will learn how to:
- Interpret decimal notation and place value.
- Multiply and divide whole numbers and decimals by 10, 100 or 1000.
- Order decimals including measurements, changing these to the same units.
- Round whole numbers to the nearest 10, 100 or 1000 and decimals, including measurements, to the nearest whole number or one decimal place.

Starting point

Do you remember …?

- what each digit represents in numbers with up to 6 digits?
  For example, what does each digit represent in the number 724 568?
- what each digit represents in numbers with up to 2 decimal places?
  For example, what does each digit represent in the number 0.43?
- how to multiply and divide whole numbers by 10, 100 or 1000 where the answer is a whole number?
  For example, calculate 234 × 100 or 7500 ÷ 10.
- how to round simple whole numbers to the nearest 10, 100 or 1000 and how to round decimals to the nearest whole number or one decimal place?
  For example, round 78 to the nearest 10.
- the relationships between different units of measurement?
  For example, how many centimetres are in 2 metres?

This will also be helpful when …

you learn how to do more complex calculations with decimals, such as multiplying and dividing by decimals.

Hook

Here is a game for 2–4 players.

You will need paper, pens and a dice.

> Aim of the game: to produce the largest number
>
> Each player draws 4 boxes like this, with a decimal point as shown:
>
>
>
> Player 1 then rolls the dice.
> All the players must write the number on the dice in one of their four boxes.
> Player 2 then rolls the dice.
> All the players must write the number on the dice in one of their remaining three boxes.
> Play continues twice more, rolling the dice and then writing the number in a box.
> Once all four boxes are complete, the players compare their numbers and the player with the largest number wins.

- If a 6 is rolled, where should you position it?
- What about if a 1 is rolled?
- Is there a way to ensure that you always win?
- Play again – this time, the player with the smallest number wins. How does this change your strategy?

Place value

> **Did you know?**
>
> In some countries the decimal point is shown as a full stop but in other countries a comma is used instead.

Key terms

A **digit** is a numeral used to show a number or part of a number. 237 is a 3-digit number with digits 2, 3 and 7.

You can use a **place value grid** (below) to show the value of each digit in a number

1 000 000	100 000	10 000	1000	100	10	1	.	0.1	0.01	0.001
millions	hundred thousands	ten thousands	thousands	hundreds	tens	units	decimal point	tenths	hundredths	thousandths
							.			

Worked example 1

State the value of the 7 in each of these numbers:

a) 437 061   b) 2.57

a) 437 061

The value of the 7 is 7000

HTh	TTh	Th	H	T	U
4	3	7	0	6	1

If the number is a whole number, without decimals, then start by putting the units in the units column.

The 7 is 7 thousands.

100 000	10 000	1000	100	10	1
hundred thousands	ten thousands	thousands	hundreds	tens	units

b) 2.57

The value of the 7 is $\frac{7}{100}$ or 0.07

u	.	t	h
2	.	5	7

If the number has a decimal point then line up the decimal points first. The 7 is 7 hundredths or 0.07.

1	.	0.1	0.01
units	decimal point	tenths	hundredths

Exercise 1

1 State the value of the 8 in each of these numbers:
  a) 872   b) 2816   c) 28 612   d) 3008   e) 2.8   f) 23.468

2 Jim is working with this number: 543 182

Jim says, "The value of the 4 in this number is ten thousand".

Do you agree with Jim? Explain your answer.

3 Here is a number: 978 654.321

Which statement is false?

A:	B:	C:	D:
The 4 digit is worth 4	The 7 digit is worth 7000	The 1 digit is worth $\frac{1}{1000}$	The 3 digit is worth 0.3

Multiplication and division by powers of 10

Worked example 2

Calculate:

a) 167 × 10   b) 1.67 × 100   c) 248 ÷ 10   d) 2.4 ÷ 100

a) 167 × 10 = 1670	When you multiply by 10 you move each digit one place value to the left. If there are empty place values between numbers and the decimal point you fill those with zeros.
b) 1.67 × 100 = 167	When you multiply by 100 you move each digit two place values to the left. If there are empty place values between numbers and the decimal point you fill them with zeros.
c) 248 ÷ 10 = 24.8	When you divide by 10 you move each digit one place value to the right. If there are empty place values between numbers and the decimal point you fill them with zeros.
d) 2.4 ÷ 100 = 0.024	When you divide by 100 you move each digit two place values to the right. If there are empty place values between numbers and the decimal point you fill them with zeros.

Exercise 2

1 Calculate:

a) 26 × 10   b) 38 × 100   c) 265 × 1000   d) 2156 × 10

e) 350 × 1000   f) 400 × 10   g) 0.05 × 10   h) 0.004 × 100

i) 3.65 × 10   j) 2.8 × 100   k) 0.48 × 1000   l) 0.104 × 100

2 Calculate:
   a) 260 ÷ 10
   b) 380 000 ÷ 1000
   c) 34 ÷ 10
   d) 28 ÷ 100
   e) 560 ÷ 100
   f) 7800 ÷ 1000
   g) 0.5 ÷ 10
   h) 0.4 ÷ 100
   i) 1.6 ÷ 10
   j) 37.8 ÷ 100
   k) 450 ÷ 1000
   l) 14.5 ÷ 100

3 Match each calculation on the left to its answer on the right.

Complete the missing calculation and answer in the empty boxes to produce 8 pairs of calculations and answers.

5.2 × 10	5200
0.52 × 1000	5.2
5.2 ÷ 10	52
52 × 100	
0.52 ÷ 10	520 000
520 ÷ 100	520
52 000 000 ÷ 100	52 000
	0.052

4 Emily is working out this calculation: 14.3 × 100.

She says, "I just need to add two 0s on to the end of my number, so the answer is 14.300".

Do you agree with Emily? Explain your answer.

Ordering decimals and measurements

Key terms

Ordering numbers means to put them in order of size.

You do this by comparing the numbers in each place value working from left to right. If the first two numbers on the left are the same you then compare the next numbers along.

41 is bigger than 38 because 4 is bigger than 3.

48 is bigger than 43 because the 4s are the same but 8 is bigger than 3.

This works with decimals too.

2.45 is bigger than 2.37 because the 2s are the same but 4 is bigger than 3.

To compare 2.338 with 2.33 you first write 2.33 as 2.330 so it has the same number of decimal numbers as 2.338.

2.338 is bigger than 2.330 because the 2s and the 3s are the same but 8 is bigger than 0.

If you are comparing more than two numbers it is often easier to write them underneath each other, in a place value table lining up the decimal points.

2.3**2**2 second largest

2.318 smallest

2.**8**90 largest

1	•	0.1	0.01	0.001
units	decimal point	tenths	hundredths	thousandths
2	•	3	2	2
2	•	3	1	8
2	•	8	9	0

Chapter 1: Place value and rounding   5

Worked example 3

a) Which of these three numbers is the largest?

    2.359   2.36   2.357

b) Order these numbers from largest to smallest.

    4.294   3.235   2.611   2.3   2.32

c) Order these lengths from shortest to longest.

    2.4 m   224 cm   2.234 m   2 m

a) 2.36 is the largest as 6 (h) is bigger than 5 (h)	Write the decimals under each other, lining up the decimal points and zeros where necessary. 2.359 2.360 2.357 Compare the numbers in each place value starting with the left-hand column.	U . t h th 2 . 3 5 9 2 . 3 ⑥ 2 . 3 5 7 ✓
b) 4.294 is the largest as 4 (U) is larger than 3 or 2 3.235 is next as 3 (U) is larger than 2 2.611 is next as 6 (t) is larger than 3 2.32 is next as 2 (h) is larger than 0 2.3 is the smallest	Write the numbers under each other, lining up the decimal points and adding zeros where necessary. 4.294 3.235 2.611 2.300 2.320 Compare the numbers in each place value starting with the left-hand column.	U . t h th 4 . 2 9 4 1 3 . 2 3 5 2 2 . 6 1 1 2 . 3 0 0 2 . 3 2 0 U . t h th 4 . 2 9 4 1 3 . 2 3 5 2 2 . ⑥ 1 1 3 2 . 3 0 0 5 2 . 3 ② 0 4
c) Writing these in metres you have 2.400 2.240 2.234 2.000 2 m is the shortest as 0 (t) is less than 2 or 4 2.234 m is next as 3 (h) is less than 4 2.240 m is next as 2 (t) is less than 4 2.4 m is the longest In order, smallest first, the lengths are 2 m, 2.234 m, 224 cm and 2.4 m	To compare these distances you must change them all to the same units. Divide 224 cm by 100 to change it into 2.24 m. Write the numbers under each other lining up the decimal points and adding zeros where necessary. Compare the numbers in the place values from left to right, but this time you are looking for the smallest numbers.	U . t h th 2 . 2 ③ 4 2 . ⓪ 0 0 U . t h th 2 . 4 0 0 4 2 . 2 4 0 3 2 . 2 ③ 4 2 2 . ⓪ 0 0 1

Unit 1A: Number and calculation

Exercise 3

1 Which is the larger number or quantity in each of these?
   a) 2.6 or 2.49
   b) 36.375 or 36.366
   c) 0.116 or 0.123
   d) 1.56 m and 1.479 m
   e) 2.79 m and 293 cm
   f) 96 g and 0.95 kg

2 Which is the smallest number or quantity in each of these?
   a) 1.43 or 1.399 or 1.322
   b) 1.2 or 1.122 or 1.109
   c) 15.198 or 14.991 or 14.910
   d) 2.61 m or 2.55 m or 2.49 m
   e) 2.31 m or 249 cm or 2.41 m
   f) 2.33 kg or 299 g or 2245 g

> **Tip**
> Remember:
> There are 100 centimetres (cm) in 1 metre (m).
> There are 1000 metres (m) in 1 kilometres (km).
> There are 1000 grams (g) in 1 kilogram (kg).
> There are 1000 millilitres (ml) in 1 litre (l).

3 Put these numbers in order from smallest to largest.
   a) 1765, 1800, 1650, 6500, 1675
   b) 13 454, 14 350, 14 503, 13 544, 14 035

4 Put these numbers in order from largest to smallest.
   a) 12.3, 13.2, 13, 12.19
   b) 0.45, 0.4, 0.54, 0.47,
   c) 0.601, 0.62, 0.6, 0.621, 0.612
   d) 16.59, 16.6, 16.599, 16.95, 16.9

5 Put these measurements in order from smallest to largest.
   a) 3.6 m, 3.36 m, 363 cm, 3.603 m
   b) 14.2 kg, 14.25 kg, 14 285 g, 14.258 kg
   c) 7.1 litres, 701 millilitres, 7000 millilitres, 0.71 litres
   d) 18.3 km, 1830 m, 17 000 m, 1.38 km, 1.835 km

6 Use each of the digits 0–5 once only to complete the missing digits to make four correct statements.

   2☐ mm < 2.1 cm   8☐ mm < 9 cm
   17.☐ km > ☐739 m   2.☐ kg > 2☐95 g

> **Think about**
> What steps should you go through to make sure you have got a set of measurements in the right order?

7 Write an ordering question with a list of 6 measurements that are difficult to order. Now write the solution.
   What makes your list of measurements hard to order?

Rounding

Key terms

If 34 237 people watched a television programme last night you would probably say that over 34 000 people watched the program. You have **rounded** the number to the nearest thousand. **Rounding** a number often makes it less accurate but easier to use.

Worked example 4

Round:
a) 27.5 to the nearest 10
b) 3562 to the nearest 10
c) 3562 to the nearest 100
d) 19.6 to the nearest whole number
e) 23.657 to 1 decimal place

a) 27.5 rounded to the nearest 10 is 30	27.5 lies between 20 and 30 and you need to decide which it is nearer to. You can do this using a number line or by looking at the number in the next place value to the right of the tens. If that number is 5 or more you increase the 2 in the tens place to 3.	20 — 27.5 — 30 T | U | . | t 2 | (7) | . | 5 3 | 0 | . | 0
b) 3562 to the nearest 10 is 3560	3562 lies between 3560 and 3570 and you need to decide which it is nearer to. The number in the units place is 2 so 3562 will be nearer 3560.	3562 ↓ 3560 — 3570 Th | H | T | U 3 | 5 | 6 | (2) 3 | 5 | 6 | 0
c) 3562 to the nearest 100 is 3600	3562 lies between 3500 and 3600. The number in the tens place is 6 so 3562 is nearer to 3600.	3562 ↓ 3500 — 3600 Th | H | T | U 3 | 5 | (6) | 2 3 | 6 | 0 | 0
d) 19.6 to the nearest whole number is 20	19.6 lies between two whole numbers 19 and 20. The number in the first decimal place is 6 so 19.6 is nearer to 20.	19.6 ↓ 19 — 20 T | U | . | t 1 | 9 | . | (6) 2 | 0 | . | 0
e) 23.657 to one decimal place is 23.7	23.657 is between 23.6 and 23.7. The number in the second decimal place is 5 so 23.657 is nearer to 23.7	23.657 ↓ 23.6 — 23.7 T | U | . | t | h | th 2 | 3 | . | 6 | (5) | 7 2 | 3 | . | 7 | 0 | 0

Exercise 4   1–12

1 Give the nearest multiples of 10 that these numbers lie between then state the multiple of 10 that the number is closest to. The first one has been done for you.

a) 367 is between 3**6**0 and 3**7**0 and is nearer to 3**7**0.

b) 648 is between 6_0 and 6_0 and is nearer to ....

c) 35 781 is between 357_0 and 357_0 and is nearer to ....

d) 2476 is between 24_0 and 24_0 and is nearer to ....

Unit 1A: Number and calculation

2 Round these numbers to the nearest 10.
   a) 35   b) 361   c) 4564   d) 1453   e) 19 963

3 Give the nearest multiples of 100 that these numbers lie between then state the multiple of 100 that the number is closest to. The first one has been done for you.
   a) 5648 lies between 5600 and 5700 and is nearer to 5600.
   b) 369 lies between _00 and _00 and is nearer to ....
   c) 6528 lies between 6_00 and 6_00 and is nearer to ....
   d) 21 477 lies between 21_00 and 21_00 and is nearer to ....

4 Round these numbers to the nearest 100.
   a) 516   b) 8341   c) 3487   d) 67 549   e) 49 655

5 Give the nearest multiples of 1000 that these numbers lie between then state the multiple of 1000 that the number is closest to. The first one has been done for you.
   i) 45 678 lies between 45 000 and 46 000 and is nearer to 46 000.
   ii) 4176 lies between ....000 and ....000 and is nearer to ....
   iii) 31 578 lies between 3......... 000 and 3......... 000 and is nearer to ....

6 Round these numbers to the nearest 1000.
   a) 7813   b) 6512   c) 63 813   d) 37 688   e) 630

7 Round these numbers to the nearest whole number.
   a) 1.87   b) 16.149   c) 173.52   d) 49.74   e) 0.35

8 Round these numbers to one decimal place.
   a) 0.46   b) 6.413   c) 12.389   d) 21.01   e) 7.98

9 Here is a number: 142 874.18
   a) Which of these statements is correct?

A:	B:	C:	D:	E:
The number rounded to the nearest 1000 is 140 000	The number rounded to the nearest 100 is 142 800	The number rounded to the nearest 10 is 142 880	The number rounded to the nearest whole number is 142 874	The number rounded to one decimal place is 142 874.1

   b) Correct the statements that are wrong.

10 Alma is rounding the number 46.419 to one decimal place. She says,
   "Because the last number is a nine, I need to round up. So the answer will be 46.5".
   Do you agree with Alma?
   Explain your answer.

11 Round 12 765.192 metres:
   a) to the nearest metre   b) to the nearest kilometre   c) to the nearest centimetre

12 Round 3734.815 grams
   a) to the nearest gram   b) to the nearest kilogram

Chapter 1: Place value and rounding

13 Set up a spreadsheet table like this:

Value A	Value B	Value A × Value B
7.3	2.915	
4.817	1.956	

Write a formula to calculate the result of Value A × Value B in the third column.

Does the spreadsheet round the answers? If so, to what degree of accuracy? If not, how can you change the settings so that it does round?

> **Did you know?**
>
> In sports competitions, measurements are often rounded because the equipment used is only accurate to a certain degree.
>
> For example, times in the 100 m race are rounded to 2 decimal places (or the nearest hundredth of a second).

14 A runner completed a 100 m race in a time of 11.39 seconds.

Give an example of a time with 3 decimal places that would be rounded to 11.39 seconds to 2 decimal places. How many times with exactly 3 decimal places are there that round to 11.39 seconds?

15 **Vocabulary feature question**

Complete the text with the words in the box.

round	ten	decimal place	decimal point	order
multiply	divide	thousand units	place value	

Our number system is based around .... columns. Each column has a value that is

.... times bigger than the previous one.

When you use a number that is not an exact whole number, you use a .... to separate the ones, tens, hundreds etc. from the tenths, hundredths, thousandths etc.

When you .... a number by ten, each digit becomes ten times larger, and thus appears in the next column to the left.

When you .... a number by ten, each digit becomes ten times smaller, and thus appears in the next column to the right.

You can compare the value of each digit in a number to help you put them in ....

Sometimes you need to .... a number. This reduces its accuracy but can make it easier to calculate with.

Numbers that have been rounded to the nearest .... will end in three 0s.

Numbers that have been rounded to one .... will have exactly one number after the decimal point.

Unit 1A: Number and calculation

End of chapter reflection

You should know that ...	You should be able to ...	Such as ...
You can organise numbers into the place value system, where each category is ten times larger than the next one: | 1 000 000 | 100 000 | 10 000 | 1000 | 100 | 10 | 1 | . | 0.1 | 0.01 | 0.001 | | millions | hundred thousands | ten thousands | thousands | hundreds | tens | units | decimal point | tenths | hundredths | thousandths |	State the value of any digit of a whole number or decimal.	State the value of the 2 in 12 356.
You can multiply or divide whole numbers and decimals by 10, 100 and 1000 by moving the place values of their digits.	Multiply or divide a whole number or decimal by 10, 100 or 1000.	Calculate: **a)** 23.6 × 100 **b)** 356.78 ÷ 10
You can order decimal numbers including measures.	Put a list of decimal numbers in order of size.	Order these decimals from the largest to the smallest 0.34, 0.4, 0.304, 0.43, 0.403
You can round numbers to the nearest 10, 100 or 1000 or to the nearest whole number or to one decimal place (sometimes written 1 d.p.).	Round numbers to a given degree of accuracy.	Round 34 567 to the nearest 100.

Unit 1A • Chapter 2

Multiplying and dividing

You will learn how to:
- Consolidate the rapid recall of number facts, including positive integer complements to 100, multiplication facts to 10 × 10 and associated division facts.
- Use known facts and place value to multiply and divide two-digit numbers by a single-digit number, for example, 45 × 6, 96 ÷ 6.
- Know and apply tests of divisibility by 2, 3, 5, 6, 8, 9, 10 and 100.
- Use known facts and place value to multiply simple decimals by one-digit numbers, for example, 0.8 × 6.

Starting point

Do you remember …?

- your multiplication facts up to 10 × 10?
  For example, can you calculate 6 × 4?
- that 3 × 4 is the same as 4 × 3?
- that (4 × 3) + (5 × 3) = 9 × 3?
- how to find the related facts for a multiplication or division?
  For example, if 7 × 5 = 35, then can you arrange these numbers to make another multiplication fact (5 × 7 = 35) and two division facts (35 ÷ 7 = 5 and 35 ÷ 5 = 7)?
- how to multiply a multiple of 10 by a single digit?
  For example, can you calculate 30 × 4?
- how to multiply and divide two-digit numbers by a single-digit number with a written method?
  For example, can you calculate 26 × 3 or 72 ÷ 3?
- how to instantly recognise odd and even numbers, multiples of 10 and multiples of 5?
  For example, is 75 odd or even, and is it a multiple of 5 or a multiple of 10?
- how to represent a decimal number on a place value table and the value of each digit in a decimal?
  For example, what is the value of the 5 in 2.357?
- that ten tenths is the same as 1 unit so 15 tenths is 1 unit and 5 tenths or 1.5?

This will also be helpful when …

you learn about calculating areas, volumes, ratios and proportions with larger numbers and decimals.

Hook

Here is a multiplication grid, with all the headers and most of the answers missing!

Can you use what you have been given to work out the missing headers and complete the answers?

- Add up the digits of the **multiples** of 9 in your table. What do you notice?
- What do you notice about the numbers that are **multiples** of 5 from your table?
- Investigate what happens when you add up the digits of **multiples** of 3. How can you use this to predict whether a number is a **multiple** of 3?

Tip

All the headings are single digits.

×				
			20	
	64			72
		18		27
			35	

Consolidation of number facts

Exercise 1

Key term

A **multiple** of a number is the result of multiplying it by a whole number.
For example, 24 is a multiple of 4 because 4 × 6 = 24.

1 Calculate the value of the missing number in each calculation.
  a) 45 + …… = 100
  b) …… + 17 = 50
  c) 0.6 + …… = 1
  d) 0.64 + …… = 1
  e) 761 + …… = 1000
  f) …… + 458 = 1000

2 Write whether these statements are true or false.
  a) 5 × 6 = 11 ………
  b) 7 × 4 = 28 ………
  c) 9 × 6 = 63 ………
  d) 8 × 7 = 54 ………
  e) 8 × 8 = 96 ………
  f) 63 ÷ 9 = 7 ………
  g) 4 × 9 = 36 ………
  h) 42 ÷ 7 = 8 ………
  i) 6 × 8 = 4 × 12 ………

3 Double each of these numbers.
  a) 58
  b) 6.5
  c) 0.52
  d) 0.89

4 Halve each of these numbers.
  a) 512
  b) 12.6
  c) 9.4
  d) 1.38

5 A shop sells T-shirts that cost $9 each.
  a) How much will 8 T-shirts cost?
  b) If I have $54, how many T-shirts can I buy?

6 Nara buys two pens for $1.85 each. She pays with $10. How much change will she receive?

7 Write a calculation problem of your own that is easy to solve. What makes it easy? Now write a calculation problem of your own that is hard to solve. What makes it hard?

Mental multiplication and division

Key term

To make mental arithmetic easier, numbers can be **partitioned** or split into two or more numbers that add up to the original number.

For example, 84 could be partitioned as:
- 80 and 4 if you want to divide by 4
- 70 and 14 if you want to divide it by 7
- 72 and 12 if you want to divide it by 6 or 12

Worked example 1

Calculate:

a) 53 × 4
b) 78 ÷ 6

a) 53 × 4 = (50 × 4) + (3 × 4) = 200 + 12 = 212	You can split 53 into 50 + 3. Mutiplying 53 by 4 is the same as multiplying 50 by 4 and multiplying 3 by 4 and adding the answers.	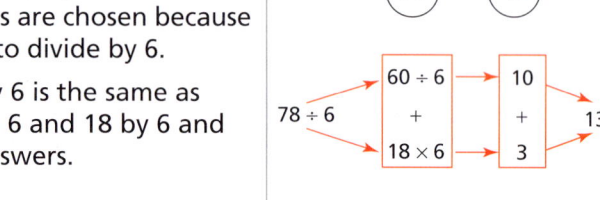
b) 78 ÷ 6 = (60 ÷ 6) + (18 ÷ 6) = 10 + 3 = 13	You can write 78 as 60 + 18 or 72 + 6 and there are other possibilities. In this example 60 and 18 are used. These numbers are chosen because they are easy to divide by 6. Dividing 78 by 6 is the same as dividing 60 by 6 and 18 by 6 and adding the answers.	

Exercise 2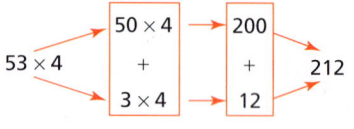

1 Use your times table knowledge to help you calculate mentally:

a) 42 × 6
b) 71 × 3
c) 91 × 5
d) 84 × 2
e) 83 × 3
f) 62 × 9
g) 3 × 27
h) 5 × 95
i) 75 × 4
j) 66 × 7

2 Use your times table knowledge to help you calculate mentally:

a) 84 ÷ 4
b) 63 ÷ 3
c) 81 ÷ 4
d) 69 ÷ 3
e) 75 ÷ 5
f) 84 ÷ 6
g) 72 ÷ 3
h) 92 ÷ 4

Think about

When is it more useful to partition the number 96 into 80 + 16 rather than 60 + 36?

Key terms

The **product** of two numbers is the answer that you get when you multiply them.
For example, the product of 2 and 10 is 20 because 2 × 10 = 20
The **quotient** of two numbers is the answer that you get when you divide them.
For example, the quotient of 24 and 3 is 8 because 24 ÷ 3 = 8

3 Calculate mentally the **product** of:

a) 52 and 3
b) 4 and 81
c) 45 and 7
d) 6 and 61

4 Calculate mentally the **quotient** of:

a) 39 and 3
b) 90 and 6
c) 65 and 5
d) 96 and 4

5 Which of these is the odd one out? Explain your answer.

96 ÷ 6   72 ÷ 4   90 ÷ 5   54 ÷ 3

6 How many different pairs of whole numbers are there with a product of 60?
List your pairs. How do you know you have got them all?

Divisibility tests

Key terms

A number is **divisible** by another number if it can be divided exactly by that number without leaving a remainder. For example, 12 is divisible by 6 as 12 ÷ 6 = 2.

There are easy ways of spotting if numbers are divisible by certain other numbers. These are called **divisibility tests**.

All even numbers are divisible by 2. Even numbers end in a digit which is an even number or 0, so 9216 is divisible by 2.

If you add the digits of a number together and the answer is divisible by 3 then the original number is divisible by 3, so 9216 is divisible by 3.

If the last two digits of a number are divisible by 4, or are 00, then the number is divisible by 4, so 9216 is divisible by 4.

If a number is divisible by 5 then the number must end in 5 or 0.

If a number is divisible by 2 and by 3 it is divisible by 6, so 9216 is divisible by 6.

There is no simple divisibility test for 7.

If the last 3 digits of a number are divisible by 8, or are 000, then the number is divisible by 8, so 9216 is divisible by 8.

If you add the digits of a number together and the answer is divisible by 9 then the original number is divisible by 9, so 9216 is divisible by 9.

If a number is divisible by 10 then it must end in a 0, so 6750 is divisible by 10.

If a number is divisible by 100 it must end in 00, so 4500 is divisible by 100.

Worked example 2

Which of these numbers is 3426 divisible by? 2, 3, 4, 5, 6, 8, 9, 10

3426 is divisible by 2 because it is an even number and all even numbers are divisible by 2	The last digit of 3426 is 6 which is divisible by 2.	342**6** is an even number
3 + 4 + 2 + 6 = 15 15 is divisible by 3 so 3426 is divisible by 3	If you add the digits of 3426, the sum is divisible by 3.	3 + 4 + 2 + 6 = 15 15 is divisible by 3
26 is not divisible by 4 so 3426 is not divisible by 4	The last two digits of 3426 are not divisible by 4.	34**26** is not divisible by 4
3426 does not end in 5 or 0 so it is not divisible by 5	All multiples of 5 end in either 5 or 0.	342**6** does not end in 0 or 5

Chapter 2: Multiplying and dividing   15

3426 is divisible by both 2 and 3 so it is also divisible by 6	You already know that 3426 is divisible by 2 and by 3. 2 and 3 have no common factors so it must also divide by 2 × 3 = 6.	Divisible by 2 – yes Divisible by 3 – yes so Divisible by 6 – yes!
The last three digits of the number are 426. 426 is not exactly divisible by 8 so 3426 is not divisible by 8	If you divide 426 by 8 you get 53 remainder 2 so the last three digits are not divisible by 8.	3426 is not divisible by 8
3 + 4 + 2 + 6 = 15. 15 is not divisible by 9 so 3426 is not divisible by 9	If a number is divisible by 9, the sum of its digits is divisible by 9.	3 + 4 + 2 + 6 = 15 15 is not divisible by 9
3426 does not end in a 0 so it is not divisible by 10	All numbers which are divisible by 10 end in a 0.	3426 is not divisible by 10

Exercise 3

Tip
You cannot say that a number that is divisible by 2 and 4 must also be divisible by 8 as 2 and 4 have a common factor of 2. 28 is divisible by 2 and 4 but not by 8.

1 Look at these numbers.
  127   144   168   219   744
  a) Which of the numbers are divisible by 2?
  b) Which of the numbers are divisible by 3?
  c) Which of the numbers are divisible by 6?

2 Look at these numbers.
  135   360   900   1248   6700
  a) Which of the numbers are divisible by 5?
  b) Which of the numbers are divisible by 10?
  c) Which of the numbers are divisible by 100?

3 Look at these numbers.
  542   639   846   1413   1732
  a) Which of the numbers are divisible by 9?
  b) Which of the numbers are divisible by 4?

4 Which of these numbers is 3600 divisible by?
  2, 3, 4, 5, 6, 8, 9, 10, 100

5 471 is divisible by:
  A: 2   B: 3   C: 6   D: 9   E: All of these numbers

6 Find a number that is divisible by 1, 2, 3, 4, 5, 6, 7 and 8. How did you do this?
  Is this the smallest possible number that is divisible by 1, 2, 3, 4, 5, 6, 7 and 8? Explain your answer.

7 Can you find, on the internet, two different divisibility tests for divisibility by 7? Test them out on the number 4057. Which is easier to use?

Multiplying decimals by integers

Worked example 3

Calculate:

a) 6 × 0.7   b) 0.8 × 3

a) 6 × 0.7 = 4.2	You can represent this calculation as six lots of seven tenths which is 42 tenths or 4 units (ten tenths) and 2 tenths.	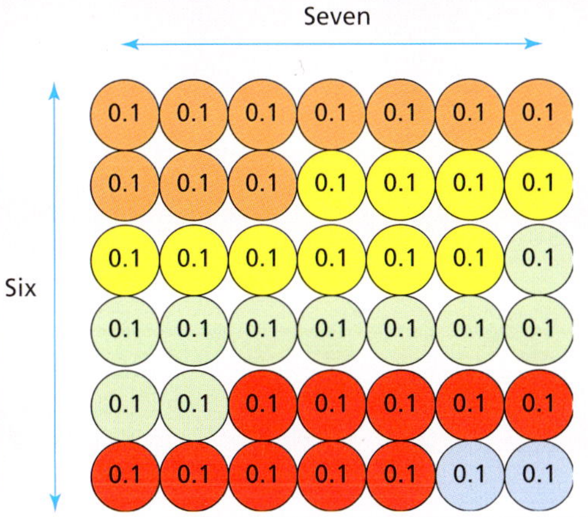 Seven → Six ↓ (grid of 0.1 circles, 6 rows × 7 columns)
b) 0.8 × 3 = 2.4	3 lots of 8 tenths is 24 tenths or two units and 4 tenths.	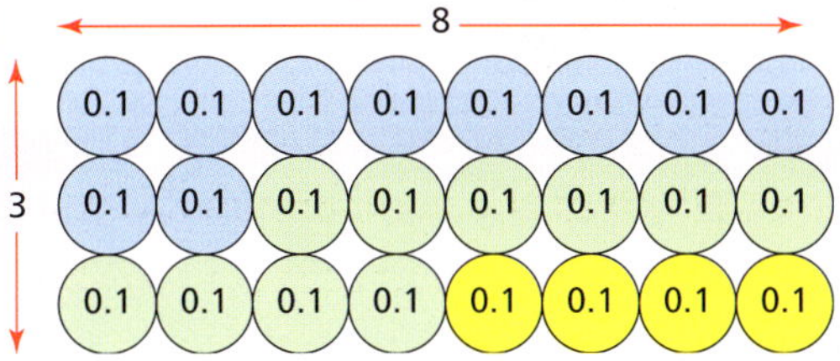 8 → 3 ↓ (grid of 0.1 circles, 3 rows × 8 columns)

Exercise 4

1 Calculate:

   a) 3 × 0.8   b) 7 × 0.5
   c) 4 × 0.9   d) 8 × 0.5
   e) 0.4 × 2   f) 0.6 × 3
   g) 0.7 × 4   h) 0.6 × 8

2 Ali calculates 0.7 × 3.

He says, "7 × 3 = 21 so the answer must be 0.21".

Ali is wrong. Explain the error that Ali has made and correct his answer.

3 How many pairs of whole numbers and decimal numbers with one decimal place can you find with a product of 7.2?

List them all. How do you know you have got them all?

Tip

Use your times table knowledge and divisibility tests to help you.

4 Vocabulary feature question

Put these words and numbers into the spaces in the sentences below.

digits   divisibility test   9   sum   divisible   divisible

A .... is a way of testing to see if a number is ....

by another number. For example, to see if 237 942 is .... by 9 you add the

.... of 237 942 together and see if the ....is divisible

by ....

End of chapter reflection

You should know that ...	You should be able to ...	Such as ...
Numbers can be partitioned to make arithmetic easier.	Multiply or divide a 2-digit number by a single digit number in your head by using partitions (splitting the 2-digit number) and times table facts.	Calculate: a) 43 × 7 = b) 75 ÷ 5 =
There are divisibility tests for certain numbers.	Test to see if a number is divisible by 2, 3, 4, 5, 6, 8, 9, 10 or 100.	Is 31 527 divisible by 9?
Simple decimals can be multiplied by a single digit number.	Work out the value of simple decimal multiplications.	Calculate: 0.8 × 7

Unit 1A • Chapter 3

Equivalent fractions

You will learn how to:
- Recognise the equivalence of simple fractions, decimals and percentages.
- Simplify fractions by cancelling common factors and identify equivalent fractions.
- Change an improper fraction to a mixed number, and vice versa.
- Convert terminating decimals to fractions. For example, $0.23 = \frac{23}{100}$.

Starting point

Do you remember …?

- the decimals and percentages equivalent to $\frac{1}{2}$, $\frac{1}{4}$, $\frac{1}{10}$, $\frac{1}{100}$?

  For example, can you complete the table below?

Fraction	Percentage	Decimal
$\frac{1}{2}$		
	25%	
		0.1
$\frac{1}{100}$		

- how to find common factors of numbers?

  For example, find the common factors of 12 and 18.

This will also be helpful when …

you learn how to use fractions, decimals and percentages as probabilities and to solve problems involving all three.

Hook

Look at the images below, which show the same square coloured in different ways:

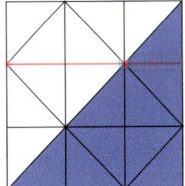 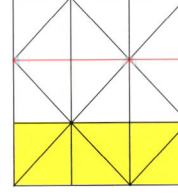 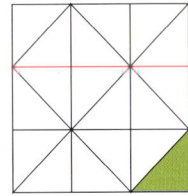 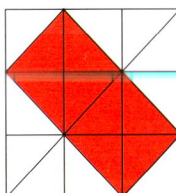

- What fraction of the square is coloured in each diagram?
- You can shade only whole triangles. Which of these fractions can you shade?
  $\frac{1}{2}, \frac{1}{3}, \frac{1}{4}, \frac{1}{5}, \frac{1}{6}, \frac{1}{7}, \frac{1}{8}, \ldots, \frac{1}{24}$

Chapter 3: Equivalent fractions

Equivalent fractions, decimals and percentages

Key terms

Fractions, decimals and percentages are **equivalent** if they have the same value.

A **percentage** represents the number of parts per hundred. For example, 17% means 17 parts per hundred or $\frac{17}{100}$.

Worked example 1

a) Find the percentage and decimal equivalent to $\frac{7}{10}$.

b) Find the percentage and decimal equivalent to $\frac{3}{4}$.

a) $\frac{1}{10} = 0.1 = 10\%$ $\frac{7}{10} = 7 \times \frac{1}{10}$ $= 7 \times 0.1 = 0.7$ $= 7 \times 10\% = 70\%$ $\frac{7}{10} = 0.7 = 70\%$	Use what you know about the percentage and decimal equivalent to $\frac{1}{10}$ to write down equivalents to $\frac{7}{10}$.	
b) $\frac{1}{4} = 0.25 = 25\%$ $\frac{3}{4} = 3 \times \frac{1}{4}$ $= 3 \times 0.25 = 0.75$ $= 3 \times 25\% = 75\%$ $\frac{3}{4} = 0.75 = 75\%$ 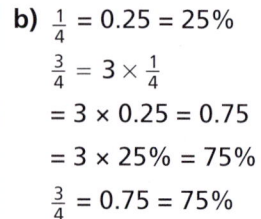	Use what you know about the percentage and decimal equivalent to $\frac{1}{4}$ to write equivalents to $\frac{3}{4}$.	

Worked example 2

a) Write a fraction and a percentage equivalent to 0.6.

b) Write a fraction and a decimal equivalent to 65%.

20 Unit 1A: Number and calculation

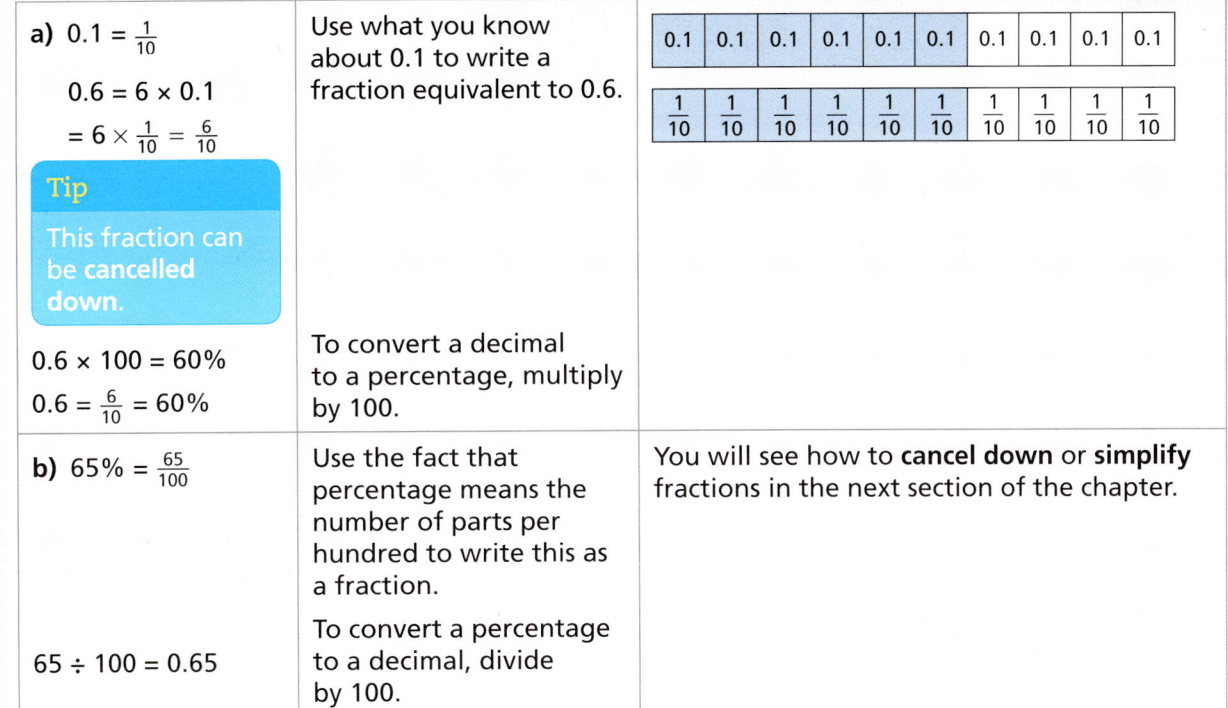

Exercise 1 1–8

1 Write these percentages as fractions.
  a) 50%   b) 10%   c) 20%   d) 75%   e) 5%   f) 15%

2 Write these percentages as decimals.
  a) 10%   b) 30%   c) 90%   d) 1%   e) 5%   f) 35%

3 Write these fractions as percentages and as decimals.
  a) $\frac{3}{10}$ b) $\frac{7}{10}$ c) $\frac{3}{5}$ d) $\frac{4}{5}$ e) $\frac{27}{100}$ f) $\frac{9}{100}$

4 Write these decimals as fractions.
  a) 0.8   b) 0.6   c) 0.03
  d) 0.08   e) 0.43   f) 0.15

> **Tip**
> 0.1 is equivalent to $\frac{1}{10}$ and 0.01 is equivalent to $\frac{1}{100}$

5 Write a percentage equivalent to $\frac{2}{3}$.

6 Which of these is the odd one out? Explain your answer.
  a) $\frac{1}{5}$ b) 0.2   c) 5%

7 Which of these is the odd one out? Explain your answer.
  a) $\frac{1}{3}$ b) 0.3   c) 30%

> **Tip**
> $\frac{1}{3}$ is equivalent to $33\frac{1}{3}\%$

8 Which of these is the odd one out? Explain your answer.
  a) $\frac{7}{100}$ b) 0.07   c) 70%

Chapter 3: Equivalent fractions

9 Match the equivalent fractions, decimals and percentages in each column.

Complete the missing values to make six equivalent trios.

0.5	$\frac{3}{4}$	
0.2		75%
0.05	$\frac{1}{2}$	10%
	$\frac{1}{20}$	5%
0.1	$\frac{1}{5}$	1%
0.75	$\frac{1}{100}$	50%

Equivalent fractions

Key terms

The **denominator** of a fraction is the number on the bottom of the fraction. It represents the number of parts in the whole.

For example, the denominator of $\frac{2}{3}$ is 3, which means there are 3 parts in the whole.

The **numerator** of a fraction is the number on the top of the fraction. It represents the number of parts you are working with.

For example, the numerator of $\frac{2}{3}$ is 2, which means you are working with 2 parts of the 3 in the whole.

Simplify means to produce something of the same value using smaller numbers.

For example, you can simplify $\frac{5}{10}$ to $\frac{1}{2}$ because you know they have the same value.

To **simplify fully** means to simplify as far as possible.

For example, we can simplify $\frac{12}{18}$ to $\frac{4}{6}$ or $\frac{6}{9}$ or $\frac{2}{3}$, but if we are asked to simplify fully $\frac{12}{18}$ then the answer is $\frac{2}{3}$ because $\frac{2}{3}$ cannot be simplified any further.

Two fractions are **equivalent** if they have the same value.

For example, $\frac{5}{10}$ and $\frac{1}{2}$ are equivalent.

Worked example 3

a) **Simplify** $\frac{6}{9}$.

b) Find an **equivalent** fraction to $\frac{3}{5}$.

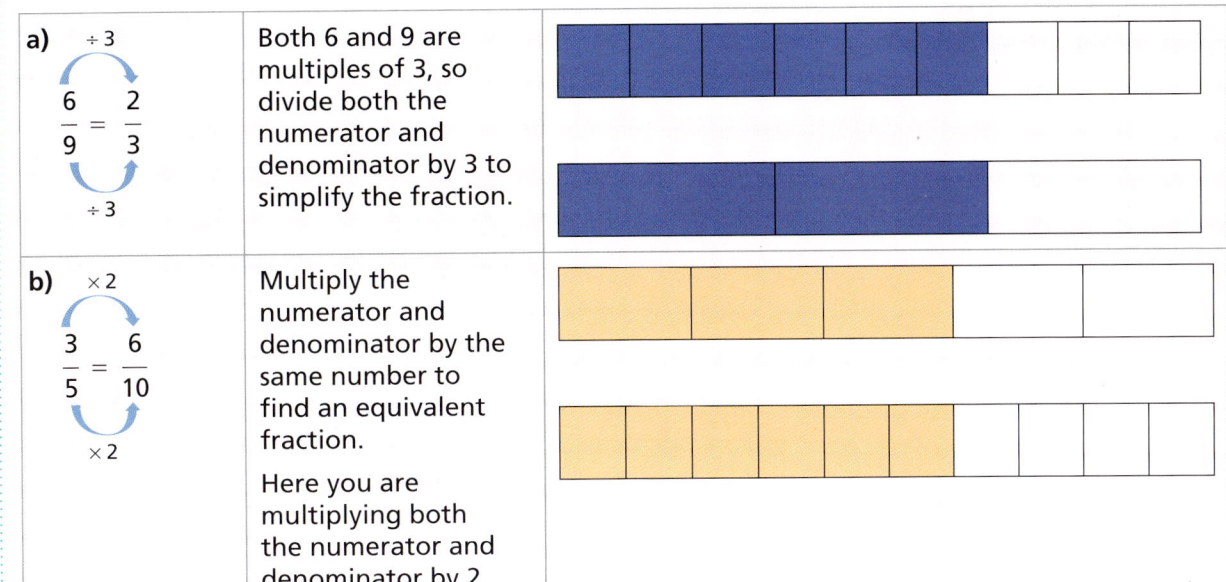

Exercise 2

1 Complete the missing digit to simplify these fractions.
   a) $\frac{6}{8} = \frac{\square}{4}$ b) $\frac{25}{30} = \frac{\square}{6}$ c) $\frac{9}{24} = \frac{3}{\square}$ d) $\frac{16}{20} = \frac{4}{\square}$ e) $\frac{32}{48} = \frac{\square}{6}$ f) $\frac{35}{56} = \frac{5}{\square}$

2 Simplify these fractions fully.
   a) $\frac{4}{10}$ b) $\frac{10}{12}$ c) $\frac{6}{15}$ d) $\frac{15}{25}$ e) $\frac{14}{21}$ f) $\frac{3}{18}$
   g) $\frac{8}{12}$ h) $\frac{20}{24}$ i) $\frac{12}{18}$ j) $\frac{30}{45}$ k) $\frac{9}{36}$ l) $\frac{30}{36}$

3 Find three fractions that are equivalent to:
   a) $\frac{1}{3}$ b) $\frac{3}{4}$ c) $\frac{2}{5}$ d) $\frac{5}{6}$ e) $\frac{1}{8}$ f) $\frac{7}{9}$

4 Complete the missing digit to find an equivalent fraction.
   a) $\frac{1}{6} = \frac{5}{\square}$ b) $\frac{2}{9} = \frac{6}{\square}$ c) $\frac{1}{8} = \frac{\square}{48}$ d) $\frac{3}{5} = \frac{\square}{45}$ e) $\frac{3}{4} = \frac{18}{\square}$ f) $\frac{7}{12} = \frac{\square}{60}$

5 For each fraction, find an equivalent fraction with a denominator of 36.
   a) $\frac{1}{4}$ b) $\frac{1}{6}$ c) $\frac{5}{9}$ d) $\frac{7}{18}$ e) $\frac{11}{12}$ f) $\frac{2}{3}$

6 Which of these fractions can be simplified to $\frac{2}{3}$?
   A: $\frac{18}{24}$ B: $\frac{10}{16}$ C: $\frac{22}{33}$ D: $\frac{18}{27}$ E: $\frac{24}{48}$

7 Write an easy simplifying fractions question. What makes it easy?
Now write a more challenging simplifying fractions question. What makes it hard?

Think about
How many equivalent fractions are there to $\frac{5}{6}$?

Mixed numbers

Key terms

In a **proper fraction** the numerator is less than the denominator. For example, $\frac{7}{11}$.

In an **improper fraction** the numerator is greater than the denominator. For example, $\frac{17}{11}$.

A **mixed number** is a combination of a whole number and a proper fraction, used to represent a quantity with a value greater than 1. For example, $3\frac{1}{4}$.

Worked example 4

a) Write $2\frac{1}{3}$ as an improper fraction.

b) Write $\frac{11}{4}$ as a mixed number.

a) $2\frac{1}{3}$ $= \frac{3}{3} + \frac{3}{3} + \frac{1}{3}$ $= \frac{7}{3}$	You can represent $2\frac{1}{3}$ as two wholes and one third of an additional whole. Write each whole as a fraction with the same denominator as the fractional part.
b) $\frac{11}{4}$ $= \frac{4}{4} + \frac{4}{4} + \frac{3}{4}$ $= 1 + 1 + \frac{3}{4}$ $= 2\frac{3}{4}$	You need to group the quarters into wholes by putting them in as many groups of four as possible. There are two groups of four and three quarters left over.

Exercise 3

1. Sort these fractions into proper and improper fractions.

   $\frac{4}{5}$ $\frac{7}{6}$ $\frac{1}{3}$ $\frac{5}{12}$ $\frac{20}{11}$ $\frac{9}{7}$ $\frac{4}{3}$ $\frac{1}{11}$ $\frac{10}{10}$

2. Convert these mixed numbers to improper fractions:
   a) $1\frac{1}{4}$ b) $1\frac{2}{5}$ c) $2\frac{2}{3}$ d) $3\frac{1}{12}$ e) $4\frac{1}{3}$
   f) $1\frac{5}{8}$ g) $3\frac{5}{6}$ h) $3\frac{4}{11}$ i) $10\frac{1}{2}$ j) $3\frac{6}{7}$

3. Here is a number line from 0 to 4.

   Draw arrows to show the positions of the following improper fractions on the line. Label each arrow clearly.
   a) $\frac{3}{2}$ b) $\frac{7}{2}$ c) $\frac{9}{4}$ d) $\frac{10}{3}$

4 Convert these improper fractions to mixed numbers.

a) $\frac{9}{4}$ b) $\frac{5}{3}$ c) $\frac{7}{2}$ d) $\frac{12}{7}$ e) $\frac{8}{5}$ f) $\frac{10}{9}$

g) $\frac{19}{8}$ h) $\frac{17}{6}$ i) $\frac{34}{11}$ j) $\frac{22}{9}$ k) $\frac{20}{3}$ l) $\frac{25}{7}$

5 Which of these improper fractions is equivalent to $4\frac{3}{5}$?

A: $\frac{23}{20}$ B: $\frac{12}{5}$ C: $\frac{23}{5}$ D: $\frac{12}{20}$ E: $\frac{15}{12}$

6 Jasper says that $\frac{12}{5}$ is equivalent to $1\frac{2}{5}$.

Do you agree with Jasper?

Explain your answer.

Key term

A **terminating decimal** is a decimal which stops after a certain number of decimal places, for example 0.6 or 0.74 or 0.71456, rather than going on forever with or without a pattern in the digits.

Changing decimals to fractions

Worked example 5

Convert these **terminating decimals** to fractions and simplify.

a) 0.9 b) 0.36

a) $0.9 = \frac{9}{10}$	You can write 0.9 as a decimal by using the smallest place value of the number. The smallest place value is tenths. You cannot cancel this fraction.
b) $0.36 = \frac{36}{100}$ $\frac{36}{100} = \frac{9}{25}$ (÷4)	You can write 0.36 as a decimal by using the smallest place value of the number. The smallest place value is hundredths. You can cancel by dividing the numerator and denominator by 4.

Exercise 4

1 Convert these terminating decimals to fractions, simplifying your answer where possible.

a) 0.7 b) 0.8 c) 0.5 d) 0.07 e) 0.29 f) 0.22

g) 0.28 h) 0.35 i) 0.65 j) 0.48 k) 0.32 l) 0.125

2 Jemima converts 0.13 to a fraction.

She says, "0.13 must be equivalent to $\frac{1.3}{10}$"

Explain what Jemima has done wrong and correct her answer.

Discuss

How would you convince someone that $\frac{3}{20}$ is the same as 15%?

3 Vocabulary feature question

Complete the sentences below using words from the box.
Some of the words may be used more than once.

terminating	proper	improper	numerator
denominator	mixed number	equivalent
percentage	decimal	fraction	simplify

A fraction represents a number of parts per whole: the size of the whole is shown by the .... and the number of parts required is shown by the ....

Usually the numerator is less than the denominator, for example in $\frac{5}{8}$, so you call this a(n) .... fraction.

When you have a number bigger than a whole, you can represent it either as a(n) .... fraction, for example $\frac{15}{8}$, or as a .... , for example $1\frac{7}{8}$.

Two fractions are .... if they have the same overall value compared to a whole. You can .... the fractions by dividing them by common factors of the numerator and denominator to show that they have the same value.

A fraction can also be .... to a .... or a .... decimals will be equivalent to fractions with a .... of 10, 100, 1000 etc.

End of chapter reflection

You should know that ...	You should be able to ...	Such as ...		
Numbers that are not whole can be expressed as fractions, decimals or percentages.	Recognise equivalent fractions, decimals and percentages in simple cases.	0.25	$\frac{1}{4}$	25%
		0.2	$\frac{1}{5}$	20%
Fractions are equivalent if they have the same proportional value of a whole.	Simplify a fraction fully.	Simplify $\frac{72}{90}$		
You can find an equivalent fraction by multiplying or dividing both the numerator and the denominator of your fraction by the same number.	Find an equivalent fraction with a given denominator.	Complete the missing digit to find an equivalent fraction: $\frac{5}{6} = \frac{\square}{42}$		
A proper fraction is one where the numerator is less than the denominator. An improper fraction is one where the numerator is greater than the denominator. A mixed number is a combination of a whole number and a proper fraction, which is used to represent a quantity greater than a whole.	Convert • an improper fraction to a mixed number. • a mixed number to an improper fraction.	Write $\frac{10}{3}$ as a mixed number. Write $5\frac{1}{4}$ as an improper fraction.		
A terminating decimal can be written as a fraction with denominator 10, 100, etc.	Convert a terminating decimal to a fraction (and simplify).	Write 0.44 as a fraction and simplify fully.		

Unit 1A • Chapter 4

Negative numbers

You will learn how to:
- Recognise negative numbers as positions on a number line, and order them.
- Add and subtract positive and negative integers in context.

Starting point

Do you remember …?
- what a negative number means?
  For example, a temperature of −4°C.
- how to add and subtract positive numbers in your head?
  For example 23 + 79 or 312 − 150.
- how to use a number line to find the difference between two numbers?
  For example, the difference between 7 and 102.

This will also be helpful when …
you learn to use negative numbers in formulae and in solving problems.

Hook

Here are some world holiday destinations and their average temperatures in January.

Chamonix	Cape Town	Yakutsk	London	Barbados	Lapland
−2°C	20°C	−34°C	7°C	29°C	−12°C

- Can you position each city in the correct place on the thermometer scale?
- Use this to list the cities in order of temperature (from coldest to warmest).
- How many degrees difference are there between each pair of neighbouring destinations in your list?
- Complete the blanks in these sentences to make a pair of true statements:
  ......Barbados...... is ......9...... degrees warmer than ......Cape Town...... .
  ......Lapland...... is ......19...... degrees colder than ......London...... .
- How many degrees difference are there altogether between the temperature of the coldest and the temperature of the hottest place? 63°C

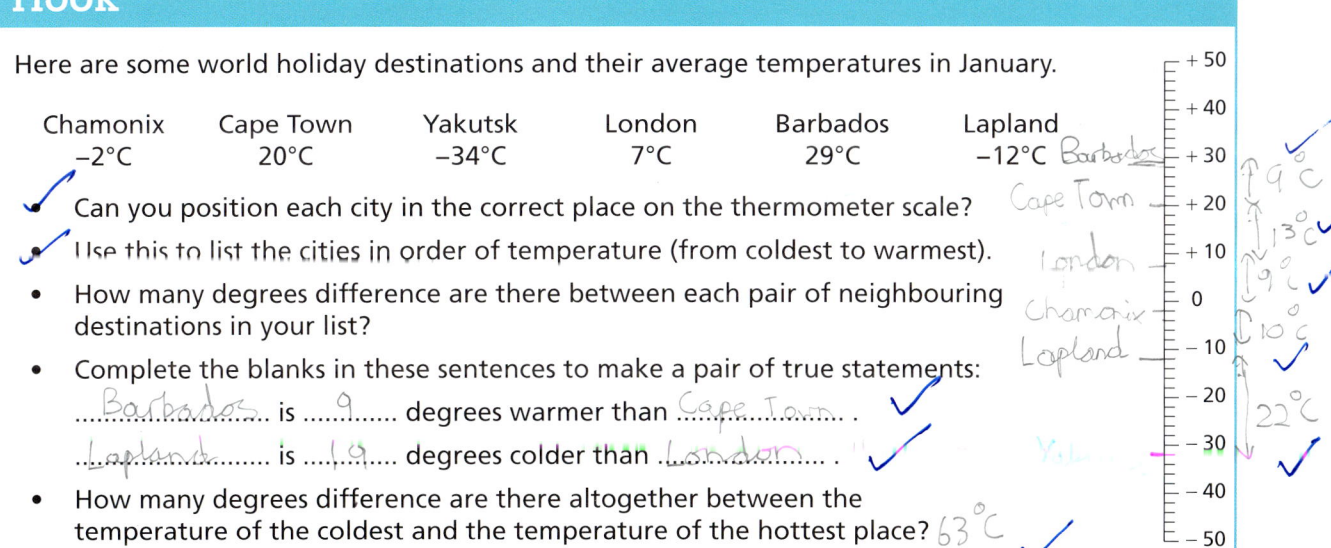

Did you know?
In some countries zero is neither positive nor negative.
In some countries zero is both positive and negative.
In some countries zero is positive.

Think about
Where else do you see negative numbers in real life?

Chapter 4: Negative numbers 27

Using negative numbers

Key terms

A **positive** number is a number that is greater than zero.
A **negative** number is a number that is less than zero.
Integers are whole numbers, whether positive, negative or zero.

Worked example 1

Put these numbers into order, smallest to largest.

4   0   −3   −1   17   −7

−7 −3 −1 0 4 17	Put the numbers on a number line.
−7, −3, −1, 0, 4, 17	You can read off the numbers in order from the number line.

Exercise 1

1 Copy the number line and draw arrows to show the position of these numbers on the number line.

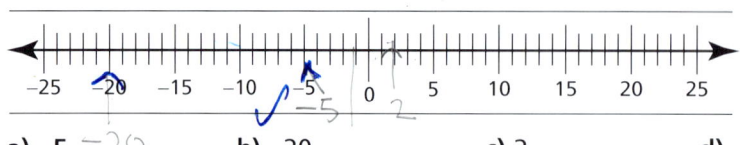

a) −5   b) −20   c) 2   d) −1   e) −16

2 Copy the number line and draw arrows to show the position of these numbers on the number line.

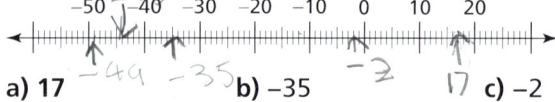

a) 17   b) −35   c) −2   d) −49

3 Use the symbol < or > to show which number in each pair is greater.

You might want to use a number line to position them both first to help you decide.

> **Tip**
> Remember that < means less than and > means greater than.

a) 3 and 15   b) 0 and 7   c) 4 and 1
d) −1 and 5   e) 3 and −4   f) −3 and −1
g) −3 and −6   h) −5 and −9   i) −91 and −93
j) −84 and −94

4 Put these quantities in order, from least to greatest.

You can use a number line to help you.

a) 7°C, −12°C, 0°C, 4°C
b) 4°C, −1°C, −5°C, 1°C
c) −11°C, −9°C, 0°C, 5°C, 9°C, −19°C
d) −65°C, −56°C, −63°C, −61°C, −60°C
e) −39, −93, −43, −49, 0
f) −12.5, −13, −12.7, −12, −12.1, −11.8

Unit 1A: Number and calculation

5. Pierre is comparing −56 and −79.

   He says, "−79 is greater than −56, because 79 is a larger number than 56".

   Do you agree with Pierre? Explain your answer. No − 79 is negative.

Adding and subtracting positive and negative integers in context

Worked example 2

The temperature outside is −8°C.

a) The temperature decreases by 5°C. Find the new temperature.

b) The temperature then increases by 20°C. Find the final temperature

−8°C	You can represent −8 on a number line, 8 places below 0.	
a) −8°C − 5°C = −13°C	If the temperature decreases by 5°C, then you need to move down the number line by 5 places, ending at −13°C.	
b) −13°C + 20°C = 7°C	Then, if the temperature increases by 20°C, you need to move up the number line by 20 places, ending at 7°C.	

Exercise 2

1. Complete the missing temperatures.
   a) 5°C warmer than 6°C is ...11... °C
   b) 5°C warmer than −12°C is ...7... °C
   c) 8°C warmer than −1°C is ...7... °C
   d) 17°C warmer than −4°C is ...13... °C
   e) 11°C warmer than ...−3... °C is 8°C
   f) ...18... °C warmer than −20°C is −2°C
   g) 3°C colder than 12°C is ...9... °C
   h) 8°C colder than −2°C is ...−10... °C
   i) 6°C colder than 2°C is ...−4... °C
   j) 15°C colder than 3°C is ...−12... °C
   k) 14°C colder than ...−7... °C is −21°C
   l) ...42... °C colder than 12°C is −30°C

2. Complete the missing numbers.
   a) 6 + 7 = ...13...
   b) −12 + 4 = ...−8...
   c) −2 + 8 = ...6...
   d) −18 + 25 = ...7...
   e) −5 + ...22... = 17
   f) ...−25... + 22 = −3
   g) 16 − 7 = ...9...
   h) −12 − 4 = ...−16...
   i) 5 − 8 = ...−3...
   j) 16 − 24 = ...−8...
   k) −5 − ...12... = −17
   l) ...19... − 22 = −3

3 In a multi-storey car park, the floors above the ground are numbered 0, 1, 2, 3, 4 and 5 and the floors below the ground are labelled −1, −2, −3 and −4.

Copy and complete this table, the first one is done for you.

	Start at floor:	Travel:	Arrive at floor:
a)	3	down 3 floors	0
b)	1	down 3 floors	−4 ✓
c)	3	down 4 floors	−1 ✓
d)	−2	up 4 floors	2 ✓
e)	−1	down 2 floors	−3 ✓
f)	−2	up 5 floors	3 ✓
g)	−2	up 6 floors	4 ✓

4 The table shows the heights above (+) and below (−) sea level of four places. The heights are given to the nearest thousand metres.

Place name	Height from sea level to the nearest thousand metres
The top of Mount Everest	+9000
El Alto	+4000
Seattle	0
Wreck of RMS Titanic	−4000
Challenger Deep	−11 000

Complete the following sentences:

a) The difference in height between the top of Mount Everest and Seattle is ......9000....... ✓ m.
b) The difference in height between the top of Mount Everest and El Alto is ......5000....... ✓ m.
c) The difference in height between the wreck of RMS Titanic and Seattle is ......4000....... ✗ m.
d) The difference in height between the Challenger Deep and El Alto is ......15 000....... m. ✗
e) The difference in height between the wreck of RMS Titanic and El Alto is ......8000....... m.
f) The difference in height between the Challenger Deep and the top of Mount Everest is ......20 000....... m.

5 Use the internet to find the difference between the highest and lowest capital cities in the world. =3697m ✓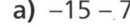

6 Which is the odd one out?

a) −15 − 7   b) −24 + 2 ✓   c) 20 − 42   d) −27 − 5   e) −21 − 1

7 How many pairs of integers between −20 and 20 can you find with a sum of 7?
How do you know you have got them all? =34 ✗

8 **Vocabulary feature question**

Complete the sentences below using words from the box.
Some of the words may be used more than once.

positive   negative   integers   zero   order

Unit 1A: Number and calculation

A ......positive...... number is one that is greater than ......negative...... .

Numbers that are less than zero are called ......negative...... numbers.

Whole numbers, whether they are ......positive......, ...0...... or ......negative...... are called ......integers...... .

You can put numbers in ......order...... from least to greatest, or from greatest to least.

End of chapter reflection

You should know that ...	You should be able to ...	Such as ...
Positive numbers, zero and negative numbers can be put in order on a number line.	Order a set of numbers.	Put these numbers in order from smallest to largest a) −15, −11, −20, −17, −30 b) −6, 0, −1, 5, −9, 4
Positive and negative numbers can be added and subtracted in context.	Answer questions involving positive and negative numbers in context.	This morning the temperature was −6°C and this afternoon the temperature is 4°C. By how many degrees has the temperature risen?

Chapter 4: Negative numbers

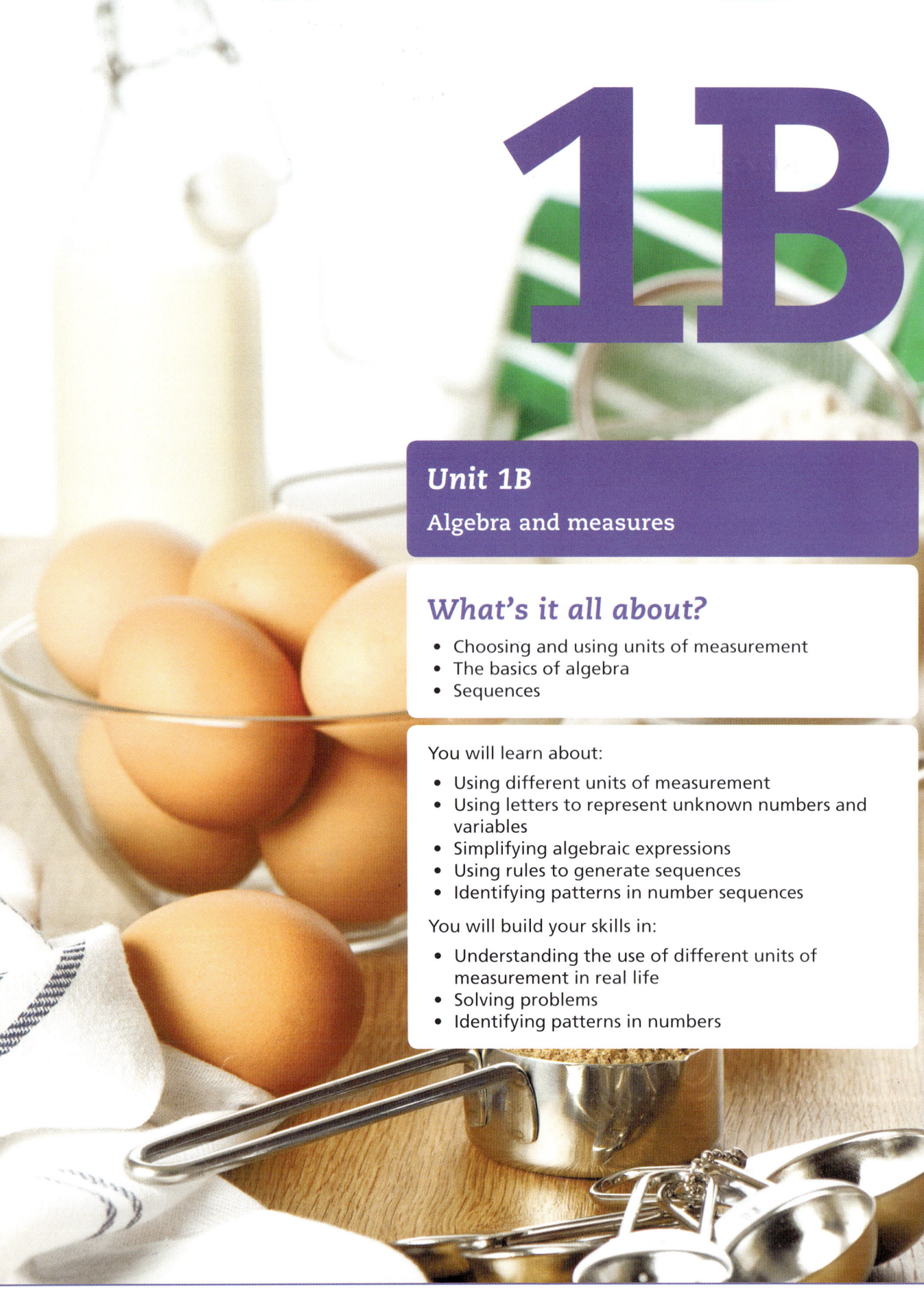

1B

Unit 1B
Algebra and measures

What's it all about?
- Choosing and using units of measurement
- The basics of algebra
- Sequences

You will learn about:
- Using different units of measurement
- Using letters to represent unknown numbers and variables
- Simplifying algebraic expressions
- Using rules to generate sequences
- Identifying patterns in number sequences

You will build your skills in:
- Understanding the use of different units of measurement in real life
- Solving problems
- Identifying patterns in numbers

Unit 1B • Chapter 5

You will learn how to:
- Choose suitable units of measurement to estimate, measure, calculate and solve problems in everyday contexts.

Units of measurement

Starting point

Do you remember …?
- learning about measures of length such as kilometres (km) and centimetres (cm)?
- learning about measures of mass such as kilograms (kg) and grams (g)?
- learning about measures of capacity, such as litres (l), centilitres (cl) and millilitres (ml), which you often use for measuring liquids such as water?

This will be helpful when …

you go on to learn about:
- converting between metric units
- square units for measuring areas

Hook

Can you tell how long a line is without using a ruler?

Use your ruler to draw 10 lines on a piece of plain, unlined paper.

They must all be an exact number of centimetres long and one of them must be exactly 1 centimetre long.

They can be at different angles.

They can be anywhere on the page but they must not cross each other.

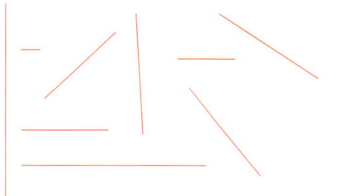

Now swap your paper with another student.

Now guess the measurement of each of the 10 lines without using a ruler or set square.

Write your answer next to the line.

Now swap back the papers and use your ruler to see how accurate the guesses are.

How did you find and use the 1 cm line?

Worked example 1

Choose a suitable unit of measurement to estimate each of the following:
a) The quantity of breakfast cereal a small family eats each morning.
b) The quantity of breakfast cereal a large hotel uses each morning.
c) The length of a pencil.
d) The height of an elephant.
e) The length of a swimming pool.

a) A packet of breakfast cereal is usually measured in grams and a very large pack is 1 kg. A small family eats less than a whole packet so the quantity will be estimated in grams.	An average person eats about 100 g of cereal for breakfast.	A paperclip has a mass of about one gram. You could easily make up the weight of cereal a family eats in paperclips so grams is the best measure.
b) The quantity of cereal used by a large hotel is estimated in kilograms because a large hotel will feed hundreds of people so will use thousands of grams and a thousand grams is a kilogram.	If one person eats about 100 g of cereal, then every 10 people will eat 1 kg.	A litre bottle of cola has a mass of about 1 kg. The mass of cereal used by a hotel would be thousands of paperclips so easier to measure in bottles of cola.
c) A pencil would be estimated in centimetres as millimetres are too small and a metre is too large.	You could use millimetres or centimetres to measure the pencil but a centimetre is about the width of a thumbnail and a millimetre is about the width of a credit card so centimetres would be a more practical estimator.	
d) The height of an elephant could be estimated in metres as centimetres are much smaller than an elephant and kilometres are much bigger.	You could use centimetres but the answer would be hundreds of centimetres so it is better to use metres.	A metre is about the length of a full size guitar. It would be easier to measure the elephant in guitars than thumbnails.
e) Although it is bigger than an elephant, the length of a swimming pool is estimated in metres as it is smaller than a kilometre.	An Olympic swimming pool is 50 m long but many local pools are smaller.	A kilometre is about the length of 10 soccer pitches, much bigger than a swimming pool.

Did you know?

Most countries use metric measures, a few countries, including the United States of America (USA), use imperial measures and some, such as the United Kingdom (UK), use a mixture of both.

In the UK small distances, such as the length of a motor car, are measured in metres and centimetres but large distances, such as the distance between two towns, are measured in miles and not kilometres.

The table shows some metric measures with some possible uses.

Tip

The third column of the Worked example above gives some ideas for getting the size of common measures. These can help when you are thinking about the correct units to use.

Unit 1B: Algebra and measures

Key terms

	Small	Medium	Large
Distance	millimetres or centimetres	centimetres and metres	kilometres
For example, these units of measurement could be used to measure:	Thickness of a book or width of a pencil	Width of a room	Distance between two towns

Mass	grams	grams and kilograms	kilograms and tonnes
For example, these units of measurement could be used to measure:	Mass of an egg	Mass of a computer	Mass of a car
Capacity	millilitres	millilitres and litres	litres and cubic metres
For example, these units of measurement could be used to measure:	Ink in a pen	Cola in a bottle	Water in a swimming pool

Exercise 1

1 Choose the most suitable unit of measurement for each item from these options.

millimetres (mm)   centimetres (cm)   metres (m)   kilometres (km)

a) The height of a room
b) The distance from London to New York
c) The width of a desk
d) The length of a football pitch
e) The thickness of a mobile phone
f) The height of a mountain
g) The height of a cupboard
h) The length of a shoe
i) The height of a giraffe
j) Your waist

2 Choose the most suitable unit of time measurement for each item from these options.

seconds (s)   minutes (min)   hours (hrs)   days (d)

a) The time taken to read a book
b) The length of your school term
c) The time taken to run 100 metres
d) The time taken to have a shower
e) The length of your school day
f) The time taken for an aeroplane to fly from Dubai to Sydney, Australia
g) The time you can hold your eyes open without blinking

Chapter 5: Units of measurement

3 Choose the most suitable unit of mass for each item from these options.

grams (g)   kilograms (kg)   tonnes (t)

a) A bag of potatoes
b) A truck
c) A lion
d) A sofa
e) A packed suitcase
f) A bar of chocolate
g) A bowl of breakfast cereal
h) A school bus
i) A table-tennis ball

4 Choose the most likely unit of measurement for each item from these options.

litres   millilitres

a) A spoonful of cough medicine
b) A tank of fuel for a car
c) The amount of water you use for a shower
d) A carton of orange juice

5 Put these measures in order from smallest to largest:

a	The mass of a tennis ball	The mass of a bowling ball	The mass of a soccer ball	The mass of a table tennis ball
b	The time it takes to run a marathon	The time it takes to boil an egg	The time it takes to clean your teeth	The time it takes to watch a film
c	The length of a family car	The length of a passenger aeroplane	The length of a bicycle	The length of a football pitch

6 Estimate the length of these items, without using your ruler, and give your answer in centimetres or millimetres.

a) The width of your thumb nail
b) Your hand span (from the tip of your thumb to the tip of your little finger with your hand stretched out)
c) The length of your foot/shoe
d) The length of your arm from your elbow to your wrist
e) The thickness of your exercise book

Now measure them with your ruler to see how accurate you are.

7 Measure these items giving your answers in centimetres.

a) The length of your pencil/pen
b) The width of your maths book
c) The height of the seat of your chair
d) The width of your desk or table

8 Which units would you use to measure the following:

a) the width of a room
b) the height you can reach above your head
c) the time it takes to boil an egg
d) the amount of liquid in a mug
e) the time it takes to put on a pair of socks
f) the distance from here to the North Pole

9 A container holds 1000 packets of sweets when it is full. Each packet of sweets has a mass of 15 grams. Which units should be used to measure the mass of the container?

10 In American recipes the quantities of ingredients, such as flour, are measured in cups. A recipe for pancakes is shown below. Find out about cup measures and change the quantities of flour and milk into appropriate metric units.

1 large egg

1 cup of self-raising flour

1 cup of milk

sea salt

End of chapter reflection

You should know that …	You should be able to …	Such as …
There are different units of measurement for length, capacity, mass and time.	Choose a suitable unit of measurement to estimate, measure, calculate and solve problems.	Write suitable units for measuring: a) the width of the room b) the time it takes to complete a piece of homework.

Unit 1B • Chapter 6

Algebra

You will learn how to:
- Use letters to represent unknown numbers or variables; know the meaning of the words *term*, *expression* and *equation*.
- Know that algebraic operations follow the same order as arithmetic operations.
- Construct simple algebraic expressions by using letters to represent numbers.
- Simplify linear expressions, for example, collect like terms.
- Multiply a constant over a bracket.

Starting point

Do you remember …?

- that the order in which you add and multiply two numbers together does not matter?
  For example, $6 + 5 = 5 + 6$ and $6 \times 5 = 5 \times 6$
- that the order you subtract and divide two numbers does matter?
  For example, $6 - 5$ is not the same as $5 - 6$ and $4 \div 2$ is not the same as $2 \div 4$
- that $3(6 + 8)$ means $3 \times (6 + 8) = 42$

Hook

Ask someone to write down a number between 1 and 20. Tell them not to show you the number.
Give them these instructions but tell them not to speak the answers until you ask:
- add 3 to the number,
- double your answer,
- add another 4,
- subtract 10, and tell me your final answer

Divide their final answer by 2 in your head. Your answer will be the number they have written down.
Try again with a different number written down.
Why does this work?
Could you use this method to find out someone's age or a number that they have written down and not shown to you?
Can you make up a puzzle of your own to finish with the number that you first thought of?

Letters for numbers

Key terms

Sometimes you don't know what a number is, but you need a way of showing a fact about the number. You could leave a space for numbers you don't know:

$7 + \ldots\ldots = 11$

or you could write a letter to represent the unknown number.

$7 + m = 11$

7 + *m* is called an **expression** and the 7 and the *m* are called the **terms** of the expression. You do not have to use *m*, you can use any letter.

Instead of writing, "My age is .... years." you could write, "My age is *t* years." *t* is an **expression** for your age. It is an expression with one term.

An **equation** has an equals sign linking two expressions or numbers which are equal.

7 + *m* = 11 and *s* − 3 = 6 are both equations.

> **Did you know?**
>
> There is evidence that the ideas of algebra were being used in ancient Babylon almost 4000 years ago.

Worked example 1

Write a letter in each of the spaces.

a) 3 + ... = 21

b) 3 + ... = 6

c) Jana is .... years old.

d) Tomas is .... years and .... months old.

e) Write the correct word in the space.

   q + 6 = 11 is an ....

f) Label the sides of this rectangle with letters to represent their lengths.

a) 3 + *t* = 21	Put in any letter instead of the space.	3, *t* / 21
b) 3 + *r* = 6	Put in any letter instead of the space.	3, *r* / 6
c) Jana is *y* years old.	Put in any letter instead of the blank.	Jana is (any letter) years old.  *y* years
d) Tomas is *y* years and *m* months old.	Put in any letters instead of the spaces. The two letters must be different as they represent different quantities.	Tomas is (any letter) years and (any different letter) months old. *y* years *m* months

Chapter 6: Algebra

e) $q + 6 = 11$ is an equation because it has an equals sign.	All equations have an equals sign.	6 | q | 11
f) (rectangle with sides labelled q and P)	You know that opposite sides of a rectangle are the same length. So you need to use the same letter on the equal sides to show that they are the same length.	Equal lengths should be labelled with the same letter.

Exercise 1

1 Write the following with letters instead of spaces.

a) $4 + \ldots\ldots = 16$ b) $\ldots\ldots - 5 = 12$ c) $4 + \ldots\ldots + \ldots\ldots = 54$

d) Samia is ………… years and ………… months old.

e) Jenny is going on holiday in ………… weeks and ………… days.

f) Danny has ………… dollars and ………… cents in his pocket.

2 Write the correct words in the spaces.

a) $q + 7 = 11$ is an ………………… .

b) $r + 4$ is an ………………… .

c) In (b) r and 4 are ………………… of an ………………… .

3 Label the sides of this isosceles triangle with letters to represent the lengths of the sides.

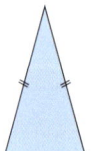

4 You are asked to label the sides of a square with letters to represent the lengths of its sides. How many different letters will you need to use?

5 You are asked to label the sides of a quadrilateral with letters to represent the lengths of its sides. What are the greatest and least number of letters that you will have to use?

Order of algebraic operations

Key terms

There are a number of **operations** in mathematics. You have learnt addition, subtraction, multiplication and division.

These operations in algebra work in the same way as they do in ordinary numbers.
For example, $6 + 7 = 7 + 6$ and $a + b = b + a$

Worked example 2

a) Is 7 + n the same as n + 7?
b) Is 7 − m the same as m − 7?
c) Is 3 × p the same as p × 3?
d) Is g ÷ 2 the same as 2 ÷ g?

a) 7 + n is the same as n + 7 as the order in which you add two numbers does not change the answer	Think of n as 'any number'. If you add 7 to a number, such as 5, it is the same as adding the 5 to 7. 7 + 5 = 5 + 7 = 12	
b) Is 7 − m the same as m − 7? No.	Think of m as 'any number'. If you take any number, such as 3, from 7 you get 4. If you take 7 from 3 you get −4 which is not the same.	
c) Is 3 × p the same as p × 3? Yes.	Think of p as 'any number'. If you multiply 3 by a number, such as 6, you get the same answer as if you multiply 6 by 3. 3 × 6 = 6 × 3 = 18	
d) Is g ÷ 2 the same as 2 ÷ g? No.	Think of g as 'any number' for example 4. 4 ÷ 2 = 2 but 2 ÷ 4 = $\frac{1}{2}$ which is not the same.	4 ÷ 2 = 2 2 ÷ 4 = $\frac{1}{2}$

Exercise 2

1 Which of the following are always true?

a) 5 + 6 = 6 + 5
b) 6 − 5 = 5 − 6
c) 6 + 4 + 3 = 3 + 4 + 6
d) 6 − 4 + 3 = 4 + 6 − 3
e) 2 × 3 = 3 × 2
f) 2 × 3 × 5 = 3 × 2 × 5
g) 6 ÷ 2 = 2 ÷ 6
h) 3 × 6 ÷ 2 = 6 × 3 ÷ 2
i) 3 × 2 ÷ 6 = 6 × 2 ÷ 3
j) 3 + r = r + 3
k) p + 3 + q = 3 + q + p
l) 9 − d = d − 9
m) 9 + 3 − k = 9 − k + 3
n) 6 × n = n × 6
o) 3 × q × 4 = 4 × 3 × q
p) 10 ÷ c = c ÷ 10
q) 2 × h ÷ 4 = 4 × 2 ÷ h
r) 3 ÷ d × 4 = 3 × 4 ÷ d

2 If p − q = q − p, what can you say about p and q? Is your statement always true?

3 If p ÷ q = q ÷ p what can you say about the values of p and q? Is your answer true if p = 0? Look up division by zero on the internet.

Forming expressions

Worked example 3

a) A ribbon of length 7 cm is joined to a ribbon of length *n* cm. Form an expression for the length of the new ribbon formed.

b) A ribbon of length 7 cm is joined to a ribbon of length *n* cm and a ribbon of length *m* cm. Form an expression for the total length of the new ribbon formed.

a) If you add 7 and *n* the expression can be written as 7 + *n* or *n* + 7. Putting in the units gives (7 + *n*) cm or (*n* + 7) cm	Add the terms 7 and *n* using a + sign to show that you are adding. This gives either 7 + *n* or *n* + 7. To show that the units of centimetres apply to both the *n* and the 7 you need to put brackets around the expressions.	7 | *n* 7 + *n*
b) Adding *m* to 7 + *n* gives 7 + *n* + *m* or *m* + 7 + *n* etc. Add brackets to show the units of centimetres apply to all 3 terms (7 + *n* + *m*) cm	The length of the new ribbon is found by adding 7 to *n* to *m*. Show this with addition signs. You can write it in different ways as the order of addition of numbers does not change the answer.	7 | *n* | *m* 7 + *m* + *n*

Exercise 3

Think about

Another answer to part (b) of the above Worked example is (*n* + 7 + *m*) cm. How many others can you find?

1 a) In each part of this question two parts of a line are shown. Form an expression, in centimetres, for the length of the line that you would get by joining the two parts.

i) _____ _____
    3 cm   *y* cm

ii) _____ _____
    t cm   4 cm

iii) _____ _____
    7 cm   *k* cm

iv) _____ _____
    8 cm   *x* cm

v) _____ _____
    b cm   10 cm

b) Form an expression, in centimetres, for the perimeter of each shape.

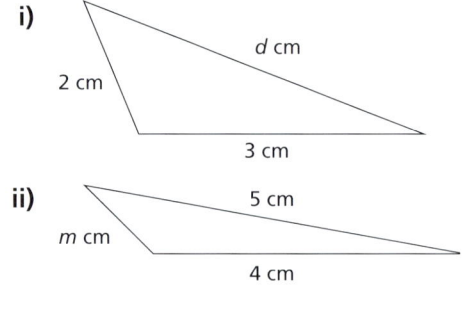
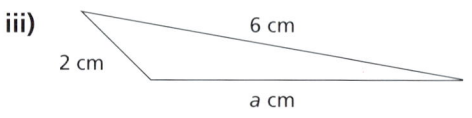
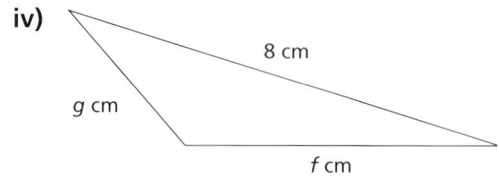

Unit 1B: Algebra and measures

2 Malia is forming expressions.

She writes 'a number 5 more than *x*' as *x* + 5.

Form an expression from each of these statements.

a) 5 plus *y*
b) *h* minus 8
c) the sum of *c* and 3
d) 6 plus *p*
e) 10 minus *f*
f) 12 more than *t*
g) 5 less than *k*
h) the difference between 10 and *w*

3 Form an expression for the perimeter of each of the shapes shown.

a)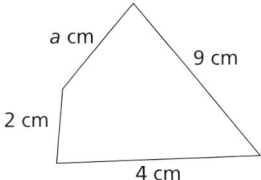
b)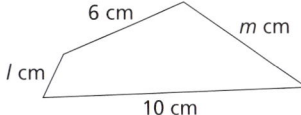
c)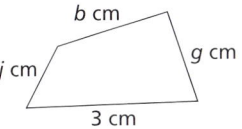
d)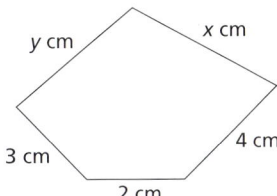
e)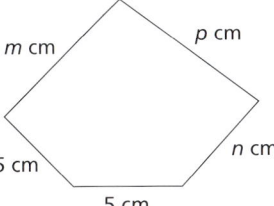
f)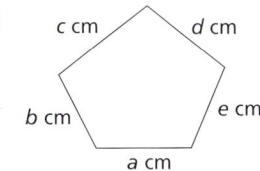

4 The perimeter of this triangle is 26 cm. Write an equation for the perimeter of the triangle using *p* and *q*. (All lengths are in centimetres.)

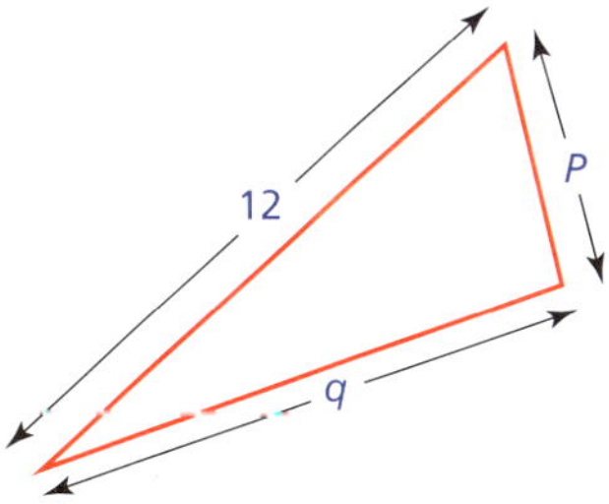

5 The perimeter of this rectangle is 26 cm. Jane says that this means that *r* = 26 − *s*. Is this true? Explain your answer.

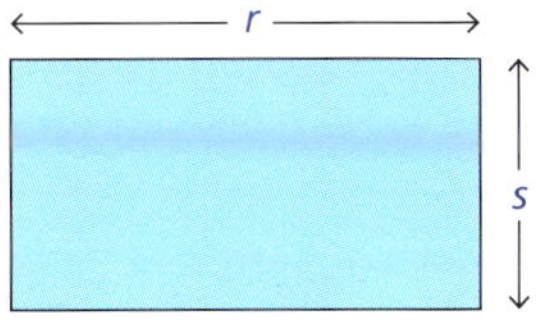

These cans all contain *n* grams of beans.

The quantity of beans in all the cans, in grams, is *n* + *n* + *n* which is 3 lots of *n* and this is the same as 3 × *n*.

In algebra 3 × *n* is written as 3*n*.

You don't use the multiplication sign to avoid confusion with the letter x.

In the same way 3*a* means 3 × *a*.

n on its own means 1 lot of *n* so *n* + 2*n* = 3*n*

n grams   *n* grams   *n* grams

Chapter 6: Algebra

Simplifying expressions

Key terms

When more than one term in the same letter is added or subtracted this is called **collecting like terms** or **simplifying by collecting like terms**.

For example, if each of these cans contain *d* grams of soup:

d grams *d* grams   *d* grams *d* grams *d* grams

the total mass of soup in the cans is   2*d* grams   +   3*d* grams   = 5*d* grams

This is because 2 lots of *d* grams added to 3 lots of *d* grams makes 5 lots of *d* grams.

Worked example 4

a) Form two expressions for the total mass of these 5 boxes from this picture.

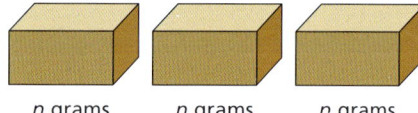

n grams   *n* grams   *n* grams   *m* grams   *m* grams

b) Form an expression for the perimeter of the triangle shown.

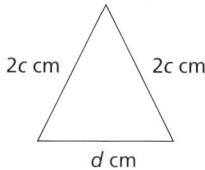

2*c* cm   2*c* cm

d cm

c) Simplify *m* + *n* + 3*m* + 2*n* − 2*m*

d) Simplify 4 × 2*z*

a) The total mass of the 3 boxes labelled *n* grams is (*n* + *n* + *n*) g = 3*n* g The total mass of the 2 boxes labelled *m* grams is (*m* + *m*) g = 2*m* g The total mass, in grams, is 3*n* + 2*m*. You can also write this as 2*m* + 3*n* The two expressions are (3*n* + 2*m*) g and (2*m* + 3*n*) g	To find the total you add 3*n* and 2*m* giving (3*n* + 2*m*) g. The brackets are used to show that all the terms inside the brackets have the same units – in this case grams. You can write this as (2*m* + 3*n*) g because it does not matter which way round you add two numbers.	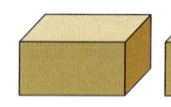 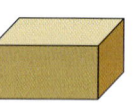

Unit 1B: Algebra and measures

b) The perimeter of the triangle is the sum of the sides which is: 2c + 2c + d = (4c + d) cm or (d + 4c) cm	Collect the terms in c by adding 2c + 2c to get 4c. Then add the d to get 4c + d or d + 4c. You often put terms in alphabetical order but either version is correct. This is the final answer as you can't mix terms in c and d.	
c) m + n + 3m + 2n − 2m = m + 3m − 2m + n + 2n = 2m + 3n	Identify the terms in m. m + 3m − 2m = 4m − 2m = 2m Then identify the terms in n. n + 2n = 3n Now combine the two. 2m + 3n or 3n + 2m	
d) 4 × 2z = 8z	2z is the same as 2 × z 4 × 2 × z = 8 × z = 8z	

Exercise 4

1 Simplify by collecting like terms.

a) m + 3m + m   5m
b) k + 3k + k   5k
c) 10g + 2g   12g
d) 15m + 7m   22m
e) 2d + 3d + d   6d
f) 5f + 7f + f   13f
g) 2b + 5b + 3b   10b
h) 6m + 10m + 4m   20m
i) y + 3y + 5y + y   10y

2 Form an expression for the length, in centimetres, of the perimeter of each shape. Simplify the expression by collecting like terms.

a) 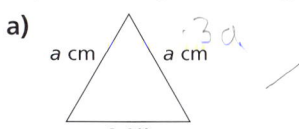 3a

b) 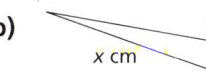 4x

c) 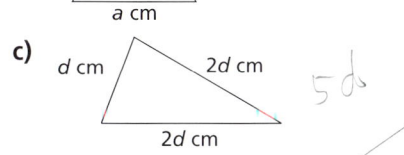 5d

d) 7f

3 Match an expression from the first column with an expression from the second column.

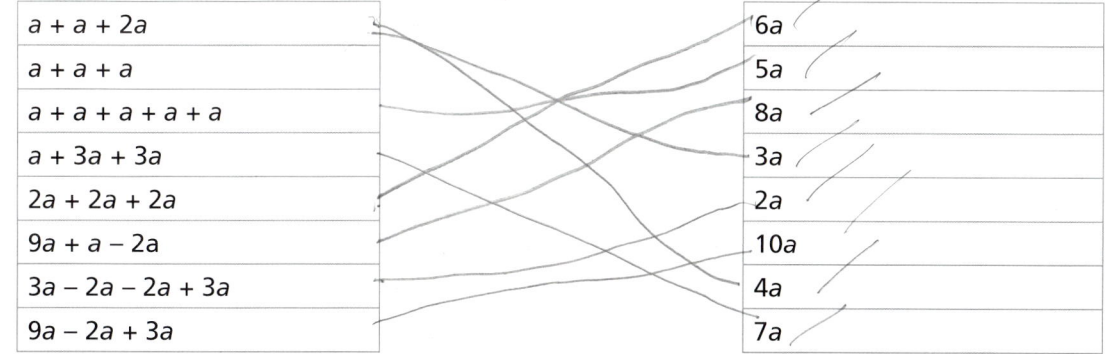

Chapter 6: Algebra   45

4. Simplify by collecting like terms.
   a) 2a – a   b) 3n – 2n   c) 5t – 3t   d) 6y – 3y
   e) 4e – 3e   f) 9j – 3j   g) 6m – 5m   h) 8y – 4y
   i) 7k – k   j) 11g – 7g   k) 13k – 2k   l) 10p – 9p
   m) b – b

5. Simplify by collecting like terms.
   a) a + b + a   b) 2x + y + y
   c) m + n + n + m   d) 3d + e – e
   e) 3y + 2x + 2y   f) 3f – f + 4g + 2g
   g) k + 4c + 2k – k   h) 3v + 2w + 5w – v

6. Form an expression, in centimetres, for the perimeter of each shape and simplify by collecting like terms.
   a) triangle with sides 2b cm, f cm, 3b cm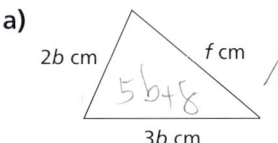
   b) triangle with sides 4g cm, 5k cm, 2k cm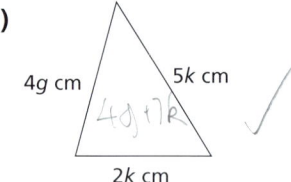
   c) rectangle 3f cm by 2m cm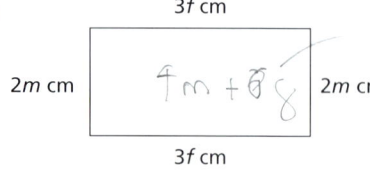
   d) kite with sides a cm, a cm, 4d cm, 4d cm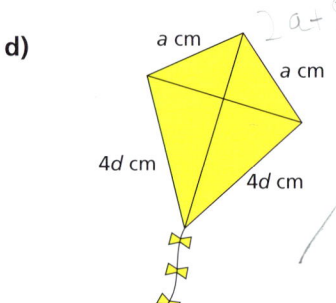
   e) parallelogram 5y cm by 3x cm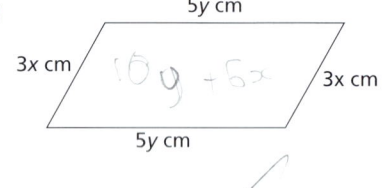
   f) parallelogram 3b cm, 5a cm, 3a cm, 2a cm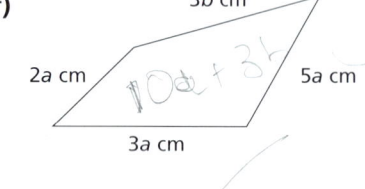

7. Simplify:
   a) 3 × x   b) 5 × t   c) 3 × 2s   d) 6 × 5b   e) 4 × 3 × c

8. The area of this rectangle is 28 cm². Write down an equation connecting v, w and 28.

9. The area of this square is g cm². The length of the side is h cm. Georgie says that this means that g = h ÷ 4. Addie says that h × h = g. Explain which person is correct.

Multiplying a constant over a bracket

Key terms

Multiplying a constant over a bracket means removing the brackets from expressions.

For example, 3(6 + w) means 3 lots of 6 + 3 lots of w

6 + w + 6 + w + 6 + w = 18 + 3w

Unit 1B: Algebra and measures

This tells you that

3(6 + w) = 18 + 3w

If you look at this you can see that both the 6 and the w have been multiplied by 3 so everything inside the bracket has been multiplied by the number outside the bracket.

In the same way 4(r + 8) = 4r + 32

and 5(7 − t) = 35 − 5t

In questions you might be asked to **expand** a bracket, this means to multiply the constant over the bracket like in these examples.

Worked example 5

Jack spends 2m minutes on his homework.

Peter spends 3 minutes more on his homework than Jack.

Daniel spends twice as much time on his homework as Peter.

Form expressions for the amount of time, in minutes, that **a)** Peter and **b)** Daniel spend on their homework.

a) Peter spends 2m + 3 minutes on his homework.	If Jack spends 2m minutes on homework and Peter spends 3 minutes more then Peter spends (2m + 3) minutes.	
b) Daniel spends 2(2m + 3) minutes 2(2m + 3) = 4m + 6	Daniel spends twice as much time as Peter which is 2 lots of 2m + 3 You write this as 2(2m + 3) Multiply out 2(2m + 3) = 4m + 6 Every term in the bracket is multiplied by the number outside the bracket.	

Exercise 5

Tip
Make sure you multiply **every** term inside the bracket by the number outside the bracket.

1 Multiply the constant over the bracket in each of these expressions:
   a) 2(a + 1)   2a+2 ✓   b) 2(d + 3) 2d+6 ✓   c) 3(c − 2) 3c−6 ✓   d) 5(h − 5) 5h−25 ✓
   e) 4(2b + 1) 8b+4   f) 5(3x − 1) 15x−5 ✓   g) 4(3a + 2b) 12a+8b   h) 3(3d − 2c) 9d−6c ✓

2 Ifrah has k stamps in her collection. Rashid has 10 more stamps than Ifrah.
   Andrew has double the number of stamps that Rashid has.
   a) Form an expression, in terms of k, for the number of stamps that Rashid has. k+10
   b) Form an expression, in terms of k, for the number of stamps that Andrew has. 2(k+10)

3 Saif has a collection of p comics in her collection. Sophie has 4 more comics than Saif. Jana has twice as many comics as Sophie. Deema has three times as many comics as Jana.
   a) Form an expression, in terms of p, for the number of comics Sophie has in her collection. p+4
   b) Form an expression, in terms of p, for the number of comics Deema has in her collection. 6p+24 ✓
   c) Form an expression for the total number of comics in the collections of all four girls. 10p+36

Chapter 6: Algebra

4 The sides of this rectangle are given by the expressions
($2a + 1$) cm and ($a + 2$) cm.

Jane knows that to find the perimeter in centimetres she needs to add $2a + 1$ to $a + 2$ and then multiply by 2.

She writes $2a + 1 + a + 2 = 3a + 3$ and then calculates $2(3a + 3)$.
She writes her answer as $6a + 6$ and then decides that it is the same as $6(a + 1)$ cm. Is she correct? Explain your answer. *She is correct*

End of chapter reflection

You should know that ...	You should be able to ...	Such as ...
You can use letters to represent unknown numbers.	Replace missing numbers with letters.	Write the following with a letter instead of the space: $6 + ... = 27$
The expression $4a + b + 6$ has 3 terms. They are $4a$, b and 6. The expression $5t$ has one term. The term is $5t$. $2a + 5 = 6$ is an equation as it has an equals sign.	Recognise terms, expressions and equations.	For each statement write True or False. a) $5n$ could be a term or an expression b) $5t + 4 = 8$ is an equation. c) $17y$ is a term of the expression $y - 17$ d) $2n - 6$ is an equation
You can construct expressions using letters for unknowns.	Construct a simple expression from the information that you are given.	Construct an expression for the perimeter of a triangle with sides of 2 cm, 5 cm and m cm.
The order of operations in algebra is the same as it is in numbers.	Know when the order of operations is correct.	Is the value of $t - 3$ always the same as the value of $3 - t$?
When more than one term in the same letter is added or subtracted this is called **collecting like terms** or **simplifying** an expression.	Collect like terms.	Simplify by collecting like terms: $3a + 4b + 2a + 4b$
You can multiply algebraic expressions in the same way as numbers.	Multiply a term by a number.	Find: $7 \times 4x$
When a constant is multiplied over a bracket, every term inside the bracket is multiplied by the term outside the bracket.	Multiply a constant over a bracket.	Expand: $3(2g + 6)$

Unit 1B: Algebra and measures

Unit 1B • Chapter 7

Sequences

You will learn how to:
- Generate terms of an integer sequence and find a term given its position in the sequence; find simple term-to-term rules.
- Generate sequences from spatial patterns and describe the general term in simple cases.

Starting point

Do you remember …?

- that integer is another name for a whole number so 20 is an integer but 20.5 is not?
- counting on in whole numbers, so counting on in 6s from 4 gives 4, 10, 16 …?
- looking at patterns of numbers in number squares?

Hook

Katie is investigating multiplication by 5. She takes a two-digit number, adds the digits and multiplies the answer by 5. She writes the answer then repeats the process with the new number. She continues to do this until she finds a pattern.

The first number she tries is 15. Adding the digits gives 6 and 6 × 5 = 30. She does the same with 30. Adding the digits gives 3 and 3 × 5 = 15. This gives her these results:

15, 30, 15, 30 …

Then she tries 24 and gets these results:

24, 30, 15, 30 …

For both of these the first repeating number is 30, and it is the second number in the pattern.

What do 15 and 24 have in common?

Which other numbers give a pattern which goes back to 30 and 15?

Now try other numbers.

What do 14 and 23 have in common?

Which starting number gives the most numbers in the pattern before you find one that repeats?

Generating sequences

Key terms

A **sequence** is a set of numbers, shapes, letters or objects, placed in order, that make a pattern or follow a rule. Each item in a sequence is called a **term**.

In the sequence 1, 3, 5, 7, 9, 11 …, the first term is 1, and the second term is 3. The dots after the 11 mean that the sequence would continue using the same rule.

The **position number** of a term is which position it has in the sequence. The first term has position number 1, and the sixth term has position number 6. In the sequence 1, 3, 5, 7, 9, 11 …, the number 9 has position number 5.

When the next number in a sequence is generated by applying a rule to the previous term it is called a **term-to-term rule**.

For example, the term to term rule 'add 3' means 'add three to a number to get the next number in the sequence'. If the first number of this sequence is 4 then the next three terms are 7, 10 and 13.

Key terms

Some sequences can be found by looking at patterns of shapes or other objects and their properties.

The **general term** of a sequence is a way of describing how you get the value of a term from its position number. If the sequence looked like this:

Position number	1	2	3	4	5	6
Value of the term	2	4	6	8	10	12

A **position-to-term** rule is the rule which relates the position number to the value of the term. In the table above, the position to term rule is to multiply the position number by 2 to get the value of the term.

For example, the 200th term would be 200 × 2 = 400.

Worked example 1

a) The first term of a sequence is 5 and the term-to-term rule is 'add six'. Find the first 6 terms of this sequence.

b) Find the term-to-term rule for this sequence: 2, 4, 8, 16 …

c) Each term of a sequence is three times its position number. What are the first, third and fifth terms of the sequence?

d) The first term of a sequence is 3. The term-to-term rule is 'multiply by 2 then add 1'. What are the first four terms of this sequence?

a) 5, 11, 17, 23, 29 and 35	The term-to-term rule tells you to add 6 to each term to get the next term. Start with the first term and follow the rule 'add six'.	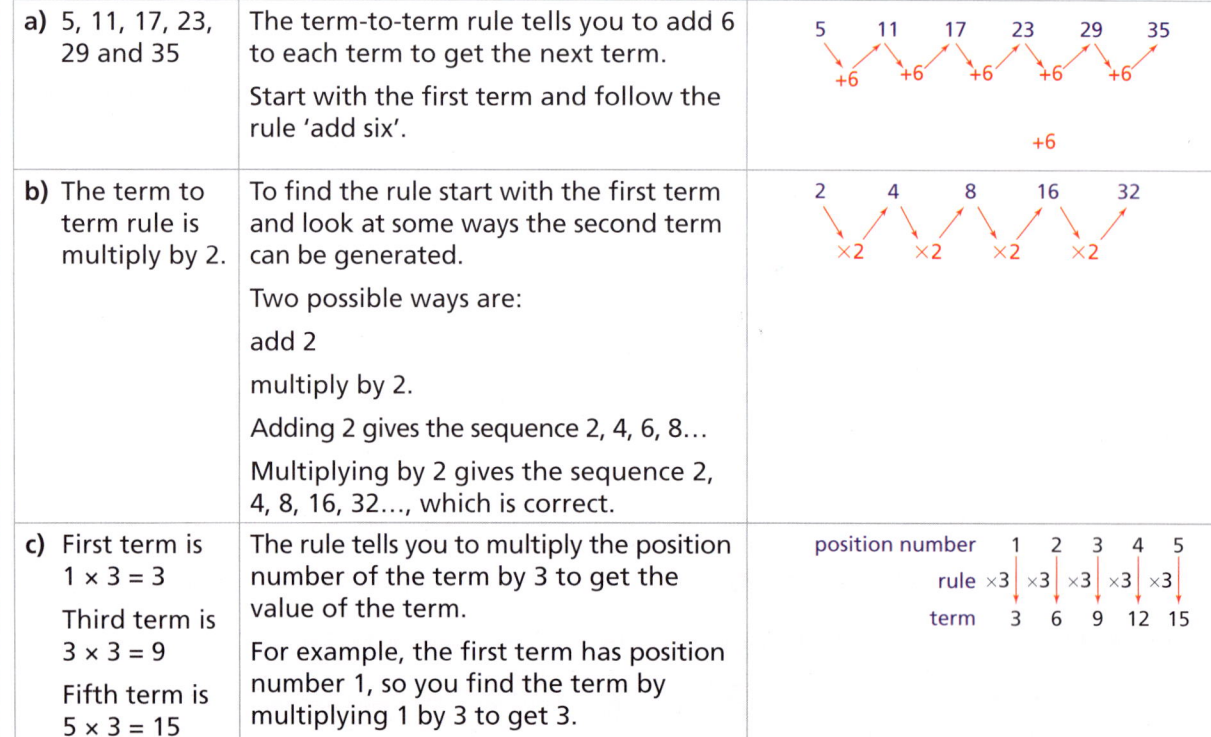
b) The term to term rule is multiply by 2.	To find the rule start with the first term and look at some ways the second term can be generated. Two possible ways are: add 2 multiply by 2. Adding 2 gives the sequence 2, 4, 6, 8… Multiplying by 2 gives the sequence 2, 4, 8, 16, 32…, which is correct.	
c) First term is 1 × 3 = 3 Third term is 3 × 3 = 9 Fifth term is 5 × 3 = 15	The rule tells you to multiply the position number of the term by 3 to get the value of the term. For example, the first term has position number 1, so you find the term by multiplying 1 by 3 to get 3.	

Unit 1B: Algebra and measures

d) The first four terms are 3, 7, 15, 31.	The first term is 3. Multiplying 3 by 2 and adding 1 to the answer gives 3 × 2 + 1 = 7 7 is the second term. The third term is 7 × 2 + 1 = 15 The fourth term is 15 × 2 + 1 = 31	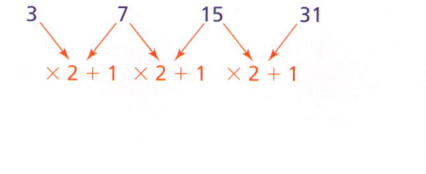

Exercise 1

1 The table below gives the first term and the term-to-term rule of a sequence. Find the first 5 terms of each sequence.

	First term	Term-to-term rule
a)	2	Add three
b)	5	Add 2
c)	−10	Add 5
d)	50	Subtract 4
e)	40	Subtract 3
f)	4	Subtract 4

	First term	Term-to-term rule
g)	1	Multiply by 2
h)	3	Multiply by 5
i)	2	Multiply by 4
j)	1 000 000	Divide by 10
k)	2000	Divide by 2
l)	1458	Divide by 3

2 Each term of a sequence is three times its position value. Which of these statements is not true? Write the correct version of the statement which is not true.
   a) The first term is 3.
   b) The seventh term is 22.
   c) The ninth term is 27.

3 In this sequence the first three terms are correct, but one term is incorrect and does not follow the term-to-term rule
   2   5   8   11   14   18   20   23 …
   a) What is the term-to-term rule?
   b) What is the value of the third term?
   c) Write the number that does not follow the term-to-term rule.
   d) What number should it be?
   e) Find the tenth term.

4 The first term of a sequence is 6. The term-to-term rule is 'multiply by 2 and subtract 3'. The first three terms of the sequence are 6, 9, 15 … What is the fifth term of this sequence?

5 The first number of a sequence is 10 and the term-to-term rule is 'multiply by 2 and subtract 5'.
   a) How many terms of this sequence are less than 100?
   b) Manish says that, after the first term, every term of this sequence has a units digit of 5. Explain why he is correct.

Chapter 7: Sequences   51

6 Copy and complete this table.

First term	Second term	Fifth term	Term-to-term rule
3	10		Multiply by 2 then add 4
5			Multiply by 3 then subtract 4
4	8		Divide by 2 then add 6
2	6		Multiply by 3 then …………
2	6		Multiply by ………… then add 2
1		41	Multiply by 3 then …………1

7 The first two terms of a sequence are 2 and 6. Complete the possible term-to-term rules for these two terms.
  a) Multiply by …………
  b) Multiply by 4 and ………… 2
  c) Add ………… and multiply by 2
  d) Multiply by 40 and …………

8 The first term of a sequence is 3.
  a) Find five possible term-to-term rules which would give a second term of 11.
  b) Can you find a term-to-term rule which gives a third term of 91?

9 Complete the table.

	Position number	1	2	3	5	100	500
a)		1	2		5		
b)		2	4	6			
c)		3	5		11		
d)		2	5		14		

Spatial patterns

Worked example 2

Claire is drawing triangle patterns using equilateral triangles of side 1 cm. Each time she adds another triangle to form the next pattern and records the perimeter of the shape in a table.

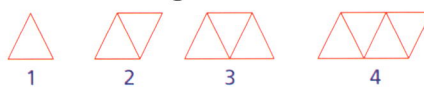

Position number	1	2	3	4	5
Perimeter in cm	3				

  a) Copy and complete the table.
  b) Write the term-to-term rule for the sequence of numbers in the perimeter row.
  c) Find a rule connecting the pattern number with the perimeter.
  d) What is the perimeter of the shape which has 150 triangles?
  e) Write a sentence describing how to find the perimeter from the number of triangles in this pattern.

Unit 1B: Algebra and measures

a) The missing numbers are 4, 5, 6 and 7	Count the perimeter of the triangles which are drawn for you. Then draw the fifth one of the pattern and count them.	The fifth one in the pattern has a perimeter of 7.
b) The term-to-term rule is 'add 1'.	The numbers in the perimeter row are 3, 4, 5, 6 and 7. Each number can be obtained by adding 1 to the previous number.	3 4 5 6 7 with +1 between each
c) To get the perimeter you add 2 to the position number.	You can see that each perimeter is 2 more than its position number.	position value 1 2 3 4 5 rule +2 +2 +2 +2 +2 perimeter 3 4 5 6 7
d) 152	To find the perimeter, you add 2 to the position number. 150 + 2 = 152	150 → +2 → 152
e) If you add 2 to the number of triangles then you get the perimeter.	There is more than one correct way of writing this sentence.	Number of triangles → +2 → perimeter

Exercise 2

Tip

When you are looking for a link between position numbers and terms, it often helps to look at the pattern and see which bit of the pattern is connected to the position number. In the next question, the position number is the same as the length of the base. Then you add one square fewer than this to complete the shape. The third shape has a base of 3 squares, and you add 2 more to make the whole shape. The fourth shape will have a base of four and you need to think about how many more squares need to be added.

1 This L shaped pattern is made by adding one square to each of the sides.

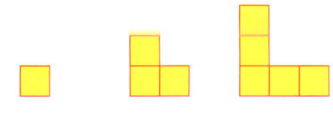

Pattern 1   Pattern 2   Pattern 3

This table records the number of squares used in each L shape.

Position number	1	2	3	4	5
Squares					

a) Copy and complete the table for patterns 1 to 5.
b) Write the term-to-term rule for the sequence you have generated.
c) Find a rule for working out the number of squares from the position number.
d) How many squares will be in pattern number 200?

2 The first 4 shapes in a pattern are shown below.

a) Draw the fifth shape and copy and complete the table.

Position number	1	2	3	4	5
Number of squares	4				

b) Describe, in words, how you work out the number of squares from the position number.

c) How many squares will be in the 200th shape?

3 These are the first three shapes in a pattern.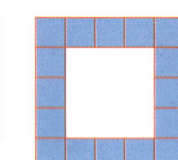

a) Draw the next two shapes in the pattern.

b) Create a table showing the position number and the number of squares in the pattern for the first 5 shapes.

c) Find a term-to-term rule for this sequence.

d) Find a position-to-term rule for this sequence.

e) How many squares are in the 100th shape?

f) Describe, in words, how you work out the number of squares from the position number.

4 These are the first four shapes in a pattern.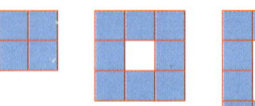

a) Draw the fifth shape and copy and complete the table.

Position number	1	2	3	4	5
Number of squares	4				

b) What is the term-to-term rule for the number of squares?

c) Write a sentence to say how to work out the number of squares from the position number.

d) How many squares are in the 100th term?

5 These are the first three shapes in a pattern.

a) Draw the fourth and fifth shapes and copy and complete the table.

Position number	1	2	3	4	5
Number of squares	8				

b) What is the term-to-term rule for the number of squares?

c) The position-to-term rule is 'multiply by 2 and then…………………'.

d) How many squares are in the 100th term?

6 These are the first three shapes in a pattern. Each shape is made up of rectangles and squares.

a) Draw the fourth and fifth shapes and copy and complete the table.

Position number	1	2	3	4	5
Number of squares	1	2			
Number of rectangles	2	3			

b) What is the term-to-term rule for the number of rectangles?
c) Write a sentence to describe how to work out the number of squares and the number of rectangles from the position number.
d) How many squares are needed to make the 100th shape in the pattern?
e) How many rectangles are needed to make the 100th shape in the pattern?

7 These patterns represent arrangements of people sitting at tables. The squares represent the tables and the small circles represent the people. Tables are added in a straight line, as shown.

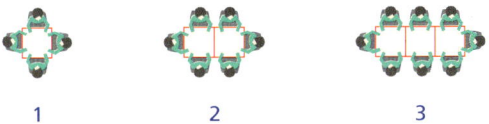

a) Draw pattern 4.
b) Copy and complete the table showing the results

Position number	1	2	3	4
Number of tables				
Number of people				

Tip

The second pattern shows two lots of two people facing each other plus one at each end of the tables. The third term shows two lots of three people facing each other plus one at each end of the tables.

c) Find a term-to-term rule for the number of people in each pattern.
d) Find a position-to-term rule for the number of people in each pattern.
e) How many people and how many tables would there be in the 50th pattern?

8 Decide on a position-to-term rule and work out the first six terms of your sequence. Now cross out every other term starting with the first term.

a) What is the position-to-term rule for your new sequence?
b) Would it be the same if you crossed out every other term starting with the second term?

Think about

Investigate with other position-to-term rules and term-to-term rules. What do you notice?

End of chapter reflection

You should know that ...	You should be able to ...	Such as ...
A term-to-term rule is a rule telling you how to find the next term in a sequence from the previous term.	Find the next term in a sequence if you know the term-to-term rule.	The third term of a sequence is 23, and the term-to-term rule is 'multiply by 2 then add 3'. What are the fourth and fifth terms of the sequence?
A position-to-term rule is a relationship between the position of a term in a sequence and the value of the term.	Find terms from a position-to-term rule.	Find the twentieth term of a sequence whose position-to-term rule is 'multiply by 2 and add 1'.
Sequences can be generated from a spatial pattern. A spatial pattern is an arrangement of objects.	Find terms in a sequence from a spatial pattern and be able to describe, in words, how to work out the value of the term from its shape.	These are the first four shapes in a spatial pattern. a) Copy and complete this table showing the number of squares in each pattern. | position	1	2	3	4	5 | |---|---|---|---|---|---| | squares | 1 | 3 | 5 | | | b) Describe the position-to-term rule for this sequence. c) Explain in words how to find the number of squares for any shape in this pattern from the position number.

1C

Unit 1C
Handling data and geometry

What's it all about?

- Properties of 2D shapes
- Estimating the size of angles
- Collecting data
- Basics of probability

You will learn about:
- Drawing 2D shapes in different orientations
- Angle, side and symmetry properties of 2D shapes
- Estimating the size of angles to the nearest 10°
- Design and use a data collection sheet or questionnaire
- The language of probability
- Finding probabilities where there are equally likely outcomes

You will build your skills in:
- Visualising properties of shapes
- Estimation
- Carrying out research tasks

Unit 1C • Chapter 8

2D shapes

You will learn how to:
- Identify, describe, visualise and draw 2D shapes in different orientations.
- Use the notation and labelling conventions for points, lines, angles and shapes.
- Name and identify side, angle and symmetry properties of special quadrilaterals and triangles, and regular polygons with 5, 6 and 8 sides.

Starting point

Do you remember …?

- what a polygon is?
- the difference between regular and irregular polygons?
- the names of polygons with 3, 4, 5, 6 and 8 sides?
- what a side is and what vertices are?
- the names and features of common 2D shapes such as equilateral triangles, squares, rectangles and parallelograms?
- how to recognise a right angle?
- how to recognise parallel lines?
- how to find lines of symmetry?

This will be helpful when …

you learn more about finding missing angles in shapes.

Hook

Here are six triangle pieces.

Some or all of these pieces can be put together on a piece of paper to make mathematical shapes, such as those shown. Can you name these three shapes?

How many different mathematical shapes can you make using any, or all, of the six pieces?

Draw these shapes and name them.

You could use isometric paper to record your shapes.

Which two mathematical shapes can you not make from these pieces?

Explain your answer.

Drawing and describing 2D shapes

Key terms

A **polygon** is a closed shape made of straight sides.

A **triangle** is a 3-sided polygon.

A **quadrilateral** is a 4-sided polygon.

Polygons with 5 sides or more have names ending in '-agon' such as **pentagon** (5 sides), **hexagon** (6 sides), **heptagon** (7 sides) and **octagon** (8 sides).

A polygon is said to be **regular** if all of its sides have equal length and all of its angles are equal. If a polygon is not regular, it is said to be **irregular**.

> Did you know?
>
> Many frameworks, such as electricity pylons, are made up of triangles because a triangle is a stable structure. A triangular frame will not bend out of shape.

Worked example 1

The diagram is made up of right angled triangles. Copy the diagram and shade:
a) A rectangle made up of 12 of the triangles
b) A parallelogram (not a rectangle) made up of 6 of the triangles
c) A hexagon made up of 10 of the triangles

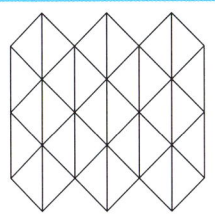

a)	A rectangle has four right angles so you need to find the right angles first and then count triangles to get the correct size.	There is more than one rectangle which can be shaded to meet this condition. One of them is shown.
b)	The parallelogram cannot be a rectangle so it must not have square corners.	There is more than one parallelogram which can be shaded to meet this condition. One of them is shown.
c)	A hexagon has 6 sides which do not have to be the same length unless it is a regular hexagon.	There is more than one hexagon which can be shaded to meet this condition. One of them is shown.

Exercise 1

1 Complete these sentences.

Shape **a** has …… sides and so it is a …………………… .

Shape **b** has …… sides and so it is a …………………… .

Shape **c** has …… sides and so it is a …………………… .

Shape **b** has …… right angles.

Shape **b** has …… pairs of parallel sides.

2 In the diagram, the red line is one side of a square.
Copy and complete the drawing.

How many dots are on the perimeter of the square?

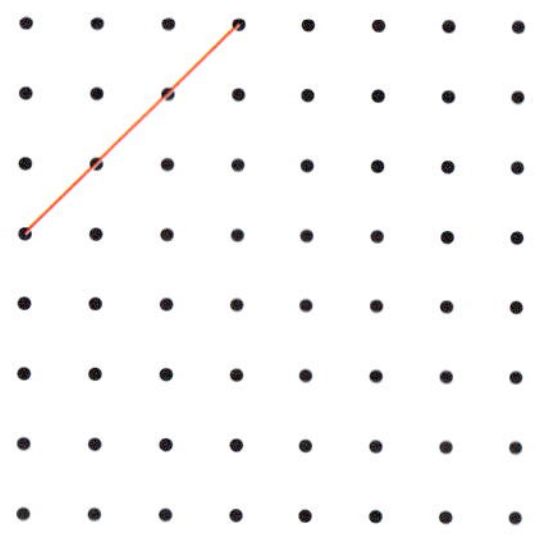

3 In the diagram, the red line is one side of an isosceles triangle.
The triangle has 6 dots on its perimeter.
Copy and complete the drawing.

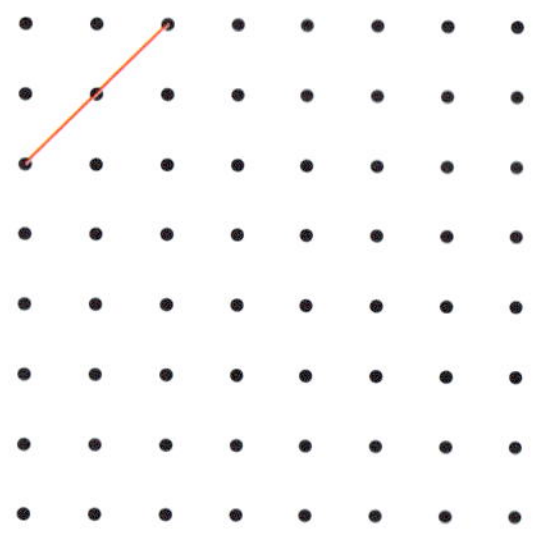

4 In the diagram, the red line is one side of an isosceles triangle.
How many different isosceles triangles can you draw on a copy of this grid using the red line as one complete side of the triangle?
The third vertex (corner) of the triangle must be on one of the dots.

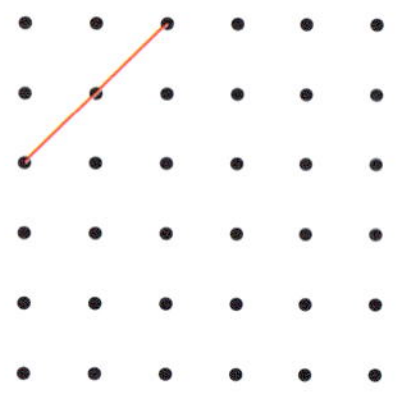

5 In the diagram, the red line is one side of a right-angled triangle.
On a copy of the grid, using the red line as one complete side of the triangle, can you draw a right-angled triangle which has:

a) 4 dots on its perimeter

b) 6 dots on its perimeter

c) 8 dots on its perimeter

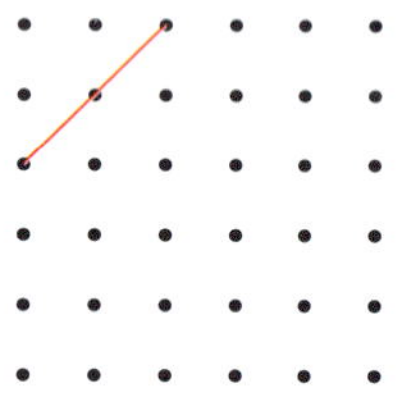

The third vertex (corner) of your triangle must be on one of the dots. How many different possible answers are there for each part of this question?

6 Imagine an irregular (scalene) triangle. It is cut into two pieces along a line drawn from the midpoint of one of its sides to the midpoint of another side. What shapes are these two pieces?

7 The square shown is divided into three triangles by joining the midpoint of one side to the two opposite corners.

Complete this sentence to describe the type of triangles.

The square is divided into two ....

triangles and one .... triangle.

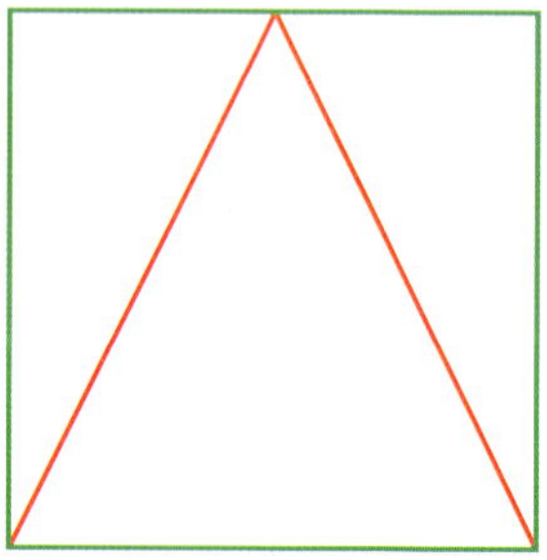

Unit 1C: Handling data and geometry

8 The regular hexagon shown has a single blue line drawn on it which divides the hexagon into two quadrilaterals.

a) What is the name of this type of quadrilateral?

b) Can a single straight line be drawn on a regular hexagon to make an isosceles triangle and a pentagon?
If your answer is yes then draw the line on a copy of this hexagon.

c) Can a single straight line be drawn on a regular hexagon to make an isosceles triangle and a hexagon?
If your answer is yes then draw the line on a copy of this hexagon.

d) What other mathematical shapes can you make by drawing a single line onto a regular hexagon?

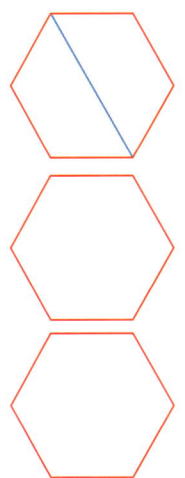

Geometrical conventions

Labelling diagrams

Capital letters are used to **LABEL** a point or vertex.

The line AB is the line joining point A to point B.

You can show that lines are equal in length by putting the same mark on each of the equal length lines. You would show another set of equal length lines using a different mark – perhaps 2 lines as shown here, or a wavy line.

In the diagram the lengths AB and DC are equal as are AD and BC.

You can mark equal angles by putting the same marks on each of the equal angles.

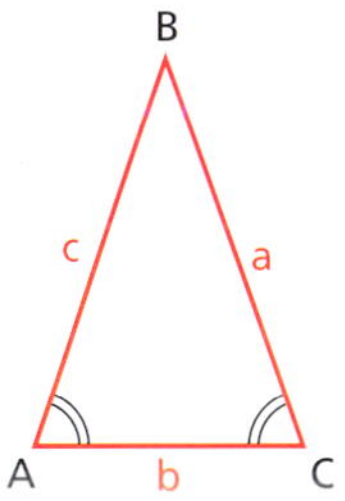

In the diagram, the angles at A and C are equal.

In a triangle lower case (small) letters can be used to label the sides of the triangle. The side a is opposite to the angle at A and the side b is opposite to the angle at B etc.

Two lines or sides are called **parallel** if they are always the same distance apart.

You mark parallel lines using arrows. The number of arrows show which lines are parallel. The first set of parallel lines that you label has a single arrow, the second set has 2 arrows etc.

In the diagram, AB is parallel to DC and DA is parallel to CB.

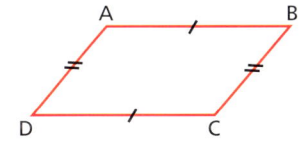

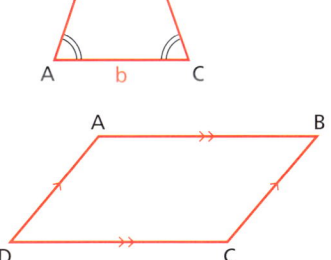

Diagrams must always be labelled with the letters going in the same direction around the diagram – usually clockwise but anticlockwise is also correct.

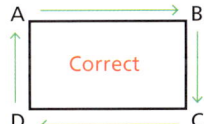
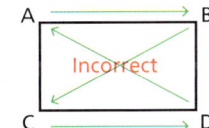

Worked example 2

a) What is wrong with the labelling of this parallelogram? Relabel it correctly leaving the label A in the same place.

In this parallelogram:

b) What is the size of the angle at R inside the parallelogram?

c) What is the size of angle PSQ? How could you label 'the angle PSQ'?

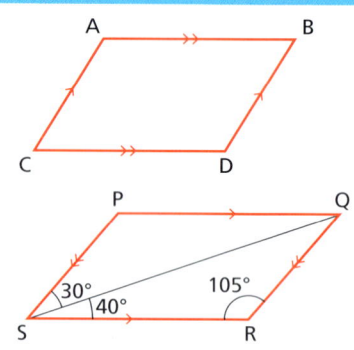

a) The labels should go around the diagram in order.	The labels for the corners are the capital letters. They should read in order as you go around the diagram and the original diagram read ABDC which is incorrect.	
b) Angle R is 105°.	The single letter R tells you which angle of the parallelogram you are looking at.	
c) Angle PSQ is 30°.	Angle PSQ is the angle at S formed by the lines PS and SQ. Another way of labelling it is ∠PSQ, where ∠ is the symbol for angle.	

Exercise 2

1 The diagram is drawn on 1 cm squared paper.

a) What is the length of the line AD?

b) What is the length of the line DC?

c) Which line is parallel to AB?

d) Which line is parallel to CD?

e) What is the size of angle ABC?

f) John says that the angle that is 67° is angle A, but Mike says that the angle that is 67° is ∠DAC. Who is correct? Explain your answer.

g) Which two angles are 23°? Give your answer using three letter notation.

h) Which two angles are right angles? Give your answer using three letter notation.

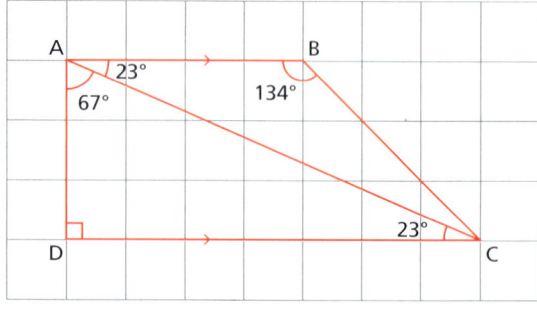

Unit 1C: Handling data and geometry

2 On the diagram opposite:

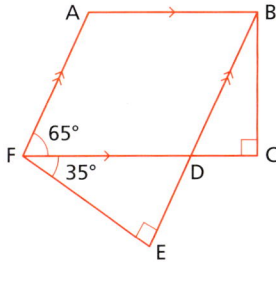

a) Which of these is a correct labelling for the parallelogram?

   ABFD   AFDB   AFBD   ABDF

b) Which of these is a correct labelling for the angle of 35°?

   F   ∠CFE   ∠DFA   ∠DFE

c) Which of these is parallel to the line AB?

   DC   FE   FD

d) Which line is parallel to EB?

e) Which two angles are right angles?

f) The point D lies on the lines .... and ....

g) The shape ABCDEF is a ....

3 Copy the drawing onto squared paper and complete the quadrilateral ABCD according to these instructions:

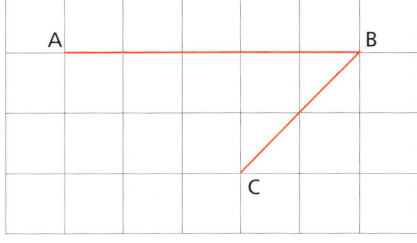

DC is parallel to AB

∠BAD = 90°

Label the parallel lines with arrows.

Label the right angles with the correct symbol.

4 Fill in the blanks in the following using the letters shown on the diagram of the regular hexagon:

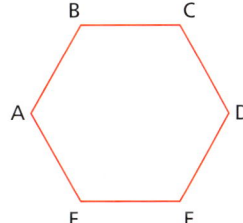

a) A B _ is an isosceles triangle.

b) A _ C _ is a quadrilateral.

c) A _ D _ is a rectangle.

d) A _ _ E _ is a pentagon.

e) _ _ _ F is a trapezium.

f) BC is parallel to _ _ .

g) ∠B _ _ is a right angle.

5 These are the instructions for drawing a quadrilateral on centimetre squared paper.

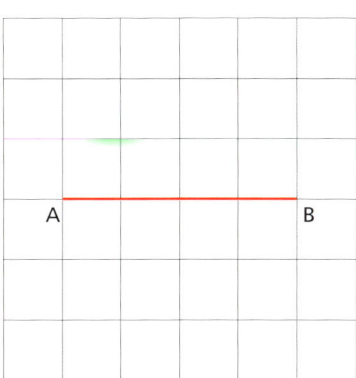

DC is parallel to AB and is the same length as AB

∠DAB = 45°

The distance between AB and DC is 2 cm.

How many different quadrilaterals can you draw using these instructions? Explain your answer.

Chapter 8: 2D shapes

Properties of special shapes

Key terms

There are special types of triangle and quadrilateral, which have particular names.

Special triangles:

equilateral   **isosceles**   **scalene**   **right-angled**

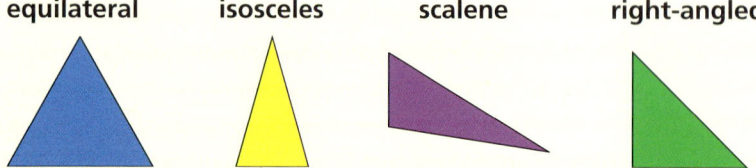

Equilateral triangles have 3 equal sides and 3 equal angles.
Isosceles triangles have 2 sides which are equal and 2 angles which are equal.
Scalene triangles have no equal sides or angles.
Right-angled triangles have one right angle.

Special quadrilaterals:

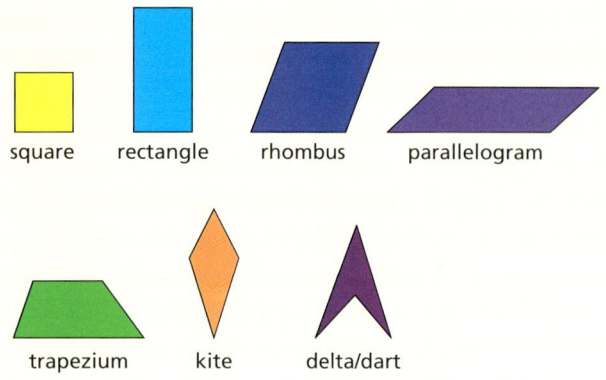

A **square** has 4 equal sides, all its angles are 90° and it has 4 lines of symmetry.

A **rectangle** has 4 angles of 90°, 2 pairs of equal sides and 2 lines of symmetry.

A **rhombus** is a parallelogram with all 4 sides the same length. It has 2 lines of symmetry.

The opposite sides of a **parallelogram** are parallel and equal in length. The opposite angles are equal. It has no lines of symmetry.

A **trapezium** has one pair of parallel sides. Some trapeziums have a line of symmetry.

A **kite** has two pairs of adjacent sides that are equal and one pair of equal, opposite angles. It has one line of symmetry.

A **delta** (or **dart** or **re-entrant quadrilateral**) has one reflex angle – an angle greater than 180°. Some deltas have a line of symmetry.

Regular polygons:

A regular pentagon has 5 sides. All its sides are equal and all its angles are equal. It has 5 lines of symmetry.

A regular hexagon has 6 sides. All its sides are equal and all its angles are equal. It has 6 lines of symmetry and 3 pairs of parallel sides.

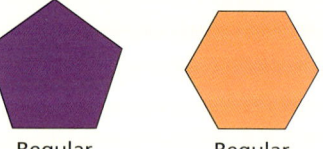 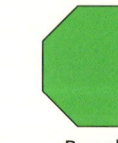

Regular pentagon   Regular hexagon   Regular octagon

A regular octagon has 8 sides. All its sides are equal and all its angles are equal. It has 8 lines of symmetry and 4 pairs of parallel sides.

Worked example 3

ABCDEF is a regular hexagon.

a) Sketch the regular hexagon ABCDEF.
b) Describe the pairs of parallel sides of ABCDEF.
c) Which of these words describe triangle BFE:

  Equilateral   Isosceles   Scalene   Right angled

d) What type of quadrilateral is ABEF? Explain your answer.
e) How many lines of symmetry does the regular hexagon ABCDEF have?

Tip

Sketch means that you do not have to measure the angles and sides exactly but they should look reasonable.

a)	A regular hexagon has all its sides and angles equal.	
b) ABCDEF has 3 pairs of parallel sides. AB is parallel to ED BC is parallel to FE CD is parallel to AF	Regular hexagons and octagons have opposite sides parallel.	
c) Triangle BFE is right-angled and scalene.	If you draw the triangle, you can see that ∠BFE is 90°. As none of the sides are the same length it is also scalene.	
d) ABEF is a trapezium as it has 4 sides and one pair of parallel sides.	ABEF has 4 sides so it is a quadrilateral. AF is parallel to BE but AB is not parallel to FE so it has one pair of parallel sides. A quadrilateral with one pair of parallel sides is a trapezium.	
e) A regular hexagon has six lines of symmetry.	There are 6 different ways that the hexagon can be folded in half.	

Chapter 8: 2D shapes

Exercise 3

1 Name these shapes from their descriptions.
   a) A triangle with all its sides the same length
   b) A quadrilateral with four equal sides and four right-angles
   c) A quadrilateral with four equal sides and no right-angles
   d) A triangle with two equal angles
   e) A five-sided shape with all of its angles equal
   f) A quadrilateral with no parallel sides but one pair of equal angles
   g) A triangle with angles of 40°, 50° and 90°
   h) An eight-sided shape with all sides of equal length

2 ABCDEFGH is a regular octagon.
   a) Which side is parallel to AB?
   b) How many pairs of parallel sides does the shape have?
   c) What type of triangle is AFE?
   d) Is AD a line of symmetry of the shape?
   e) Fill in the missing letter: B _ is a line of symmetry of this shape.

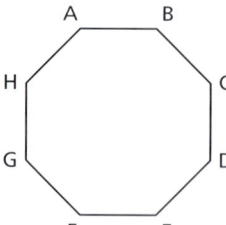

3 Copy and complete each of these statements.
   a) A square has ……… sides. ……… of these sides are equal in length and it has ……… pairs of parallel sides.
   b) A scalene triangle has ……… sides. ……… of these sides are equal in length and it has ……… pairs of parallel sides.
   c) A regular hexagon has ……… sides. ……… of these sides are equal in length and it has ……… pairs of parallel sides.
   d) A rhombus has ……… sides. ……… of these sides are equal in length and it has ……… pairs of parallel sides.
   e) An isosceles triangle has ……… sides. ……… of these sides are equal in length and it has ……… pairs of parallel sides.
   f) An equilateral triangle has ……… sides. ……… of these sides are equal in length and it has ……… pairs of parallel sides.
   g) A regular pentagon has ……… sides. ……… of these sides are equal in length and it has ……… pairs of parallel sides.

4) Match the quadrilateral to a correct statement about its properties. Complete the missing shape and property.

Shape
Square
Trapezium
Parallelogram
Rectangle
Rhombus

Property
Has exactly two lines of symmetry
Always has four lines of symmetry
Has only one pair of parallel lines
Always has one line of symmetry
Always has four right angles

5) Sort these shapes into the correct place on the Carroll Diagram.

Rectangle   Equilateral triangle   Regular Hexagon   Kite
Square   Rhombus   Trapezium   Scalene triangle

	Quadrilateral	Not a quadrilateral
Regular		
Irregular		

6) Which 3 types of quadrilateral have diagonals which always cross at right angles?

7) Use the internet to find out what an isosceles trapezium is.
   a) Does it have any sides which are equal to each other?
   b) Describe its symmetries.
   c) How many pairs of equal angles does it have?

Discuss

Is a square a parallelogram?

Chapter 8: 2D shapes

End of chapter reflection

You should know that ...	You should be able to ...	Such as ...
You can recognise, visualise, describe and draw two dimensional shapes.	Pick out shapes in unfamiliar settings and describe them.	The broken line cuts the regular pentagon into two other shapes. Name these shapes.
There are mathematical rules for identifying points, lines, shapes and angles using letters.	Identify and label points, lines, shapes and angles.	a) What is the size of angle BDA? b) Name two angles which are 36°. c) Which vertex has an angle of 108° marked? d) What shape is ABCDE?
Triangles can be equilateral, isosceles or scalene depending on how many equal sides or angles they have.	Identify and describe the side, angle and symmetry properties of a special triangle given its name.	Describe the side, angle and symmetry properties of an isosceles triangle.
Squares, rectangles, parallelograms, rhombuses, kites, deltas (darts) and trapeziums are special types of quadrilateral.	Identify and describe the side, angle and symmetry properties of a special quadrilateral given its name.	Describe the side, angle and symmetry properties of a rectangle.
Regular polygons have all their sides and angles equal.	Describe the side, angle and symmetry properties of a regular polygon with 5, 6 or 8 sides.	Describe the symmetry of a regular hexagon.

Unit 1C • Chapter 9

Estimating angles

You will learn how to:
- Estimate the size of acute, obtuse and reflex angles to the nearest 10°.

Starting point

Do you remember …?
- that an angle is a measure of turn and is measured in degrees?
- how to draw a right angle of 90°?
- how to say whether an angle is acute or obtuse?

This will be helpful when …
you learn to calculate missing angles in diagrams to help you sense check your answers.

Hook

Here is an image of a compass.

It shows the usual four points North (N), South (S), East (E) and West (W) as well as the points in between them. For example North-East (NE) lies exactly halfway between North and East. North-North-East then lies exactly halfway between North and North-East.

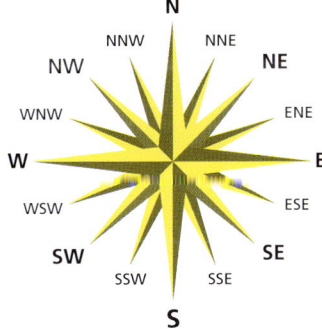

Starting at North with 0°, how many degrees turn, clockwise, will it be to get to East?

Can you work out how many degrees turn, clockwise, it is from North to North-East?

What about North-North-East? And East-North-East?

Label the rest of the compass points with the correct number of degrees.

Did you know?

Military organisations use angles called bearings to plan routes all the time.

They are usually measured in a standard way by measuring from North (as 0°), measuring clockwise and giving exactly 3 digits to help with communicating over a radio.

Chapter 9: Estimating angles   **69**

Key terms

An **estimate** is an approximate value (rather than an accurate value) made using information and knowledge about the situation.

In contrast, a **measure** is an accurate value obtained using equipment and/or calculations.

You measure angles in **degrees** or °; there are 360° in a full turn.

An angle, *x*, is **acute** if *x* < 90°

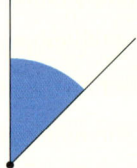

An angle, *x*, is **obtuse** if 90° < *x* < 180°

An angle, *x*, is a **straight line** if *x* = 180°

An angle, *x*, is a **right angle** if *x* = 90°

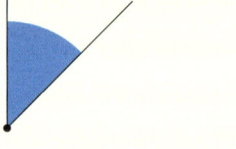

An angle, *x*, is **reflex** if 180° < *x* < 360°

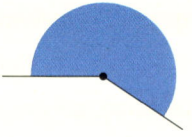

Worked example 1

Estimate the size of these angles to the nearest 10°.

a)    b)    c)

a) The angle is approximately 70° as it is about halfway between 45° and 90°.	You can see that the angle is clearly less than a **right angle**. Mark on the right angle line and the midpoint at 45° to help. The angle is more than half a right angle but less than a whole one; it is approximately half-way between these two markers or about halfway between 45° and 90°.	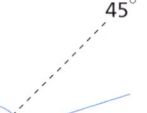
b) The angle is between 90° and 135° but nearer to the 135° line.	The angle is **obtuse** because it is more than a **right angle** but less than a **straight line**. Mark on the right angle line and the straight line as well as the midpoint at 135° to help. The angle is a little less than half way between 90° and 180°.	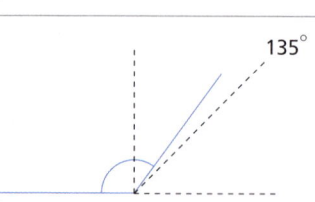

70   Unit 1C: Handling data and geometry

By drawing the line at approximately 112.5° the angle can be estimated at 120°.	Add a marker at 112.5°, which is halfway between the right angle and the 135° line. The angle is approximately halfway between these two markers, so at 120° to the nearest 10 degrees.	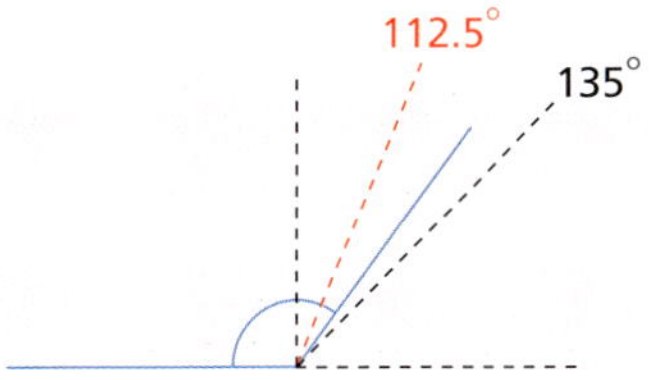
c) The angle is more than 270° but less than 360°.	The angle is **reflex** and it is more than three right angles or 270°. Mark on the line at 270° as well as the line halfway between 270° and 360° at 315°.	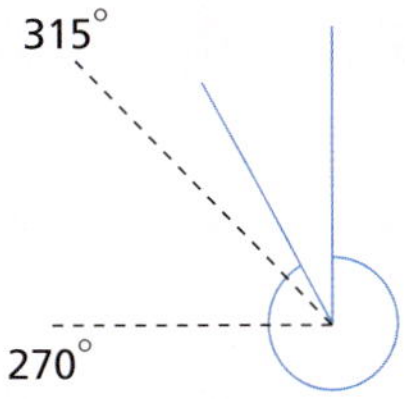
By drawing the lines at 315° and 337.5° you can see that the angle is slightly smaller than 337.5° and is approximately 330°.	The angle is a little more than the 315° that is marked, so add a line that is halfway between 315° and 360°, that is 337.5°. The angle is only just smaller than this, so 330° to the nearest 10 degrees.	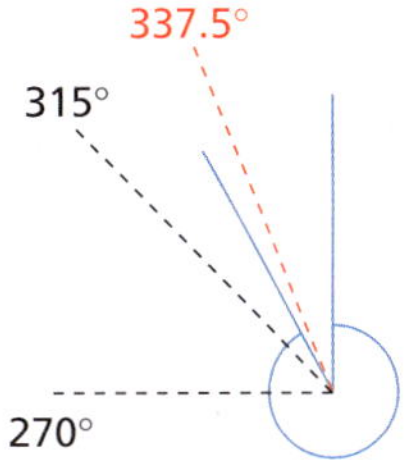

Think about

Can you have an angle of more than 360°?

Exercise 1

1 Estimate the value of these acute angles to the nearest 10 degrees.

Tip

Check your work – all your answers should be between 0° and 90°.

a)  b)  c)  d)

2 Estimate the value of these obtuse angles to the nearest 10 degrees.

a) 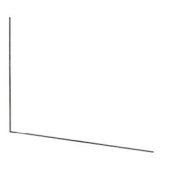 b)    c) 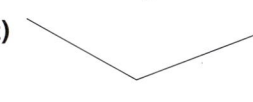 d)

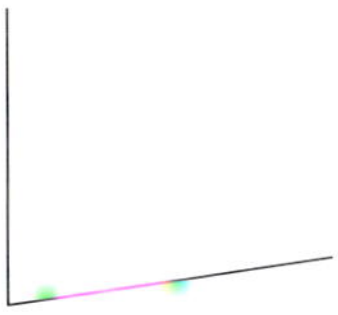

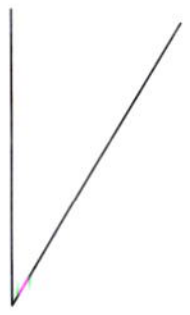

Chapter 9: Estimating angles 71

3 Estimate the value of these reflex angles to the nearest 10 degrees.
a)    b)    c) 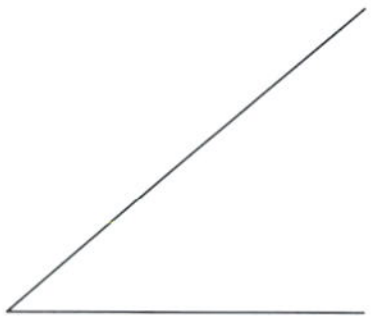   d)

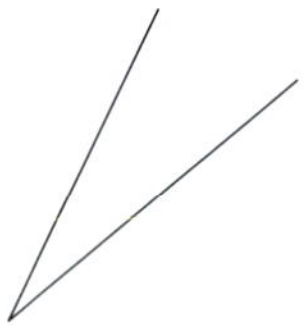

Tip
In parts (c) and (d) it may be easier to estimate the size of the acute angle and then subtract it from 360° to find the size of the reflex angle.

4 i) State whether these angles are acute, obtuse or reflex.
ii) Estimate the value of these angles to the nearest 10 degrees.

a) 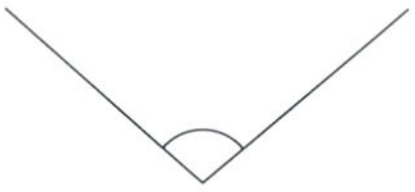   b)    c)    d)

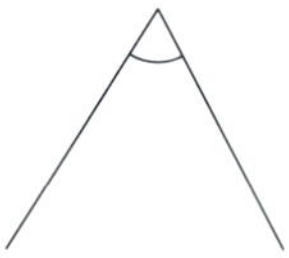

e) 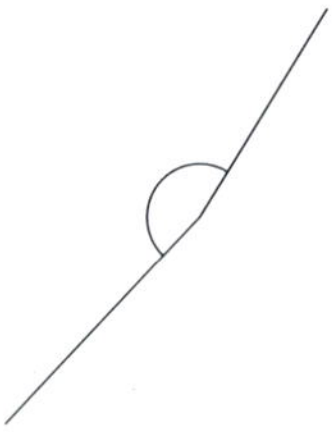   f)    g) 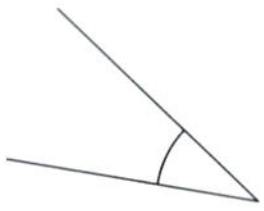   h)

5 a) Estimate the value of this acute angle.

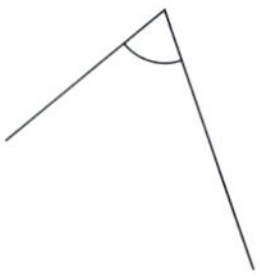

b) Use your answer to part (a) to estimate the value of this reflex angle.

c) How can you use this to help you estimate the value of reflex angles such as in question 4 part (c)?

Discuss
What's the same and what's different? 15° and 345°

6 Vocabulary feature question
Complete the text with the words from the box.

acute	obtuse	reflex	estimate
measure	right-angle	straight line
degrees	acute	obtuse	reflex

If you do not have a protractor, you cannot .... an angle accurately; however you can .... it by comparing it to a ....

72   Unit 1C: Handling data and geometry

Angles that are less than a right angle are called .... and are usually the easiest to estimate.

Angles that are more than a right angle but less than a .... are called ....

If you know the value of an .... or .... angle, you also know the value of a .... angle, because they pair with it to form a full turn. These .... angles lie between 180 and 360 ....

End of chapter reflection

You should know that ...	You should be able to ...	Such as ...
An acute angle is an angle of less than 90°.	Estimate the size of an acute angle.	Estimate the size of this angle. 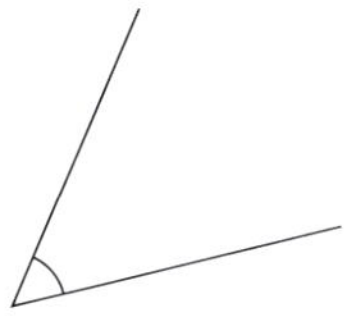
An obtuse angle is an angle between 90° and 180°.	Estimate the size of an obtuse angle.	Estimate the size of this angle. 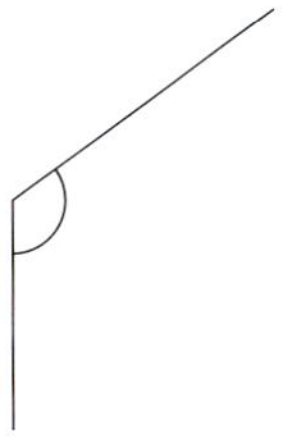
A reflex angle is an angle between 180° and 360°. Angles around a point sum to 360°.	Recognise the relationship between reflex angles and acute/obtuse angles.	Estimate the value of the acute angle and use this to estimate the value of the reflex angle. 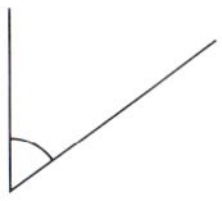 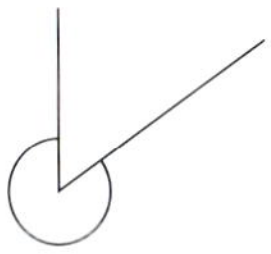

Unit 1C • Chapter 10

Data collection

You will learn how to:
- Decide which data would be relevant to an enquiry and collect and organise the data.
- Design and use a data collection sheet or questionnaire for a simple survey.

Starting point

Do you remember …?

- how to read and use a frequency table of data?
- how to fill in a questionnaire or survey to collect data?
- collecting data yourself?

This will also be helpful when …

you learn more about calculating averages from data to help analyse it.

Hook

A person's pulse rate is the number of beats per minute made by their heart.

Everyone's pulse rate is different but generally a normal resting pulse rate for a person older than 10 is between 60 and 100 beats per minute.

What do you think might happen to your pulse rate when you exercise? When you are asleep? When you are ill?

Let's find out!

Measure your pulse rate while you are sitting down by positioning your fingers on your wrist and counting the beats.

Record the number of beats per minute.

Then run on the spot for 1 minute and repeat the experiment.

Record the number beats per minute immediately after you stop running.

- What happened to your pulse rate? How do you know?
- Compare your results to others in your group – what do you notice?
- To investigate further, what other information would you collect?

Collecting data

Key terms

A **questionnaire** is a series of questions for people to complete.

Questionnaires can include yes/no answers, tick boxes, numbered responses, word responses and questions requiring a longer written answer.

Data is information that can be analysed. You refer to the results of a questionnaire as **data**.

Worked example 1

A website wants to find out about the age and gender of people who use the site, and how often they use it. Design a short questionnaire for users to complete to collect this data.

A website wants to find out about the age and gender of people who use the site and how often they use it.	The website wants to know three things: 1. age 2. gender 3. how often people use the site so you will need three questions.

1. What is your age?
  • Under 18   • 18–30
  • 31–60   • 61 or over
	The first question is about age so you can either ask for an exact age or provide categories.
	 Categories are easier to analyse. Be careful to ensure that the options do not overlap and that every possible age has an option to select.

2. What is your gender? • Female • Male	The second question is about gender, so you can ask a simple male or female question here.

3. How often do you use this site per week?
  • 0 or 1 times
  • 2 or 3 times
  • 4–10 times
  • more than 10 times
	The third question is about how often people use the site.
	 Again you can use option boxes to make the data easier to analyse as long as you make sure the options do not overlap and that every possible answer has an option to select.
	 You need to make sure you give a time period for people to base their answer on, for example, per month or per week.

Exercise 1

1 Mo has been asked to explore the question:

Do adults sleep more than children?

He has decided to collect data from people in a local town centre.

Which two of these things will it be most useful for him to collect data about?

A	B	C	D
Gender of person	Age of person	Number of hours slept last night	Time they woke up this morning

2 Geraldine is investigating the average height of people in different countries around the world. Which would be the most sensible way for her to collect useful data? Explain your answer.

A	B	C	D
Measure her own height	Measure the height of people in her class	Look on the internet	Phone up people in different cities and ask them what their height is

Chapter 10: Data collection

3 A mobile phone company believes that young people use their phones more than older people do. Write a questionnaire of at least three questions to help the company collect data to test their theory.

4 Astrid is collecting data to find out about how much television people watch.

She has the following information about each person:
- age
- gender
- favourite colour
- number of hours of television they watched last week
- favourite television programme
- type/manufacturer of their television set
- number of days they watched television in the last week

Which three pieces of data are not relevant to Astrid's research? Explain your answer.

5 Jaspreet wants to collect information about how many times people play sport.

Here is the question she has written:

How many times do you play sport?

0 to 2 ☐   2 to 4 ☐
4 to 6 ☐   more than 6 ☐

a) Identify two things that are wrong with this question.

b) Write a suitable question for Jaspreet to use.

Data collection sheets and questionnaires

Key terms

A **data collection sheet** is a way of recording the results of a questionnaire or experiment.

The most common way to record data is using a **table**.

You use a **frequency table** to list categories and record their frequency or totals.

Worked example 2

You are collecting data about how students travel to school.
You intend to ask 24 students how they travelled to school today.
Design a suitable data collection sheet to record the responses and complete it.

Transport Type	Tally	Frequency

For each student, you need to record a type of transport.

The easiest way to count all the data is to use a tally chart and mark off each piece using a line, with every fifth item creating a 'bundle'.

So you will add a 'Tally' column to our table and a 'Frequency' column to find the total afterwards.

Transport Type	Tally	Frequency
Car		
Walk		
Bus		
Cycle		
Train		

You can predict some of the responses to help when collecting the data. Let's add:

Car
Walk
Bus
Train
Cycle

to the Transport Type column.

Transport Type	Tally	Frequency
Car		
Walk		
Bus		
Cycle		
Train		
Other		

It is possible that someone will give you a Transport Type that you have not included, so add an 'Other' row.

Now you can start collecting data!

Key terms

A question is said to be **biased** if it is worded so that a particular answer is favoured over others. This can mean that the data collected is not representative.

Data is **representative** if it accurately reflects the real situation.

Think about

How likely are people to tell the truth when completing a questionnaire?

Suggest some situations or topics where they are less likely to be honest.

Exercise 2

1 A café is trying to find out which drinks are its bestsellers.

They will go through the records from a morning to see which drinks have sold the most.

Copy and complete the data collection sheet for the café to record their results.

Drink	Tally	Frequency
....		
....		
....		
....		
....		
....		

2 Valeria is researching students' favourite subjects.

She completes a survey of students and asks them, "What is your favourite subject?"

Design a table for Valeria to use to record her results.

Chapter 10: Data collection   77

3 Kim is finding out about the hobbies of students of different age groups.

She asks students aged 11 and 16 what their favourite hobby is.

Design a data collection sheet for Kim to record her data.

4 Elliot is researching what people think about libraries. He designs a survey to complete. Which would be the best group of people for him to survey? Explain your answer.

A	B	C	D
People in his local library	Children at a school	People in a town centre	People in a local bookshop

5 Peter is conducting an experiment that tests the strength of springs using weights.

He records the maximum weights held by springs in grams.

The highest weight Peter will use is 50 g.

Which of these data collection sheets would be most suitable? Explain your answer.

Weight (g)	Tally	Frequency
....		
....		
....		
....		
....		
....		

Weight (g)	Tally	Frequency
1		
2		
3		
4		
5		
More than 5		

Weight (g)	Tally	Frequency
0–9		
10–19		
20–29		
30–39		
40–49		
50		

6 Design a questionnaire to find out whether people would be in favour of or against building a new shopping mall in the nearest town. Include a data collection sheet.

7 Use a word processing program to design a questionnaire to find out how students rate the quality of meals served in the school canteen. Include a data collection sheet.

8 There are three maths teachers in Catalina's school – Teacher A, Teacher B and Teacher C.

Catalina is investigating whether the three different teachers set the same amount of homework. She conducts a survey of the students and asks them:
- Who is your maths teacher?
- How many hours of homework were you set last week?

Design a data collection sheet for Catalina to use.

9 Rewrite the following questions so they are not biased.

a) Do you agree that the environment is important?

b) The business has made a profit for the last 5 years. Do you think the business is successful?

c) Are you in favour of opening a new cinema to give young people more to do?

10 **Vocabulary feature question**

Complete the sentences with the words from the box.

tally	frequency table	data	
category	overlap	biased	totals

Unit 1C: Handling data and geometry

If you use a questionnaire, you need to be careful that your questions are not .... and that any option boxes you use do not .... or exclude any possible answers.

Once .... is collected, it can be organised in a .... using a .... to record the number of responses in each .... before finding the ....

End of chapter reflection

You should know that ...	You should be able to ...	Such as ...
Data can be collected from an experiment or from a questionnaire.	Design a questionnaire to find out relevant data.	Design a questionnaire to find out how much money people spend on chocolate.
You need to collect data appropriate to your enquiry.	Say whether data is relevant or not.	Bob is investigating how much time men and women spend exercising. He has collected the following data from 100 people: • age • gender • time spent exercising per week • favourite exercise Which two items are the most relevant?
A data collection sheet can be used to collect information from a survey.	Design a data collection sheet.	a) Cindy is collecting information about how many pets people have. Design a data collection sheet to record her results. b) Dylan is investigating whether adults go to the cinema more than children. He asks 100 people their age and the number of times they have been to the cinema in the last month. Design a data collection sheet to record his results.

Unit 1C • Chapter 11

Probability 1

You will learn how to:
- Use the language of probability to describe and interpret results involving likelihood and chance.
- Understand and use the probability scale from 0 to 1.
- Find probabilities based on equally likely outcomes in simple contexts.

Starting point

Do you remember ...?

- the meaning of words like chance, certain, impossible and likely?
- how to write fractions and decimals?
- how to place numbers on number scales?

This will be helpful when ...

you learn how to find probabilities of two or more combined events.

Hook

A game for 2 or more players

You will need:
- 2 dice
- a 3 × 3 grid like this for each player, filled in with numbers of your choice from 1 to 12 (no repeats)

Rules:

Players take it in turns to roll both dice and find the total of the scores.

Any player with this total on their grid may cross it out.

The winner is the first to cross out a line!

12	5	9
2	11	7
8	4	10

- Play the game!
- Then discuss your strategy with the other players before playing again, to see if you can improve your performances.
- Are all the different scores equally likely to occur?
- If not, which are the most likely and which are the least likely? Are any of them certain? Are any of them impossible?
- Does it matter which number is in the middle of your grid?

Probability words

Key terms

An **outcome** is a possible result of an **event**.

For example, the outcomes of a football match are win, lose or draw. The event is the football match. The outcomes from rolling a six-sided dice are the numbers 1, 2, 3, 4, 5 and 6. The event is rolling the dice.

A **probability** is the chance that a particular outcome, or result, will happen. If a fair coin is tossed, there are two possible outcomes as the coin has two different sides. Fair means that all outcomes are equally likely.

You measure and describe a probability as a number on the **probability scale** from 0 to 1, where the probability of an outcome happening which is impossible is zero, and the probability of an event happening which is certain to happen is 1.

You can use fractions, decimals or percentages to express probabilities as well as represent them visually on a probability scale. For a coin toss there are two possible, equally likely outcomes so the probability of either outcome is one chance in two. You can write this as $\frac{1}{2}$ or 0.5 or 50%. These are different ways of writing the same thing.

An outcome positioned halfway along the probability scale with a value of 0.5 or $\frac{1}{2}$ is one where the probability of it happening is the same as the probability of it not happening. This is sometimes described as evens.

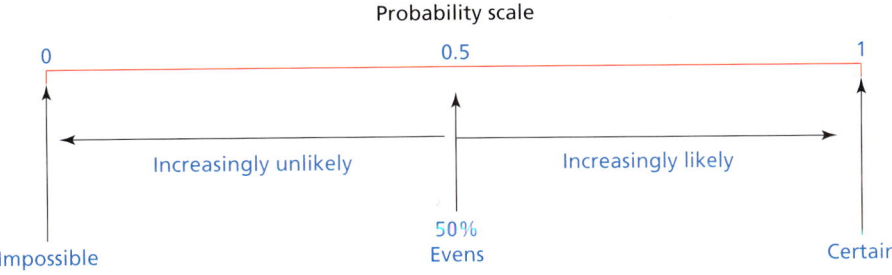

Outcomes with probabilities of less than $\frac{1}{2}$ are said to be **unlikely**. Outcomes with probabilities of more than $\frac{1}{2}$ are said to be **likely**. An outcome with a probability of $\frac{3}{4}$ is more likely to happen than an outcome with a probability of $\frac{1}{4}$.

Worked example 1

Here is a probability scale:

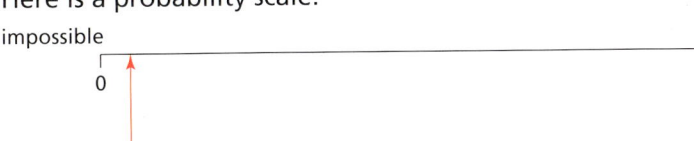

a) On the scale, mark and estimate the probability that you will fall asleep before midnight tonight.

b) Describe something with a probability matching the arrow marked on the probability scale.

Chapter 11: Probability 1

a) impossible ——————————————— certain 0 1 The probability that you will fall asleep before midnight	It is very likely that you will fall asleep before midnight tonight – however, there is a small chance that you may not. You need to position your mark close to 1, but not at 1 because this is not a certain event.
b) You will get an increase in your pocket money tomorrow.	The arrow is pointing to a number close to 0. This means the probability is low. So you are looking for an event that is very unlikely, but not impossible. For example, the arrow could represent the probability that you get an increase in your pocket money tomorrow – it could happen but is unlikely.

Exercise 1

1 Choose one of the following probability words to describe the likelihood of each outcome happening.

Impossible   Unlikely   Evens   Likely   Certain

a) Getting a particular side when you toss a coin
b) You arriving at school on time on the next school day
c) A person chosen at random from the population of a large city being female
d) Studying probability in maths next lesson
e) A day old baby being able to talk in sentences
f) The sun rising tomorrow morning

2 a) Put the following outcomes in order of probability, from the least likely to the most likely.
 – You will get homework tomorrow.
 – It will snow tomorrow.
 – You will eat breakfast tomorrow.
 – It will rain tomorrow.
 – It will be sunny tomorrow.

b) Use one of the following to describe the probability of each of the outcomes in (a) happening.

Certain   Very likely   Likely   Evens   Unlikely   Very Unlikely   Impossible

3 a) Describe an outcome which could be placed on this probability scale at the places marked A, B, C and D.

b) Give an estimate of the probability of outcomes B and C as a decimal or fraction.

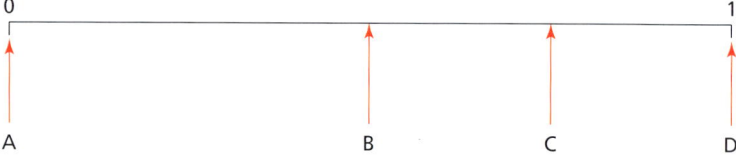

Unit 1C: Handling data and geometry

4 Here is a probability scale showing the probability that the 08:15 train will arrive late.

a) Write a sentence to describe how likely it is that the 08:15 train will be late.

b) The probability that an aeroplane from London arriving at 12:00 will be late is estimated as $\frac{3}{4}$.

Show this probability on a probability scale.

5 Sally has a pack of counters. She will select one without looking (**at random**).

Draw a probability scale and mark on it where each of the outcomes below should be.

a) Sally selects an orange counter.
b) Sally selects a yellow counter.
c) Sally selects a green counter.
d) Sally does not select an orange counter.

6 Sama has a bag that contains 11 red counters, 4 orange counters and 5 green counters. She takes out a counter at random and does not put it back in the bag. She then picks out another counter. The second counter is twice as likely to be red as it is to be green. What was the colour of the first counter that was removed?

Calculating probabilities

Key term

When items are chosen **at random**, this means that every item is equally likely to be chosen. Therefore, the probability of picking each item will be the same.

When all the **outcomes** are equally likely, you can calculate the probability of an event occurring as:

$$\frac{\text{number of favourable outcomes}}{\text{total number of outcomes}}$$

An event is described as **fair** if all the outcomes of the event are equally likely. If a fair spinner, which is a regular hexagon with sides numbered from 1 to 6, is spun then it is equally likely to land on any of the six numbers.

Using decimals and fractions to describe a probability

How likely is likely? Assigning a probability to a number means you can be more specific about how likely an outcome is to happen. Look at these two statements.

- I'm likely to win my next basketball match, and I'm likely to win my next tennis match.
- The probability I win my next basketball match is 0.7. The probability I win my next tennis match is 0.8.

Both statements say that I am likely to win both matches, but the second statement also tells me that I am more likely to win the tennis match.

> **Did you know?**
>
> You write **P(outcome)** to mean the probability of a particular outcome of an event.
>
> For example, P(it will rain tomorrow) means 'the probability that it will rain tomorrow'.

Worked example 2

Jess has a bag of sweets.
She selects one at random.
Calculate the probability that:

a) Jess selects a red sweet.
b) Jess selects a green or an orange sweet.
c) Jess does not select a purple sweet.
d) Jess selects a blue sweet.

a) There are 5 red sweets out of a total of 12 sweets so: P(red sweet) = $\frac{5}{12}$	There are 5 red sweets in the bag out of 12 sweets altogether. Jess has 5 chances out of 12 to select a red or $\frac{5}{12}$.	
b) There are a total of 4 green or orange sweets out of a total of 12 sweets so: P(green or orange sweet) = $\frac{4}{12}$	There are 3 green sweets and 1 orange sweet, so altogether Jess has 4 chances out of 12 to select a green or orange sweet or $\frac{4}{12}$. You could simplify this fraction to $\frac{1}{3}$.	
c) 11 of the 12 sweets are not purple so: P(not a purple sweet) = $\frac{11}{12}$	There is 1 purple sweet in the bag, so there are 11 that are not purple. Jess has 11 chances out of 12 to select a non-purple sweet or $\frac{11}{12}$.	
d) There are 0 blue sweets in the bag of 12 sweets so: P(a blue sweet) = 0	There are no blue sweets in the bag so it is impossible for Jess to choose one.	

Tip

When you are working out probabilities remember that a probability can never be bigger than 1. If your probability is greater than 1 then you need to recheck your working.

Discuss

Why must a certain event have a probability of 1?

Exercise 2   1–9

1. Tick which of these events **must** have equally likely outcomes.
   - A sweet is chosen from a bag which has 5 red sweets and 5 green sweets without looking. ✓
   - I spin this spinner.
   - A letter is chosen from my name at random.

2. The eleven letters in the word PROBABILITY are written on eleven separate cards with one letter on each card. One card is chosen at random.
   a) Write all the possible outcomes for this event. P/R/O/B/A/I/L/T/Y
   b) Are there any outcomes that are more likely than others? Explain your answer. Yes - letters that are there more than 1x.

3. Esme rolls a fair six-sided dice.
   What is the probability that she obtains:
   a) a five? 1/6
   b) a one or a two? 1/3
   c) a number less than six? 5/6
   d) an odd number? 1/2

4. Jamal has some counters in front of him.

   He says, 'the probability of selecting a red counter is 3/5 because there are 3 reds but 5 blue counters'.
   Do you agree with Jamal? Explain your answer. No it's 3/8

5. Felix spins the spinner shown.
   What is the probability that the spinner stops on:
   a) a blue sector? 3/8
   b) a sector with a negative number on it? 0
   c) a sector not coloured red? 7/8
   d) a yellow sector with an even number on it? ✱ 1/2
   e) a sector with a number greater than 3 on it? 5/8
   f) a sector with a number less than 20 on it? 1

6. A jar contains 1 gold coin, 6 silver coins and 3 copper coins and no other coins.
   One coin is selected at random.
   What is the probability that the coin selected is:
   a) gold? 1/10
   b) silver? 3/5
   c) not gold? 9/10
   d) platinum? 0

7. Nidia picks one of these eight cards at random.

   | 1 | 2 | 3 | 4 | 5 | 6 | 7 | 8 |

Chapter 11: Probability 1   85

Mark on the scale with an arrow the probability of these outcomes:

|—+—+—+—+—+—+—+—+—|
0   0.5   1

Event A: The card shows an even number.

Event B: The card shows a number 7.

Event C: The card shows a number which can be drawn using only straight lines.

Event D: The card shows a factor of 48.

Event E: The card shows a number less than 10.

8 Draw a spinner containing only 5 sectors, coloured red, yellow and green, which meets the following conditions:

P(green) = $\frac{3}{5}$

P(yellow) = P(red)

9 Katy says, "I am running for election as school captain and I have marked the probability of me winning on this probability scale. I think it is evens as I can only win or lose."

|————————|————————|
0   0.5   1
     ↑
equally likely to win or lose

Do you agree with Katy? Explain your answer.

10 Roll two dice and calculate the total score shown on the two dice.

Repeat this 50 times.

Use a spreadsheet to record your results.

Then use your spreadsheet to calculate the probability of each score from your experiment.

11 Vocabulary feature question

Complete the sentences with the words in the box.

| Probability | chance | likely | equally | outcomes | fractions | scale |
| certain | event | impossible | likelihood | 0 | 1 | unlikely | at random |

Probability is defined as the .... or .... of an .... occurring.

The .... of an event with .... likely outcomes can be calculated as the total number of favourable outcomes ÷ the total number of possible ...., as long as the outcome is selected ....

The highest possible value of a probability is ...., which represents a .... outcome.

The lowest possible value of a probability is ...., which represents an .... outcome.

You can represent probabilities on a .... or as decimals, or ....

A probability with a value of higher than 0.5 but less than one is said to be ...., while a probability with a value of less than 0.5 but greater than zero is said to be ....

Unit 1C: Handling data and geometry

End of chapter reflection

You should know that ...	You should be able to ...	Such as ...
The probability of a particular outcome of an event can be described using probability words such as certain, likely, evens, unlikely and impossible.	Describe the probability of an outcome in words.	Describe the probability that it will rain tomorrow.
You can tell how likely an outcome is from its position on the probability scale.	Describe how likely an outcome is from its position on the probability scale.	The arrow shows the probability of tomorrow being sunny. How likely is it to be sunny tomorrow? 0 ──────────↑── 1
An impossible outcome has a probability of 0 and an outcome which is certain has a probability of 1.	Position an outcome on a probability scale between 0 and 1.	Mark on a probability scale an estimate of the probability that Norway will win the next ski-jumping world cup.
When the outcomes of an event are equally likely, you can calculate the probability as the $\frac{\text{number of favourable outcomes}}{\text{total number of outcomes}}$	Calculate the probability of an event with equally likely outcomes.	Tracey has a jar of buttons. There are 9 black buttons, 5 brown buttons and 1 white button. Tracey selects a button at random. Calculate the probability that Tracey selects: **a)** a brown button. **b)** a button that is not black.

Unit 2A
Number and calculation

What's it all about?

- Working with time in 12- and 24-hour clock formats
- Properties of numbers
- Calculations with fractions
- Describing parts of shapes, quantities and measures using fractions or percentages
- Finding fractions or percentages of amounts
- Simplifying calculations
- Rounding

You will learn about:

- Interpreting timetables and finding the length of time something takes
- Reading scales
- Factors, multiples, primes, square numbers and square roots
- Adding, subtracting and multiplying fractions
- Finding fractions and percentages of amounts
- Writing one amount as a fraction or percentage of another
- Simplifying calculations
- When to round answers

You will build your skills in:

- Reading scales
- Interpreting timetables
- Arithmetic
- Mental maths

Unit 2A • Chapter 12

Time and scales

You will learn how to:
- Know the relationships between units of time; understand and use the 12-hour and 24-hour clock systems.
- Interpret timetables and calculate time intervals.
- Read the scales on a range of analogue and digital measuring instruments.

Starting point

Do you remember…?

- how to read an analogue watch?
- the relationships between different units of time such as days and weeks?

Hook

How accurate is your sense of time? This is a game for two players.

In a turn of this game:
- One player says 'start' and starts a timer or a watch which shows seconds.
- The second player then says 'stop' when they think one minute has passed.
- The time is recorded in seconds.
- Each person has three turns.
- The winner of the turn is the person who is more accurate.
- The person who wins most turns is the winner of the game.

Emma and Dexter play the game for three turns. These are their results:

Turn number	Dexter	Emma	Winner of turn
1	44 seconds	72 seconds	
2	69 seconds	48 seconds	
3	62 seconds	57 seconds	

a) Who won the game?

b) Now play the game with another member of the class. Make a table for the results. You could have a class competition to see who is the most accurate.

Units of time and the 24-hour clock

Key terms

Units of time

1 minute = 60 seconds   1 hour = 60 minutes   1 day = 24 hours   7 days = 1 week

$\frac{1}{4}$ of an hour = 15 minutes $\frac{1}{2}$ an hour = 30 minutes $\frac{3}{4}$ of an hour = 45 minutes

1 year = 12 months = 365 days (or 366 days in a leap year)

The number of days in a month varies.

> **Did you know?**
>
> There is a poem to help you remember how many days there are in each month:
>
> 30 days has September, April, June and November
>
> All the rest have 31 except February alone
>
> Which has 28 days clear but 29 each leap year.

Worked example 1

Convert these times to the units given in the brackets:

a) 142 seconds (minutes and seconds)
b) 2 and a quarter hours (minutes)
c) 72 hours (days)
d) 43 days (weeks and days)

a) To change seconds to minutes you divide by 60. 142 ÷ 60 = 2 remainder 22 so 142 seconds = 2 minutes 22 seconds	You could use repeated subtraction. 142 − 60 = 82 82 − 60 = 22 There are 2 whole minutes and 22 seconds left.	
b) To change hours to minutes, multiply by 60. 2 and a quarter hours = 2 × 60 + 15 minutes = 135 minutes	Convert the hours to minutes first and then add 15 minutes (quarter of an hour). 2 × 60 = 120 120 + 15 = 135	
c) There are 24 hours in a day. 72 ÷ 24 = 3	72 − 24 = 48 48 − 24 = 24 24 − 24 = 0 There are 3 lots of 24 in 72.	
d) There are 7 days in a week so divide 43 by 7. = 43 ÷ 7 = 6 r1 so 43 days = 6 weeks and 1 day	There are 7 days in a week. So divide by 7 to find out how many 7s are in 43. Any remainder will be days.	

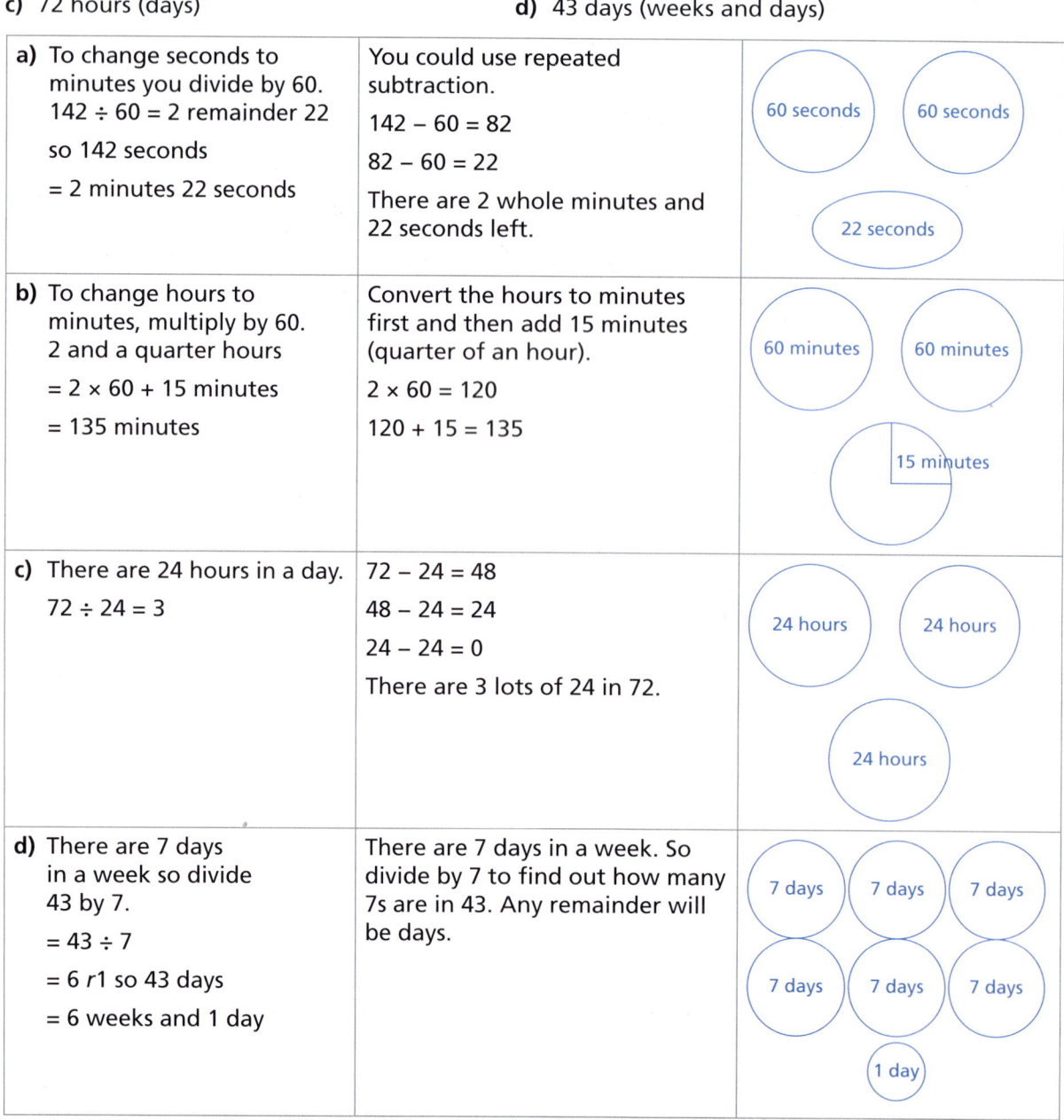

Key terms

Times of day can be written in two ways:

- you can use the **12-hour clock** using a.m. – before noon – and p.m. – after noon. 10 a.m. or 10:00 a.m. means 10 o'clock in the morning. 10 p.m. or 10:00 p.m. means 10 o'clock at night.
- you can use the **24-hour clock** where times are measured from midnight, which is written as 00:00. 9 a.m. is written as 09:00 and 9 p.m. is written as 21:00 because it is 9 hours past 12 noon and so is 21 hours after midnight. The 24-hour clock always uses 4 digits so 7 a.m. is written 07:00 and not 7:00.

Worked example 2

Copy and complete this table.

12-hour clock time	24-hour clock time
7:35 a.m.	
8:15 p.m.	
	11:50
	18:25

12-hour clock	24-hour clock
7:35 a.m.	07:35
8:15 p.m.	20:15
11:50 a.m.	11:50
6:25 p.m.	18:25

For times in the morning you rewrite in 4 digits so 07:35.

For times in the afternoon you add 12 hours so 8 hours 15 minutes + 12 hours = 20 hours 15 minutes written as 20:15

If the number of hours is less than 12, then the time is before noon so 11:50 is 11:50 a.m.

If the number of hours is more than 12, you subtract 12 to give the time after noon. 18:25 becomes 6:25 p.m. as 18 − 12 = 6.

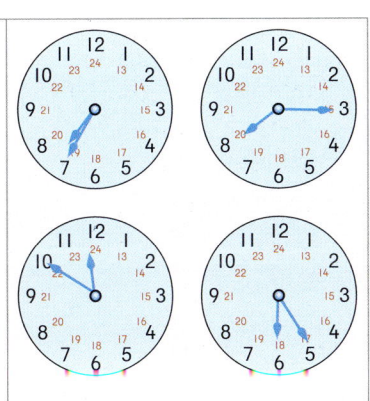

Exercise 1

1 Convert these times to seconds.
   a) 4 minutes
   b) 10 minutes
   c) 20 minutes
   d) 30 minutes
   e) 45 minutes
   f) 8 minutes 20 seconds

2 Convert these times from seconds to minutes and seconds.
   a) 60 seconds
   b) 120 seconds
   c) 180 seconds
   d) 360 seconds
   e) 75 seconds
   f) 90 seconds
   g) 150 seconds
   h) 605 seconds

3 Convert these times to minutes.
   a) 3 hours
   b) 5 hours
   c) 10 hours
   d) 15 hours
   e) 2 hours 30 minutes
   f) 4 hours 15 minutes

4 Convert these times from minutes, to hours and minutes.
   a) 120 minutes
   b) 240 minutes
   c) 480 minutes
   d) 1200 minutes
   e) 73 minutes
   f) 95 minutes
   g) 125 minutes
   h) 610 minutes

5 Convert these times to hours.
   a) 2 days
   b) 5 days
   c) 10 days
   d) 4 days 12 hours
   e) 3 days 5 hours
   f) 5 days 17 hours

6 Convert these times from hours to days and hours.
   a) 48 hours
   b) 55 hours
   c) 144 hours
   d) 29 hours

7 Match each analogue clock face with two digital times.

a)    b)    c)    d)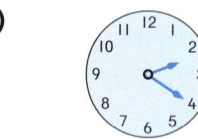

18:30   12:25   02:20   11:20   14:20   23:20   06:30   00:25

8 Copy and complete this table.

12-hour clock time	24-hour clock time
7:32 a.m.	
11:25 a.m.	
3:17 p.m.	
10:20 p.m.	
12:15 p.m.	
10 past midnight	
	00:35
	03:30
	11:20
	12:30
	14:50
	23:15

9 Saraya changes 125 hours to days and says it is 2 days and 5 hours. Explain her mistake.

10 Some chronograph watches have telemetric scales for measuring distances. Investigate how telemetric scales work.

Time intervals and timetables

Key term

A **time interval** is the amount of time between two given times.

Worked example 3

a) What is the time 1 hour and 35 minutes after 10:20?

b) Olivia is going ice skating. The journey takes 38 minutes. At what time should she leave to arrive at the ice rink at exactly 10 a.m.?

c) What is the time interval between 10:30 and 14:20?

d) What is the time interval between 22:40 on Tuesday and 07:30 on Wednesday?

a) 1 hour after 10:20 is 11:20 35 minutes after 11:20 is 11:55	Count on 1 hour and then count on 35 minutes.	
b) 30 minutes before 10 a.m. is 9:30 a.m. 8 minutes before 9:30 a.m. is 9:22 a.m.	Do this in two steps. Take away the 30 minutes first and then take away the 8 minutes.	
c) From 10:30 to 11:00 is 30 minutes. From 11:00 to 14:00 is 3 hours. From 14:00 to 14:20 is 20 minutes. The total is 3 hours 50 minutes.	Count on to the next hour. Then count on in whole hours. From 11:00 to 14:00 is 3 hours. Then count on to the time you need. Add together to get 3 hours and 50 minutes.	
d) From 22:40 to 23:00 is 20 minutes. From 23:00 to 07:00 is 8 hours. From 07:00 to 07:30 is 30 minutes. The total is 8 hours and 50 minutes.	Count on to the next hour. Next count on in hours to 07:00. And then count on the minutes from 07:00 to 07:30. Add together to get 8 hours and 50 minutes.	

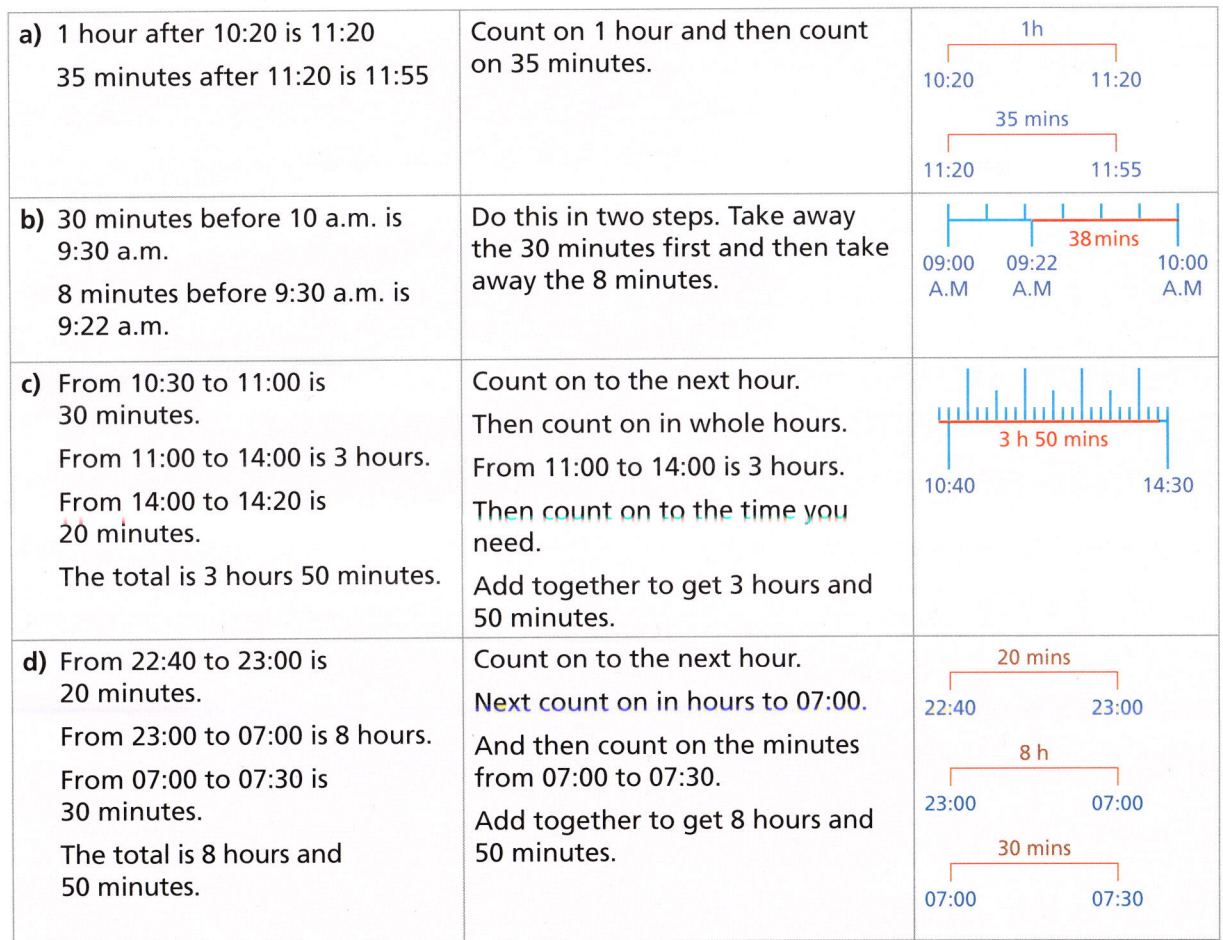

Chapter 12: Time and scales

Key term

A **timetable** is a schedule showing the times at which things will happen. Often they are shown as charts to make them easy to read. On timetables the times are usually in the 24-hour clock but the colon (:) between the hours and the minutes is sometimes left out so 0732 means 07:32.

Worked example 4

Sheila catches the bus to get to work in the morning. She works in West Town Lane and needs to get there before 8 a.m. She catches the latest possible bus from Southmead. This is a section of the bus timetable that shows the times of the buses in the morning for bus service 1 and bus service 2.

Service No.:	2	1	2	1	2	1	2	1	2	1	2
Notes:											
Kingsville	0510	0540	0610	0620	0628	0633	0638	0643	0648	0653	0657
Henbury	—	0554	—	0634	—	0647	—	0657	—	0707	—
Southmead	0525	—	0625	—	0643	—	0653	—	0704	—	0713
Westbury	—	0604	—	0644	—	0657	—	0707	—	0717	—
Henley	0532	—	0632	—	0650	—	0700	—	0711	—	0721
Ballam	0539	0612	0639	0652	0657	0705	0707	0715	0720	0725	0732
Broadmead	0552	0625	0652	0705	0710	0718	0720	0728	0733	0741	0750
Temple Meads	0600	0633	0700	0713	0718	0726	0728	0736	0742	0752	0801
West Town Lane	0610	—	0710	—	0728	—	0738	—	0754	—	0814
Broomhill	—	0645	—	0725	—	0738	—	0750	—	0806	—
Stockwood	0619	—	0719	—	0737	—	0747	—	0804	—	0824

a) Which bus service does Sheila use?
b) What time does her bus get to West Town Lane?
c) What time does this bus leave Southmead?
d) How long does the journey take?

a) Sheila uses service number 2.	Read the timetable across from West Town Lane and then up to the top of the timetable to show Sheila uses service number 2.	
b) 07:54	Sheila can catch any bus that gets in before 8 a.m. The latest bus that gets to West Town Lane before 8 a.m. arrives at 07:54.	Service No: 2 Southmead 0704 West Town Lane 0754
c) The bus leaves Southmead at 07:04	Reading up the timetable from 0754 to 0704.	
d) The journey takes 50 minutes.	The difference in time between 07:54 and 07:04 is 54 − 04 = 50 minutes	50 mins 7:04 ———— 7:54

Unit 2A: Number and calculation

Exercise 2

1 Find the difference in hours and minutes between the two times.
   a) 6 p.m. and 7:30 p.m.
   b) 10 a.m. and 1 p.m.
   c) 1:15 a.m. and 4 a.m.
   d) 11:15 a.m. and 2:45 p.m.
   e) 12:05 p.m. and 3:50 p.m.
   f) 6:20 a.m. and 11:10 p.m.
   g) 4:15 p.m. and 5:08 p.m.
   h) 12:32 a.m. and 3:48 p.m.
   i) 10:52 p.m. and 1:18 a.m.

2 Find the difference in hours and minutes between the two successive times.
   a) 00:10 and 03:50
   b) 15:25 and 16:35
   c) 07:20 and 18:35
   d) 11:45 and 11:53
   e) 02:17 and 05:13
   f) 04:38 and 09:49
   g) 18:50 and 21:13
   h) 19:44 and 13:34
   i) 23:46 and 02:13

3 Add 45 minutes to the following times.
   a) 09:00
   b) 13:10
   c) 10:30
   d) 2:20 p.m.
   e) 16:50
   f) 11:50 a.m.
   g) 23:15

4 Frankie subtracts 55 minutes from 07:00. He writes down this subtraction sum rather than counting back.

```
  7 00
-   55
------
  6 45
```

Is he correct? Explain your answer.

5 The calendar which you use is a Gregorian calendar. Investigate why years which are divisible by 4, such as 2016, are usually leap years and 2400 will be a leap year but 2100 will not be.

6 Neil is flying from Manchester airport to Belfast airport and back on the same day. This is the flight timetable for that day.

Manchester	Belfast	Belfast	Manchester
08:40	09:35	07:10	08:10
15:50	16:45	17:15	18:10
19:55	20:50	21:20	22:20

   a) Write all the possible journeys Neil could make from Manchester to Belfast and back again on the same day.
   b) Neil decides to catch the 08:40 plane. He lives 30 minutes from the airport and must arrive at least 2 hours before he flies. What is the latest time he could leave home and still catch the flight?
   c) Neil's meeting is 45 minutes by taxi from Belfast airport.
   Assuming that his plane is on time and that it takes him 20 minutes from the time that the plane arrives to get to the taxi, what time will he arrive at his destination?
   d) Neil wants to catch the 17:15 flight back to Manchester. His meeting finishes at 3 p.m. His journey time back to the airport is the same as when he arrived and he needs to be at the airport at least 2 hours before his flight. Will he catch this flight? Explain your answer.

7

Service No.:	2	1	2	1	2	1	2	1	2	1	2
Notes:											
Kingsville	0510	0540	0610	0620	0628	0633	0638	0643	0648	0653	0657
Henbury	—	0554	—	0634	—	0647	—	0657	—	0707	—
Southmead	0525	—	0625	—	0643	—	0653	—	0704	—	0713
Westbury	—	0604	—	0644	—	0657	—	0707	—	0717	—
Henley	0532	—	0632	—	0650	—	0700	—	0711	—	0721
Ballam	0539	0612	0639	0652	0657	0705	0707	0715	0720	0725	0732
Broadmead	0552	0625	0652	0705	0710	0718	0720	0728	0733	0741	0750
Temple Meads	0600	0633	0700	0713	0718	0726	0728	0736	0742	0752	0801
West Town Lane	0610	—	0710	—	0728	—	0738	—	0754	—	0814
Broomhill	—	0645	—	0725	—	0738	—	0750	—	0806	—
Stockwood	0619	—	0719	—	0737	—	0747	—	0804	—	0824

Use the timetable to answer the following questions.

a) i) What what time does the 0610 bus from Kingsville arrive in Ballam?

   ii) How long does the journey take?

b) i) What time does the 0657 bus from Kingsville arrive in Broadmead?

   ii) How long does the journey take?

c) Which service stops at Broomhill?

d) Konrad catches the service 1 bus at 06:33 in Kingsville. He wants to travel to Stockwood which is on the service 2 route.

   i) Write the stops where Konrad could change from service 1 to service 2.

   ii) He catches the 0633 bus. What is the earliest he could arrive in Stockwood?

   iii) How long is his journey?

e) How much longer does the 0648 from Kingsville take to get to Stockwood than the 0638?

8 This is a section of a train timetable between Ibadan and Lagos.

Ibadan	Lagos	Cost $ (single fare)
12:57	14:25	15.30
13:57	15:27	15.30
14:57	16:25	11.20
15:57	17:22	20.80
16:57	18:25	15.30

Lagos	Ibadan	Cost $ (single fare)
15:40	17:13	15.30
15:50	17:53	34.70
16:41	18:13	15.30
17:44	19:15	11.20
17:50	20:09	34.70
18:45	20:22	11.20
19:42	21:13	20.80

a) i) What time does the 15:57 from Ibadan arrive in Lagos?

   ii) How long does the journey take?

   iii) How much does it cost?

b) i) What time does the train that arrives in Ibadan at 20:09 leave Lagos?

   ii) How long does the journey take?

   iii) How much does it cost?

Abeni is travelling to Lagos to see a friend and keeps the cost as low as possible by taking the cheapest trains.

c) i) Which train should she take from Ibadan to Lagos?

   ii) How long does the journey from Ibadan to Lagos take?

d) i) Which trains could she take from Lagos to Ibadan?

   ii) How long does each of these journeys from Lagos to Ibadan take?

e) i) If Abeni wants to spend at least 2 hours in Lagos which trains should she take?

   ii) For this journey, work out the total length of time between Abeni leaving Ibadan and returning there.

9 Iona is looking at two journeys to see her mother in Summer City. The first train leaves at 07:40 and arrives at Summer City 5 hours and 35 minutes later. The next train leaves 25 minutes later and arrives in Summer City at 13:40. She decides that the second train is the shorter journey time. Is she correct?

10 The time is different in the different time zones across the world. Jana lives in Mumbai. She says that she can find the time in London by turning her analogue watch upside down because there is a 5.5 hour time difference. Is this true? Investigate.

Reading scales

Key term

Measurements of quantities are often shown on **scales**. An **analogue** watch uses a form of scale and so does your ruler. Scales are used when you are drawing graphs. Instruments used for measuring quantities in science often have scales.

Worked example 5

a) Write the quantity shown on this scale by the arrows at (i), (ii) and (iii).

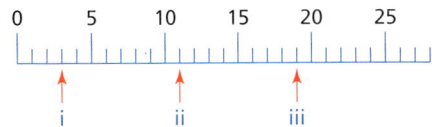

b) Write the quantity shown on this scale by the arrows at (i), (ii) and (iii).

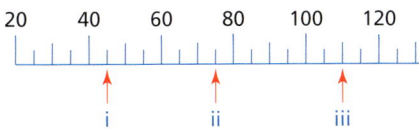

c) Write the quantity of liquid in the jug:

   i) in millilitres

   ii) in litres

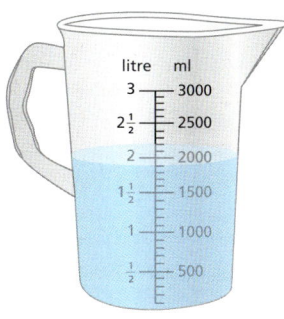

a) Each small division is 1 unit so: i) shows 3 ii) shows 11 iii) shows 19	The difference between each number marked is 5. There are 5 spaces between each number so each space represents 5 ÷ 5 = 1. (Count the spaces and not the marks.) i) is 3 marks past 0 so is 0 + 3 = 3 ii) is 1 mark past 10 so is 10 + 1 = 11 iii) is 4 marks past 15 so is 15 + 4 = 19	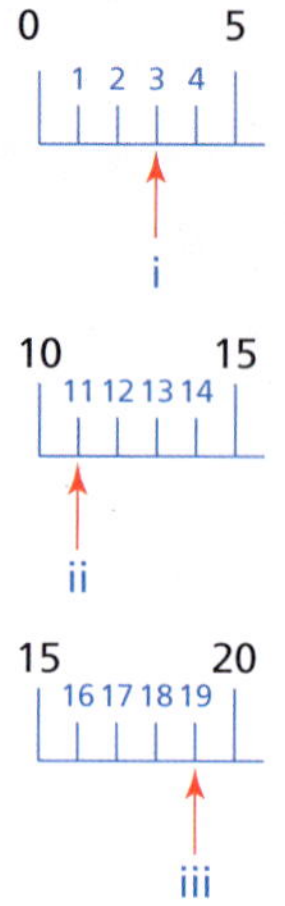
b) 4 small divisions make 20 so 1 small division represents 5 units. i) shows 45 ii) shows 75 iii) shows 110	The difference between each number marked is 20. There are 4 spaces between each mark so each space represents 20 ÷ 4 = 5 units. i) is 1 space past 40 so 40 + 1 × 5 = 45 ii) is 3 spaces past 60 so is 60 + 3 × 5 = 75 iii) is 2 spaces past 100 so is 100 + 2 × 5 = 110	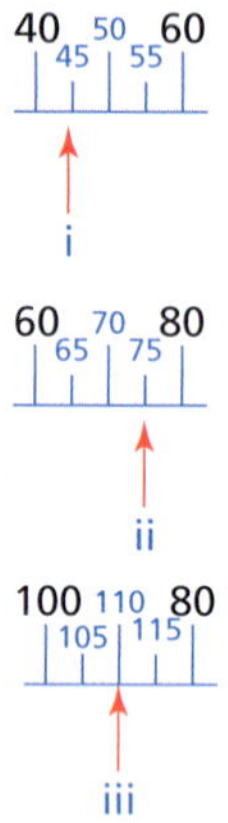
c) i) 1900 ml ii) 1.9 l	i) The difference between the numbers marked in millilitres is 500 and there are 5 spaces so each space represents 500 ÷ 5 = 100. The liquid is 4 spaces above 1500 so is 1500 + 4 × 100 = 1900 ii) The difference between the numbers marked in litres is $\frac{1}{2}$ or 0.5 and there are 5 spaces so each space is 0.5 ÷ 5 = 0.1. The liquid is 4 spaces above 1.5 so is 1.5 + 4 × 0.1 = 1.9 l	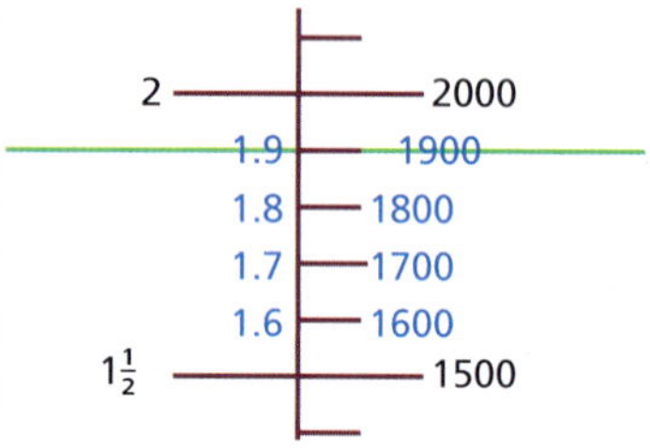

Exercise 3

1 Write the numbers indicated by the letters a, b, c, d, e and f on the diagram.

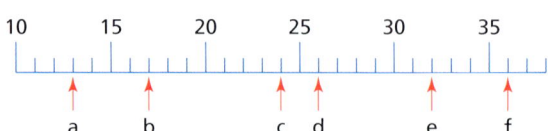

2 Write the numbers indicated by the letters a, b, c, d, e and f on the diagram.

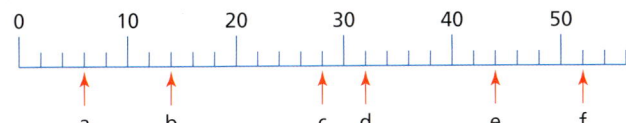

3 Write the numbers indicated by the letters a, b, c, d, e and f on the diagram.

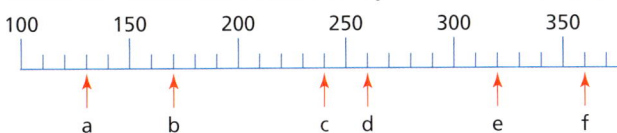

4 Write the numbers indicated by the letters a, b, c, d, e and f on the diagram.

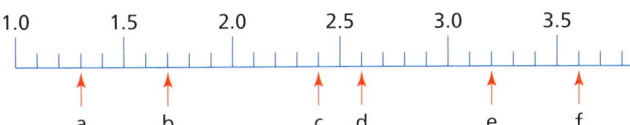

5
```
40        70   a
|ııılııılıı|
```
What is the value of a in the diagram?

6 Ilaria has a recipe which needs 1 pint of milk. Her measuring jug measures in millilitres (ml) only. She looks at this picture of a measuring jug and says that, as a pint is the same as 20 fluid ounces (fl oz), a pint is about 530 millilitres. Is she correct? Explain your answer.

End of chapter reflection

You should know ...	You should be able to ...	Such as ...
The relationships between units of time.	Convert between units of time.	Convert these times to the given units: a) 35 hours; days and hours b) 2 minutes 25 seconds; seconds c) 650 seconds; minutes and seconds
How to use the 12- and 24-hour clock systems and the relationships between them.	Read analogue and digital clocks and convert times shown on each.	Write 4:35 p.m. as a time in the 24-hour clock.
How to read a timetable and calculate time intervals.	Find the difference between two times.	Find the difference in time between 7:15 a.m. and 1:20 p.m.
How to read scales on a range of analogue and digital instruments.	Read scales to measure weight and other measures.	Write the weight shown on the scale:

Chapter 12: Time and scales

Unit 2A • Chapter 13

Numbers

You will learn how to:
- Recognise multiples, factors, common factors, primes (all less than 100), making use of simple tests of divisibility;
- Find the lowest common multiple in simple cases; use the 'sieve' developed by Eratosthenes for generating primes.
- Recognise squares of whole numbers to at least 20 × 20 and the corresponding square roots; use the notation 7^2 and $\sqrt{49}$.

Starting point

Do you remember…?

- your times tables up to 12?
- how to check whether a number is divisible by 2, 3, 4, 5, 6, 9, 10?
- the prime numbers up to 100?

This will be helpful when…

- you learn how to write numbers as a product of primes.
- you learn about indices (powers).
- you write fractions over a common denominator.

Hook

This is a picture of the Lorenz cipher machine. It was used by the Germans in World War II to encrypt messages.

Prime numbers are important in cryptography and in computers. They are used by computer security experts to devise codes to protect information that is sent between computers. These codes are based on multiplying together very large prime numbers.

All of these numbers have been generated by multiplying two prime numbers. Can you find the pairs of prime numbers that have been multiplied in each case?

   6   77   35   39   14   39   34

Did you know?

Prime numbers are really important when sending secure messages electronically, for example in internet banking.

Multiples, factors and primes

Key terms

A **multiple** of a number is in the times table of that number.

For example, 30 is a multiple of 5 because 6 x 5 = 30 and 30 ÷ 5 = 6 with no remainder.

A **factor** is a number that divides into another number without a remainder.

For example, 1, 2, 3 and 6 are all factors of 6 as 6 ÷ 1 = 6, 6 ÷ 2 = 3, 6 ÷ 3 = 2 and 6 ÷ 6 = 1.

Factors usually come in pairs. In this example 1 and 6 are a factor pair and 2 and 3 are a factor pair.

Prime numbers are numbers with exactly two factors; 1 and the number itself. This means that 1 is **not** a prime number.

Tests of divisibility are methods for quickly finding out whether one number is divisible by another. (The tests for divisibility can be found in Chapter 2.)

Worked example 1

a) Write all the factors of i) 18, ii) 25

b) Why does 25 have an odd number of factors?

a) i) Write all the factors of 18. 1, 2, 3, 6, 9 and 18	Find the pairs of numbers that multiply together to make 18. As all these numbers divide into 18 without leaving a remainder they are factors of 18.	
a) ii) Write all the factors of 25. 1, 5 and 25	Find the pairs of numbers that multiply together to make 25. 5 is a repeated factor, but is only listed once.	
b) Why does 25 have an odd number of factors? 25 has an odd number of factors because: 5 × 5 = 25 so 5 pairs with itself to make 25.	25 is a square number so it has a factor that multiplies by itself to make 25.	

Chapter 13: Numbers   101

Worked example 2

Write the first 10 multiples of **a)** 6, **b)** 8

a) Multiples of 6: 6, 12, 18, 24, 30, 36, 42, 48, 54, 60	Write the first 10 numbers in the 6 times table. 6 is the first number in the list.	(multiplication grid 1–10 with row 6 highlighted: 6, 12, 18, 24, 30, 36, 42, 48, 54, 60)
b) Multiples of 8: 8, 16, 24, 32, 40, 48, 56, 64, 72, 80	Write the first 10 numbers in the 8 times table. 8 is the first number in the list.	(multiplication grid 1–10 with row 8 highlighted: 8, 16, 24, 32, 40, 48, 56, 64, 72, 80)

Worked example 3

a) Use a test of divisibility to determine whether 5 is a factor of these numbers:
   i) 463
   ii) 650

b) Use a test of divisibility to determine whether 9 is a factor of these numbers:
   i) 846
   ii) 1082

a) i) 463 is not divisible by 5 so 5 is not a factor of 463.	463 does not end 0 or 5 so is not divisible by 5.
a) ii) 650 is divisible by 5 so 5 is a factor of 650.	650 ends in a 0 so it is divisible by 5.

Unit 2A: Number and calculation

b) i) 9 is a factor of 846 as 846 is divisible by 9.	Add the digits of the number 846 to get 8 + 4 + 6 =18 18 is divisible by 9 so the number is divisible by 9.
b) ii) 9 is not a factor of 1082 as 1082 is not divisible by 9.	Add the digits of 1082. 1 + 0 + 8 + 2 = 11 11 is not divisible by 9 so the number is not divisible by 9.

Exercise 1   3–5, 7–9

1 Write the first 5 multiples of each number. (Remember that the first multiple is the number itself.)
   a) 2   b) 5   c) 7   d) 10   e) 11

2 a) Which of these numbers are multiples of 3?
   6   11   12   18   24   28   30   36   63
   b) Which of these numbers are multiples of 8?
   16   24   38   42   48   56   64   78   80
   c) Which of these numbers are multiples of 9?
   9   27   37   45   54   72   83   90   100

3 a) Which of these numbers are multiples of both 2 and 3?
   1   6   9   12   15
   b) Which of these numbers are multiples of both 3 and 4?
   6   12   15   18   24
   c) Which of these numbers are multiples of both 5 and 6?
   15   18   30   40   60
   d) Which of these numbers are multiples of both 2 and 5?
   10   15   20   25   30

4 Cameron says that, "Multiples of odd numbers can only be odd because any number multiplied by an odd number is always odd." Give an example to show that Cameron is wrong.

5 a) Which of these numbers are factors of 15?
   3   4   5   6   10   15   30
   b) Which of these numbers are factors of 28?
   4   8   12   14   26   28
   c) Which of these numbers are factors of 11?
   1   2   3   6   7   11   22
   d) Which of these numbers are factors of 24?
   3   6   9   12   24   36
   e) Which of these numbers are factors of 17?
   1   2   5   7   10   17
   f) Which of these numbers are factors of 40?
   1   4   8   16   32   40

6 Write all the factors of each number.

a) 4 b) 8 c) 9 d) 11
e) 20 f) 36 g) 49 h) 100

7 Anna says that, "The bigger a number is the more factors it has. For example, 24 has eight factors (1, 2, 3, 4, 6, 8, 12 and 24) and 20 has six factors (1, 2, 4, 5, 10 and 20) so this proves this is true."
Give at least two examples that show Anna is wrong.

8 Each number in a green box is a factor of the number in the row or column. For example, 3 is a factor of 12 and 75, and 4 is a factor of 12 and 40.

```
        3
    4  12  40
       75 125 25
            5
```

Copy and complete these number squares with factors that work for every row and column. You should not use 1 in your answers.

a) 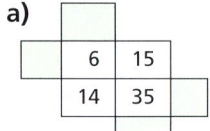   b) 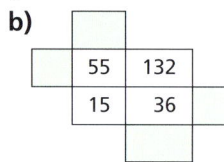   c) 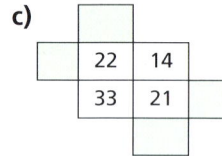   d)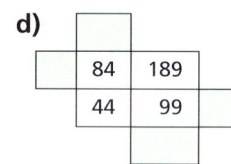

9 For each statement answer True or False.

If the statement is false, write the statement correctly.

a) The sum of the factors of 6 is equal to the sum of the factors of 11.

b) The sum of the factors of 14 is less than the sum of the factors of 15.

c) The sum of the factors of 16 is greater than the sum of the factors of 18.

Common multiples and the sieve of Eratosthenes

Key terms

A **common factor** is a number that divides exactly into more than one number.

For example, 3 is a common factor of 15 and 18

The **lowest common multiple (LCM)** is the lowest multiple of two or more integers.

For example, 20, 40 and 60 are all multiples of 4 and 5 but 20 is the lowest common multiple.

The **sieve of Eratosthenes** is a method for finding small prime numbers in a given range.

> **Did you know?**
>
> The **highest common factor (HCF)** is the highest number that divides into more than one number.
>
> For example, 18 and 24 have more than one common factor (1, 2, 3 and 6) but 6 is the highest common factor.
>
> You will learn more about this in Stage 8.

Worked example 4

Find the lowest common multiple of 6 and 10.

| 6, 12, 18, 24, 30, 36 …
 10, 20, 30, 40, 50 …
 Lowest common multiple = 30 | Write multiples of 6 and multiples of 10 until you find a number that appears in both lists. The smallest number that appears in both lists is the lowest common multiple. | |

Think about

How would you find the lowest common multiple of 3 numbers?

Think about

How could you use Venn diagrams to represent the factors and common factors of two numbers?

How could you find the lowest common multiple from this Venn diagram?

There is a method of finding prime numbers that was developed by Eratosthenes in Greece over 2200 years ago and this method is still used in computer algorithms today. You can find interactive versions on the internet.

This number square shows the method for finding all the prime numbers from 1 to 25. The idea is to cross out or colour all the numbers which are not prime.

You start by colouring 1 which is not a prime number.

The next uncoloured number is 2, which is a prime number. Leave the 2 square blank and colour all the multiples of 2.

The next uncoloured number is 3, which is prime. Leave the 3 square blank and colour all the multiples of 3.

Continue with the next uncoloured number, which is 5.

After colouring the multiples of 5 the next unshaded number is 7 but all its multiples are already coloured. This is because 7 x 7 is bigger than 25 and all its multiples by 2, 3, 4 and 5 have been coloured already.

The uncoloured numbers, 2, 3, 5, 7, 11, 13, 17, 19 and 23, are all the prime numbers between 1 and 25 and you have found them without using divisibility tests to check the 25 numbers one at a time.

Exercise 2   1–7

1 Write the lowest common multiple of:
   a) 5 and 7
   b) 7 and 11
   c) 3 and 13
   d) 4 and 8
   e) 6 and 15
   f) 10 and 12

2 Find the lowest common multiple of:
   a) 3, 4 and 6   b) 4, 5 and 6
   c) 5, 6 and 8   d) 6, 8 and 9

3 a) Which of these numbers are common factors of 12 and 18?
   1   3   6   9
   b) Which of these numbers are common factors of 8 and 14?
   1   2   3   7
   c) Which of these numbers is a common factor of 17 and 34?
   2   4   7   17
   d) Which of these numbers are common factors of 8 and 32?
   2   4   6   8
   e) Which of these numbers are common factors of 15 and 45?
   1   3   5   7   9
   f) Which of these numbers are common factors of 24 and 36?
   3   4   6   8   12

4 Praneeth has used the Venn diagram shown to find the common factors of two numbers. He has made some errors. Find the errors and rewrite his Venn diagram correctly.

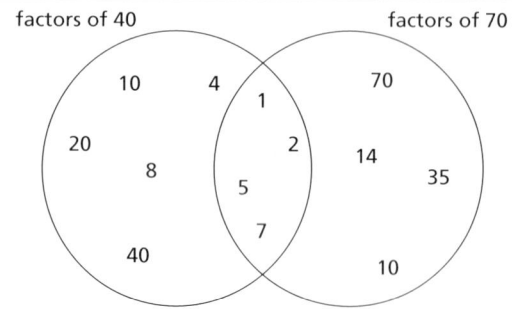

5 Write the highest common factor of:
   a) 4 and 6   b) 10 and 15   c) 12 and 18
   d) 14 and 24   e) 14 and 35   f) 27 and 36

6 Use a sieve of Eratosthenes to find all the prime numbers between 1 and 49.

7 Find an interactive sieve of Eratosthenes on the internet and use it to find all the prime numbers between 1 and 100.

Squares and square roots

Key terms

A **square number** is the product of an integer multiplied by itself.

For example, $36 = 6 \times 6$, so 36 is a square number and is written as 6^2. You need to recognise all the square numbers up to 20^2.

The **square root** of a number multiplied by itself gives the number.

For example, the square root of 9 is 3 because $3 \times 3 = 9$

Square roots do not have to be integers (whole numbers).

This symbol means square root $\sqrt{}$. For example, $\sqrt{9} = 3$.

Unit 2A: Number and calculation

You can find square numbers and square roots using a calculator. For example,

- to find 28^2 use this button
- to find $\sqrt{961}$ use this button

Worked example 5

Match the pairs of numbers that are equal.

4^2 $\sqrt{25}$ 4   16   5 2^2

4^2 $\sqrt{25}$ 4 16 5 2^2 16 5 4 The pairs of equal numbers are: 4^2 and 16 $\sqrt{25}$ and 5 2^2 and 4	$4^2 = 4 \times 4 = 16$ $5 \times 5 = 25$ so $\sqrt{25} = 5$ $2^2 = 2 \times 2 = 4$

Worked example 6

A square has an area of 49 cm². Find the side length of the square.

area = length² = 49 length = $\sqrt{49}$ length = 7 cm	The area of a square is found by multiplying the side length by itself. You can write: area = length² To find the side length you can square root the area.	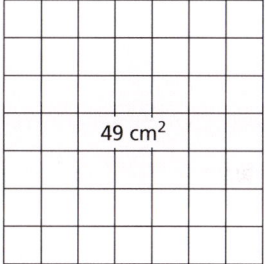 Counting the squares along the side you can see the side length is 7 cm.

Exercise 3   1–3, 6, 7

1 Write the value of:
  a) 5^2 b) 10^2 c) 9^2 d) 11^2 e) 15^2
  f) 19^2 g) 17^2 h) 12^2 i) 13^2 j) 18^2

2 Write the value of:
  a) $\sqrt{36}$ b) $\sqrt{64}$ c) $\sqrt{100}$ d) $\sqrt{81}$
  e) $\sqrt{144}$ f) $\sqrt{400}$ g) $\sqrt{121}$

3 Find:
   a) $2^2 + 5^2$
   b) $3^2 + 7^2$
   c) $8^2 + 10^2$
   d) $7^2 + 11^2$
   e) $9^2 + 10^2$
   f) $12^2 - 4^2$
   g) $10^2 - 6^2$
   h) $14^2 - 8^2$
   i) $15^2 - 3^2$
   j) $20^2 - 15^2$

4 Use a calculator to find:
   a) 25^2
   b) 32^2
   c) 53^2
   d) 99^2
   e) $\sqrt{729}$
   f) $\sqrt{1156}$
   g) $\sqrt{3721}$
   h) $\sqrt{9409}$

5 Tommy says that $\sqrt{49} - \sqrt{9}$ is $\sqrt{40}$. He is wrong. Explain where Tommy went wrong and write down the correct answer.

6 Find:
   a) $\sqrt{36} + \sqrt{16}$
   b) $\sqrt{100} + \sqrt{49}$
   c) $\sqrt{100} + \sqrt{36}$
   d) $\sqrt{121} + \sqrt{81}$
   e) $\sqrt{100} - \sqrt{49}$
   f) $\sqrt{169} - \sqrt{144}$
   g) $\sqrt{225} - \sqrt{196}$
   h) $\sqrt{400} - \sqrt{289}$

7 Find:
   a) $4^2 + \sqrt{36}$
   b) $7^2 + \sqrt{100}$
   c) $11^2 + \sqrt{121}$
   d) $14^2 + \sqrt{225}$
   e) $\sqrt{324} - 4^2$
   f) $\sqrt{361} - 32$
   g) $17^2 - \sqrt{256}$
   h) $19^2 - \sqrt{361}$

8 Write these numbers and calculations in ascending order.
   a) 2^2, 5, $\sqrt{9}$, 4^2, 12
   b) 15, $\sqrt{100}$, 4^2, $\sqrt{144}$, 11
   c) $\sqrt{121}$, 7, $\sqrt{81}$, 10, 3^2
   d) 16, 5^2, 17, $\sqrt{361}$, 22

9 Use a calculator to find the length of the side of each square from the area given.

   a) 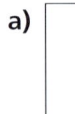 81 cm²
   b) 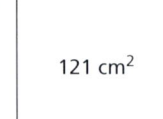 121 cm²
   c) 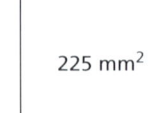 225 mm²
   d) 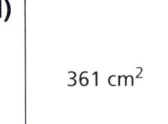 361 cm²
   e)  256 mm²
   f) 289 cm²

10 A perfect number is a number where all of its factors apart from itself add up to the number.
6 is the smallest perfect number because the factors of 6 are 1, 2, 3 and 6 and 6 = 1 + 2 + 3
There is one other perfect number between 1 and 30. Find this number.

11 Vocabulary feature question

Some number words from this chapter have been changed using a code. To decode a letter you first find the letter in a copy of the alphabet. You then move to the right the same number of letters as the second prime number.

Decode each of these words and show their meaning by giving an example in context.
   i) JRIQFMIB
   ii) CXZQLO
   iii) AFSFAB
   iv) MOFJB
   v) PNRXOB
   vi) PNRXOB OLLQ

Unit 2A: Number and calculation

End of chapter reflection

You should know that ...	You should be able to ...	Such as ...
A **multiple** of a number is a number in its times table. A **factor** of a number divides into that number without a remainder. **Common factors** are factors that numbers share. **Prime numbers** are numbers with exactly two factors The lowest common multiple (LCM) of a set of numbers is the smallest number which is a multiple of each of them.	Recognise multiples, factors, primes and common factors.	2 3 4 8 16 24 From these numbers which is/are: a) Multiples of 4? b) Factors of 24? c) Prime numbers? d) Common factors of 12 and 48? e) The LCM of 6 and 8?
Prime numbers can be generated using the sieve of Eratosthenes.	Generate prime numbers.	Find the prime numbers between 0 and 64.
A **square number** is the product of an integer multiplied by itself. The **square root** of a number multiplied by itself gives the number.	Recognise square numbers to at least 20^2 and match to the corresponding square roots.	Match the numbers that are the same. 9 $\sqrt{64}$ 10 3^2 8 $\sqrt{100}$

Unit 2A • Chapter 14

Fractions

You will learn how to:
- Add and subtract two simple fractions, for example, $\frac{1}{8} + \frac{9}{8}$, $\frac{11}{12} - \frac{5}{8}$; find fractions of quantities (whole number answers); multiply a fraction by an integer.

Starting point

Do you remember …?

- the meaning of the words **numerator** and **denominator**?
- how to simplify fractions?
  For example, cancel $\frac{12}{18}$.
- how to find equivalent fractions?
  For example, $\frac{3}{4} = \frac{?}{20}$.

This will be helpful when …

you learn more about calculating with fractions.

Hook

A rectangle is divided into 8 equal pieces. Each piece is $\frac{1}{8}$ of the whole rectangle.

The diagram could show the fraction sum $\frac{3}{8} + \frac{2}{8} = \frac{5}{8}$.

This is the same as $\frac{2}{8} + \frac{3}{8} = \frac{5}{8}$ as it does not matter in which order you write two numbers that you are adding.

The diagram could also show $\frac{3}{8} - \frac{2}{8} = \frac{1}{8}$ as the difference between the number of blue squares and purple squares is 1 square or $\frac{8}{8} - \frac{5}{8} = \frac{3}{8}$ as the number of uncoloured squares.

Write as many different fraction calculations as you can find by using two colours to colour different numbers of squares in this rectangle.

Adding and subtracting fractions

Key term

In a **fraction** the **denominator** is the bottom number which indicates how many parts the whole is divided into and the **numerator** is the top number which indicates how many of those parts you have.

For example,

$\frac{5}{6}$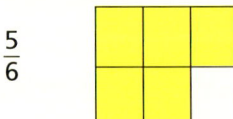

To add or subtract fractions the denominators must be the same.

Key term

Equivalent fractions are fractions with different denominators that are worth the same.

For example, $\frac{3}{4}$ is equivalent to $\frac{6}{8}$

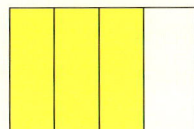 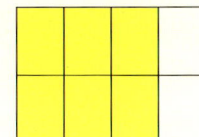

You can find equivalent fractions by multiplying or dividing the numerator (top) and denominator (bottom) of the fraction by the same number.

For example,

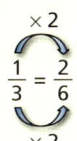

Key term

To give your answer in its **simplest form** write the fraction as an equivalent fraction with the lowest possible values for the numerator and denominator. Find common factors of the numerator and denominator and divide.

For example,

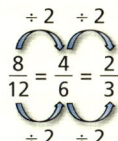

so $\frac{8}{12}$ can be simplified to $\frac{2}{3}$.

A fraction where the numerator and denominator do not have a common factor cannot be simplified. For example, $\frac{7}{12}$.

> **Did you know?**
>
> The word fraction comes from the Latin "fractio" which means to break.

Worked example 1

a) Find $\frac{3}{7} + \frac{2}{7}$ b) Find $\frac{7}{8} - \frac{3}{8}$ c) Find $\frac{3}{4} - \frac{5}{8}$

a) 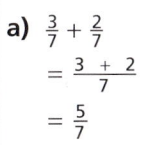	The denominators are the same. Add the numerators.	(diagram: $\frac{3}{7} + \frac{2}{7} = \frac{5}{7}$)
b) 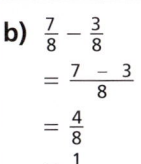	The denominators are the same. Subtract one numerator from the other. You can simplify (cancel down) the answer by dividing the numerator (top) and denominator (bottom) of the fraction by the same number.	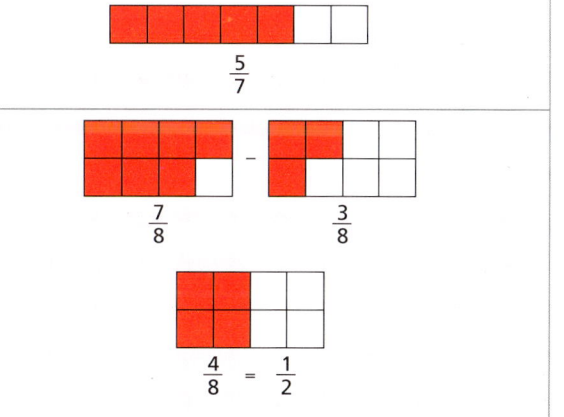

Chapter 14: Fractions   111

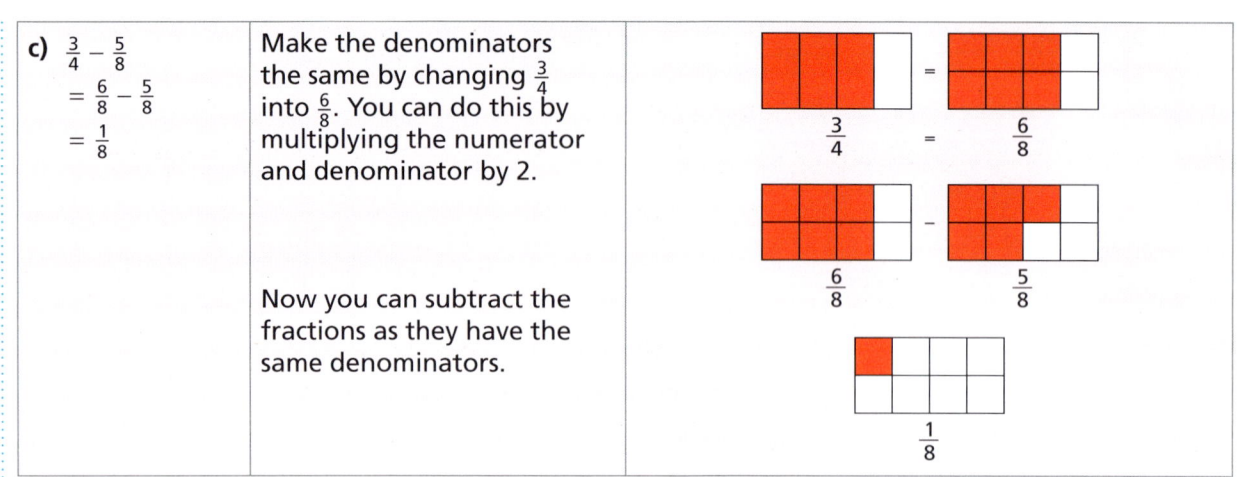

c) $\frac{3}{4} - \frac{5}{8}$ $= \frac{6}{8} - \frac{5}{8}$ $= \frac{1}{8}$	Make the denominators the same by changing $\frac{3}{4}$ into $\frac{6}{8}$. You can do this by multiplying the numerator and denominator by 2. Now you can subtract the fractions as they have the same denominators.	

Key terms

An **improper fraction** is a fraction where the value of the numerator is higher than the value of the denominator, for example, $\frac{5}{4}$ and $\frac{22}{5}$ are both improper fractions.

A **mixed number** is a number that has both integer values and fractions. For example, $1\frac{1}{4}$ and $4\frac{2}{5}$ are both mixed numbers.

$\frac{5}{4}$ and $1\frac{1}{4}$ are equivalent

$\frac{22}{5}$ and $4\frac{2}{5}$ are equivalent.

Worked example 2

Find $\frac{2}{3} + \frac{5}{9}$

$\frac{2}{3} + \frac{5}{9}$ $= \frac{6}{9} + \frac{5}{9}$ $= \frac{11}{9}$ $= \frac{11}{9}$ or $1\frac{2}{9}$	Make the denominators the same by changing $\frac{2}{3}$ into $\frac{6}{9}$. You can do this by multiplying the numerator and denominator by 3. Now the denominator is the same, add the numerators. The answer is an improper fraction so write this as a mixed number.	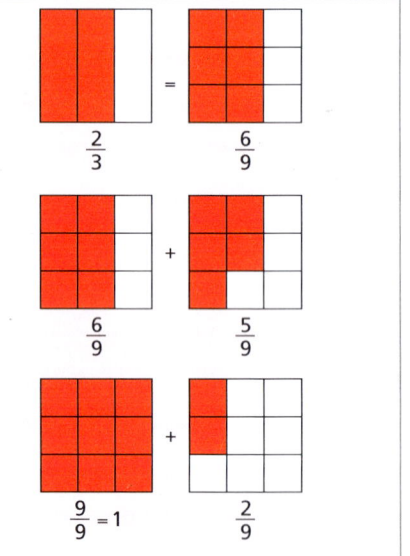

Unit 2A: Number and calculation

Worked example 3

a) Write the answer to $\frac{5}{12} + \frac{3}{4}$ in its simplest form.

b) Dan and Eloise are house painters. Dan has $\frac{3}{4}$ of a pot of red paint left and Eloise has $\frac{11}{12}$ of a pot of red paint the same size left.

How many pots of red paint do they have altogether?

a) $\frac{5}{12} + \frac{3}{4}$ $= \frac{5}{12} + \frac{9}{12}$ $= \frac{14}{12}$ $= 1\frac{2}{12}$ $= 1\frac{1}{6}$	The fractions do not have a common denominator (bottom number). Use equivalent fractions to write $\frac{3}{4}$ as $\frac{9}{12}$ by multiplying the numerator (top) and denominator (bottom) by 3. Add the two fractions. Write the improper fraction as a mixed number. Cancel $\frac{2}{12}$ to $\frac{1}{6}$.	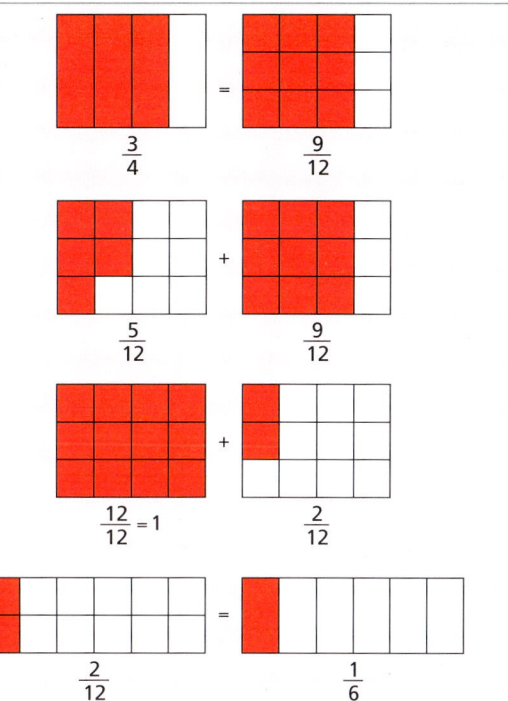
b) Add $\frac{3}{4}$ and $\frac{11}{12}$ $= \frac{3}{4} + \frac{11}{12}$ $= \frac{9}{12} + \frac{11}{12}$ $= \frac{20}{12}$ $= 1\frac{8}{12}$ $= 1\frac{2}{3}$	The fractions do not have a common denominator (bottom number). Use equivalent fractions to write $\frac{3}{4}$ as $\frac{9}{12}$ by multiplying the numerator (top) and denominator (bottom) by 3. Add the two fractions. Write the improper fraction as a mixed number. Cancel $\frac{8}{12}$ to $\frac{2}{3}$.	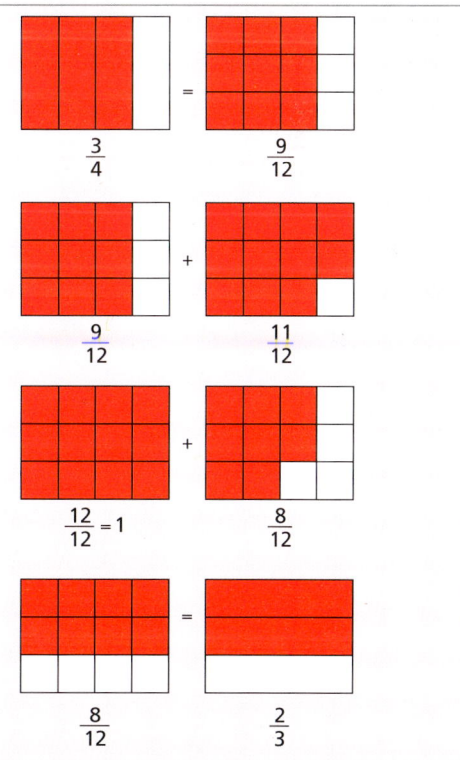

Chapter 14: Fractions

> **Think about**
> Where can you use addition and subtraction of fractions in real life?
> What real life addition and subtraction of fractions problems could you write?

Exercise 1

1 Write an addition calculation for each of the following pictures. Add the two fractions in each case.

a) 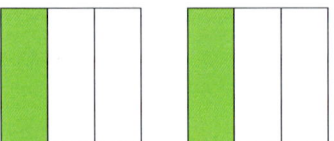   b)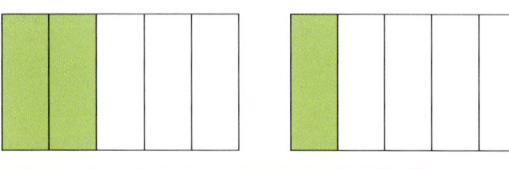

c) 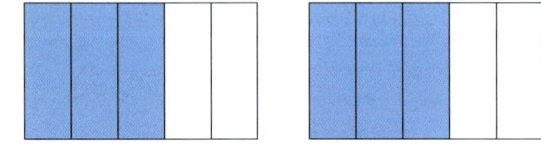   d)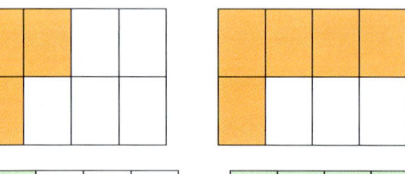

e)    f)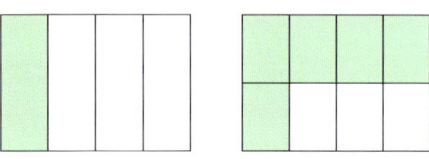

2 Write a subtraction calculation for each of the following pictures. Subtract the second fraction from the first fraction in each case.

a) 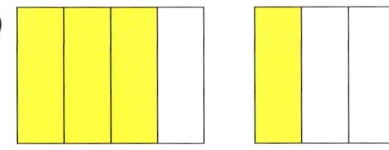   b)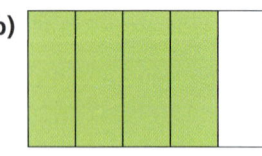

c) 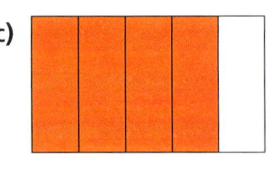   d)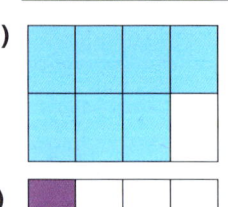

e) 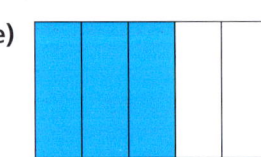   f)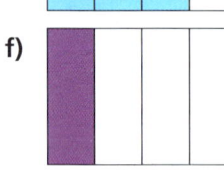

3 Work out. Give your answer as a mixed number where appropriate.

a) $\frac{1}{4} + \frac{3}{4}$ b) $\frac{1}{2} + \frac{1}{2}$ c) $\frac{1}{3} + \frac{1}{3}$ d) $\frac{2}{3} + \frac{1}{3}$

e) $\frac{1}{8} + \frac{7}{8}$ f) $\frac{3}{8} + \frac{2}{8}$ g) $\frac{5}{8} + \frac{5}{8}$ h) $\frac{1}{7} + \frac{4}{7}$

i) $\frac{3}{7} + \frac{6}{7}$ j) $\frac{3}{12} + \frac{5}{12}$ k) $\frac{7}{12} + \frac{11}{12}$

4 Work out:

a) $\frac{2}{3} - \frac{1}{3}$ b) $\frac{4}{5} - \frac{2}{5}$ c) $\frac{7}{8} - \frac{3}{8}$ d) $\frac{5}{12} - \frac{1}{12}$

e) $\frac{7}{12} - \frac{5}{12}$ f) $\frac{7}{10} - \frac{4}{10}$ g) $\frac{1}{2} - \frac{1}{4}$ h) $\frac{3}{4} - \frac{1}{2}$

5 Work out. Show the stages in your working.

a) $\frac{1}{4} + \frac{3}{8}$ b) $\frac{2}{5} + \frac{3}{10}$ c) $\frac{3}{4} + \frac{1}{8}$ d) $\frac{1}{6} + \frac{1}{3}$

e) $\frac{1}{3} + \frac{5}{6}$ f) $\frac{3}{8} + \frac{3}{4}$ g) $\frac{7}{10} + \frac{4}{5}$ h) $\frac{7}{8} + \frac{3}{4}$

i) $\frac{5}{12} + \frac{1}{4}$ j) $\frac{3}{4} + \frac{1}{12}$ k) $\frac{1}{2} + \frac{7}{12}$ l) $\frac{2}{3} + \frac{7}{9}$

6 Work out. Show the stages in your working.

a) $\frac{1}{2} - \frac{1}{8}$ b) $\frac{3}{4} - \frac{1}{8}$ c) $\frac{1}{2} - \frac{3}{8}$ d) $\frac{2}{3} - \frac{1}{6}$

e) $1 - \frac{1}{4}$ f) $1 - \frac{3}{4}$ g) $\frac{5}{6} - \frac{1}{3}$ h) $\frac{7}{12} - \frac{1}{6}$

i) $\frac{4}{5} - \frac{3}{10}$ j) $\frac{7}{10} - \frac{2}{5}$ k) $\frac{5}{12} - \frac{1}{4}$ l) $\frac{1}{2} - \frac{3}{10}$

7 Asha is adding two fractions.

Here is her working.

$\frac{3}{8} + \frac{1}{4} = \frac{4}{12} = \frac{1}{3}$

Is Asha correct? Explain your answer.

8 In a magic square the rows, columns and diagonals have the same total. Here is part of a magic square made with fractions. Find the missing fractions in the magic square.

$\frac{4}{15}$	$\frac{3}{5}$	$\frac{2}{15}$
	$\frac{1}{3}$	

Finding fractions of numbers

> **Tip**
> To find **the fraction of an amount** multiply the amount by the numerator of the fraction and then divide by the denominator.

Worked example 4

a) Find $\frac{1}{5}$ of 70.

b) Find $\frac{3}{4}$ of 80.

| a) $\frac{1}{5}$ of 70
$= 70 \div 5$
$= 14$ | To find $\frac{1}{5}$ of an amount, you divide by 5. |  |

Chapter 14: Fractions

b) $\frac{1}{4}$ of 80
  $= 80 \div 4$
  $= 20$
  $\frac{3}{4}$ of 80
  $= 20 \times 3$
  $= 60$
  $\frac{3}{4}$ of 80
  $= \frac{3 \times 80}{4}$
  $= 3 \times 80 \div 4$
  $= 60$

First find $\frac{1}{4}$ of 80 by dividing by 4.

Next find $\frac{3}{4}$ of 80 by multiplying your answer by 3.

You can also find $\frac{3}{4}$ of 80 in one calculation.

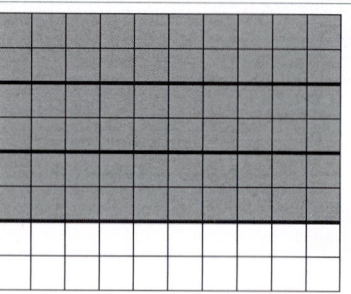

Exercise 2

1 Find the fraction of each amount.
  a) $\frac{1}{2}$ of 10
  b) $\frac{1}{4}$ of 12
  c) $\frac{1}{8}$ of 64
  d) $\frac{1}{5}$ of 20
  e) $\frac{1}{12}$ of 36
  f) $\frac{3}{4}$ of 32
  g) $\frac{3}{10}$ of 50
  h) $\frac{3}{4}$ of 16
  i) $\frac{3}{8}$ of 80
  j) $\frac{4}{5}$ of 25
  k) $\frac{3}{12}$ of 60
  l) $\frac{11}{12}$ of 144

2 Find the fraction of each amount
  a) $\frac{1}{2}$ of 24 ml
  b) $\frac{1}{4}$ of $52
  c) $\frac{1}{12}$ of $288
  d) $\frac{3}{5}$ of 100 m
  e) $\frac{2}{5}$ of 500 ml
  f) $\frac{3}{8}$ of 64 miles
  g) $\frac{7}{10}$ of 500 g
  h) $\frac{7}{8}$ of 56 cm
  i) $\frac{3}{4}$ of 72 km
  j) $\frac{3}{12}$ of 84 litres
  k) $\frac{2}{3}$ of $435
  l) $\frac{4}{5}$ of 1980 mm

Tip
Remember to include the units with your answers.

3 Which is larger in each pair?

a	$\frac{4}{5}$ of 10	$\frac{2}{5}$ of 25	b	$\frac{1}{2}$ of 20	$\frac{3}{4}$ of 16
c	$\frac{3}{4}$ of 12	$\frac{1}{5}$ of 50	d	$\frac{3}{5}$ of 45	$\frac{1}{2}$ of 60
e	$\frac{3}{12}$ of 24	$\frac{2}{6}$ of 12	f	$\frac{7}{10}$ of 100	$\frac{2}{5}$ of 200
g	$\frac{2}{3}$ of 21	$\frac{1}{8}$ of 80	h	$\frac{7}{8}$ of 56	$\frac{3}{5}$ of 90
i	$\frac{2}{7}$ of 49	$\frac{4}{9}$ of 36	j	$\frac{2}{11}$ of 110	$\frac{3}{20}$ of 220

4 Suki says, "To find a fraction of an amount you just have to divide the amount by the denominator of the fraction."

Is Suki correct? Explain why or why not.

5 Find the missing numbers in the calculations.
  a) $\frac{2}{5}$ of ___ = 10
  b) $\frac{\square}{7}$ of 28 = 24
  c) $\frac{3}{\square}$ of 48 = 9

Try creating your own questions like these and test them on your classmates.

Multiplying fractions by integers

Key terms

To **multiply a mixed fraction by an integer** first change the fraction into an improper fraction and multiply the numetrator. Then write your answer in simplified form and as a mixed number if the answer is greater than 1.

Worked example 5

a) i) Find $6 \times \frac{2}{3}$

  ii) Helena works in a supermarket. She has 7 boxes of potatoes that are each $\frac{3}{4}$ full. How many boxes of potatoes does she have in total?

b) Find $5 \times 1\frac{1}{5}$

a) i) $6 \times \frac{2}{3}$ $= \frac{6 \times 2}{3}$ $= \frac{12}{3}$ $= 4$	To find 6 lots of $\frac{2}{3}$ multiply the numerator of the fraction by 6. Simplify the answer $= 4$.	
ii) To find out how much 7 lots of $\frac{3}{4}$ is you need to multiply 7 by $\frac{3}{4}$. $= \frac{7 \times 3}{4}$ $= \frac{21}{4}$ $= 5\frac{1}{4}$ 5 and $\frac{1}{4}$ boxes of potatoes altogether.	You need to find 7 lots of $\frac{3}{4}$ so you multiply $\frac{3}{4}$ by 7. Multiply the numerator of the fraction by 7. Change from an improper fraction to a mixed fraction $= 5\frac{1}{4}$	$7 \times \frac{3}{4}$ $5\frac{1}{4}$
b) $5 \times 1\frac{1}{5}$ $= 5 \times \frac{6}{5}$ $= \frac{30}{5}$ $= 6$	Change $1\frac{1}{5}$ to an improper fraction before multiplying the numerator by 5. Change from an improper fraction to a mixed number or, in this case, an integer.	$5 \quad + \quad \frac{5}{5}$ $= 6$

Chapter 14: Fractions   117

Exercise 3

1 Multiply the fractions by the integers shown. Give your answer as an improper fraction.
a) $3 \times \frac{1}{2}$ b) $2 \times \frac{1}{5}$ c) $4 \times \frac{1}{3}$ d) $2 \times \frac{3}{4}$ e) $5 \times \frac{2}{3}$
f) $3 \times \frac{2}{8}$ g) $3 \times \frac{1}{7}$ h) $4 \times \frac{2}{5}$ i) $3 \times \frac{2}{3}$ j) $10 \times \frac{1}{3}$

2 Multiply the fractions by the integers shown. Give your answer as a mixed number.
a) $7 \times \frac{1}{2}$ b) $3 \times \frac{3}{4}$ c) $8 \times \frac{3}{4}$ d) $10 \times \frac{1}{5}$ e) $6 \times \frac{3}{5}$
f) $5 \times \frac{3}{8}$ g) $9 \times \frac{2}{5}$ h) $10 \times \frac{7}{8}$ i) $8 \times \frac{5}{12}$ j) $11 \times \frac{3}{12}$

3 Multiply the fractions by the integers shown. Give your answer as an improper fraction.
a) $3 \times 1\frac{1}{2}$ b) $4 \times 1\frac{1}{4}$
c) $4 \times 1\frac{3}{4}$ d) $10 \times 3\frac{1}{5}$

> **Tip**
> Write the mixed numbers as improper fractions first.

4 Ricardo writes the following working:

$1\frac{1}{3} \times 5 =$

$\frac{11}{3} \times 5 =$

$\frac{11 \times 5}{3 \times 5} =$

$\frac{55}{15} =$

$3\frac{10}{15} =$

$3\frac{2}{3}$

Ricardo has made two mistakes. Find these mistakes and explain what Ricardo should have done.

5 Find the missing numbers in the calculations.
a) $2\frac{1}{6} \times \underline{} = \frac{39}{6}$ b) $1\frac{\square}{5} \times 6 = 9\frac{3}{5}$ c) $\frac{\square}{3} \times 9 = 24$

Try creating your own questions like these and test them on your classmates.

6 **Vocabulary feature question**

Copy the sentences and complete the missing words.

In a .... the .... indicates how many parts the whole is divided into and the .... indicates how many of those parts you have.

To give your answer in its .... write the fraction as an equivalent fraction with the lowest possible values for the numerator and denominator.

An .... is a fraction where the value of the numerator is higher than the value of the denominator.

A .... is a number that has both integer values and fractions.

End of chapter reflection

You should know that …	You should be able to …	Such as …
In a **fraction** the **denominator** indicates how many parts the whole is divided into and the **numerator** indicates how many of those parts you have.	Add and subtract two simple fractions with the same denominator. Add and subtract two simple fractions where the denominators are not the same.	Find $\frac{2}{5} + \frac{1}{5}$ $\frac{2}{3} + \frac{1}{6}$
To give your answer in its **simplest form** write the fraction as an equivalent fraction with the lowest possible values for the numerator and denominator.	Simplify fractions in answers.	Find $\frac{3}{8} + \frac{1}{8}$ giving your answer in its simplest form.
To find **the fraction of an amount** multiply by the numerator and divide by the denominator.	Find fractions of quantities.	Find $\frac{7}{8}$ of $112
In an **improper fraction** the value of the numerator is higher than the value of the denominator A **mixed number** is a number that has both integer values and fractions. To multiply a simple fraction by an integer multiply the numerator by the integer. To multiply a mixed number by an integer, write the mixed number as an improper fraction and multiply the numerator by the integer.	Multiply a simple fraction by an integer. Multiply a mixed number by an integer.	Find $3 \times \frac{3}{4}$ Find $1\frac{2}{3} \times 5$

Unit 2A • Chapter 15

Percentages and fractions

You will learn how to:
- Understand percentage as the number of parts in every 100; use fractions and percentages to describe parts of shapes, quantities and measures.
- Calculate simple fractions and percentages of quantities, e.g. one quarter of 64, 20% of 50 kg.

Starting point

Do you remember …?

- how to find equivalent fractions?
  For example, $\frac{2}{3} = \frac{?}{12}$

- how to simplify fractions?
  For example, simplify $\frac{10}{25}$

- how to find simple fractions of an amount?
  For example, find $\frac{3}{5}$ of 40

This will be helpful when …

you learn more about percentage increases and decreases.
For example, a dress costs $80 and it is reduced in a sale by 20%. What is the sale price?

Hook

A film review website gives the percentages of positive reviews to show how popular a film is.

These are the reviews of three films:

Jungle Jumble was reviewed by 200 people and 80% were positive reviews.

Hotel Bombay was reviewed by 250 people and 80% were positive reviews

Moon Walker was reviewed by 150 people and 50% were positive reviews.

a) How many people gave a positive review to each film?

b) Which of the films was the most popular and which was the least popular? Can you rely on the percentage of positive reviews to know this?

Percentages and fractions

Fractions can be used to describe parts of a shape.

For example,

4 out of 9 squares are unshaded. You can write $\frac{4}{9}$ of the shape is unshaded.

5 out of 9 squares are shaded. You can write $\frac{5}{9}$ of the shape is shaded.

Worked example 1

Here is a shape.

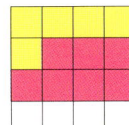

a) Write down the fraction of the shape shaded like this:
b) Write down the fraction of the shape that is not shaded.
c) Write down the fraction of the shaded squares that are shaded like this: ▨

a) 16 squares in total 5 shaded ▯ Fraction = $\frac{5}{16}$	Count the total number of squares that make up the shape. Count the number of squares shaded with this pattern. Fraction = $\frac{\text{number shaded with this pattern}}{\text{total number of squares}}$	
b) 16 squares in total 4 not shaded Fraction = $\frac{4}{16}$ $= \frac{1}{4}$	Count the total number of squares that make up the shape. Count the number of squares that are unshaded. Fraction = $\frac{\text{number not shaded}}{\text{total number of squares}}$ You can simplify this answer by dividing the numerator and denominator by 4.	
c) ▨ 12 shaded squares in total 7 shaded with this pattern Fraction = $\frac{7}{12}$	Count the number of squares that are shaded. Count the number of squares that are shaded with this pattern. Fraction = $\frac{\text{number shaded with this pattern}}{\text{total number of shaded squares}}$	

Key terms

Percentage means parts per hundred.

25% is 25 out of 100   and   64% is 64 out of 100.

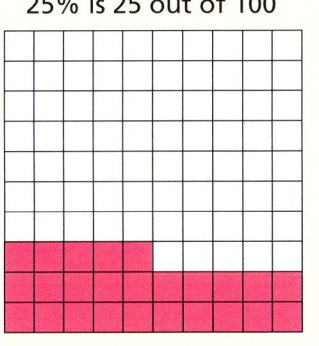
25%

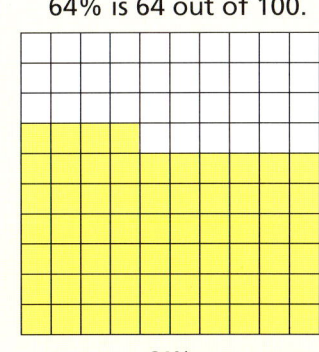
64%

This diagram has 8 parts out of 50 shaded or $\frac{8}{50}$

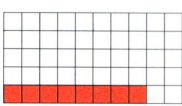

By doubling it you can see that this is equivalent to 16 parts out of a hundred or $\frac{16}{100}$ or 16%, so 8 parts out of 50 is the same as 16%.

$$\frac{8}{50} = \frac{16}{100} = 16\%$$

This diagram has 16 parts out of 25 shaded or $\frac{16}{25}$

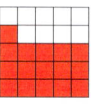

By joining 4 of these you can see that this is equivalent to 64 parts out of a hundred or 64%.

$$\frac{16}{25} = \frac{64}{100} = 64\%$$

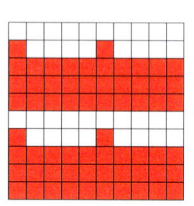

Worked example 2

a) What percentage of this square is shaded?
b) i) Write 24 as a percentage of 100.
   ii) Write 13 as a percentage of 50.
c) There are 25 pupils in Claire's class. Six wear glasses. What is the percentage of pupils in Claire's class who wear glasses?

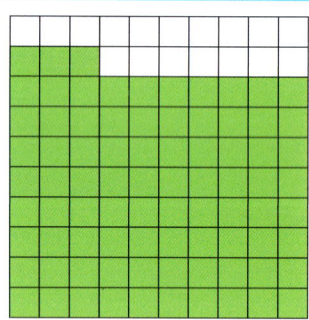

a) There are 100 squares and 83 are shaded so 83% is shaded.	83 squares from 100 are shaded.	
b) i) $\frac{24}{100}$ = 24%	Convert 24 out of a 100 into a fraction. The denominator is 100 so this is already 'per 100'.	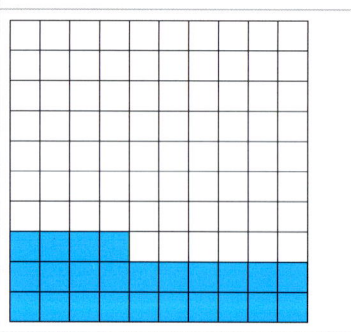

122   Unit 2A: Number and calculation

ii) $\frac{13}{50}$

$\frac{13}{50} = \frac{26}{100}$ (×2)

$= 26\%$

Convert 13 out of 50 into a fraction.

Multiply the numerator and denominator by 2 so the denominator is 100.

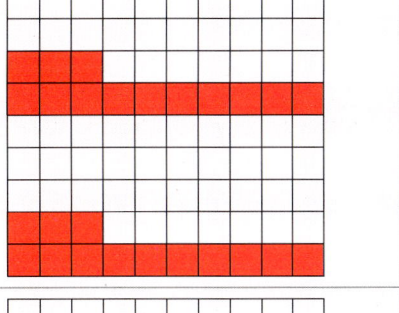

c) $\frac{6}{25}$

$\frac{6}{25} = \frac{24}{100}$ (×4)

$= 24\%$

Write the number with glasses as a fraction of the total number of pupils.

Find an equivalent fraction with a denominator of 100 by multiplying the numerator and denominator by 4 as $4 \times 25 = 100$

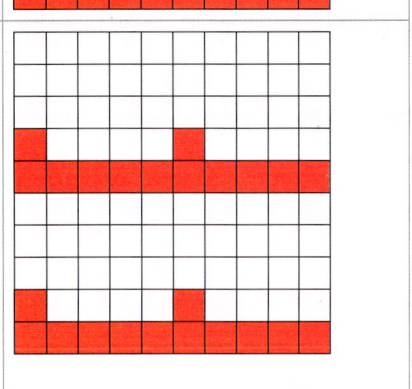

Exercise 1

1 Write down the fraction of each shape that is shaded. Simplify your answers where possible.

a) 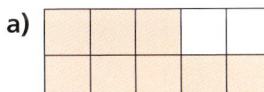 b)   c)   d)

2 Copy the shapes into your book. Shade the fraction indicated.

a) 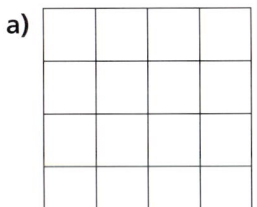 b) 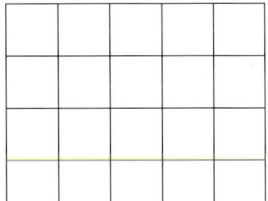 c) 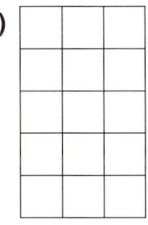 d)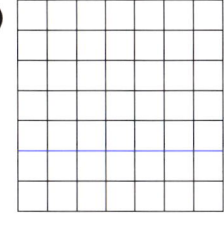

Shade $\frac{5}{8}$ Shade $\frac{3}{4}$ Shade $\frac{2}{3}$ Shade $\frac{2}{7}$

3 Write down the shaded squares as a percentage of the whole block of squares.

a) 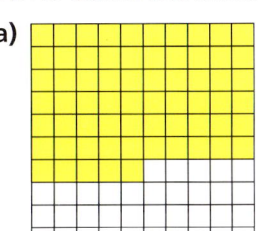 b) 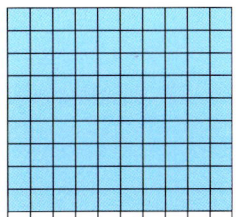 c) 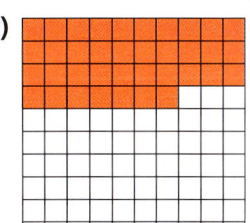 d)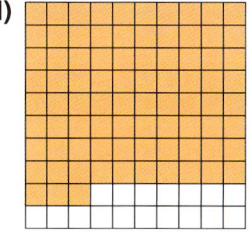

4 Write down these percentages as fractions of 100. (a) is done for you. Simplify your fractions where possible.
   a) 27% = $\frac{27}{100}$ b) 36%   c) 63%   d) 29%
   e) 22%   f) 95%   g) 70%   h) 58%

5 Write down these fractions as percentages.
   a) $\frac{12}{100}$ b) $\frac{34}{100}$ c) $\frac{51}{100}$ d) $\frac{83}{100}$

6 Find the percentage of each shape that is shaded.
   a)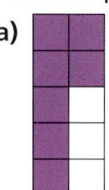
   b)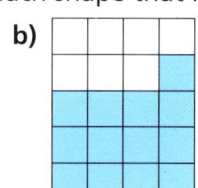
   c)
   d)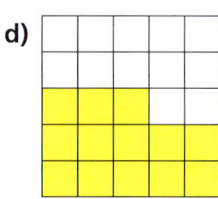
   e)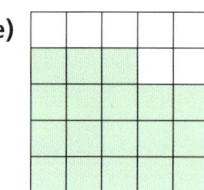

7 Write down these percentages as fractions in their simplest form.
   a) 30%   b) 80%   c) 15%   d) 45%   e) 60%   f) 22%

8 Write down the first quantity as a percentage of the second quantity.
   a) $25, $100   b) $60, $100   c) $45, $100   d) 24 cm, 50 cm
   e) 15 mm, 50 mm   f) 20 m, 50 m   g) 16 litres, 25 litres   h) 13 litres, 25 litres
   i) 28 grams, 50 grams   j) 9 grams, 25 grams   k) $17, $20   l) $23, $25

9 Afia says that $\frac{12}{25}$ is the same percentage as $\frac{24}{50}$. Is Afia right? Explain your answer.

10 Write the first number as a percentage of the second number.
   a) 5, 10   b) 5, 20   c) 1, 10   d) 2, 10   e) 3, 4
   f) 5, 25   g) 4, 5   h) 20, 50   i) 16, 50

11 Mia and Lata are comparing their favourite cricket teams.

Mia says, 'My favourite team is better as they have won 14 matches out of the last 25. They have won more matches.'

Lata says, 'My favourite team are better as they have won 12 matches out of the last 20. They have lost fewer matches.'

Use your knowledge of percentages to explain which team is better. Give reasons for your answer.

12 In each part of this question, write the first number as a percentage of the second number.
   a) 20, 200   b) 30, 200   c) 50, 200   d) 60, 300   e) 15, 300   f) 75, 300

Mental methods

Worked example 3

Four candidates stood for the school council. 200 pupils voted and the votes were cast as follows:

Candidate A received $\frac{1}{5}$ of the votes.

Candidate B received $\frac{1}{4}$ of the votes.

Candidate C received $\frac{3}{10}$ of the votes.

Candidate D received the remaining votes.

a) Work out how many votes were cast for each candidate.

b) Who won the election?

a) Candidate A 200 ÷ 5 = 40 votes	To find $\frac{1}{5}$ of a number you divide by 5 or you could divide by 10 and multiply by 2 because $\frac{2}{10}$ is the same as $\frac{1}{5}$.	200 40 | 40 | 40 | 40 | 40
Candidate B 200 ÷ 4 = 50 votes	To find $\frac{1}{4}$ of a quantity, you divide by 4.	200 50 | 50 | 50 | 50
Candidate C $\frac{1}{10}$ of 200 = 200 ÷ 10 = 20 $\frac{3}{10}$ of 200 = 20 × 3 = 60 60 votes	To find $\frac{3}{10}$ of a quantity, you first find $\frac{1}{10}$ by dividing by 10, and then multiply the answer by 3 to get $\frac{3}{10}$.	200 20 20 20 20 20 20 20 20 20 20 60
Candidate D 200 – 40 – 50 – 60 = 50 votes	Candidate D received the remaining votes so you can find the number of votes by taking the number of votes for the other candidates away from 200.	200 – 40 – 50 – 60
b) The winner was candidate C with 60 votes.	To see who is the winner you need to see who has the most votes.	

Chapter 15: Percentages and fractions

> **Think about**
>
> Where have you seen percentages used in real life?

Worked example 4

Ravina has been finding out about students in her year at school.

There are 120 students in Ravina's year.

    10% of the students play a musical instrument.   30% of the students play in a sports team.

    70% of the students can ride a bike.   15% of the students can juggle.

Find the number of students who:

a) can play a musical instrument.   b) play in a sports team.

c) can ride a bike.   d) can juggle.

a) To find 10% you divide by 10. 120 ÷ 10 = 12 12 students	The whole amount (120 students) is 100%. You want to find 10%. You can do this by dividing by 10 to go from 100% to 10%.	Bar model: 100% = 120, split into ten 10% sections of 12 each.
b) To find 30% you find 10% and multiply by 3. 10% = 12 students 30% = 12 × 3 = 36 students	You know 10% of the amount is 12. To find 30% you can add three lots of 12 or multiply 12 by 3.	Bar model with three 10% sections highlighted.
c) To find 70% you find 10% and multiply by 7. 10% = 12 students 70% = 12 × 7 = 84 students	To find 70% you can multiply 12 by 7.	Bar model with seven 10% sections highlighted.

d) To find 15% you add 10% and 5%.
10% = 12 students
5% = 12 ÷ 2
      = 6 students
15% = 10% + 5%
      = 12 + 6
      = 18 students
	You know 10% of the amount.
	You can find 5% by halving 10%.
	You can find 15% by adding 10% and 5%.
		Bar model showing 10% (12) and two 5% (6) sections highlighted.

> **Discuss**
>
> Can you find a way to build all percentages that end in a 5 using the method in part (d)?
>
> What other percentages could you build up using this method? How would you build the percentages?

Unit 2A: Number and calculation

Exercise 2

1 Find $\frac{1}{5}$ of:
 a) 75c
 b) 150 g
 c) 90 cm
 d) $12.50
 e) 7.5 kg

2 Find $\frac{3}{4}$ of:
 a) 40c
 b) 16 kg
 c) 60 cm
 d) 240 g
 e) $8.40

3 Find $\frac{2}{5}$ of:
 a) 70c
 b) 750 g
 c) 250 cm
 d) $1.50
 e) 3.5 kg

4 Find $\frac{7}{10}$ of:
 a) 50c
 b) 600 g
 c) 80 cm
 d) $3
 e) 4.5 kg

5 Find 50% of:
 a) 30c
 b) 36 kg
 c) 22 cm
 d) 68 g
 e) $1.50

6 Find 25% of:
 a) 12c
 b) $2.40
 c) 44 cm
 d) 320 g
 e) 14 kg

> **Tip**
> Finding 25% is the same as finding $\frac{1}{4}$. You can either divide by 4 or divide by 2 twice.

7 Find 75% of:
 a) 80c
 b) $16
 c) 120 cm
 d) 48 g
 e) 22 kg

> **Tip**
> To find 75% you can find 25% and multiply the answer by 3.

8 Find 20% of:
 a) 15c
 b) $3.50
 c) 25 cm
 d) 450 g
 e) 5.5 kg

9 Find 10% of:
 a) 90c
 b) $4.60
 c) 340 cm
 d) 230 g
 e) 15 kg

10 Find 70% of:
 a) 60c
 b) $2.50
 c) 20 cm
 d) 200 g
 e) 8 kg

11 Match the question with the answer.

50% of $230	$36
25% of $500	$39
10% of $360	$115
20% of $170	$125
75% of $52	$120
60% of $200	$34
80% of $40	$42
70% of $60	$32

12 Which is larger:

a) $\frac{1}{4}$ of 2.5 m or 20% of 2.4 m?
b) $\frac{1}{4}$ of 4 kg or 30% of 5 kg?
c) $\frac{1}{3}$ of $3.60 or 70% of $2?
d) $\frac{1}{5}$ of 15 litres or 25% of 14 litres?
e) $\frac{3}{10}$ of $8.50 or 75% of $3.60?
f) $\frac{4}{5}$ of 275 cm or 40% of 560 cm?

13 Marta wants to find 80% of $130.

Can you find different ways to work out 80% of $130?

Find as many different ways as possible.

14 Find examples of percentage calculations from the real world, for example from shops or newspapers. Use these to produce percentage questions of your own.

Include answers for your questions.

15 **Vocabulary feature question**

ACROSS

2 $\frac{3}{4}$ is _____ to 75%

3 It has a numerator and a denominator

DOWN

1 Means per hundred

End of chapter reflection

You should know that ...	You should be able to ...	Such as ...
Percentage is the number of parts in every 100.	Use fractions and percentages to describe parts of shapes, quantities and measures.	50 people voted for their preferred school council representative. Find the percentage of votes for each candidate from these results: Candidate A 8 votes Candidate B 14 votes Candidate C 28 votes
Percentage amounts can be built up by finding 10%, 5% and 1% and adding multiples of these.	Calculate simple fractions and percentages of quantities by using non-calculator methods, e.g. one quarter of 64, 20% of 50 kg.	Graeme has been following a strict exercise regime. He has lost 10% of his body weight. If he started at 95 kg, how much weight has he lost?

Unit 2A: Number and calculation

Unit 2A • Chapter 16
Calculations

You will learn how to:
- Use the laws of arithmetic and inverse operations to simplify calculations with whole numbers and decimals.
- Know when to round up or down after division when the context requires a whole-number answer.

Starting point

Do you remember …?

- how to add or subtract numbers?
  For example, 173 + 249 or 564 − 237?
- how to multiply or divide two numbers?
  For example, 58 × 7 or 63 ÷ 9?
- how to round to the nearest whole number?
  For example, round 4.5 to the nearest whole number?

This will be helpful when …

you meet the Order of Operations.
For example, in what order should you work out the steps in this calculation: $20 - (4 - 2) \times 3^2$?

Hook

Usma and her brother want to bake some biscuits.

They find a recipe which makes 12 biscuits:

175 g softened butter

85 g caster sugar

200 g plain flour

They want to make 36 biscuits. How many packs of each ingredient do they need to buy?

Butter comes in 250 g packs.

Caster sugar comes in 500 g packs.

Plain flour comes in 500 g packs.

Simplifying calculations

Worked example 1

Work out 59 + 83 + 31

59 + 83 + 31 = 50 + 9 + 80 + 3 + 30 + 1 = 50 + 80 + 30 + 9 + 3 +1 =	You can treat each of the two digit numbers as their tens part plus their units part.	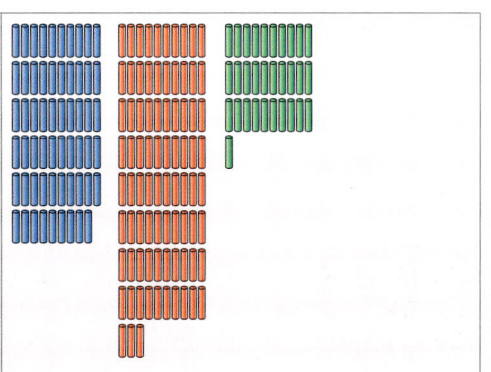

Chapter 16: Calculations 129

	You can then add the tens parts and add the units parts separately.	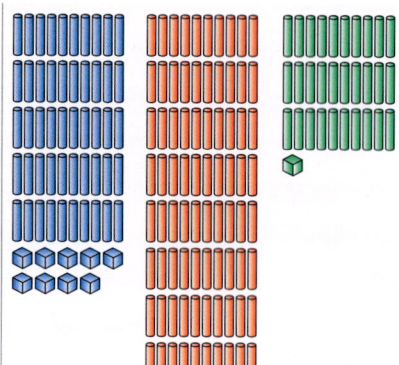
160 + 13 = 173	You then add the total of the tens parts and the total of the units parts to get your answer.	

Worked example 2

Work out:

a) 12 × 9 + 8 × 9   b) 17 × 4   c) 16 × 8 − 6 × 8   d) 27 × 9 − 14 × 9

a) 12 × 9 + 8 × 9 =		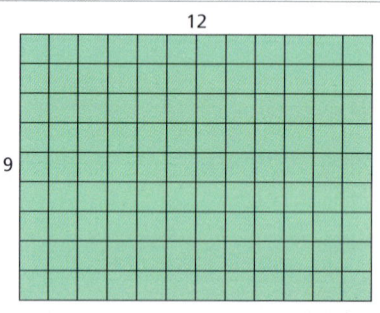 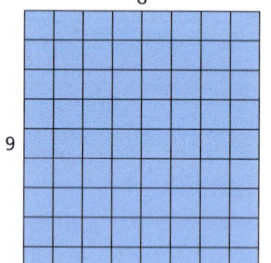
(12 + 8) × 9 =	You can group the twelve lots of nine with the eight lots of nine to make twenty lots of nine.	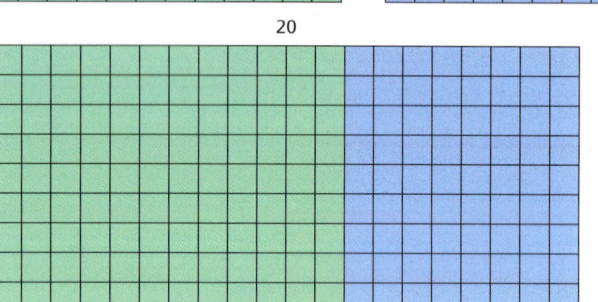
20 × 9 = 180		
b) 17 × 4 =		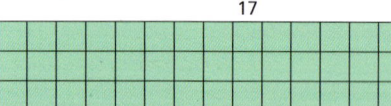
(10 + 7) × 4 =	You can split the seventeen lots of four into ten lots of four and 7 lots of four.	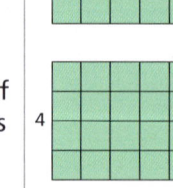 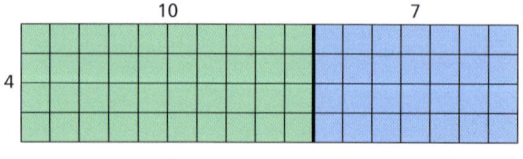
10 × 4 + 7 × 4 = 40 + 28 = 68		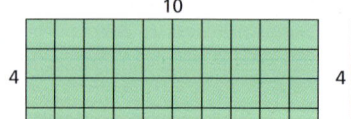 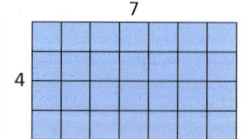

Unit 2A: Number and calculation

c) $16 \times 8 - 6 \times 8 =$		
$(16 - 6) \times 8 =$ $10 \times 8 =$ 80	You can take away 6 groups of 8 from 16 groups of 8 to leave you with 10 groups of 8.	
d) $27 \times 9 - 14 \times 9 =$ $(27 - 14) \times 9 =$ $13 \times 9 =$ $10 \times 9 + 3 \times 9 =$ $90 + 27 =$ 117	If you start with 27 groups of 9, and take away 14 groups of 9, then you are left with 13 groups of 9. You can split 13 groups of 9 into 10 groups of 9 and 3 groups of 9.	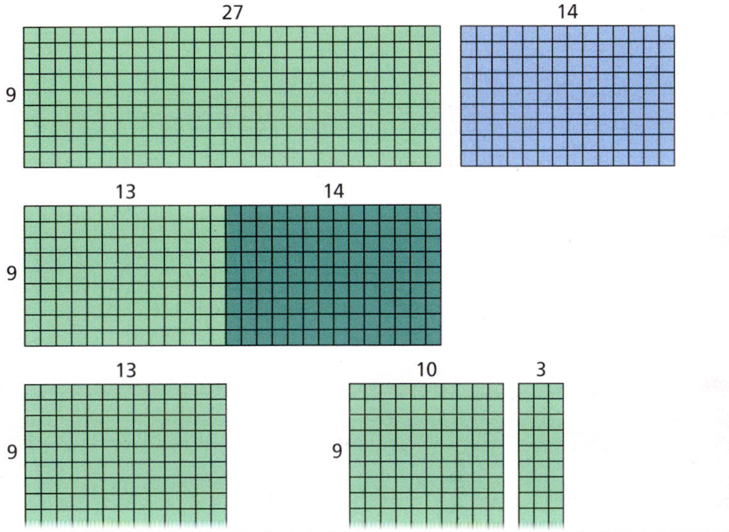

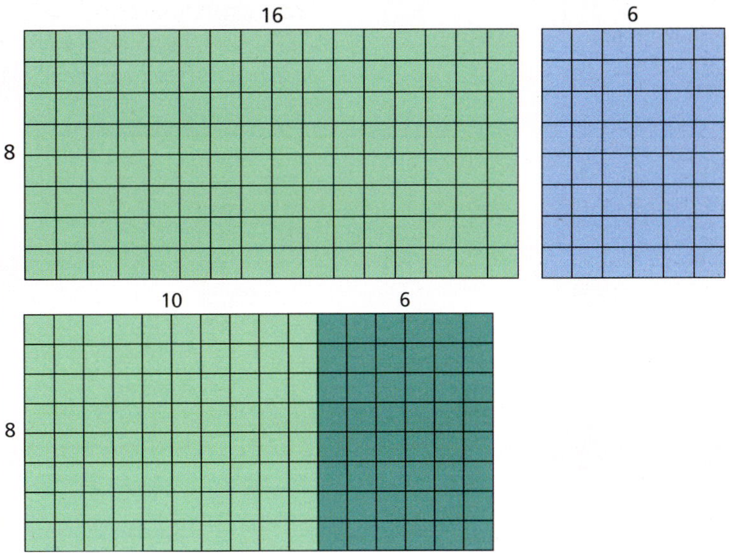

Worked example 3

Work out:

a) $145 + 76 - 145$ b) $7.2 \times 3 \div 7.2$ c) $\sqrt{6^2}$

a) $145 + 76 - 145 =$ $76 + 145 - 145 =$ 76	145 plus 76 is the same as 76 plus 145 so you can swap the two numbers in the addition. You can see that if you add 145 and then subtract 145 you will be back at the number you started with.
b) $7.2 \times 3 \div 7.2 =$ $3 \times 7.2 \div 7.2 =$ 3	7.2 times 3 is the same as 3 times 7.2 If you multiply by 7.2 and then divide by 7.2 you will be back at the number you started with.
c) $\sqrt{6^2} =$ 6	Square rooting is the inverse operation to squaring, so the square root of the square of 6 is 6.

> **Think about**
>
> Which calculations can you swap around numbers in without changing the calculation?
>
> For example, 45 + 17 = 17 + 45
>
> Can you swap the numbers in:
> - additions?
> - subtractions?
> - multiplications?
> - divisions?
>
> Try to write explanations or give examples for each type of calculation.

Worked example 4

Work out $3 \times 4.6 \div 6$

$3 \times 4.6 \div 6 =$	You can rewrite 4.6 as 2×2.3
$3 \times (2 \times 2.3) \div 6 =$	
$3 \times 2 \times 2.3 \div 6 =$	
$6 \times 2.3 \div 6 =$	6 times 2.3 is the same as 2.3 times 6
$2.3 \times 6 \div 6 =$	
2.3	

Worked example 5 – Extension

$7.5 \times 8 =$	You can split 7.5 times 8 into 7 times 8 and 0.5 times 8	7.5×8
$(7 + 0.5) \times 8 =$		$\downarrow$
$7 \times 8 + 0.5 \times 8 =$		$7 \times 8 + 0.5 \times 8$
		$\downarrow \quad \downarrow$
$7 \times 8 + \frac{1}{2} \times 8 =$		$7 \times 8 + \frac{1}{2} \times 8$
	0.5 is the same as $\frac{1}{2}$ so you can replace the decimal with a fraction.	$\downarrow \quad \downarrow$
		$56 + 4$
		$\searrow \swarrow$
	Work out the two multiplications and add the answers.	60
$56 + 4 = 60$		

Exercise 1

1 Work out:

   a) 37 + 54 + 63   b) 65 + 134 + 35   c) 57 + 82 + 48 + 53   d) 93 + 44 + 126 + 37

2 Work out:

   a) 36 + 27 + 53   b) 67 + 19 + 32   c) 39 + 45 − 18   d) 37 + 51 − 24

3 Write down the value of:

   a) 247 + 63 − 247   b) 7.578 + 37.76 − 37.76   c) 23 + 76 + 15 − 76   d) 2754 + 293 − 43 − 293

   e) $8.7 \times 15 \div 15$ f) $1.3 \times 26 \div 1.3$ g) $3.07 \times 7 \div 7$ h) $243 \times 15.7 \div 243$

   i) $\sqrt{19^2}$ j) $(\sqrt{121})^2$

4 Complete each calculation.

a) 27 + …… − 27 = 36
b) 235 + …… − 235 = 38
c) 217 + 97 − …… = 97
d) 374 + 216 − …… = 374
e) 87 × 325 ÷ …… = 325
f) …… × 67 ÷ 67 = 185
g) 155 ÷ 9. 3 × …… = 155
h) 317 × 5.8 ÷ …… = 5.8

5 Match each calculation on the first line with an equivalent calculation from the second line.

A	B	C	D
(7 × 57) + (3 × 57)	(34 × 57) − (4 × 57)	(57 × 19) + (43 × 19)	(19 × 21) − 19

P	Q	R	S
100 × 19	10 × 57	20 × 19	30 × 57

6 Work out:

a) 9 × 32 + 32
b) (17 × 29) − (7 × 29)
c) (43 × 8) + (2 × 43)
d) (30 × 27) + (30 × 3)
e) (87 × 47) + (13 × 47)
f) (112 × 5.3) − (12 × 5.3)
g) (34 × 2.6) + (16 × 2.6)

7 Work out:

a) 2 × 73 × 5
b) 4 × 18 × 25
c) 20 × 23 × 5
d) 4 × 12.3 × 2.5
e) 700 × 24.6 ÷ 7
f) 70 × 32.7 ÷ 7
g) 60 × 34 ÷ 15
h) 96 × 0.7 ÷ 12

8 Amina says that 4.5 × 8 ÷ 3 = 4.5 × 3 ÷ 8
Is Amina correct? Explain your answer.

9 Work out:

a) 4.5 × 12
b) 3.25 × 8
c) 3.75 × 4

Interpreting results of calculations

Key term

To **round** to the nearest whole number you look at the number in the tenths place value. If the tenths are 5 or above you round up, if the tenths are less than 5 you round down.

For example,

15.73 = 16 to the nearest whole number

7.34 = 7 to the nearest whole number

9.5 = 10 to the nearest whole number

If you are told to round 7.8 down to the nearest whole number you get 7.

If you are told to round 12.4 up to the nearest whole number you get 13.

Worked example 6

Howard sold 45 tickets to a small concert. He is putting seats out in rows of 8. How many rows does he need if everyone with a ticket must have a seat?

| To find how many rows he needs to divide 45 by 8. $$\begin{array}{r}5\ r5\\8\overline{)45}\end{array}$$ | Divide 45 by 8

If Howard puts out 5 rows of 8 chairs there will be 5 people without chairs so he needs 6 rows.

In this case the answer must be rounded up to the next whole number which is 6. | 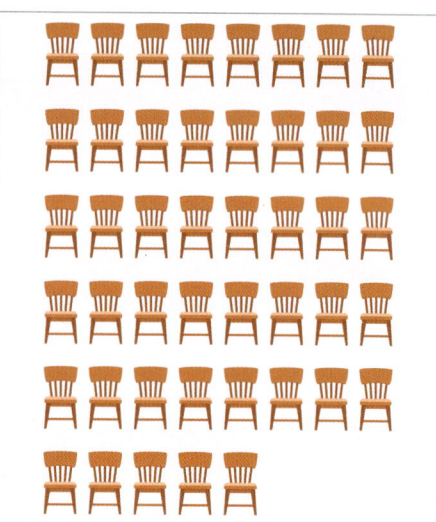 |

Did you know?

There are special types of rounding used in different subjects and settings. Some of these have their own names like 'floor' and 'ceiling' which are used in computing.

You might like to find out about the different types of rounding that are used.

Exercise 2   8

1 Round the answers to each calculation to the nearest whole number.
   a) 12 ÷ 5   b) 20 ÷ 7
   c) 13 ÷ 6   d) 27 ÷ 4
   e) 42 ÷ 8   f) 53 ÷ 5
   g) 84 ÷ 6   h) 93 ÷ 7

2 Round the answer to each calculation **up** to the nearest whole number.
   a) 19 ÷ 5   b) 25 ÷ 6
   c) 43 ÷ 5   d) 28 ÷ 10
   e) 53 ÷ 7   f) 68 ÷ 8
   g) 100 ÷ 7   h) 100 ÷ 9

3 Round the answer to each calculation in question 2 **down** to the nearest whole number.

4 When computers are shipped to computer shops they can only have up to 8 computers in each box. What is the smallest number of boxes needed to ship each of these computer deliveries?
   a) 24   b) 14
   c) 33   d) 131

Unit 2A: Number and calculation

5 Apples are being packed in boxes which can hold up to 120 apples. What is the smallest number of boxes needed to pack:

a) 480 apples   b) 375 apples   c) 613 apples
d) 729 apples   e) 2 500 apples   f) 3 152 apples

6 Work out how many complete loads of washing each of these bottles will give. One complete wash uses 15 millilitres of liquid.

50 ml

750 ml

1 litre

7 Tobias is tiling the kitchen floor with 30 cm by 30 cm tiles. The kitchen measures 3 metres by 2.5 metres.

a) Work out how many tiles Tobias needs.
b) The tiles are sold in boxes of 12. How many boxes of tiles should Tobias buy?

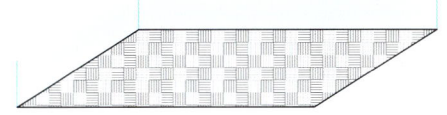

8 Chen and Yuri want to tile the bathroom floor in the house they share.
The bathroom floor is 2.4 metres by 1.6 metres. The tiles they will use are 25 cm by 25 cm.

Chen does this working:
2.4 m = 240 cm, 1.6 m = 160 cm
Area of floor = 240 × 160 = 38 400 cm²
Area of one tile = 25 × 25 = 625 cm²
Number of tiles needed = 38 400 ÷ 625 = 61.44 so 62 tiles

Yuri does this working:
2.4 m = 240 cm, 1.6 m = 160 cm
Number of tiles along the 240 cm side = 240 ÷ 25 = 9.6 so 10 tiles
Number of tiles along the 160 cm side = 160 ÷ 25 = 6.4 so 7 tiles
Number of tiles needed = 10 × 7 = 70 tiles

How many tiles should Chen and Yuri buy? Explain your answer.

9 Use the internet to find out about different types of rounding and why these are used.

10 Vocabulary feature question

Complete the sentences with these words.

accurate   easier   round   close   simpler

When you .... you make a number .... but you keep its value .... to what it was. The result is less ...., but .... to use.

Chapter 16: Calculations

End of chapter reflection

You should know that …	You should be able to …	Such as …
Numbers in addition and multiplication calculations can be swapped without changing the calculation.	Simplify calculations by rearranging.	Work out, without using a calculator: 1. 357 + 45 − 357 2. 8 × 7.3 ÷ 8 3. 3 × 6.4 ÷ 6
Calculations involving multiplication by a common number can be simplified by grouping or splitting.	Simplify multiplication calculations by combining or splitting terms.	Work out, without using a calculator: 1. 64 × 71 + 36 × 71 2. 13 × 67
Some answers need to be rounded up and some answers need to be rounded down. This depends on the setting for the question.	Know when to round up or down after division when the context requires a whole-number answer.	Ilias fills empty salt pots with salt. Each salt pot holds 9 grams of salt. How many pots can he fill from a 100 gram bag of salt?

2B

Unit 2B
Algebra and measures

What's it all about?

- Working with metric units of length, mass, area and capacity
- The area and perimeter of rectangles and shapes made from rectangles
- Writing and using simple formulae
- Plotting coordinates
- Plotting, and recognising the equation of, straight line graphs
- Constructing and solving equations

You will learn about:

- How to convert between metric units of length, mass, area and capacity
- How to find the area and perimeter of rectangles and shapes made from rectangles
- Writing simple formulae
- Substituting into formulae
- Solving problems involving coordinates in all four quadrants
- Different representations of functions
- Plotting straight line graphs
- Constructing and solving linear equations

You will build your skills in:

- Working with a range of metric units
- Problem solving
- Visualising shapes

Unit 2B • Chapter 17

Area and perimeter

You will learn how to:
- Know abbreviations for and relationships between metric units; convert between:
  - kilometres (km) and metres (m), centimetres (cm) and millimetres (mm)
  - tonnes (t), kilograms (kg) and grams (g)
  - litres (l) and millilitres (ml)
  - square metres (m^2), square centimetres (cm^2) and square millimetres (mm^2).
- Derive and use formulae for the area and perimeter of a rectangle; calculate the perimeter and area of compound shapes made from rectangles.

Starting point

Do you remember …?

- how to multiply and divide whole and decimal numbers by 10, 100 and 1000?
- how to convert between metric units?

  For example, know that 435 cm is the same as 4 m 35 cm?
- how to construct simple algebraic expressions and how to multiply a constant across a bracket?

  For example, know that $3(x + y) = 3x + 3y$?
- how to find the perimeter of a shape if you are given the lengths of its sides?
- how to find the area of a rectangle or square shape by counting squares or by calculation?

This will also be helpful when …

you learn to solve problems involving area of rectangles, triangles and other polygons.

Hook

Using only 12 connecting lines from one dot to another vertically and horizontally, create a closed shape on a copy of the dotty grid.

- How many different shapes can you make?
- Count the number of squares enclosed by each of your shapes.
- What is the maximum number of squares you can enclose with 12 lines? What shape have you made?

Converting between metric units

Key terms

Length is measured in **kilometres** (km), **metres** (m), **centimetres** (cm) or **millimetres** (mm).

1 kilometre = 1000 metres

1 metre = 1000 millimetres or 100 centimetres

1 centimetre = 10 millimetres

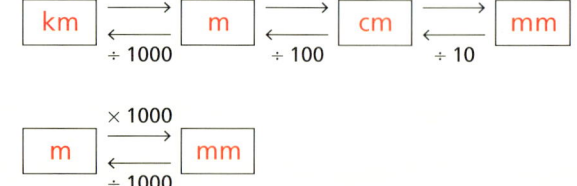

Mass is measured in **tonnes** (t), **kilograms** (kg) or **grams** (g).

1 tonne = 1000 kilograms

1 kilogram = 1000 grams

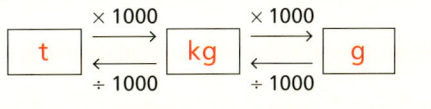

Capacity (usually volume of liquids) is measured in **litres** (l) or **millilitres** (ml).

1 litre = 1000 millilitres

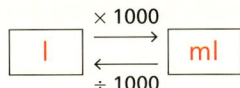

> **Did you know?**
>
> These units of length, mass and capacity can be given different prefixes to make them larger or smaller.
>
> For example, the prefix 'micro' means something 1000 times smaller than a 'milli', so a micrometre is 1/1000 of the size of a millimetre.
>
> The prefix 'mega' is 1000 times larger than a 'kilo', so a megametre is 1000 times the size of a kilometre.
>
> Can you find any other prefixes for units like this?

Worked example 1

Convert:

a) 5 kilograms into grams
b) 6.42 metres into centimetres
c) 14 350 grams into kilograms
d) 3.6 litres into millilitres

a) 5 kg = 5000 g	To convert kilograms to grams you multiply by 1000 so you move every number 3 place values to the left. 5 × 1000 = 5000	1000	100	10	1			
		thousands	hundreds	tens	units			
					5			
		5	0	0	0			
b) 6.42 m = 642 cm	To convert metres to centimetres you multiply by 100 so move every number 2 place values to the left. 6.42 × 100 = 642	100	10	1	.	0.1	0.01	
		hundreds	tens	units	decimal point	tenths	hundredths	
				6	.	4	2	
		6	4	2	.			
c) 14 350 g = 14.35 kg	The convert from grams to kilograms you divide by 1000 so you move every number 3 place values to the right. 14 350 ÷ 1000 = 14.350 or 14.35	10 000	1000	100	10	1	.	0.1	0.01	0.001
		ten thousands	thousands	hundreds	tens	units	decimal point	tenths	hundredths	thousanths
		1	4	3	5	0	.			
					1	4	.	3	5	0

d) 3.6 l = 3600 ml	To convert from litres to millilitres you multiply by 1000 so you move every number 3 place values to the left 3.6 × 1000 = 3600	1000	100	10	1	.	0.1	0.01	0.001
		thousands	hundreds	tens	units	decimal point	tenths	hundredths	thousanths
					3	.	6		
		3	6	0	0				

Exercise 1

1 Convert these lengths into the units given:
   a) 4 m to cm b) 12 km to m c) 15 cm to mm d) 40 m to cm
   e) 40 cm to mm f) 6.2 m to cm g) 17.14 m to cm h) 1.35 km to m
   i) 6.25 cm to mm j) 200 cm to m k) 3500 mm to m l) 120 mm to cm
   m) 1.2 m to mm n) 413 cm to m o) 19 mm to cm p) 7540 m to km

2 Convert these masses into the units given:
   a) 19 kg to g b) 40 t to kg c) 2.3 kg to g d) 13.5 t to kg
   e) 3000 g to kg f) 43 000 kg to t g) 4250 g to kg h) 7531 kg to t
   i) 135 g to kg j) 465 kg to t

3 Convert these capacities into the units given:
   a) 24 l to ml b) 754 l to ml c) 2.3 l to ml d) 0.57 l to ml
   e) 13 000 ml to l f) 5160 ml to l g) 360 ml to l h) 23 ml to l

4 Which of these is the odd one out?
   A: 3600 cm   B: 360 m   C: 36 000 mm   D: 0.036 km

5 Complete the missing units.
   a) 4.56 m = 4560 ....
   b) 3 450 000 .... = 3.45 t
   c) 27.25 .... = 272.5 ....

Perimeter and area of shapes made from rectangles

Key terms

The **perimeter** of a shape is the total distance all the way around the outside.

If the sides of the rectangle have lengths x and y. then the length all the way round the outside is: Perimeter = $x + y + x + y = 2x + 2y$.

The **area** of a shape is the amount of space it covers.

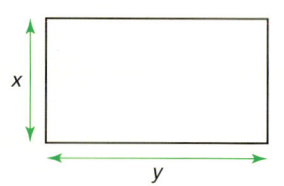

Unit 2B: Algebra and measures

For a rectangle the area is length × width:

Area = $x \times y$ which you can write as xy.

Area is measured in **square metres** (m^2), **square centimetres** (cm^2) or **square millimetres** (mm^2).

$1 m^2 = 1 m \times 1 m = 100 cm \times 100 cm = 10\,000 cm^2$

$1 cm^2 = 1 cm \times 1 cm = 10 mm \times 10 mm = 100 mm^2$

Worked example 2

a) Find the perimeter of this shape which is made up of two rectangles.

b) Find area of the shape in part a).

c) Find the shaded area of the shape below.

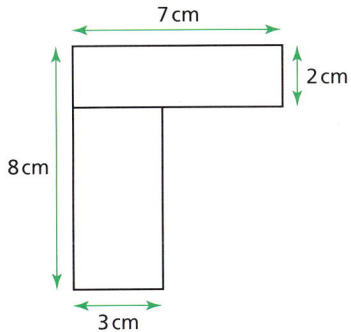

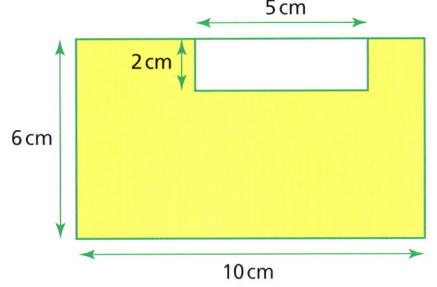

a) The perimeter of the shape is: $(7 + 2 + 4 + 6 + 3 + 8)$ cm $= 30$ cm	First find all the lengths on the outside of the shape. The 4 cm is 7 cm − 3 cm The 6 cm is 8 cm − 2 cm Add all the lengths on the outside of the shape together to get the perimeter. $7 + 2 + 4 + 6 + 3 + 8 = 30$	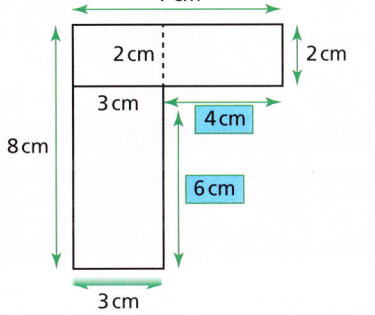
b) The area of the shape is: $18 cm^2 + 14 cm^2 = 32 cm^2$	Split the shape into two rectangles. (There are two ways to do this.) The area of the shaded rectangle is $6 \times 3 = 18 cm^2$ The area of the unshaded rectangle is $7 \times 2 = 14 cm^2$ The whole area is $18 cm^2 + 14 cm^2 = 32 cm^2$	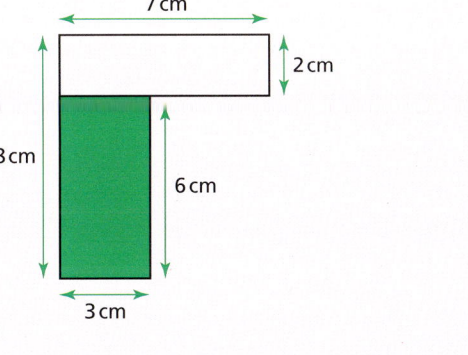

Chapter 17: Area and perimeter   141

c) The shaded area is:

$60 \text{ cm}^2 - 10 \text{ cm}^2 = 50 \text{ cm}^2$

The shaded area is the area of a whole rectangle measuring 10 cm × 6 cm with a rectangle of area 2 cm × 5 cm removed.

60 − 10 = 50

Tip

If you are finding an area and the lengths are in m then the area is in m^2.

If you are finding an area and the lengths are in cm then the area is in cm^2.

If you are finding an area and the lengths are in mm then the area is in mm^2.

Key term

A **compound shape** is one that is made from connecting two or more simple shapes.

For example, this compound shape has been made from two rectangles

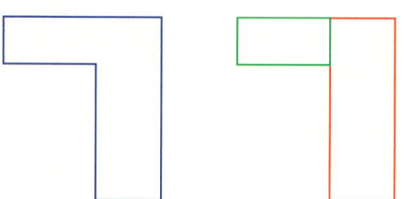

Think about

Do any objects in your classroom have a surface that is a rectangle? What are their perimeter and area?

Can you see any surfaces that are a compound shape made of two rectangles? What are their perimeter and area?

Unit 2B: Algebra and measures

Exercise 2 1–6

1 Find the perimeter of these rectangles, which are not drawn to scale.

a)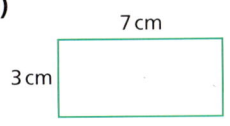
b)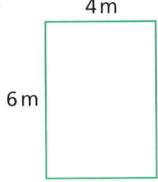
c)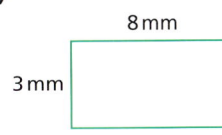

d)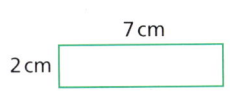
e)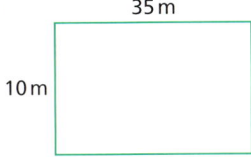
f)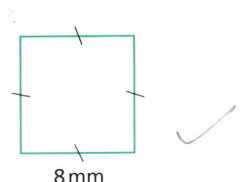

Tip: Remember to state the units with your answer.

2 Find the perimeter of these **compound shapes** which are made up of rectangles and are not drawn to scale.

a)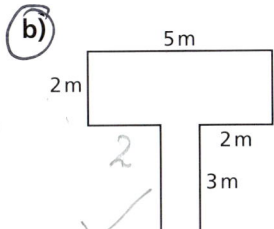
b)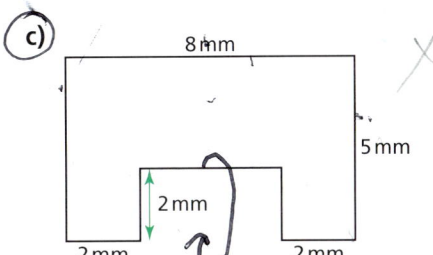
c)

3 Find the areas of the rectangles in question 1.

4 Find the areas of the compound shapes in question 2.

5 Fill in the missing measurements on these rectangles.

a) 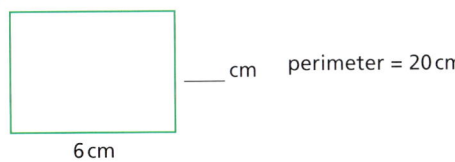   perimeter = 20 cm
b) 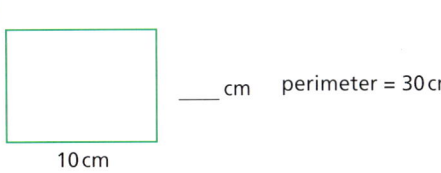   perimeter = 30 cm

c) 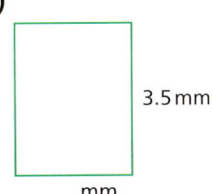   perimeter = 11 mm
d) 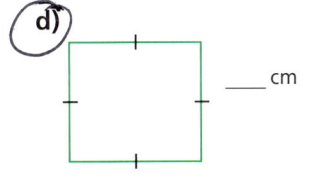   perimeter = 28 cm

Chapter 17: Area and perimeter 143

6 Fill in the missing measurement on these rectangles.

a)  ___ cm area = 15 cm²

5 cm

b) 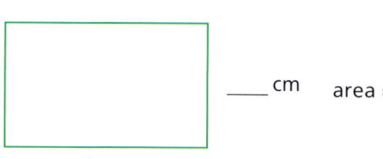 ___ cm area = 40 cm²

8 cm

c) 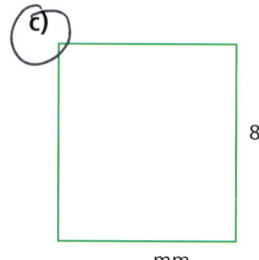 8 mm area = 48 mm²

___ mm

d) 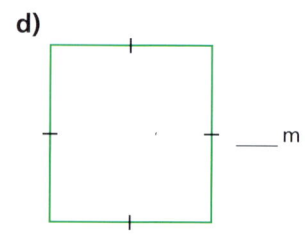 ___ m area = 9 m²

___ m

7 Find the shaded area in each of these shapes made of rectangles.

a)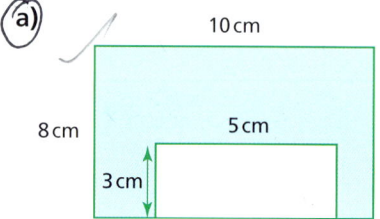
10 cm, 8 cm, 5 cm, 3 cm

b)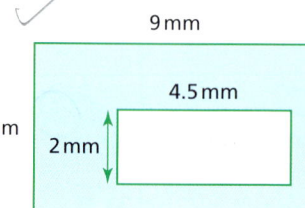
9 mm, 5 mm, 4.5 mm, 2 mm

c)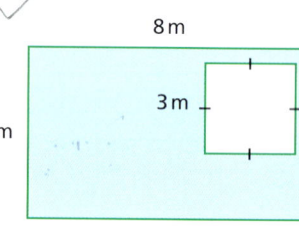
8 m, 4.5 m, 3 m

8 a) A rectangle has sides of 5 cm and 8 cm.

Esther says that the perimeter is 5 cm + 8 cm + 5 cm + 8 cm = 26 cm.

Jana says that it is quicker to add the 5 and 8 and then multiply the answer by 2. She calculates 2 × (5 cm + 8 cm) = 2 × 13 cm = 26 cm.

Are both methods correct? Which do you think is faster?

b) A rectangle has sides of *a* and *b*.

Esther says that the perimeter is $a + b + a + b = 2a + 2b$.

Jana adds the *a* and *b* and then multiplies the answer by 2 giving $2(a + b)$.

Is $2(a + b)$ the same as $2a + 2b$? Explain your answer.

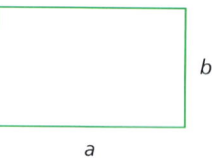

9 a) A rectangle has sides of 3 cm and 4 cm.

Emanuel finds the area of the shape by dividing it into 1 cm squares and counting the squares. His answer is 12 centimetre squares or 12 cm².

Owen says that it is quicker to multiply the 3 cm by the 4 cm to get 12 cm².

Are both boys correct? Explain your answer.

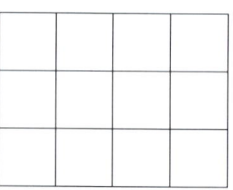

b) A rectangle has sides of lengths *a* and *b*. To find the area, John multiplies the two lengths together and gets the answer $a \times b$ which he writes as ab. Is he correct? Explain your answer.

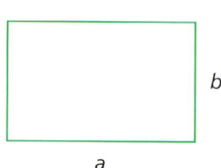

144   Unit 2B: Algebra and measures

10 A rectangle has an area of 30 m².

a) Sketch three possible rectangles that it could be. Show the lengths and widths clearly on your sketches.

b) Will the perimeters of your three rectangles be the same? Calculate the perimeter of each of your rectangles to check.

11 Use a spreadsheet to create a table like this to find the perimeters and areas of rectangles when you input their sides.

Length	Width	Perimeter	Area
2	3	10	6
		..3	

End of chapter reflection

You should know that …	You should be able to …	Such as …
There are standard metric units (with abbreviations) used for measuring length, area, mass and capacity.	Recognise a unit by its name or abbreviation and say what it used to measure.	a) tonne is a unit of……… b) ml is a unit of ……… c) cm² is a unit of ………
You can convert between metric units.	Convert between units efficiently.	Convert a) 4500 m to km b) 3.6 kg to g
The perimeter of a shape is the total distance around it and is measured in units of length.	Find the perimeter of a rectangle and shapes made from rectangles.	Find the perimeter of this shape which is made up of rectangles. (15 m, 8 m, 6 m, 5 m)
The area of a shape is the total space and is measured in squares, for example m² or cm² or mm².	Find the area of a rectangle and shapes made from rectangles.	Find the area of this shape which is made up of rectangles. (15 m, 8 m, 6 m, 5 m)
For a rectangle of length a, width b, perimeter P and area A, $P = 2a + 2b$ or $P = 2(a + b)$ and $A = a \times b$ or $A = ab$	Derive the formula for perimeter and area of a rectangle.	(rectangle with sides p and q) Explain why the perimeter of this rectangle is $2(p + q)$.

Unit 2B • Chapter 18

Formulae

You will learn how to:
- Derive and use simple formulae. For example, to change hours to minutes.
- Substitute positive integers into simple linear expressions/formulae.

Starting point

Do you remember …?

- how to use letters to represent unknown numbers?
- how to write and simplify algebraic expressions?
  For example, writing $x + x + x = 3x$
- what a term, an expression and an equation are?
- the correct order of operations used to calculate with numbers and algebra?

This will also be helpful when …

you learn to draw graphs and solve equations to find missing numbers.

Hook

The cost of a mobile phone contract is made up from:
- a fixed charge of $8 per month. This is the charge that you pay whether or not you use any data.

  plus
- a cost of $1.20 per megabyte of data used.

If you use 5 megabytes of data every month, how much will your bill be each month?

If you use 10 megabytes of data every month, how much will your bill be each month?

What is the minimum price you could pay each month?

Is there a maximum price you could pay each month?

If you are charged $12.80 for the month, how many megabytes of data did you use?

The cost of the mobile phone contract can be written as a **formula** so that you can work out the cost of any number of megabytes and compare charges between different providers.

Constructing and using formulae

Key terms

A **variable** is a letter that represents a number that can take different values.

A **formula** is a mathematical relationship between 2 or more variables expressed algebraically.

For example, for the phone contract above, if C is the cost of the mobile phone contract for a month, and m is the number of megabytes of data used, $C = 8 + 1.20m$ is a **formula** connecting the variables.

A formula does not mean anything unless you say what your variables represent.

Unit 2B: Algebra and measures

Worked example 1

a) Write in words a formula to change years into months.
b) Write a formula to calculate the number of months, m, in y years.
c) Use your formula to calculate the number of months in 6 years.

a) number of months = number of years × 12	To change years into months you multiply the number of years by 12.	1 year / 12 months
b) The total number of months, m, can be written as m = y × 12 or 12 × y m = 12y	To find the number of months in y years, you need to multiply y by 12.	y years — 1 year, 1 year, 1 year, 1 year, 1 year … 1 year / 12 months each / 12y months
c) m = 12y m = 12 × 6 m = 72 so there are 72 months in 6 years	You want to find the number of months in 6 years, so y = 6. Replace the y in the formula with 6 to find the number of months, m.	6 years / 1 year × 6 / 12 months × 6 / 72 months

Exercise 1   1–5

1 Kerri uses this formula to find out how many medium sized potatoes she needs to make one portion of French Fries:

number of potatoes = number of portions of French Fries × 2

a) How many potatoes does she need to make 5 portions of French Fries?
b) How many potatoes does she need to make 20 portions of French Fries?

2 Janina charges $20 per hour for decorating. She works out how much to charge by using this formula:

Total charge in dollars = number of hours × 20

a) How much does she charge for 10 hours of decorating?
b) How much does she charge for 50 hours of decorating?

3 Which is the correct formula for converting weeks (w) into days (d)?
   w = 7d   d = 7w   d = 7 + w   d = w ÷ 7

4 a) Write a formula for the number of minutes, m, in h hours.
    b) Use your formula to find the number of minutes in 50 hours.

Chapter 18: Formulae   147

5 a) Write a formula for the number of grams, x, in y kilograms.
   b) Use your formula to find the number of grams in 14 kilograms.

6 There are 8 tomatoes in a can of tomatoes.
   a) Write a formula for the number of tomatoes, t, in c cans of tomatoes.
   b) Use your formula to find the number of tomatoes in 7 cans of tomatoes.

7 Maya buys books from a website that charges $5 for postage and packing.
   a) Write a formula for her total bill, $t, if the cost of the books is $b.
   b) What is her total bill if she orders books costing $35.

8 Rahman is writing a formula to find the number of hours, h, in d days.
   He says, "There are 24 hours in a day, so $24h = d$".
   Rahman is wrong. Explain the mistake he has made and correct his formula.

9 The cost $c of buying b loaves of bread and having them delivered is given by the formula:
   $c = 2b + 5$
   A cafe uses 100 loaves of bread each week. They can buy 50 loaves twice a week or buy all 100 loaves once a week. What is the difference in cost for the week?

Substitution

Key term

You **substitute** for a variable in a formula by replacing the letter with its known value.

Worked example 2

If $p = 6$ and $q = 4$, find the value of:

a) $p + 7$ b) $15 - p$ c) $3q - 5$ d) $2p + 3q$ e) $2q - p$

a) $p + 7 =$ $6 + 7 = 13$	$p + 7$ means add 7 to the value of p.
b) $15 - p =$ $15 - 6 = 9$	$15 - p$ means subtract the value of p from 15.
c) $3q - 5 =$ $3 \times 4 - 5 = 7$	$3q$ means $3 \times q$ so you need to multiply the value of q by 3 and then subtract 5.
d) $2p + 3q$ $= 12 + 12$ $= 24$	You need to find the value of $2p$ which is $2 \times 6 = 12$ and $3q$ which is $3 \times 4 = 12$ and add them together.
e) $2q - p =$ $2 \times 4 - 6 = 2$	You need to find the value of $2q$, which is $2 \times 4 = 8$ and then subtract the value of p.

Exercise 2   1–6

1 If $x = 5$, find the value of:
   a) $x + 8$ b) $x - 3$ c) $15 - x$
   d) $2x$ e) $3x - 1$ f) $50 - 4x$

2 If $p = 2$ and $q = 6$ find the value of:
   a) $3 + 2p$ b) $20 - 3q$ c) $p + q$
   d) $2p + q$ e) $3q - 6p$ f) $\frac{q}{2}$
   g) $p - \frac{q}{3}$ h) $4p + 6q - 20$

3 If $a = 5$, $b = 6$, $c = 1$ and $d = 9$, find the value of:
   a) $2a + b$ b) $11 + 3b$ c) $3b - a$
   d) $d - 2c$ e) $10c + d$ f) $8a - 3c$

4 A formula states that $p = 4q - 12$
   Find the value of p if:
   a) $q = 6$ b) $q = 3$ c) $q = 12$

5 A formula states that $x = a + 4b$
   Find the value of x if:
   a) $a = 6$ and $b = 4$ b) $a = 9$ and $b = 1$ c) $a = 100$ and $b = 25$ d) $a = 2$ and $b = 9$

6 The cost of hiring a babysitter, C, in dollars for n hours can be found using the formula:
   $C = 8n + 5$
   a) Calculate the cost of hiring the babysitter for 2 hours.
   b) Calculate the cost of hiring the babysitter for 10 hours.

7 The perimeter of a shape, p, can be found using the formula
   $p = 3a + 2b$, where a and b are the lengths of two marked sides.
   Calculate the value of p if:
   a) $a = 5$ and $b = 3$ b) $a = 11$ and $b = 2$
   c) $a = 500$ and $b = 75$ d) $a = 7$ and $b = 3$

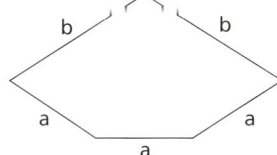

8 Maha has been given this formula:
   $y = 5x + 4$
   Maha has to find the value of y when $x = 3$.
   She says,
   "When $x = 3$, $y = 53 + 4 = 57$"
   Do you agree with Maha? Explain your answer.

9 $A = 2x - 17$
   Use a spreadsheet to enter a formula to work out the value of A for different values of x.

Chapter 18: Formulae   **149**

10 Vocabulary feature question

Match the key term on the left to an example of it on the right.

Expression	$C = 4x - 3$
Formula	The x in $13 = 4x - 3$
Variable	$4x - 3$
Substituting	The x in $C = 4x - 3$
Equation	Replacing the x in $C = 4x - 3$ with a 7
Unknown	$13 = 4x - 3$

End of chapter reflection

You should know that ...	You should be able to ...	Such as ...
A **variable** is a letter that represents a number that can take different values.	Derive a simple formula to connect two variables.	Derive a formula for the number of days, d, in n weeks.
A **formula** represents a mathematical relationship between two or more variables.	Use a simple formula to find missing information.	The cost of hiring a taxi, C, for m miles is represented by $C = 3 + \frac{m}{2}$ Find the cost of hiring the taxi for 10 miles.
Substitution is when you replace a variable with a known value.	Substitute positive numbers into expressions and formulae.	If $A = 5p - q$, calculate the value of A when $p = 3$ and $q = 9$.

Unit 2B • Chapter 19

Coordinates, functions, graphs and equations

You will learn how to:
- Read and plot coordinates of points determined by geometric information in all four quadrants.
- Represent simple functions using words, symbols and mappings.
- Generate coordinate pairs that satisfy a linear equation, where y is given explicitly in terms of x; plot the corresponding graphs; recognise straight-line graphs parallel to the x- or y-axis.
- Construct and solve simple linear equations with integer coefficients (unknown on one side only), for example, $2x = 8$, $3x + 5 = 14$, $9 - 2x = 7$.

Starting point

Do you remember …?

- how to plot a coordinate?
  For example, plot the point (3, 1).
- how to substitute into a formula?
  For example, substitute $x = 4$ into the formula $A = 3x + 5$?
- how to solve a problem using inverse operations?
  For example, I think of a number and multiply it by 2. I then subtract 4. What number did I start with?

This will be helpful when …

you learn how to plot the graphs of more complex functions and solve equations with unknowns in more than one place.

Hook

COORDINATE GAME!

A game for 3 or more players.

You will need:
- two sets of number cards −5 to 5
- a copy of the axes shown

How to play:

Each player draws three lines on their axes: one horizontal, one vertical and one at an angle.

Players take it in turns to choose a card at random from each set to generate a coordinate. For example, if the cards selected were a 2 and then a 3, the coordinate would be (2, 3).

Players mark off the coordinates on their grid as they occur.

A player wins when they get 3 coordinates on any of their lines.

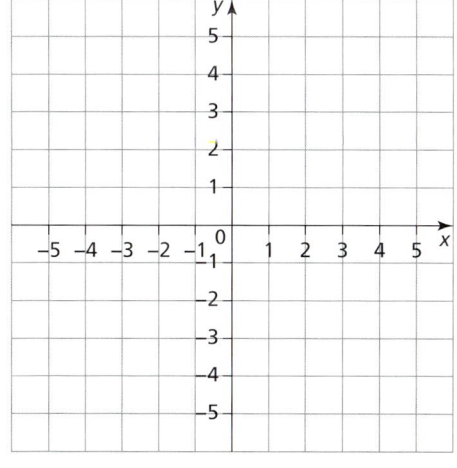

Chapter 19: Coordinates, functions, graphs and equations

Coordinates

In this chapter you will explore how coordinates that lie on a line together are related.

> **Think about**
> What do you notice about the coordinates of the points on each of your horizontal lines? The vertical lines? What about the diagonal ones?

Worked example 1

a) Plot these points with the coordinates shown:

   A (2, 4)   B (2, –1)   C (–4, –3)

b) Shape ABCD is a parallelogram.

   Write the coordinates of point D.

a) A = (2, 4) 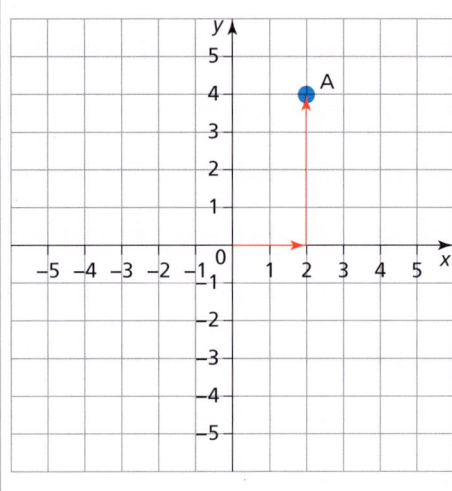	You read a coordinate as a position relative to (0, 0). The first number tells you how far to move horizontally. The second number tells you how far to move vertically. So (2, 4) can be represented by the point that is 2 units right and 4 units up from (0, 0).
B = (2, –1) 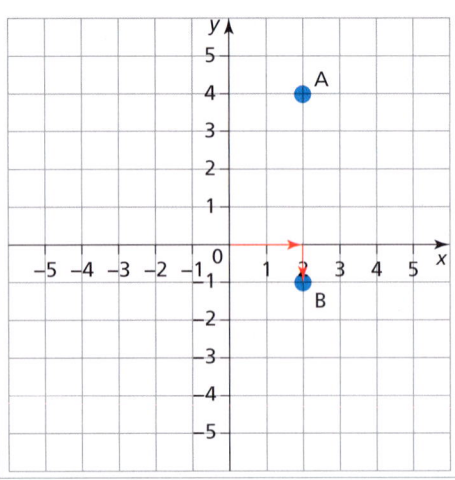	(2, –1) is a point that is 2 units right and one unit down from (0, 0).

152   Unit 2B: Algebra and measures

C = (−4, −3)

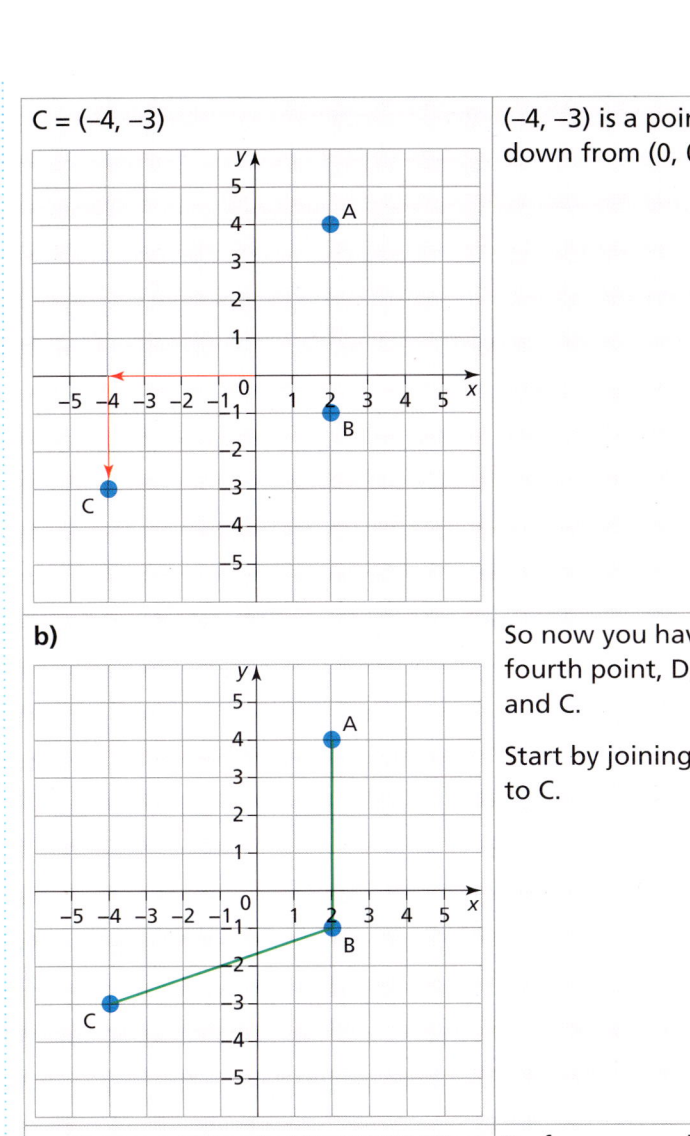

(−4, −3) is a point that is found 4 units left and 3 units down from (0, 0).

b)

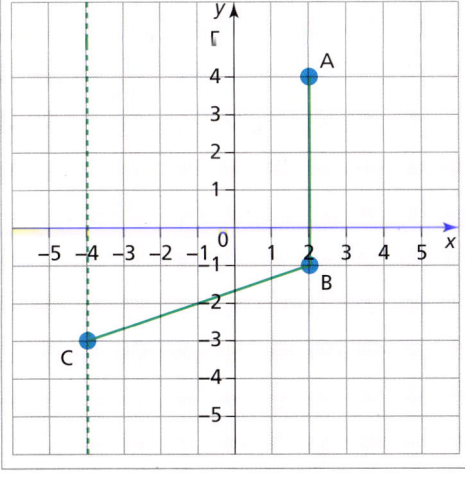

So now you have all three points, you have to find a fourth point, D, that forms a parallelogram with A, B and C.

Start by joining the points together in order: A to B then to C.

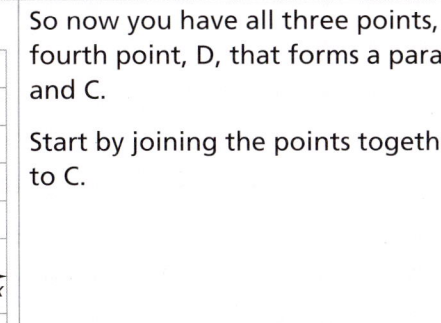

To form a parallelogram, point D must lie on a vertical line from C.

D is (−4, 2)

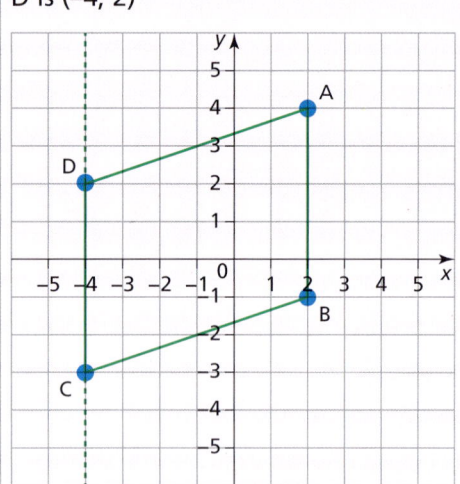

Point D must be 5 squares above the point C as the sides AB and CD must have the same length.

So point D is at (−4, 2).

Exercise 1

1 Write down the coordinates of points A to J in this diagram.

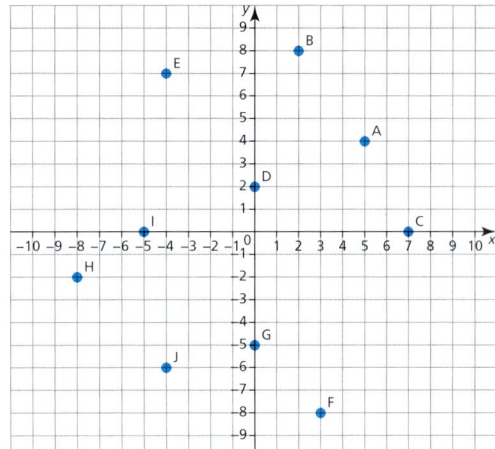

2 Make a copy of these axes and plot the points with coordinates listed.

A) (6, 3)
B) (2, 9)
C) (0, 3)
D) (−2, 5)
E) (0, −6)
F) (−3, −7)
G) (−2, 0)
H) (4, −9)

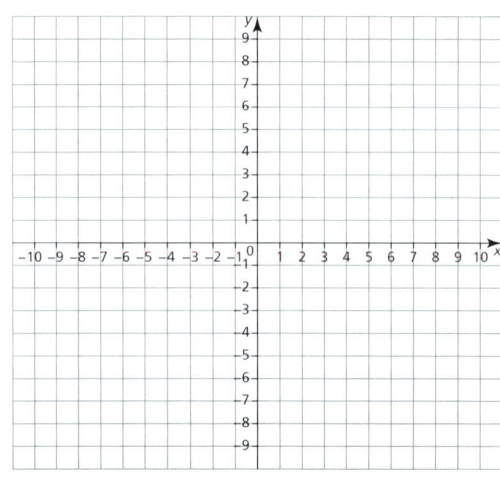

154   Unit 2B: Algebra and measures

3 **a)** Plot these coordinates:

A = (−2, 8)   B = (1, 8)   C = (1, −3)

b) Shape ABCD is a rectangle.

Write down the coordinates of point D.

4 **a)** Plot these coordinates:

A = (−2, −3)   B = (4, −3)

b) Shape ABC is an isosceles triangle.

Write down two of the possible sets of coordinates of point C.

5 **a)** Plot these coordinates:

A = (−5, −2)   B = (−3, 3)   C = (4, 3)

b) Shape ABCD a parallelogram.

Write down the coordinates of point D.

6 **a)** Plot these coordinates:

A = (−2, 1)   B = (0, −2)   C = (−2, −5)

b) Shape ABCD a rhombus.

Write down the coordinates of point D.

c) Shape ABCE is a kite.

Write down a possible set of coordinates for point E.

7 How many different coordinate pairs can you form using the numbers 4 and −3? How do you know you have got them all?

What shape will they form when you plot them?

Is this always true for every pair of numbers that you can choose?

Mappings

Key term

A **function** is a mathematical process that converts an **input** value to an **output** value.

You can express a **function** as a series of operations (like a **function machine**) or using algebra as an **equation** or **mapping**.

You use a $\mapsto$ sign to represent a **mapping**, for example $x \mapsto x + 5$ means that the **input** x goes to an **output** of $x + 5$.

You can show the effect of a function using a **table** of input and output values or a **mapping diagram**.

Worked example 2

a) Here is a function machine.

Copy and complete the table of inputs and outputs for the machine.

input	output
1	
5	12
7	18
10	

b) Another function machine has the function $x \mapsto 2x - 1$.

Represent this function on a copy of this mapping diagram.

```
0  1  2  3  4  5  6  7  8  9  10

0  1  2  3  4  5  6  7  8  9  10
```

a) For an input of 1, $1 - 1 = 0$ $0 \times 3 = 0$ the output will be 0. For an input of 10, $10 - 1 = 9$ $9 \times 3 = 27$ the output will be 27. 	input	output
---	---
1	**0**
5	12
7	18
10	**27**		You need to work out the output when the input is 1 and when the input is 10.	The function machine tells you to take each input, then subtract one and then multiply by 3. $1 \rightarrow$ Subtract 1 $\xrightarrow{0}$ Multiply by 3 $\rightarrow 0$ $10 \rightarrow$ Subtract 1 $\xrightarrow{9}$ Multiply by 3 $\rightarrow 27$
b) $x \mapsto 2x - 1$ You need to multiply your number by 2... and then subtract 1. Input Output 1 $2 \times \mathbf{1} - 1 = 1$ 2 $2 \times \mathbf{2} - 1 = 3$ 3 $2 \times \mathbf{3} - 1 = 5$ 4 $2 \times \mathbf{4} - 1 = 7$ 5 $2 \times \mathbf{5} - 1 = 9$ 6 $2 \times \mathbf{6} - 1 = 11$	$x \mapsto 2x - 1$ means that an input of x becomes an output of $2x - 1$. You need to multiply your number by 2 and then subtract 1.	You could write this mapping as a function machine like: 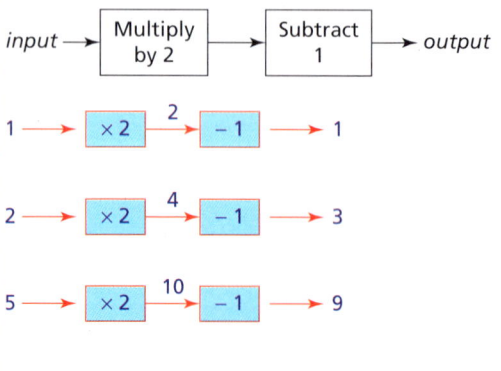

Unit 2B: Algebra and measures

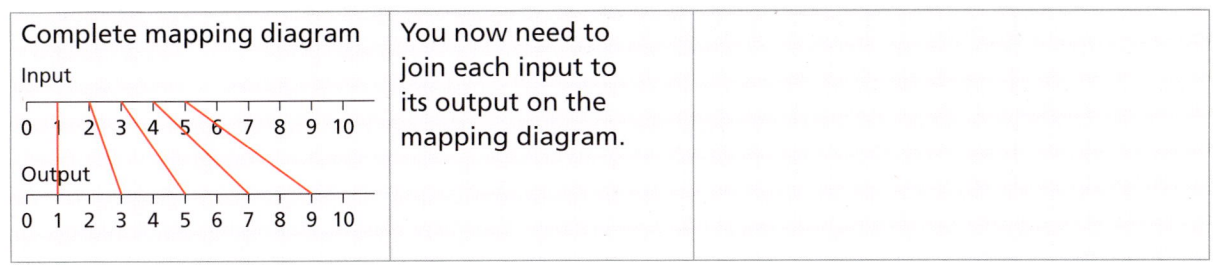

Exercise 2

1 Here is a function machine:

input ⟶ [Multiply by 5] ⟶ output

Copy and complete the table of inputs and outputs for this machine.

input	output
1	5
4	20
7	
10	
	25

2 Here is a function machine:

input ⟶ [Add 3] ⟶ [Divide by 2] ⟶ output

Copy and complete the table of inputs and outputs for this machine.

input	output
1	2
11	7
5	
9	
12	

3 Here is a function machine.

input ⟶ [Multiply by 10] ⟶ [Subtract 7] ⟶ output

Chapter 19: Coordinates, functions, graphs and equations 157

Copy and complete the table of inputs and outputs for this machine.

input	output
1	3
5	43
10	
13	
	193

4 For each table of inputs and outputs, suggest a function machine.

a)
input	output
1	3
2	6
3	9
4	12
5	15

b)
input	output
1	5
2	6
3	7
4	8
5	9

c)
input	output
1	11
2	21
3	31
4	41
5	51

5 Copy and complete these mappings for the function $x \mapsto 3x - 1$.

a) $1 \mapsto$ b) $4 \mapsto$ c) $10 \mapsto$ d) $11 \mapsto$ e) $50 \mapsto$

6 Afia is using this function machine.

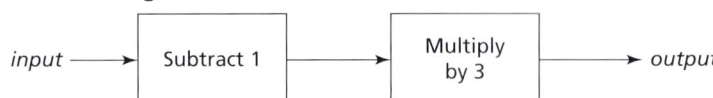

Afia says, "I can work out what the input was by multiplying the output by 3 and subtracting 1."

Do you agree with Afia? Explain your answer.

7 a) For each function produce a mapping diagram.

i) $x \mapsto x + 2$ ii) $x \mapsto 2x$ iii) $x \mapsto x - 3$

iv) $x \mapsto 3x$ v) $x \mapsto \frac{x}{2}$ vi) $x \mapsto 2x + 1$

vii) $x \mapsto 3x - 4$

b) Look at your diagrams. What do you notice about the gap between the numbers on the bottom of each diagram and the number in front of x?

8 Draw a function machine to represent these mappings.

a) $x \mapsto x + 2$ b) $x \mapsto 4x$ c) $x \mapsto x - 9$

d) $x \mapsto \frac{x}{3}$ e) $x \mapsto 3x + 2$ f) $x \mapsto \frac{x}{2} + 1$

Linear equations and their graphs

Worked example 3

Here is the equation of a line: $y = 2x - 3$

a) Find the coordinates of three points on this line.

b) Plot the graph of $y = 2x - 3$ for values of x between 0 and 6 inclusive.

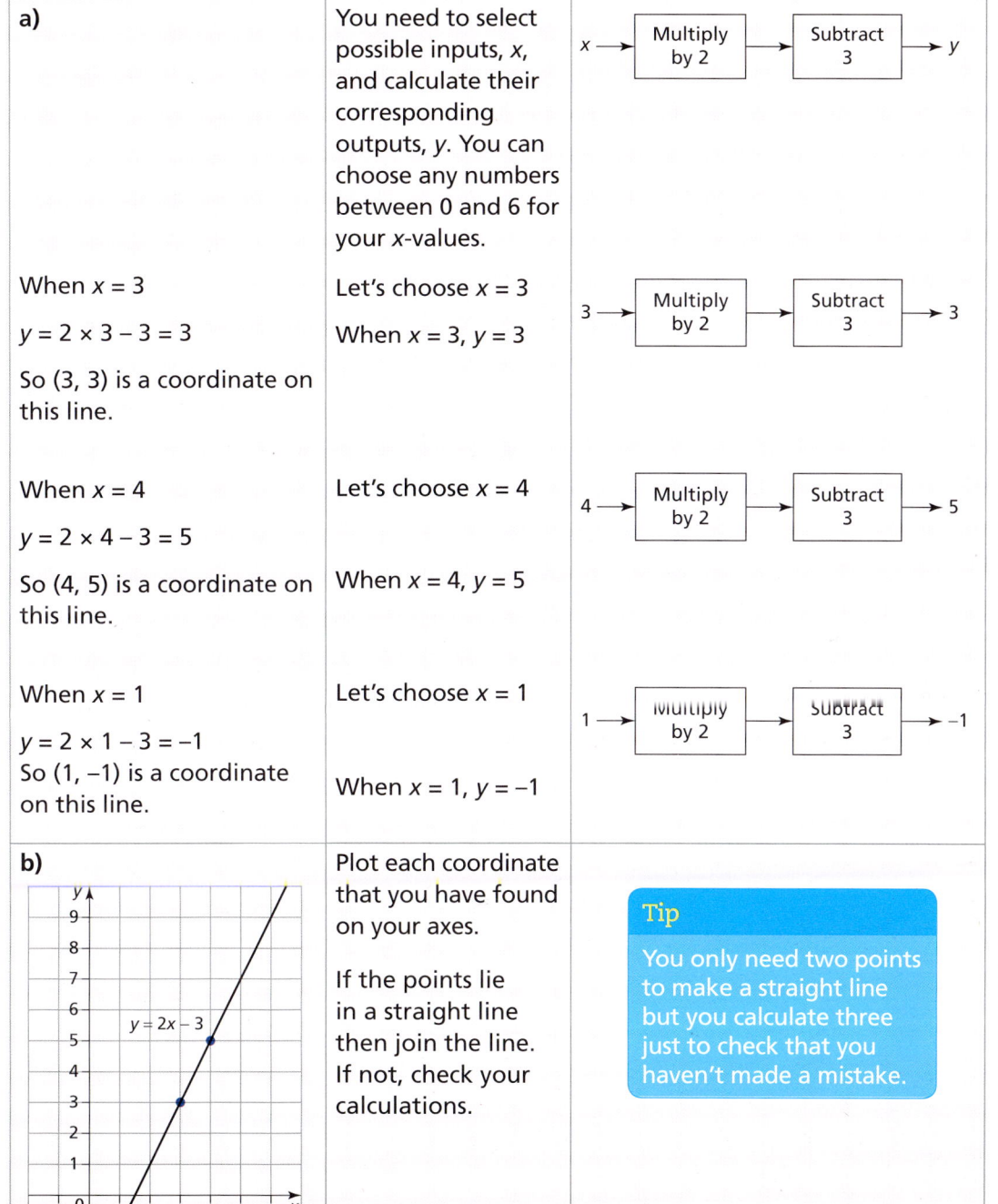

a)

You need to select possible inputs, x, and calculate their corresponding outputs, y. You can choose any numbers between 0 and 6 for your x-values.

When $x = 3$
$y = 2 \times 3 - 3 = 3$
So (3, 3) is a coordinate on this line.

Let's choose $x = 3$
When $x = 3$, $y = 3$

When $x = 4$
$y = 2 \times 4 - 3 = 5$
So (4, 5) is a coordinate on this line.

Let's choose $x = 4$
When $x = 4$, $y = 5$

When $x = 1$
$y = 2 \times 1 - 3 = -1$
So (1, -1) is a coordinate on this line.

Let's choose $x = 1$
When $x = 1$, $y = -1$

b) Plot each coordinate that you have found on your axes.

If the points lie in a straight line then join the line. If not, check your calculations.

Tip

You only need two points to make a straight line but you calculate three just to check that you haven't made a mistake.

Chapter 19: Coordinates, functions, graphs and equations   159

Worked example 4

Identify the equations of lines A and B shown in the diagram.

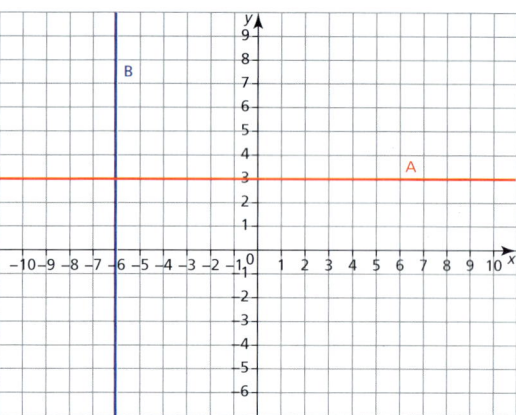

A: Points on the line are (0, 3), (1, 3), (2, 3) … . Every point on line A has a *y*-coordinate of 3.

Therefore, the equation of line A is *y* = 3.

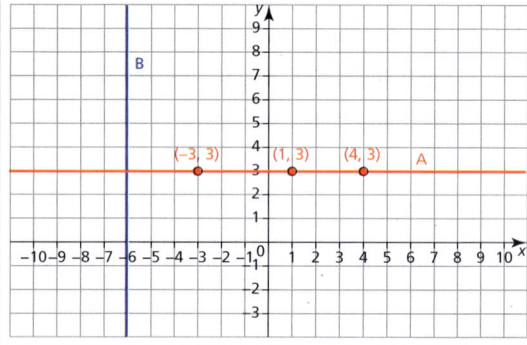

B: Points on this line are (–6, 0), (–6, 1), (–6, 2) … .
The *x*-coordinate of every point is –6.

Therefore, the equation of line B is *x* = –6.

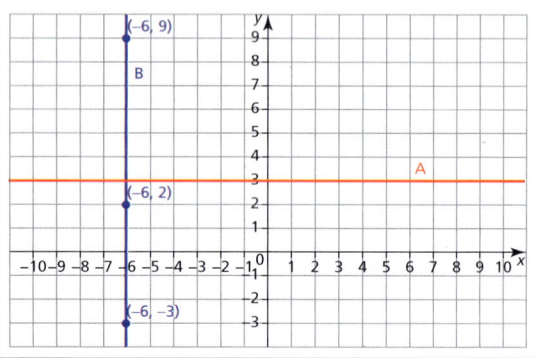

Exercise 3   1–9

1 Copy and complete the missing coordinates of points on the line *y* = 4*x* + 1.
   a) (2, ….)   b) (5, ….)   c) (0, ….)   d) (1, ….)   e) (–2, ….)

2 Copy and complete this table of coordinates for the line *y* = 3*x* + 7.

x	0	1	2	3	4	5
y						

160   Unit 2B: Algebra and measures

3 Copy and complete this table of coordinates for the line $y = 2x - 4$.

x	0	1	2	3	4	5
y						

4 Give the coordinates of three points on each of these lines. Use values of x from 0 to 6.
  a) $y = 2x$
  b) $y = 3x$
  c) $y = x + 1$
  d) $y = x - 3$
  e) $y = 2x + 5$
  f) $y = 3x - 1$

5 Draw a graph of each of the equations in Question 4.
Use values of x from 0 to 6.

6 Using values of x from 0 to 6 inclusive:
  a) Calculate the coordinates of three points on the line $y = x + 4$
  b) Use these three coordinates to draw the line $y = x + 4$

7 Using values of x from 0 to 6 inclusive:
  a) Calculate the coordinates of three points on the line $y = 2x - 1$
  b) Use these three coordinates to draw the line $y = 2x - 1$

8 a) For each of the lines A to H in the diagram, give the coordinates of three points on the line.
  b) Use your answers to part a) to give the equation of each of the lines.

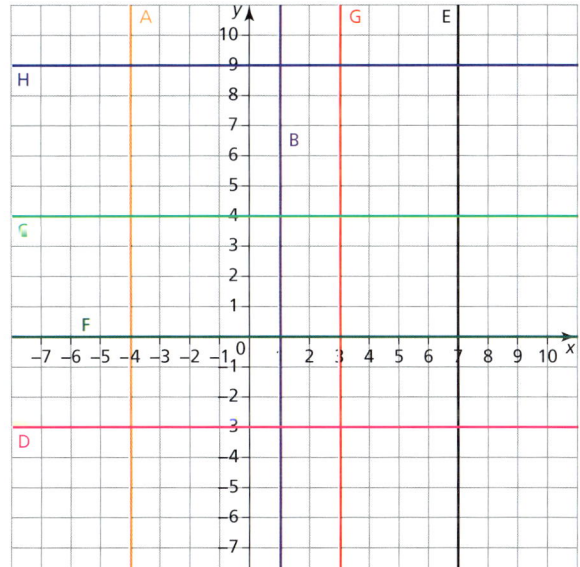

9 Give the coordinates of three points on each of these lines.
  a) $y = 2$
  b) $x = 5$
  c) $y = 0$
  d) $y = -4$

Chapter 19: Coordinates, functions, graphs and equations

10 Which of the following points lie on the line $y = 2x - 6$?

a) (3, 0)   b) (4, 2)   c) (8, 12)   d) (15, 26)   e) (20, 34)

11 On the same set of axes, draw the graphs of:

a) $y = -4$ b) $x = -2$ c) $x = 0$ d) $y = 3$

12 True or false?

The x-axis has equation $y = 0$.

13 a) Which horizontal and vertical lines does the point (3, 1) lie on?

b) Which horizontal and vertical lines does the point (a, b) lie on?

14 Use graphing software to plot the graphs of:

- $y = x + 5$
- $y = x + 8$
- $y = x - 3$

If you do not have graphing software then draw the lines on graph paper.

What do you notice about where each of your graphs crosses the y-axis?

Can you predict what the graph of $y = x + 12$ will look like?

Check your answer.

> **Think about**
>
> Can you think of a quick method for drawing the graph of a line like $y = 4$ without generating lots of coordinates?

Solving equations

Key term

Sometimes you use a letter to represent an **unknown** value that you want to find.

You can find the value of an **unknown** when you have an **equation**. You often use x to represent an unknown, but any letter can be used.

An **equation** is a mathematical statement that includes an equals sign (=).

Solving an equation means finding the value of the unknown quantity. If the equation is $2x + 3 = 17$ then solving it means finding the value of x on its own.

> **Tip**
>
> To keep an equation balanced you must always do exactly the same things to both sides of the equation. Think about $4 + 2 = 6$. If you add 3 to the left hand side you will get $4 + 2 + 3$. To keep the two sides equal you would then need to add 3 to the right hand side too because $4 + 2 + 3 = 6 + 3$.

Worked example 5

Solve these **equations**:

a) $3x = 12$ b) $2x + 3 = 17$ c) $20 = 3x - 1$

| a) $3x = 12$ $\div 3 \downarrow \quad \downarrow \div 3$ $x = 4$ | Divide both the 12 and the $3x$ by 3 to find the value of each x. So each x is worth 4. | You can represent the equation $3x = 12$ using a bar model.

 \| x \| x \| x \|
 \| 12 \|

 \| x \| x \| x \|
 \| $12 \div 3$ \| $12 \div 3$ \| $12 \div 3$ \|

 \| x \|
 \| 4 \| |

Unit 2B: Algebra and measures

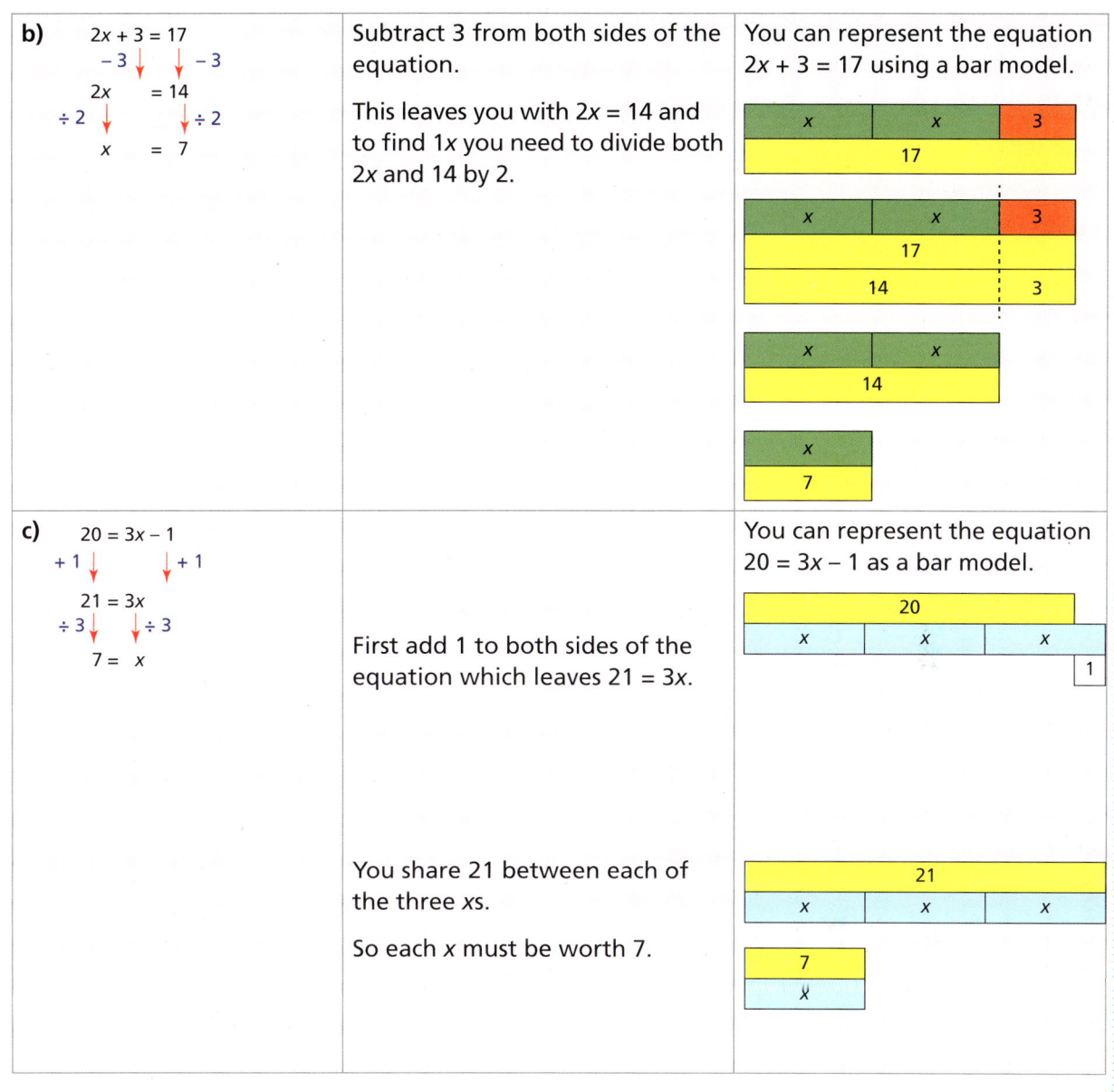

b)	$2x + 3 = 17$ $-3 -3$ $2x = 14$ $\div 2 \div 2$ $x = 7$	Subtract 3 from both sides of the equation. This leaves you with $2x = 14$ and to find $1x$ you need to divide both $2x$ and 14 by 2.	You can represent the equation $2x + 3 = 17$ using a bar model.
c)	$20 = 3x - 1$ $+1 +1$ $21 = 3x$ $\div 3 \div 3$ $7 = x$	First add 1 to both sides of the equation which leaves $21 = 3x$. You share 21 between each of the three xs. So each x must be worth 7.	You can represent the equation $20 = 3x - 1$ as a bar model.

> **Tip**
>
> It does not matter if you swap around the two sides of an equation, they are still equal.
>
> $3 + 4 = 7$ is the same as
>
> $7 = 3 + 4$

> **Tip**
>
> You can check that you have the correct value for x by putting that value of x back into the equation. In part c) of Worked example 5 you saw that if $20 = 3x - 1$ then $x = 7$. To check you need to see if $20 = 3 \times 7 - 1$, which it does.

Chapter 19: Coordinates, functions, graphs and equations

Worked example 6

Solve $20 - 3x = 11$

$20 - 3x = 11$
$+ 3x \downarrow \quad \downarrow + 3x$
$20 = 11 + 3x$
$-11 \downarrow \quad \downarrow -11$
$9 = 3x$
$\div 3 \downarrow \quad \downarrow \div 3$
$3 = x$

Add $3x$ to both sides of the equation.

Subtract 11 from both sides of the equation.

So you have $9 = 3x$. Share 9 between each of the three xs.

Each x must be worth 3.

You can represent the equation $20 = 11 + 3x$ as a bar model.

This shows us that $20 = 11 + 3x$

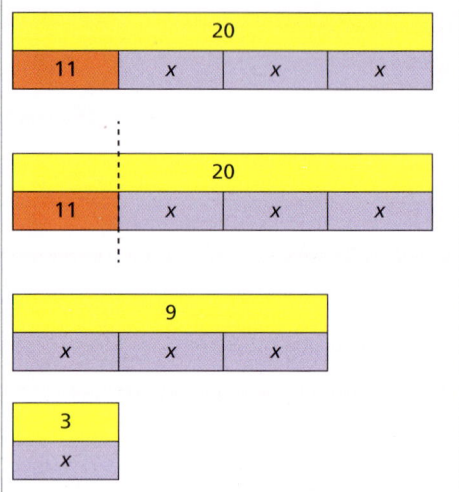

Exercise 4

1. Solve these equations to find the value of x:
   a) $2x = 16$
   b) $3x = 21$
   c) $9x = 36$
   d) $22 = 2x$
   e) $18 = 3x$

2. Solve these equations to find the value of x:
   a) $x + 5 = 11$
   b) $x - 2 = 20$
   c) $14 = x + 3$
   d) $8 = x - 5$
   e) $2 = x - 3$

3. Solve these equations to find the value of x:
   a) $2x + 3 = 11$
   b) $3x + 9 = 21$
   c) $4x + 7 = 27$
   d) $2 + 6x = 26$
   e) $5 + 3x = 14$
   f) $20 = 3x + 2$
   g) $31 = 7x + 3$
   h) $38 = 3x + 14$

4. Solve these equations to find the value of x:
   a) $2x - 3 = 13$
   b) $6x - 9 = 21$
   c) $5x - 2 = 23$
   d) $7x - 1 = 27$
   e) $4x - 3 = 17$
   f) $25 = 8x - 7$
   g) $21 = 3x - 6$
   h) $34 = 7x - 8$

5. Solve these equations to find the value of the unknown:
   a) $12 - x = 4$
   b) $14 = 19 - x$
   c) $11 - 2x = 7$
   d) $18 - 4x = 6$
   e) $25 - 3x = 16$
   f) $32 - 5x = 7$
   g) $40 - 6x = 4$
   h) $17 = 31 - 2x$

6. Which is the odd one out? Explain your answer.

   A: $3x - 4 = 23$
   B: $1 + 2x = 19$
   C: $40 = 6x - 8$
   D: $7x = 63$
   E: $39 = 4x + 3$

7 Pamela is solving the equation $2x + 1 = 33$.

Here is her working out:

$$2x + 1 = 33$$
$$3x = 33$$
$$x = 11$$

Explain what Pamela has done wrong and correct her solution.

8 Quentin is solving the equation $2x - 7 = 17$

Here is his working out:

$$2x - 7 = 17$$
$$2x = 10$$
$$x = 5$$

Explain what Quentin has done wrong and correct his solution.

9 Here is a shape with a perimeter of 42 cm:

a) Write an expression, in terms of x, for the perimeter of this shape.

b) Use this expression to write an equation for the perimeter.

c) Solve this equation to find the value of x.

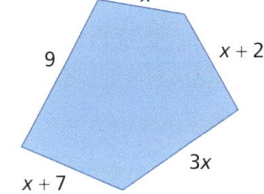

10 Ellen thinks of a number, x. She multiplies her number by 3 and then adds 2. She gets an answer of 23.

a) Write an equation in x to represent this number puzzle.

b) Solve your equation to find x.

11 Pedro has 4 identical packets of biscuits. Each packet contains x biscuits.

One packet has been opened and 3 biscuits have been removed.

a) Write an expression using x for the number of biscuits that Pedro has in total.

Pedro has 53 biscuits.

b) Write an equation in x to show this information

c) Solve your equation to find x, the number of biscuits in a packet.

12 Ajay's mother is 42. Ajay notices that if he triples his age and subtracts 3, the answer is his mother's age. Let x be Ajay's age.

Write and solve an equation to find the value of x.

13 **Vocabulary feature question**

Complete the sentences with a key term selected from the box.

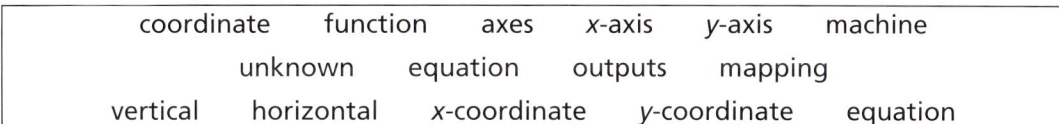

You can plot a point on a graph if you have its .... and a set of ....

In a coordinate the first number is the ...., which tells you how far to move horizontally.

The second number is the .... which tells you how far to move vertically.

Chapter 19: Coordinates, functions, graphs and equations

When points lie on a line together, their coordinates fit a rule connecting x and y – this is called a ....

You can represent a function using a function .... to show how the rule converts different inputs into ....

You can also represent a function using a .... diagram, which shows how each input connects with its output.

Some straight line graphs have special equations. Graphs that are .... have equations like x = a and graphs that are .... have equations like y = a.

Another name for the .... is the line x = 0 and another name for the .... is the line y = 0.

You can find the value of a letter or an .... by solving an ....

To solve an equation you must carry out the same operations to each side of the ....

End of chapter reflection

You should know that ...	You should be able to ...	Such as ...
A coordinate (x, y) represents a point that is reached by moving x units horizontally and y units vertically from (0,0).	Solve geometric coordinate problems.	Shape ABCD is a parallelogram. A = (–2, 6), B = (5, 6), C = (3, –2). Find the coordinates of point D.
A function is a mathematical process linking inputs to outputs.	Use a function machine to find output values and input values in simple cases.	Here is a function machine. input → Add 4 → Multiply by 5 → output Use the machine to copy and complete this table of inputs and outputs. | x	2x – 1
---	---
2	30
5	
	100	
A function can be expressed as a function machine, as a mapping or as an equation and its graph.	Use a mapping to find outputs from given inputs. Create a mapping diagram to show the effect of a function.	Here is a mapping $x \mapsto x + 7$ Copy and complete these outputs $2 \mapsto$ $5 \mapsto$ Represent $x \mapsto x + 7$ using a mapping diagram. 0 1 2 3 4 5 6 7 8 9 10 0 1 2 3 4 5 6 7 8 9 10

Unit 2B: Algebra and measures

You should know that ...	You should be able to ...	Such as ...
	Suggest a function given the inputs and outputs.	Here are some inputs and outputs of a function. $2 \mapsto 8$ $5 \mapsto 20$ $10 \mapsto 40$ What is the function? Give your answer as a mapping.
	Generate coordinates for a given equation.	Generate three coordinates on the line $y = 6x - 5$.
	Plot a graph of a given equation.	Plot a graph of $y = 2x - 1$ for values of x between 0 and 5.
	Say whether a coordinate lies on a given line.	Does the coordinate (2, 3) line on the line $y = 3x - 5$?
	Name the equation of a horizontal or vertical line.	State the equations of these two lines.
An equation is a mathematical statement containing an equals sign. You can solve an equation to find the value of an unknown by carrying out the same operations to both sides of the equation.	Solve an equation to find the value of its unknown.	Solve: a) $3x = 27$ b) $21 = 2x - 1$ c) $25 - 4x = 17$
	Construct an equation to solve a problem.	The perimeter of this rectangle is 34 cm. Write and solve an equation to find the value of the width and length.

Chapter 19: Coordinates, functions, graphs and equations

2C

Unit 2C
Handling data and geometry

What's it all about?
- Angle facts
- Symmetry
- Displaying data using a range of graphs
- Theoretical and experimental probabilities

You will learn about:
- Angle properties related to parallel lines, perpendicular lines and transversals
- The angle sum at a point, on a straight line, in a triangle and in a quadrilateral
- How to identify line symmetry and rotational symmetry
- How to find the mode, median, mean and range of a data set
- How to draw and interpret a range of diagrams
- How to identify all the possible mutually exclusive outcomes of a single event
- Using experimental data to estimate probabilities
- Comparing theoretical and experimental probabilities

You will build your skills in:
- Problem solving in geometry
- Presenting data

Unit 2C • Chapter 20

Angles

You will learn how to:
- Start to recognise the angular connections between parallel lines, perpendicular lines and transversals.
- Calculate the sum of angles at a point, on a straight line and in a triangle, and prove that vertically opposite angles are equal; derive and use the property that the angle sum of a quadrilateral is 360°.

Starting point

Do you remember …?

- what is meant by parallel lines?

  For example, can you draw a pair of parallel lines?

- what is meant by perpendicular lines?

  For example, can you draw a pair of perpendicular lines?

- what is meant by an acute angle, a right angle and an obtuse angle?

  For example, identify an acute angle, a right angle and an obtuse angle in the shape shown.

- the side and angle properties of special triangles and quadrilaterals?

  For example, what are the properties of an equilateral triangle?

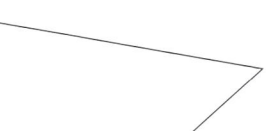

This will be helpful when …

- you learn more about solving geometrical problems.

Hook

Mia is investigating quadrilaterals. She has drawn a square and measured its angles.

She notices that the angles add up to 360°.

Mia wants to know whether the angles in all quadrilaterals add up to 360°.

Draw some different quadrilaterals and investigate the sum of their angles. You could draw a rectangle, a parallelogram, a rhombus, a trapezium, a kite, a delta, etc.

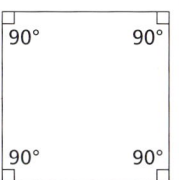

Angles and parallel lines

Discuss

If you know three angles in a quadrilateral, can you always work out the fourth angle?

If you know fewer than three angles in a quadrilateral, is it possible to work out the other missing angles? What properties might help you to do this?

- Parallel lines are shown using sets of arrows

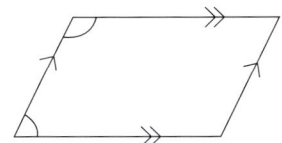

Worked example 1

Use your protractor to measure the angles in this diagram. Find as many 60° angles as possible.

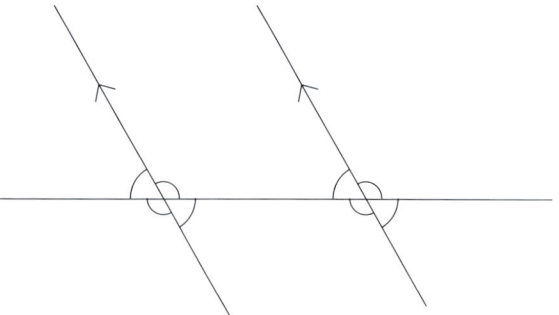

Use your protractor to measure the angles.	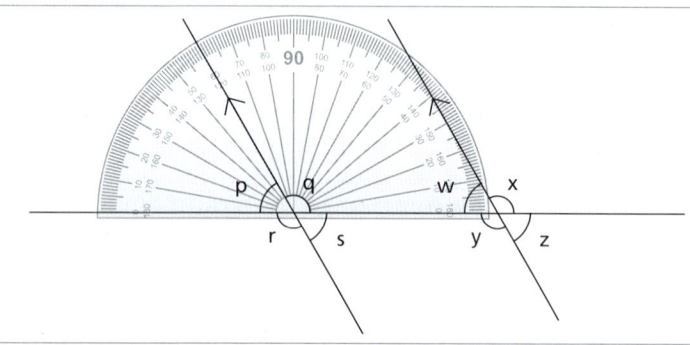
p = 60° s = 60° w = 60° z = 60°	If you measure the angles you can see that these angles are all 60°.

Worked example 2

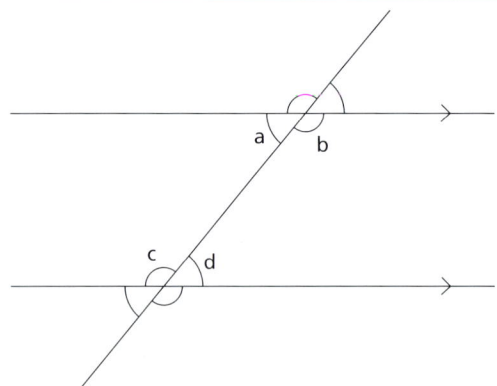

a) Write down a pair of angles that are the same size in this diagram.
b) Write down a second pair of angles that are the same size in this diagram.

170   Unit 2C: Handling data and geometry

a) Measure the angles using a protractor. 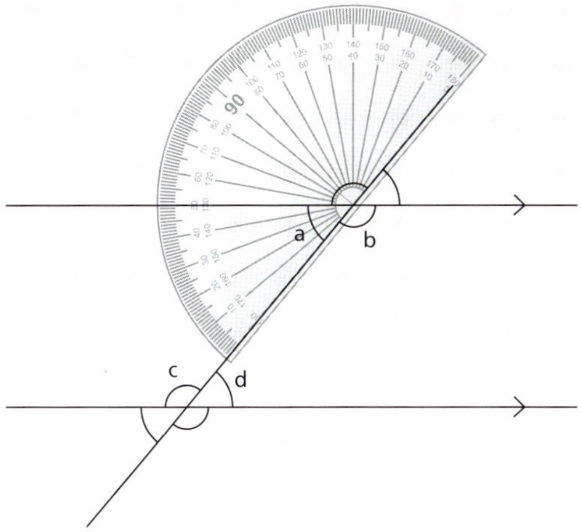 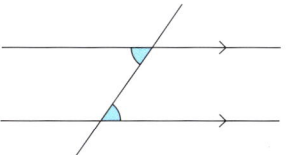 a = 50° b = 130° c = 130° d = 50° a = d = 50°	Start by comparing the sizes of the angles in the diagram. Now look at the angle sizes and identify a pair of angles the same size.	Use tracing paper to draw around one angle and then compare this to the others to see which are the same size.
b) b = c = 130°	Now look at the angle sizes and identify a second pair of angles that are the same size.	Use tracing paper to draw around a different angle and compare this with the others to see which are the same size.

The pair of angles shaded in blue in each of these diagrams are equal.

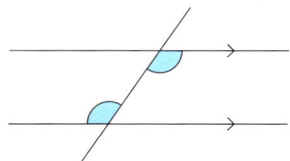

These are called **alternate angles**. You will work with this rule now, but you won't need to remember that these are called alternate angles until stage 8.

Worked example 3

In this diagram, which labelled angle is equal to angle a?

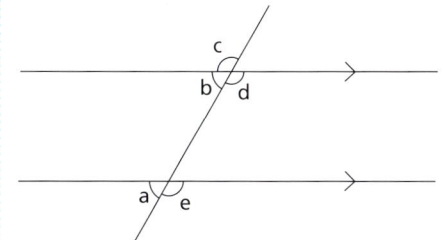

Chapter 20: Angles   **171**

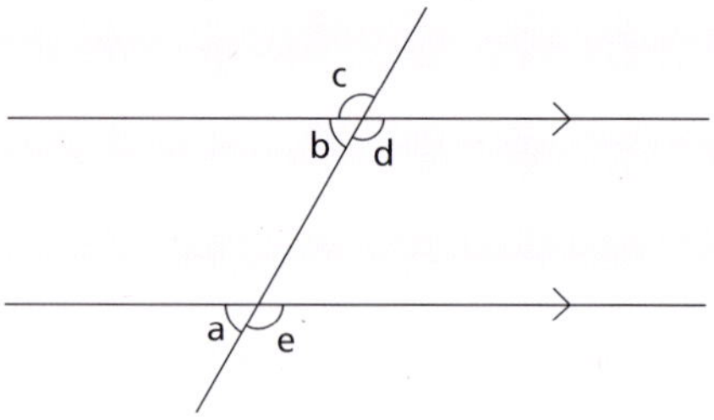 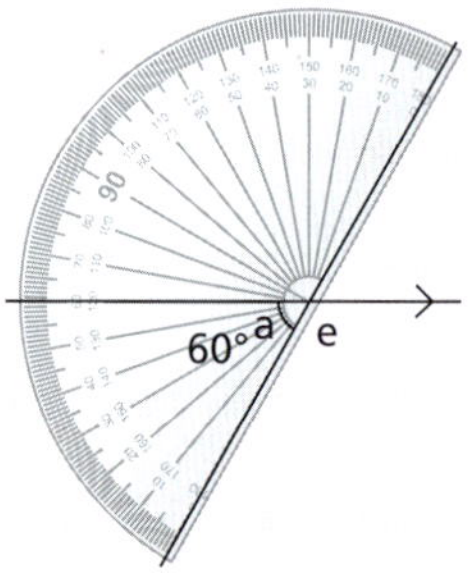 Measure the angles in the diagram using your protractor.	To identify the angle that is equal to angle a, you need to compare the size of the angles.	Use tracing paper to draw around angle a. 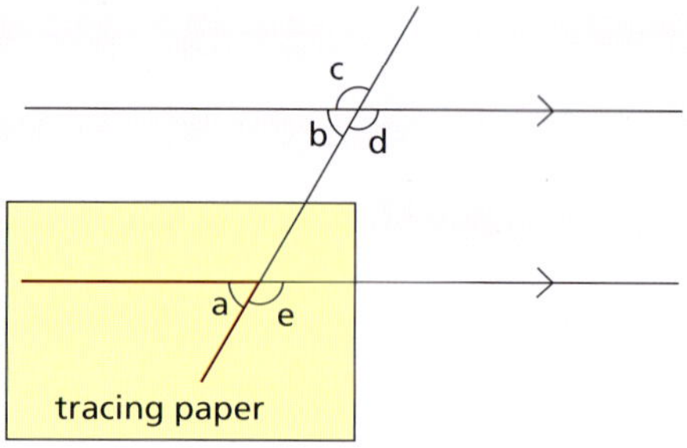
a = 60° b = 60° c = 120° d = 120° e = 120°		
Comparing the sizes of the angles you have measured, you can see that angle a and angle b are the same size.	Compare the size of the angles.	Compare angle a to the other angles using the tracing paper. Angle b is the only labelled angle that matches the tracing of angle a.

The pair of angles shaded in green in each of these diagrams are equal.

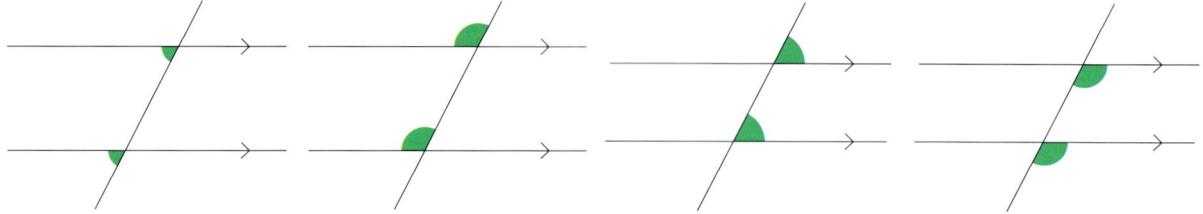

These are called **corresponding angles**. You will work with this rule now, but you won't need to remember that these are called corresponding angles until Stage 8.

Key term

A **transversal** is a line crossing two or more parallel lines.

Exercise 1

In these questions use the angle properties we have identified (alternate angles and corresponding angles).

1 Work out the size of the angle marked with a letter in each part.

a)   b)   c)   d)

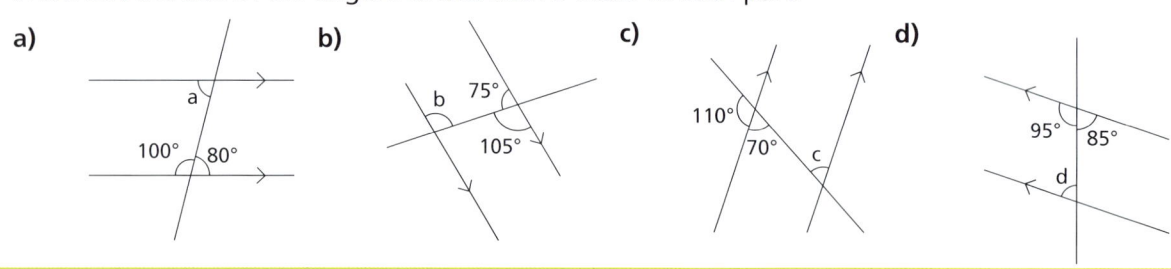

2 Write down pairs of angles that are equal in this diagram.

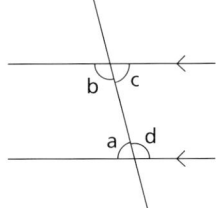

3 Work out the size of the angle marked with a letter in each part.

a)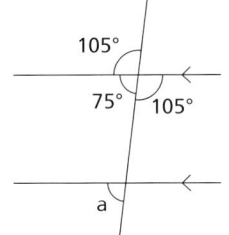
b)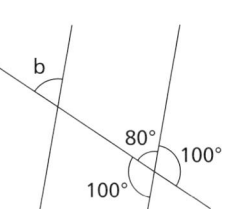
c)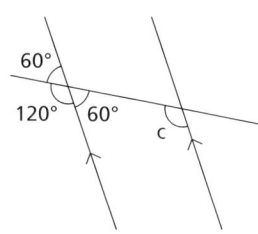
d)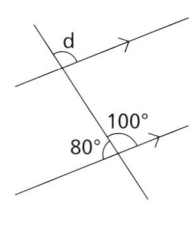

4 Write down pairs of angles that are equal in each of these diagrams.

a)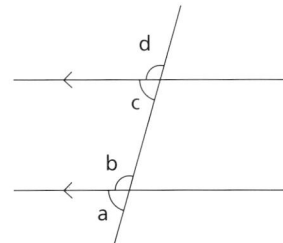
b)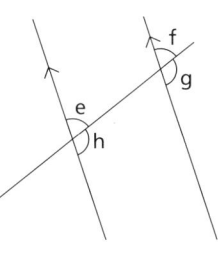

5 Work out the size of the angle marked with a letter in each part.

a)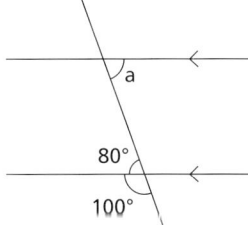
b)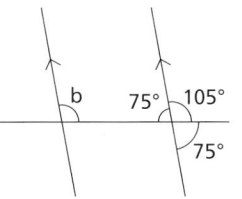
c)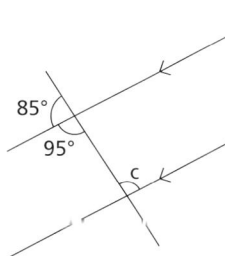
d)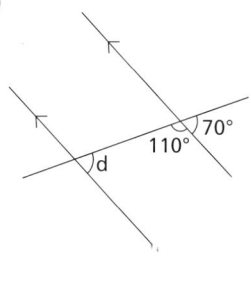

6 Safia has been investigating angles formed by parallel lines and transversals.

She has drawn this diagram.

Safia says that all of the angles formed by a line crossing a pair of parallel lines are equal.

Is Safia correct? Explain your answer.

7 Write an equation linking a and b in this diagram.

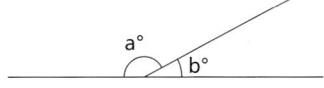

Chapter 20: Angles **173**

8 **Vocabulary feature question**

Using the diagram, complete the statements using words from the boxes.

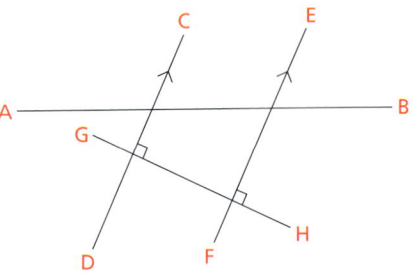

| TRANSVERSAL | PARALLEL | PERPENDICULAR |

CD and EF are _____ .

CD and GH are _____ .

AB is a _____ .

Calculating angles

Key term

Vertically opposite angles at a point are equal.
The angles shaded green in the diagram are equal.
The angles shaded blue in the diagram are equal.

Worked example 4

Find the size of angle a. Explain your answer.

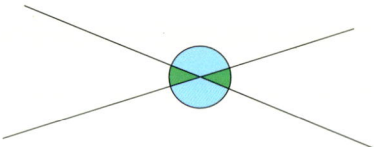
Not accurate

Angle a is equal to the angle labelled 55°. 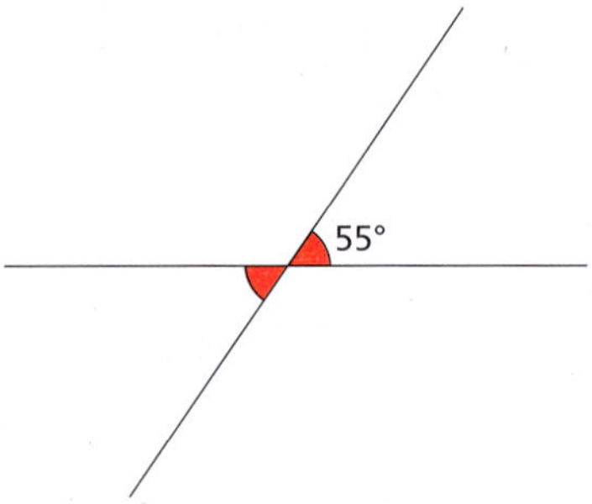 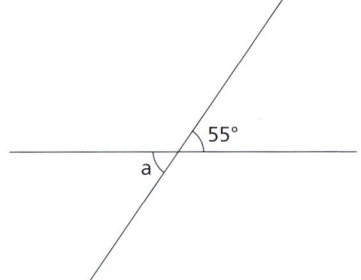 a = 55°	You need to find the size of angle a.
The 55° angle and angle a are vertically opposite. Vertically opposite angles are equal.	You are asked to give a reason – you need to give an angle fact.

174   Unit 2C: Handling data and geometry

Key term

The **angles on a straight line** add up to **180°**.

Worked example 5

Find the size of angle b. Explain your answer.

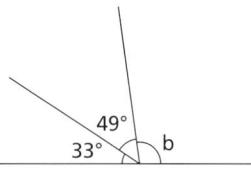

180 − 33 − 49 = 98 So b = 98°.	You need to work out the size of the missing angle. You can do this by taking the two angles that you do know away from 180°.
The three angles are on a straight line. Angles on a straight line add up to 180°.	You are asked to explain our answer. You need to state the angle fact that you have used.

Key term

The **angles around a point** add up to **360°**.

Discuss

If you have a pair of parallel lines and a transversal how many angles do you need to be told to be able to work out all of the angles formed?

Worked example 6

Find the size of angle c. Explain your answer.

One of the angles is a right angle 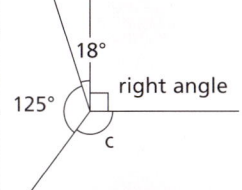 360 − 90 − 18 − 125 = 127 So c = 127°.	The four angles meet at a point. Angles at a point add to 360°. You need to take the angles that you do know away from 360°.
The four angles meet at a point. Angles at a point add up to 360°.	You are asked to explain your answer. You need to state the angle fact that you have used.

Chapter 20: Angles   **175**

> **Think about**
>
> Draw a triangle on a sheet of paper. Cut out the triangle. Shade in the angles using colours. Cut off the angles and rearrange them next to each other.
>
> What can you tell from doing this?

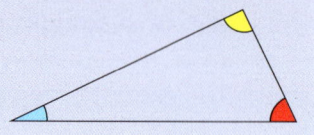

Key term

The **angles** in a **triangle** add up to **180°**.

Worked example 7

Find the size of angle d. Give reasons for your answer.

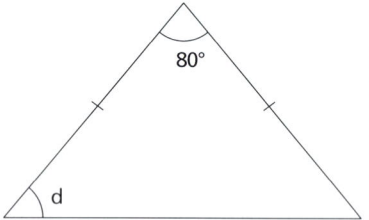

The marks on the two sides tell you that this is an isosceles triangle. This means that the base angles are equal. 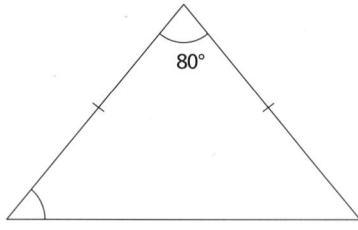	You need to start by thinking about what you know about this triangle.
180 − 80 = 100 So the sum of the two unknown angles is 100°.	You can work out what the two base angles add up to.
100 ÷ 2 = 50 So d = 50°.	As the two angles are equal you can divide by 2 to find the size of one angle.
The reasons are: • base angles of an isosceles triangle are equal • the angles in a triangle add up to 180°	You are asked to give reasons for your answer. You need to give a geometrical reason for each step.

Key term

The **angles** in a **quadrilateral** add up to **360°**.

Worked example 8

Find the size of angle e. Give a reason for your answer.

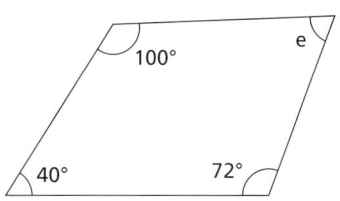

360 − 40 − 72 − 100 = 148 So e = 148°.	The shape is a quadrilateral. You know that the angles will add up to 360°. You need to take the angles that you do know away from 360°.
Angles in a quadrilateral add to 360°.	You are asked to explain your answer. You need to state the angle fact that you have used.

Exercise 2

Tip

In some of these diagrams the same letter is used to label a missing angle more than once. If this happens, then those angles must be equal.

1 Find the size of each labelled angle.

a)

b)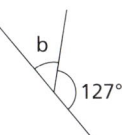

c)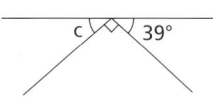

d)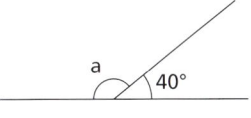

e)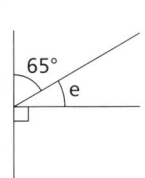

f)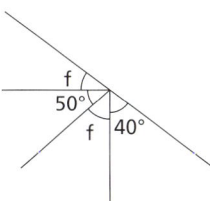

2 Find the size of each labelled angle.

a)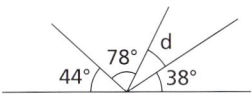

b)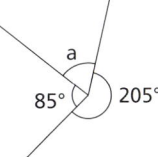

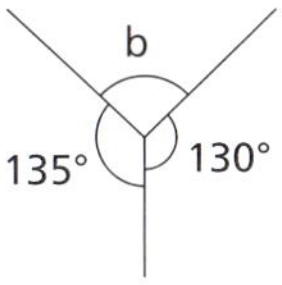

c)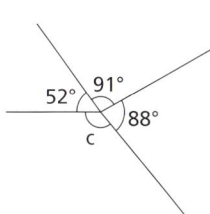

d)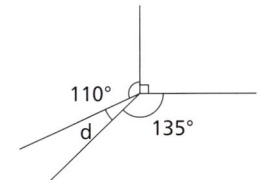

e)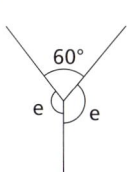

f)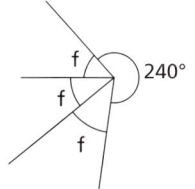

Chapter 20: Angles   177

3 Find the size of each labelled angle.

a)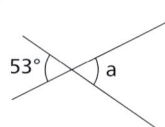
b)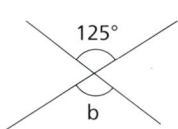
c)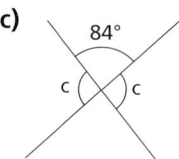

> **Did you know?**
>
> In some countries, vertically opposite angles are called 'vertical angles'

4 Find the size of each labelled angle.

a)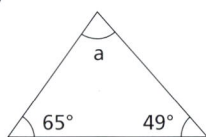
b)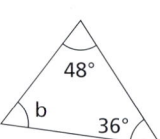
c)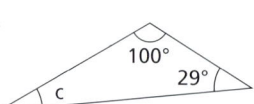
d)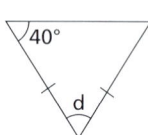

5 Find the size of each labelled angle.

a)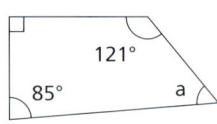
b)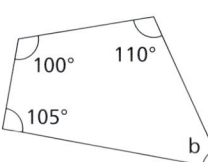
c)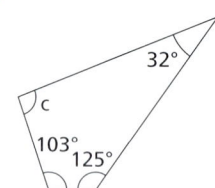
d)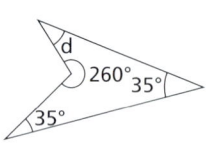

6 Are the following statements true or false? Explain your answers.
   a) A triangle can have only one acute angle.
   b) A triangle can have exactly two acute angles.
   c) A triangle can have only one obtuse angle.
   d) A triangle can have exactly two obtuse angles.

7 Find the size of each angle in the triangle. Give reasons for each step in your working.

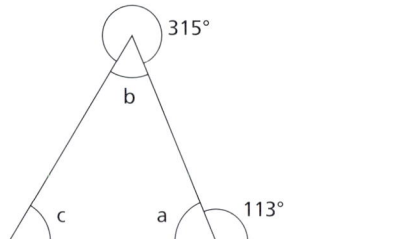

8 One angle in an isosceles triangle is 38°.
What could the other two angles be? Explain your answer.

> **Tip**
>
> There is more than one solution to this problem.

End of chapter reflection

You should know that …	You should be able to …	Such as …
A transversal on a set of parallel lines creates sets of equal angles.	Identify the equal angles on a diagram involving parallel lines.	On this diagram, mark equal angles with the same letter. 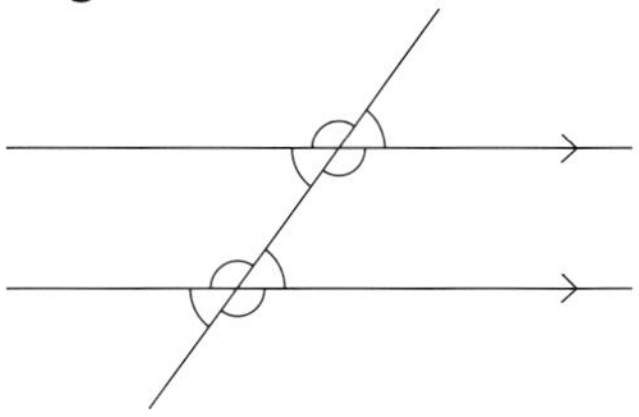
Angles on a straight line sum to 180°. Angles at a point sum to 360°. Angles in a triangle sum to 180°. Vertically opposite angles are equal. Angles in a quadrilateral sum to 360°.	Select and use the facts needed in order to find missing angles in geometrical problems.	What is the value of the angle marked a? 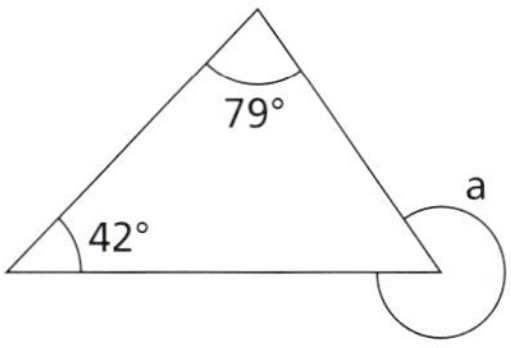

Unit 2C • Chapter 21

Symmetry

You will learn how to:
- Recognise line and rotation symmetry in 2D shapes and patterns; draw lines of symmetry and complete patterns with two lines of symmetry; identify the order of rotation symmetry.

Starting point

Do you remember …?
- names of special quadrilaterals and triangles?
- properties of special quadrilaterals and triangles?
- what a full turn is?

This will be helpful when …
you go on to learn about:
- transformations of shapes
- constructions

Hook

Butterflies

You are going to cut out the shape of a butterfly. First, fold a piece of paper in half. Then draw the shape of half of a butterfly.

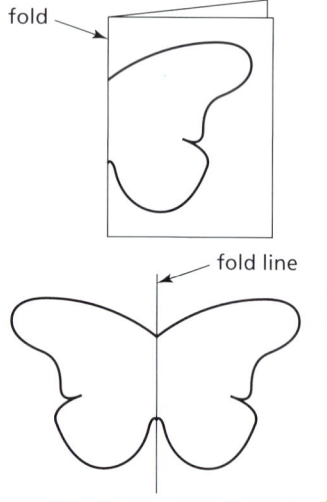

Now cut out the shape and unfold the piece of paper.

The shape that you get is the same on both sides of the fold line. Each side is a mirror image of the other side and the 'mirror' is the fold line.

Can you shade or colour your butterfly so that the two wings are still mirror images of each other?

Now fold another piece of paper in half and draw the shape of half an animal's face. Then open it out to see if it looks like the animal you were thinking about.

Line and rotational symmetry

Key terms

A shape has **line symmetry** if it can be folded in half exactly along a straight line. The straight line is called a **line of symmetry**.

A shape has **rotational symmetry** if it fits into its outline more than once as you rotate it a full turn.

The **order of rotational symmetry** is the number of times a shape fits into its outline in a full turn.

Unit 2C: Handling data and geometry

The rectangle shown has two lines of symmetry – two lines where you can fold it in half exactly.

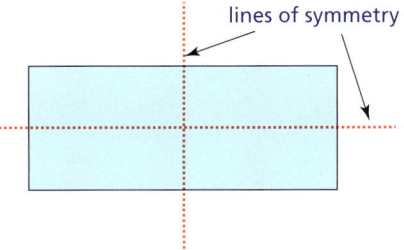

If you cut out an object, such as the rectangle above, draw around it and then rotate the rectangle about its centre for one full turn, the rectangle fits back, exactly, into its outline twice.

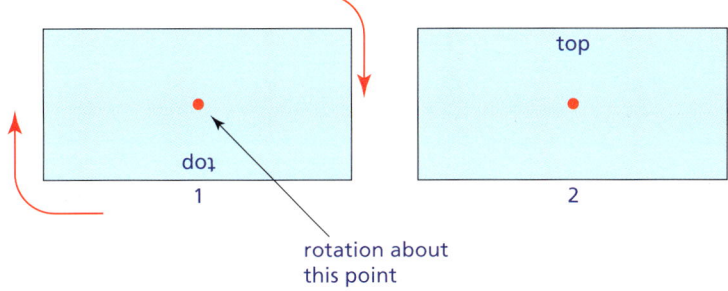

A rectangle has **rotational symmetry** of **order** 2 as it fits back into its outline twice in one full turn. Order 2 tells you how many times it fits back into its outline.

Worked example 1

For each shape, state how many lines of symmetry it has and whether or not it has rotational symmetry. If it has rotational symmetry, state the order of that rotational symmetry. State 'no rotational symmetry' if it does not have rotational symmetry.

a) 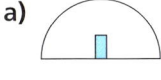   b) 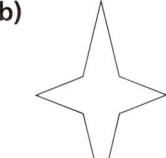   c) 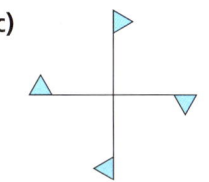   d)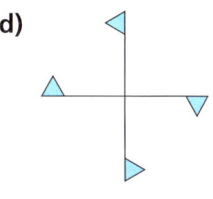

a) The shape has **one line of symmetry** as it can be folded in half along a vertical line. It has **no rotational symmetry** as it will not fit back onto its outline more than once in a full turn.

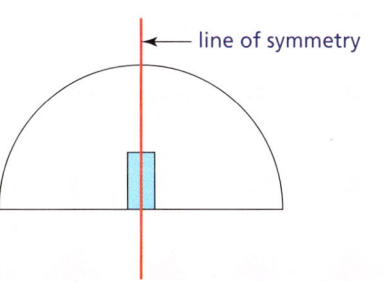

Chapter 21: Symmetry   **181**

b) The shape has **two lines of symmetry** as it can be folded in half along a vertical line through its centre and also along a horizontal line through its centre.

It fits back into its outline twice in one full turn, so it has **rotational symmetry of order 2**.

c) There are **no lines of symmetry** as you cannot fold the shape exactly in half along a straight line. The shape has **rotational symmetry of order 4** as it will fit into its outline four times in one full turn.

d) This shape has **two lines of symmetry** as you could fold it exactly in half along two different lines.

It has **rotational symmetry of order 2** as it would fit back into its outline twice as it was turned through a full turn.

Tip

When you are thinking about lines of symmetry think about cutting out the shape and then trying to fold it exactly in half so that one half fits exactly onto the other half.

Did you know?

Snowflake patterns such as this one have rotational symmetry of order 6. Real snowflakes are rarely perfectly symmetrical, but all have a base design with 6 spokes and rotational symmetry of order 6, or, very rarely, 12 spokes and rotational symmetry of order 12.

Exercise 1

1 In this question, one half of each shape has been drawn with one of its lines of symmetry. Copy and complete each diagram.

a)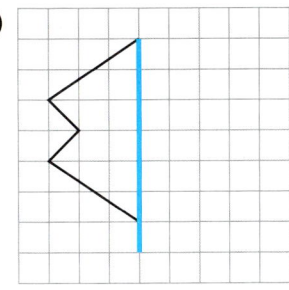
b)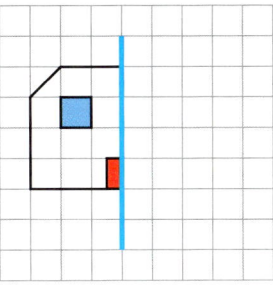
c)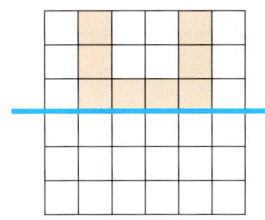
d)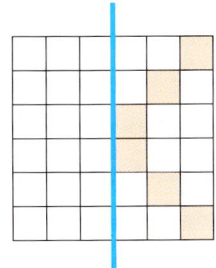
e)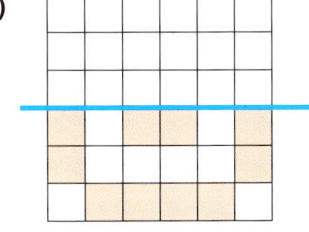
f)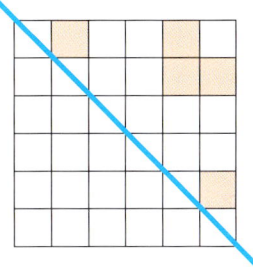

2 How many lines of symmetry does each of these capital letters have?
a) A
b) B
c) C
d) D
e) E
f) F

3 Do these capital letters have rotational symmetry? If they have rotational symmetry, state the order of rotational symmetry.
a) A
b) H
c) N
d) S
e) T

4 Name two quadrilaterals with exactly two lines of symmetry.

5 For each of these shapes state how many lines of symmetry it has and (if it has rotational symmetry) its order of rotational symmetry.

a)
b)
c)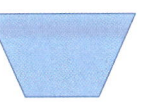
d)
e)
f)
g)
h)
i)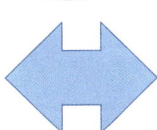
j)

Chapter 21: Symmetry

6 For each of these patterns state how many lines of symmetry it has and (if it has rotational symmetry) its order of rotational symmetry.

a) 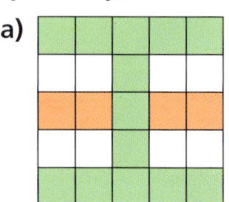 b) 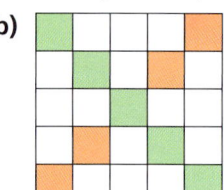 c) 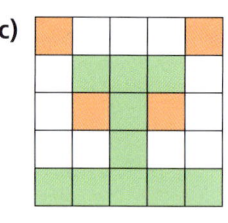 d)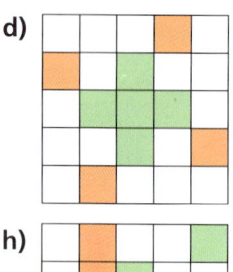

e) 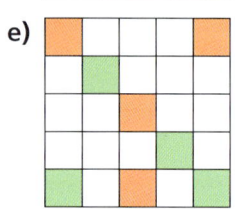 f) 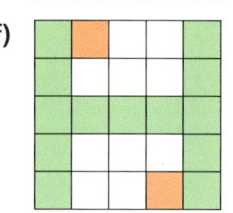 g) 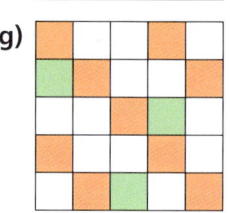 h)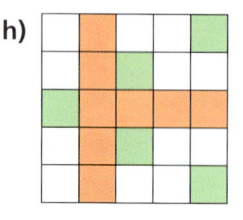

7 Each diagram has two lines of symmetry (shown in blue) when completed. Some of the shape has been drawn for you. Copy and complete each diagram.

a) 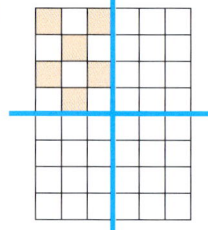 b) 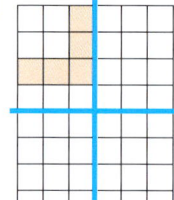 c) 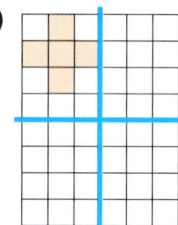 d)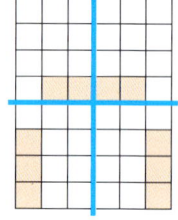

8 Copy and complete each diagram so that the finished pattern has rotational symmetry of order 4. The centre is marked.

a) 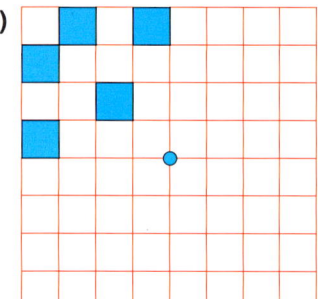 b) 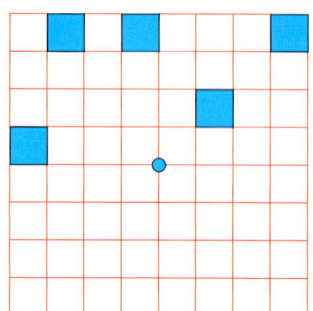 c)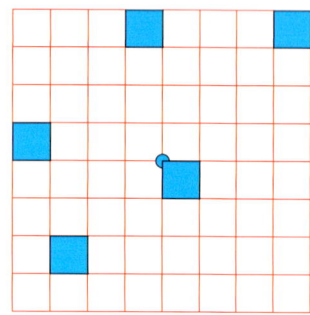

9 a) Draw two quadrilaterals, both with two lines of symmetry and rotational symmetry of order 2.

b) Draw a quadrilateral with one line of symmetry and no rotational symmetry.

c) Make a table of all the quadrilaterals that you know with the number of lines of symmetry and the order of rotational symmetry.

184 Unit 2C: Handling data and geometry

End of chapter reflection

You should know that ...	You should be able to ...	Such as ...
An object has **line symmetry** if it can be folded in half exactly along a straight line.	Recognise when a shape has a line of symmetry.	Does this pattern have line symmetry?
	Draw lines of symmetry and complete patterns with two lines of symmetry.	Copy and complete this pattern so it has two lines of symmetry.
The **order** of rotation in symmetry is the number of times a shape or pattern would fit exactly back into its own outline when rotated through a full turn.	Find the order of rotational symmetry of a shape.	What is the order of rotational symmetry of this shape?
If the order of rotational symmetry of a shape or pattern is less than two then it has no rotational symmetry.	Decide if a shape or pattern has rotational symmetry.	Does this triangle have rotational symmetry?

Chapter 21: Symmetry

Unit 2C • Chapter 22

Averages

You will learn how to:
- Find the mode (or modal class for grouped data), median and range.
- Calculate the mean, including from a simple frequency table.

Starting point

Do you remember …?

- how to find the mode and range from a list of results?

  For example, find the mode and range of these long jump results:

  5.4 m, 4.8 m, 5 m, 4.6 m, 4.8 m, 3.7 m, 4.8 m, 4.5 m

- how to use a frequency table?

  For example, here is a frequency table showing the number of brothers and sisters students in a class have.

  How many students have fewer than 2 brothers or sisters?

  How many students are in this class?

Number of brothers and sisters	Frequency
0	4
1	7
2	8
3	5
4	3

This will be helpful when …

you learn how to compare two sets of data using averages and spreads.

Hook

Here are two ice skaters' scores in a competition:

	Judge 1	Judge 2	Judge 3	Judge 4	Judge 5	Judge 6	Judge 7	Judge 8
Skater 1	101	99	107	89	121	115	105	103
Skater 2	96	102	113	109	108	105	105	102

- Which skater do you think has done better just by looking?
- How could you check your answer?
- What is the total score for each skater?
- Skater 3 was awarded a total score of 784. Each judge gave the same score. What was that score?
- Find the highest and lowest scores for each skater and work out how far apart they are.
- Which skater has a bigger spread of scores?

You have just found an average and a measure of spread for this data!

Unit 2C: Handling data and geometry

> **Did you know?**
>
> In lots of sports the awarding of points is done by finding averages of individual judges' scores. Computers usually calculate these instantly once the judges have entered their scores.

Mode, median and range

Key terms

The **mode** is an average.

The **mode** is the value in a set of data that occurs most frequently.

For example, for the data:

   7, 18, 3, 6, 3, 23, 14, 3, 8,

the mode is 3.

A set of data can have more than one mode (or no mode at all).

You can also find the mode for a set of data that are not numerical.

The **median** is an average.

The **median** is the middle value of data, once the data is arranged in order of size.

For example, for the data:

   5, 7, **10**, 11, 16,

the median is 10, because this is the middle number.

If there are two numbers in the middle, the median is the value half way between them.

For example, for the data:

   5, 7, **10**, **12**, 17, 20,

the median is 11, because this is halfway between 10 and 12.

The **range** is a measure of spread.

The **range** is the difference between the highest data value and the lowest data value. It shows how spread out the data is.

For example, for the data:

   8, 10, 15, 21, 39,

the range = 39 − 8 = 31.

Worked example 1

Here are the ages of students in a music club.

13   13   10   9   14   12   12   13

a) Find the **mode**.
b) Find the **median** age.
c) Find the **range** of ages.

a) 13 13 10 9 14 12 12 13 Mode = 13	The mode is the most common data item in the list. So you are looking for the age that appears most frequently.
b) 9 10 12 12 13 13 13 14 9 10 12 12 13 13 13 14 9 10 12 12 13 13 13 14 9 10 12 12 13 13 13 14 9 10 12 12 13 13 13 14 Median = 12.5	The median is the middle number when you put the data in order. So, first you need to order the data. You need to find the middle value, so you will cross out a number from each end until you reach the middle. You are left with two pieces of data in the middle, so you have to find the value which is halfway between 12 and 13, which is 12.5.
c) Range of 5 9 lowest value — 14 highest value Range = 14 − 9 = 5	The range is the spread of the data. Your highest value is 14. Your lowest value is 9. So the range is 5.

Exercise 1

1 Find the mode for each of these sets of data.

a) Favourite colour of 12 people:

| red | blue | purple | blue | yellow | blue |
| purple | blue | purple | green | orange | pink |

b) Age of children at a cinema:

15   12   9   7   11   12   8   12

c) Height of young plants in a greenhouse:

7 cm   6 cm   7 cm   4 cm   5 cm

d) Shoe size of 10 people:

39   42   45   38   40   42   36   39   47   41

2 Find the median and range of each set of data.

a) Age of 11 children at a playgroup:

   3   4   2   3   3   3   2   1   4   0   4

b) Weights of 9 people:

   57 kg   64 kg   59 kg   61 kg   68 kg   61 kg   56 kg   67 kg   63 kg

c) Number of goals scored in 8 football matches:

   2   3   0   1   2   2   1   5

d) Heights of gymnasts in a national team:

   154 cm   151 cm   146 cm   159 cm   139 cm
   160 cm   143 cm   140 cm   137 cm   147 cm

e) Number of cups of coffee sold by a café each day:

   17   57   50   50   55   47   48   54   29
   45   42   34   50   36   36   24   37   40

3 Write a set of five numbers with:

a) a mode of 3

b) a median of 7

c) a range of 6

d) a mode of 3 and a range of 6

e) a mode of 3 and a median of 7

f) a mode of 3, a median of 7 and a range of 6

4 Jasmine has a set of four number cards.

| 9 | 11 | 12 | ? |

The numbers have a range of 5. Which two possible values could the last card have?

5 Which is the odd one out? Explain your answer.

A: Mode   B: Median   C: Range

6 Here are the numbers of students absent from Class A over the last two weeks.

| 0 | 3 | 2 | 0 | 0 | 1 | 2 | 4 | 3 | 2 |

Paula says, "On average there were 4 students absent because the range is 4 − 0 = 4".

Do you agree with Paula? Explain your answer.

The mean

Key terms

The **mean** is an average.

The **mean** is the total value of all the data divided by the number of pieces of data.

For example, for the data:

   8, 10, 10, 16,

the mean = $\frac{8+10+10+16}{4} = \frac{44}{4} = 11$

Chapter 22: Averages

Worked example 2

Sadia notes how many minutes the school bus is late during a week. The results are:

Monday	Tuesday	Wednesday	Thursday	Friday
5 minutes	0 minutes	8 minutes	6 minutes	1 minute

What is the mean number of minutes that the bus is late?

The mean = (5 + 0 + 8 + 6 + 1) ÷ 5 = 20 ÷ 5 = 4 minutes	Add all the numbers and divide by how many numbers there are. Remember to count the zero.	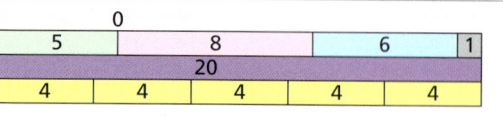

Worked example 3

Julian is investigating the number of sweets in boxes of fruit drops. Here are his results:

Number of sweets in a box	Frequency
19	1
20	1
21	4
22	8
23	3
24	3

a) Find the mode.
b) Calculate the mean.
c) Find the range.

a) Mode = 22

The mode is the data value that occurs most often, which is 22 since this appears 8 times.

Number of sweets in a box	Frequency
19	1
20	1
21	4
22	**8**
23	3
24	3

b) Mean

Number of sweets in a box		Frequency		
19	×	1	=	19
20	×	1	=	20
21	×	4	=	84
22	×	8	=	176
23	×	3	=	69
24	×	3	=	72
		20		440

You need to find the total number of sweets and divide by the number of boxes.

You need to start by finding the total number of sweets.

Number of sweets in a box	Frequency
19	1
20	1
21	4
22	8
23	3
24	3

19, 20, 21, 21, 21, 21, 22, 22, 22, 22, 22, 22, 22, 22, 23, 23, 23, 24, 24, 24

Total =

19 + 20 + 21 + 21 + 21 + 21 + 22 + 22 + 22 + 22 + 22 + 22 + 22 + 22 + 23 + 23 + 23 + 24 + 24 + 24

= 440

Total number of sweets = 19 × 1 + 20 × 1 + 21 × 4 + 22 × 8 + 23 × 3 + 24 × 3 = 440 Total frequency = 1 + 1 + 4 + 8 + 3 + 3 = 20 Mean = $\frac{440}{20}$ = 22	Altogether there are 20 boxes of sweets in the sample. So mean = 440 ÷ 20 = 22	(19, 20, 21, 21, 21, 21, 22, 22, 22, 22, 22, 22, 22, 22, 23, 23, 23, 24, 24, 24)
c) Range = 24 − 19 = 5	The highest number of sweets in a box in the sample was 24. The lowest number of sweets in a box in the sample was 19. So the range is the difference between these, which is 5.	Number of sweets in a box / Frequency 19 / 1 20 / 1 21 / 4 22 / 8 23 / 3 24 / 3 Range of 5 19 ← → 24 lowest value / highest value

Think about

Does the range need to be a number from the data set?

What does it mean if the range is a large or small number?

Exercise 2   1, 4

1 Find the mean of these data sets.

a) Number of applications for jobs advertised by a company:
   20   31   27   19   23

b) Times in the 100 m race at Sports Day (in seconds):
   14.3   13.5   16.7   14.2   13.9   15.1   14.8   13.9

c) Number of students in each class in Year 7:
   25   28   23   24   26

2 Karen has a set of four number cards.

| 6 | 8 | 11 | ? |

The numbers have a mean of 10.

a) What must the total of the numbers be?   b) Find the value of the missing number.

3 A set of 5 numbers has a mean of 7. Four of the numbers are 4, 5, 11 and 10.
What is the final number?

4 Here are the number of minutes that trains were late to arrive at a station on 20 consecutive days:

| 22 | 8 | 6 | 0 | 1 | 0 | 52 | 1 | 10 | 0 |
| 0 | 1 | 2 | 0 | 7 | 1 | 1 | 5 | 0 | 0 |

a) Calculate the mean, median and mode of this data set.

b) Which of the three averages that you calculated in part a) would be best to use if you wanted to argue that trains arrive late too often? Explain your answer.

c) Which of the three averages that you calculated in part a) would be best to use if you wanted to argue that trains are often on time? Explain your answer.

5 Use a spreadsheet to create a set of 20 pieces of data.

Calculate the mean of your data. Adjust the data so that the mean of the data is 11.

Now adjust the data again so that the mean stays as 11 but the range is 35.

6 Jessie rolled an ordinary dice and recorded the scores in this table.

Score	Frequency
1	7
2	8
3	7
4	9
5	6
6	5

a) How many times did Jessie roll the dice?
b) What was Jessie's modal score?
c) What was the range of scores?

> **Key term**
>
> The **modal score** is the name given to the category or class of data that is the most frequent.

7 Lars completed a survey of the number of hours of maths homework students received each week. Here are his results:

Number of hours	Frequency	Number of hours × frequency
0	1	
1	4	
2	5	
3	6	
4	4	

a) Copy and complete the final column of the table.
b) Then find the total number of hours of homework completed by the students.
c) Calculate the number of students in Lars's survey.
d) Then calculate the mean number of hours of homework completed by the students.

8 Find the mean from these tables.

a)
Value	Frequency	Value × frequency
13	2	
14	1	
15	7	
16	5	
17	5	

b)
Value	Frequency	Value × frequency
0	7	
1	5	
2	1	
3	3	

> **Think about**
>
> How can you check whether your answer is reasonable when checking the mean?
>
> Would it be possible to have data going from a lowest value of 3 to a highest value of 13 and a mean of 20?

9 Fatima keeps a record of the number of portions of fruit and vegetables that she eats per day over a number of days. Here are her results.

a) What is the modal number of portions of fruit and vegetables eaten by Fatima?

b) Calculate the number of portions of fruit and vegetables eaten by Fatima in total

c) How many days did Fatima record data for?

d) Calculate the mean number of portions of fruit and vegetables eaten by Fatima.

e) Fatima says, "The range of my data is 12 – 2 = 10." Do you agree with Fatima? Explain your answer.

Number of portions	Frequency
0	3
1	5
2	8
3	12
4	10
5	10
6	2

10 Jamie recorded the number of cars that used the school car park each day.

Here are his results.

Number of cars	Frequency
0–19	12
20–29	15
30–39	19
40–49	14

State the **modal class** of Jamie's data.

Key term

The **modal class** is the name given to the category or class of data that is the most frequent.

11 Allegra recorded the ages of people attending a play at a theatre.
Here are her results.

Age	Frequency
0–18	6
19–30	11
30–39	19
40–49	34
50–65	58
66–100	54

What is the modal class of Allegra's data?

12 Hannah has collected some data about the number of pets that students in her class own.

Number of pets	Frequency
0	3
1–2	18
3–4	15
5–8	12
9–12	1

Hannah says, "The modal class is 18, because this is highest frequency".

Do you agree with Hannah? Explain your answer.

13 **Vocabulary feature question**

Match each of these key terms to its description.

Median	A single value to represent the typical value of data in a set
Mean	The middle value of the data when it is arranged in order
Mode	The difference between the highest and lowest data values
Range	The most common data value
Modal class	The category that has the highest frequency

Unit 2C: Handling data and geometry

End of chapter reflection

You should know that …	You should be able to …	Such as …
An average is a single value that sums up the typical value of data in a set. The mode, median and mean are all examples of averages. The mode is the most common value in a data set. The median is the middle value in a data set when the data is arranged in order of size. The mean is the total of all the data values divided by the number of pieces of data.	Calculate the mode from a list of data. Calculate the median from a list of data. Calculate the mean from a list of data. Find a missing value from a list of data given information about the mode, median or mean.	Calculate the mode, median and mean for this data set: 3, 10, 12, 9, 12, 8 Emily, Fiona and Grace have a mean age of 7. Emily and Fiona are both 4. How old must Grace be?
The range is a measure of spread. The range is the difference between the highest data value and the lowest data value.	Calculate the range from a list of data. Find a missing value from a list of data given information about the range.	Calculate the range for this data set: 3, 10, 12, 9, 12, 8 The highest value in a data set is 24. The range of the data is 11. What must the lowest value in the data set be?
Averages and the range can be found from data in a frequency table.	Find the mean, mode or range from a simple frequency table.	Amy completes a survey of the number of people living in each house in her street. Here are the results. | Number of people	Frequency
---	---
1	2
2	3
3	2
4	7
5	1
6	3	 a) Write down the mode. b) Calculate the range. c) Calculate the mean.
The modal class is the category or class with the highest frequency in a frequency table.	State the modal class for a frequency table.	Here are the results of a survey of how many hours of exercise students complete per week. | Hours	Frequency
---	---
0–4	9
5–8	7
9–12	5
13–16	1	 What is the modal class of the data?

Chapter 22: Averages

Unit 2C • Chapter 23

Displaying data

You will learn how to:

Draw and interpret:
- pictograms, bar-line graphs and bar charts
- frequency diagrams for grouped discrete data
- simple pie charts

Starting point

Do you remember …?

- how to draw and interpret a simple pictogram?

  For example, here is an incomplete pictogram representing the favourite colour of students in a class in Year 7.

  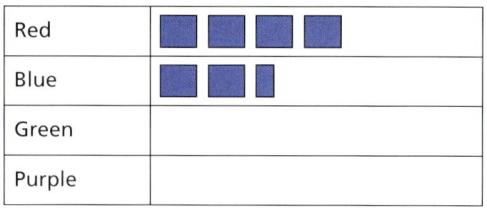
  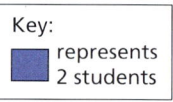

  a) How many more students said red than said blue?

  6 students said that green was their favourite colour.
  There were a total of 22 students in the class.

  b) Copy and complete the pictogram.

- how to draw and interpret a simple bar chart?

  For example, here is a bar chart showing how students in Year 8 travel to school.

  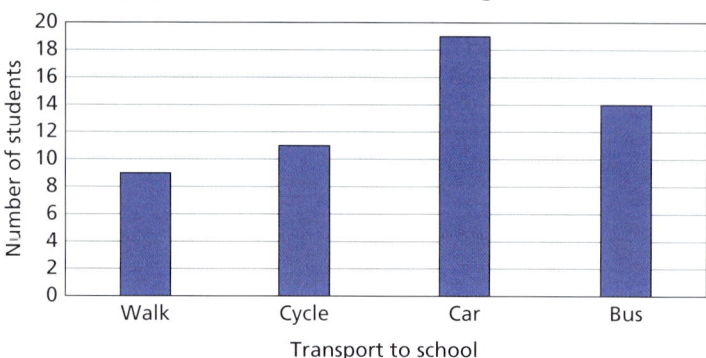

  a) Write down the number of Year 8 students who travel by car.
  b) Work out how many more Year 8 students travel by bus than cycle.

This will be helpful when …

you go on to learn about: drawing conclusions from diagrams.

Hook

Lata has drawn this pictogram to show the favourite fruit of students in her class.

Apple	●●
Orange	⬤ ⬤ ⬤
Banana	● ● ● ●
Pear	💧💧💧
	●●

What is wrong with Lata's pictogram? Find as many errors as you can.

Can you draw a bar chart with errors in it? Give your bar chart to another student and see if they can spot the errors you have included.

Pictograms, bar charts and bar-line graphs

Key terms

A **pictogram** is a chart where you use pictures to represent data. The **frequency** (how many times something happens) is worked out using the key.

	Vehicles passing school
Motorbike	▦ ▦
Car	▦ ▦ ▦ ▦ ▦
Van	▦ ▦ ▦
Lorry	▦

Key: ▦ represents 5 vehicles

A **bar chart** uses the height of the bar to represent the frequency. There are gaps between the bars on a bar chart.

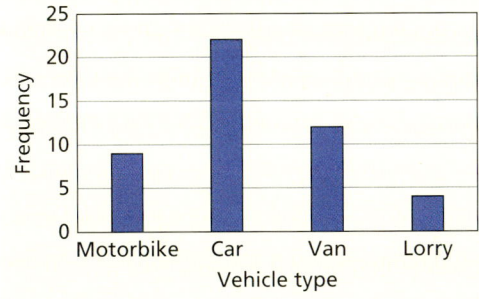

A **bar-line graph** is like a bar chart, but you use lines rather than bars to show the frequency.

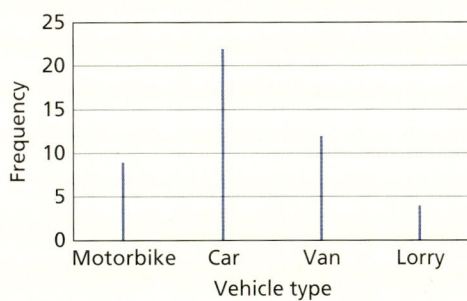

Chapter 23: Displaying data   **197**

Worked example 1

The bar chart shows information about eye colour in a group of children in Year 7.
The pictogram shows information about the eye colour in a group of children in Year 9.

Eye colour for children in Year 7
(Bar chart: Grey ~15, Green ~26, Brown ~60, Blue ~48; x-axis Frequency 0–80)

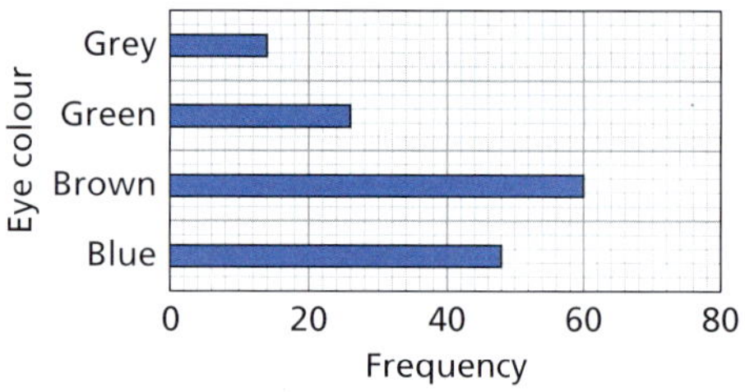

Eye colour for children in Year 9
Blue	👁👁👁👁👁👁👁
Green	👁👁👁👁👁👁👁👁◐
Brown	👁👁👁👁◐
Grey	👁◐

Key: 👁 represents 8 children

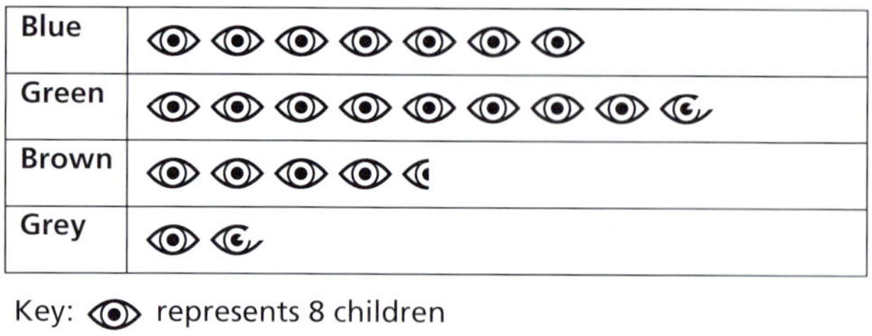

a) How many children in Year 7 have green eyes?
b) How many children in Year 9 have grey eyes?
c) What is the difference between the number of children with blue eyes in Year 7 and Year 9?

a) There are 10 small squares between the 0 and the 20 labels. $20 \div 10 = 2$ Each small square is worth 2. $20 + 3 \times 2 = 26$	Start by working out the scale on the bar chart. Work out what each small square represents. Work out how many children are represented by the bar for green eyes. There are 3 small squares beyond the 20 mark.	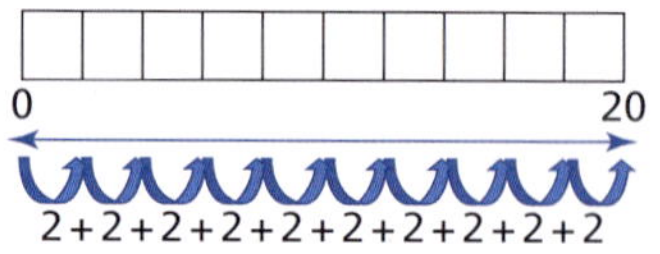 (Diagram showing 0 to 20 split into 10 steps of +2) Each small step is worth 2. (Diagram: 20 to 26, +2+2+2) 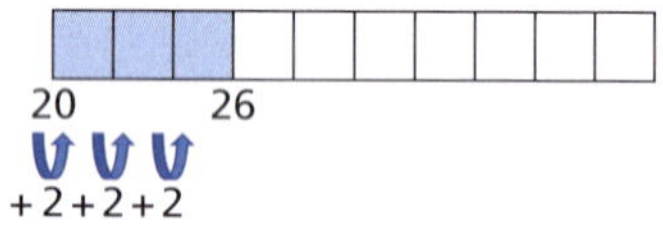
b) $1\frac{7}{8}$ of 8 $= 8 + \frac{7}{8}$ of 8 $= 8 + 7$ $= 15$	Work out the number of children represented by $1\frac{7}{8}$ of the eye symbols.	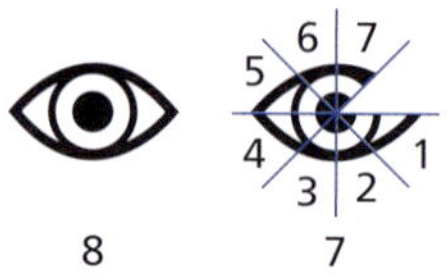 (Eye symbol = 8; partial eye divided in 8ths showing 7) 8 7
c) $40 + 4 \times 2 = 48$ $8 \times 7 = 56$ $56 - 48 = 8$	Work out the number of children with blue eyes in Year 7. There are 4 small squares beyond the 40 mark. Work out the number of children with blue eyes in Year 9. There are 7 symbols each representing 8 children. Work out the difference.	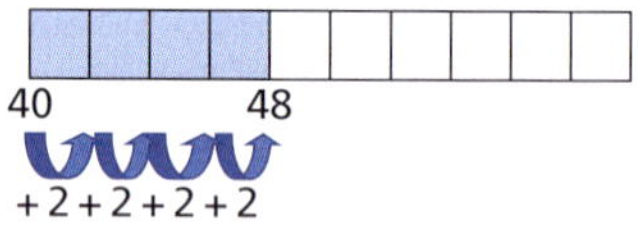  (Diagram: 40 to 48, +2+2+2+2) 👁👁👁👁👁👁👁 $8+8+8+8+8+8+8 = 56$

198   Unit 2C: Handling data and geometry

Worked example 2

The incomplete dual bar chart shows some information about the favourite types of television programme for two classes in Year 8, class 8r and class 8s.

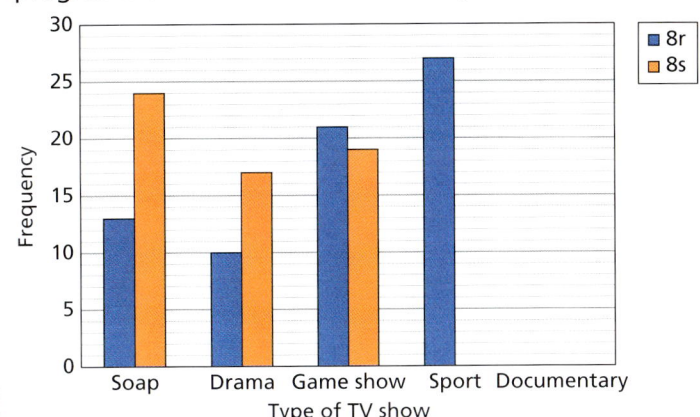

The number of class 8s who said that 'Sport' was their favourite type of television show was one third of the number of class 8r who said that 'Sport' was their favourite type of television show.

9 of class 8r and 11 of class 8s said that 'Documentary' was their favourite type of television show.

a) Complete the bar chart.
b) Write down the most popular type of television show for class 8s.

a) 27 of class 8r said 'Sport'. $27 \div 3 = 9$ 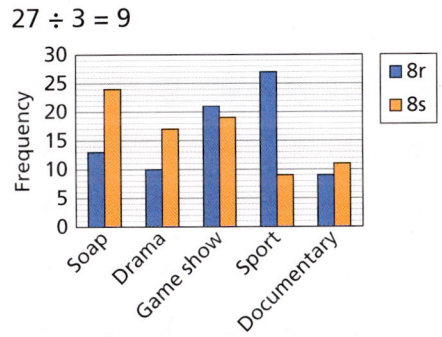	Start by working out how many of class 8s said that 'Sport' was their favourite type of television show. You need to find $\frac{1}{3}$ of the number of class 8r who said 'Sport'. You need to add the bars for students in class 8s who said 'Sport' and for 'Documentary' to the bar chart. **Tip** Remember to use the key to check the colour for the bars for class 8r and for class 8s.
b) Looking at the orange bars, you can see that 'Soap' has the tallest bar. 'Soap' is the most popular type of television show for class 8s.	The key shows you that the bars for class 8s are orange. To find the most popular type of television show for class 8s you need to find the tallest orange bar.

Chapter 23: Displaying data 199

Exercise 1

1. The frequency table shows information about the number of people who visited a local library each day last week.

Day	Number of people
Monday	25
Tuesday	32
Wednesday	28
Thursday	22
Friday	18
Saturday	46
Sunday	29

Draw a pictogram to represent this information.

Tip
Think about the number of people that your symbol will represent and remember to include a key.

2. The incomplete frequency table and pictogram show information about the number of people in cars passing a school over a 30-minute period.

Number of people in car	Frequency
1	30
2	
3	9
4	6
5	

Key: ■ represents _____

a) Using the information in the frequency table, copy and complete the pictogram.

b) Using the information in the pictogram, copy and complete the frequency table.

3. Sarika wants to check whether her dice is fair. She has rolled the dice 90 times and recorded her results in the bar chart.

a) Which number did Sarika roll most often?

b) How many more rolls landed on 2 than landed on 5?

c) Do you think the dice is fair? Explain your answer.

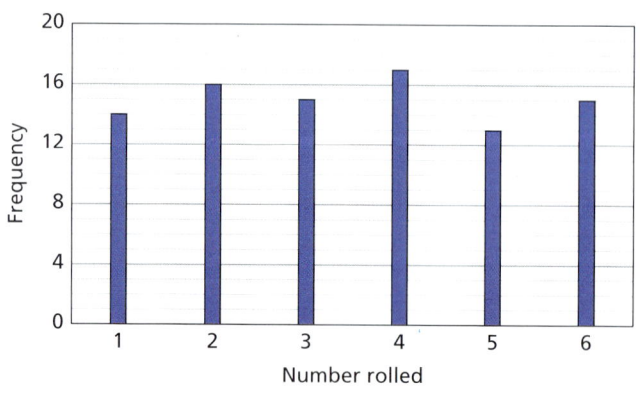

200   Unit 2C: Handling data and geometry

4) Ross manages two teams for a football club. He keeps a record of the number of goals scored in their matches. Here are his results.

Number of goals	A team	B team
0	5	11
1	6	6
2	6	4
3	4	1
4	2	1
5	1	0

a) Construct a bar chart to show this information.

b) Write some questions that you can use your bar chart to answer. Include the answer to each of your questions.

5) Pedro has drawn a bar chart to represent the number of bedrooms in a sample of houses from his town.

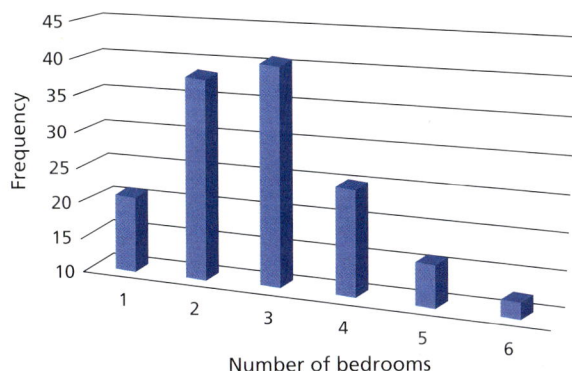

Write anything that is wrong or could be misleading about this bar chart.

6) A mountaineering club keeps information about its members.

Information about people's preferred activity is shown in the bar chart.

a) What is the most popular activity?

b) Freya thinks that the difference between those who prefer mountain biking and those who prefer kayaking is 4. Do you agree? Explain your answer.

c) How many people are in the mountaineering club?

d) True or false: the number of people who prefer climbing is three times greater than the number of people who prefer mountain biking. Explain your answer.

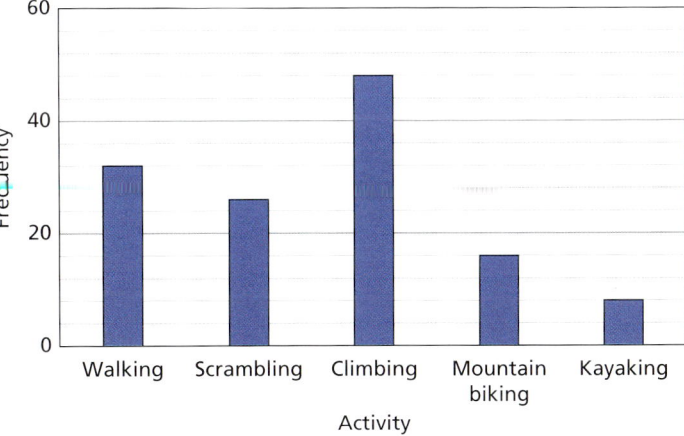

Chapter 23: Displaying data   201

7 Sayed has asked his friends what their favourite hobby is. He has asked 30 friends from his Biology class and 30 friends from his French class. He has collected his results in this table.

Hobby	Biology class	French class
Playing sport	12	9
Reading	6	7
Craft	3	10
Computer games	9	4

Use a computer to produce bar charts and bar-line graphs to represent this information.

> **Discuss**
> Are there any errors with the graphs that the computer produces? Are some of the graphs that the computer produces misleading?

8 **Vocabulary feature question**

Complete the statements using the words in the box.

| bar chart | pictogram | bar-line graph | key | frequency |

A .... uses symbols to show the frequency of different categories. This chart needs a .... so that you know how many each symbol represents.

In a .... the height (or length) of each bar shows the .... A .... is like a bar chart, but the frequencies are shown by the lengths of the lines.

Frequency diagrams for grouped discrete data

Key term

Discrete data is data that can only take certain values, for example,
- the number of students in a class (you can't have half a student)
- the number of letters in a word (you can only have whole numbers of letters)
- shoe sizes.

Worked example 3

Blessy is investigating the number of letters in words in a science textbook. She has collected data on the number of letters in 40 words. Here is her data:

3	11	3	3	4	2	5	2
4	5	4	2	3	4	10	3
4	7	2	5	10	6	3	7
9	5	2	8	4	8	8	4
3	11	11	6	5	2	5	3

a) Draw a frequency diagram for this data.
b) Comment on the lengths of words in the science textbook.

a)

Number of letters in word	Tally	Frequency
1 to 3		
4 to 6		
7 to 9		
10 to 12		

Start by collecting together the data in a frequency table.

If you collected the number of words with each length separately then you would have lots of rows in the table and lots of bars in your bar chart so you need to group the data. Use groups with the same width.

When you are deciding the groups to use you need to think about how many groups you want.

Tip
You can use tallies to help you to put the data into a frequency table.

Number of letters in word	Tally	Frequency
1 to 3	|||| |||| ||||	14
4 to 6	|||| |||| ||||	15
7 to 9	||||		6
10 to 12	||||	5

Next, complete the grouped frequency table.

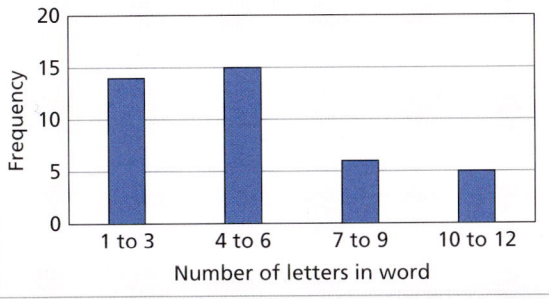

Now you can draw a bar chart to represent the information in the grouped frequency table.

The bars have equal widths and gaps in between them.

b) More words have between 4 and 6 letters than other lengths.

There are much fewer words with 7 letters or more than with up to 6 letters.

You can see that the bars for 1 to 3 and 4 to 6 have higher frequencies than the bars for 7 to 9 and 10 to 12.

Exercise 2

1 Pierre has collected information about the number of pieces of homework that students in his class got this week. Here is his data.

9	7	6	2	1
5	2	7	3	5
6	5	3	4	5
3	4	4	3	1
4	5	8	0	6

Chapter 23: Displaying data

a) Copy and complete this grouped frequency table for Pierre's data.

Number of pieces of homework	Tally	Frequency
0 or 1		
2 or 3		
4 or 5		
6 or 7		
8 or 9		

b) Draw a bar chart to show the information in the grouped frequency table.

c) Write down the modal class for number of pieces of homework.

Tip
The modal class is the group with the highest frequency.

2 Here are the marks for a maths test for 30 students.

24	31	31	35	19	37
29	32	25	34	36	17
32	29	30	28	37	38
39	34	27	30	33	26
28	20	23	22	31	31

a) Create a grouped frequency table for the marks.

b) Draw a bar chart to show the information in your grouped frequency table.

c) Use your bar chart to write a comment on the marks for the maths tests.

Tip
You do not have to start your groups with 0.

3 The incomplete grouped frequency table and bar chart give information about the number of CDs owned by 70 students.

Number of CDs	Frequency
	9
10 to 19	
20 to 29	
	19
40 to 49	

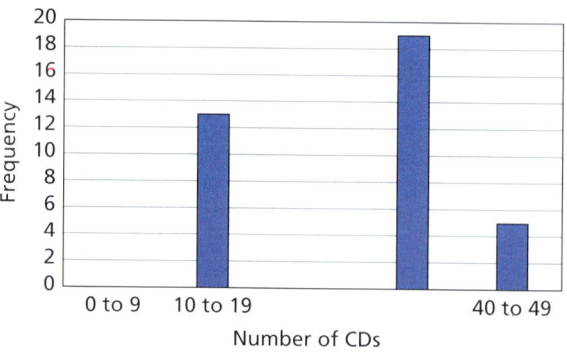

a) Use the information in the bar chart to copy and complete the grouped frequency table.

b) Use the information in the grouped frequency table to copy and complete the bar chart.

c) Which group has the highest frequency?

Unit 2C: Handling data and geometry

4 This bar chart shows the number of cakes sold by a local shop on each of 60 days.

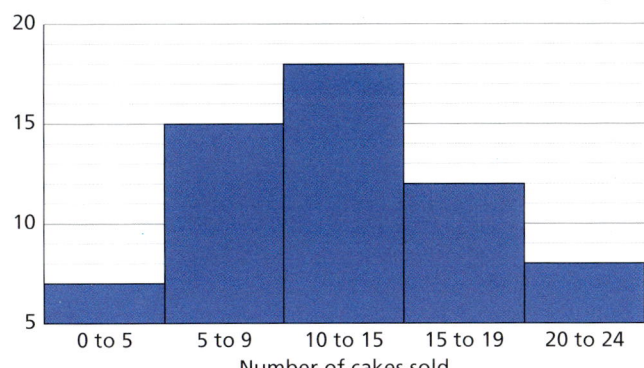

Write anything that is wrong or could be misleading about this bar chart.

5 Marco and Angelique have collected data about the number of visitors to their local park between 9 a.m. and 10 a.m. each day for 50 days. They have used their data to make this bar chart.

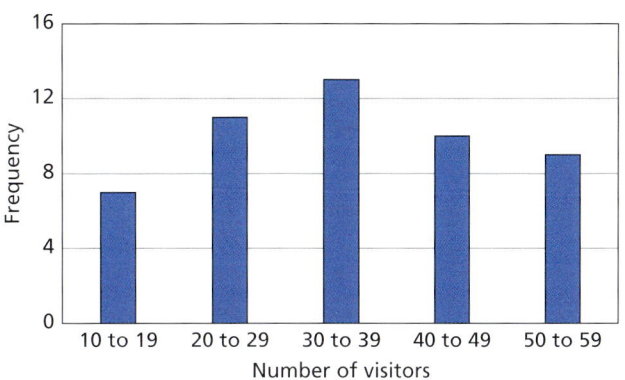

a) Marco says, "On half of the days there are more than 35 visitors". Is Marco correct? Explain your answer.

b) Angelique says, "It is not possible to tell from the bar chart if there were more than 55 visitors between 9 a.m. and 10 a.m. on any of the days". Is Angelique correct? Explain your answer.

Simple pie charts

Key terms

A **pie chart** is another way to represent data. A pie chart shows the proportions of the whole rather than information about frequencies.

A **sector** of a circle is a slice of the circle formed by two radii.

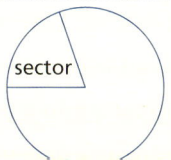

Worked example 4

The pie chart shows information about the method of transport to school for 32 students.

a) What fraction of students travelled by bus?
b) Which two methods of transport were used equally?
c) Which method of transport was used most? How many students used this method of transport?

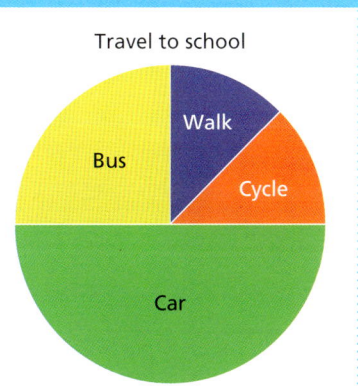

Chapter 23: Displaying data **205**

a) Look at the fraction of the pie chart that shows 'bus'.

$\frac{1}{4}$ of the students travelled by bus.

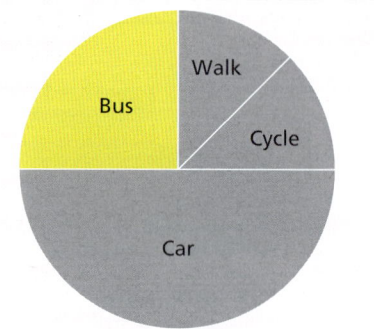

b) You need to see which two sectors of the pie chart are equal in size.

Walk and cycle are each $\frac{1}{8}$ of the pie chart so were used equally.

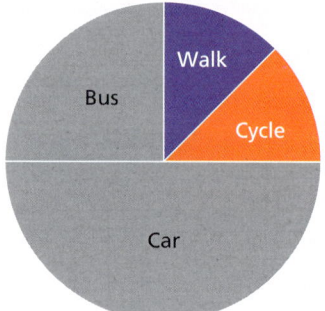

c) The method of transport which was used the most is the one with the biggest sector of the pie chart.

Car is the method of transport used most.

You know that $\frac{1}{2}$ of the students travel by car. You need to find $\frac{1}{2}$ of the total number represented by the pie chart.

$\frac{1}{2}$ of 32 = 16

16 students travelled by car.

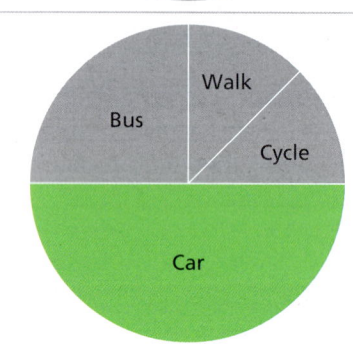

Worked example 5

The frequency table gives information about the favourite type of film for 50 people. Use the information in the frequency table to copy and complete the pie chart.

Type of film	Frequency
Action	10
Comedy	10
Romance	25
Science fiction	5

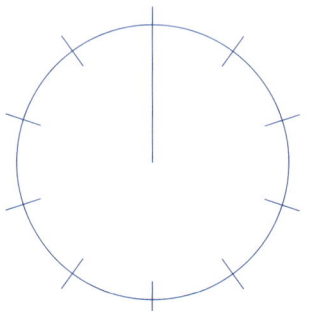

Each sector represents 50 ÷ 10 = 5 people	The pie chart has markings around the circumference dividing it into 10 equal parts. Start by working out how many people each of these parts represents.	(pie chart with 10 equal sectors, each labelled 5)
Action 10 people = 2 × 5 people 2 sectors Comedy 10 people = 2 × 5 people 2 sectors Romance 25 people = 5 × 5 people 5 sectors Science Fiction 5 people = 1 × 5 people 1 sector	Work out how many sectors are needed to represent each of the frequencies.	(completed pie chart showing science fiction, action, comedy, romance sectors)

Exercise 3

1 The table shows information about hair colour in a group of students. Use the diagram to draw a pie chart for this data.

Hair colour	Frequency
Blonde	6
Brown	12
Black	6

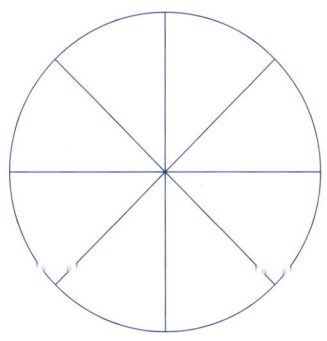

2 The table shows information about the 60 passengers travelling on a train. Use the diagram to draw a pie chart for this data.

Passengers	Frequency
Men	18
Women	24
Boys	6
Girls	12

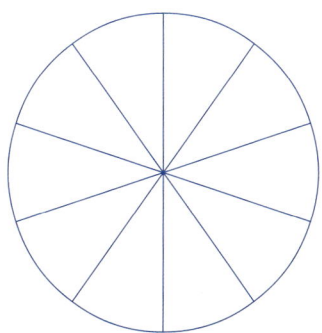

Chapter 23: Displaying data

3 Students in Amandeep's school choose some of the subjects that they will study in Year 10. Amandeep has drawn a pie chart to show the proportion of 100 students that chose each subject.

Write anything that is wrong or could be misleading about this pie chart.

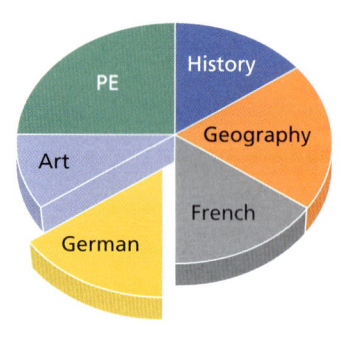

4 The pie charts show the favourite type of chocolate for 40 boys and 40 girls.

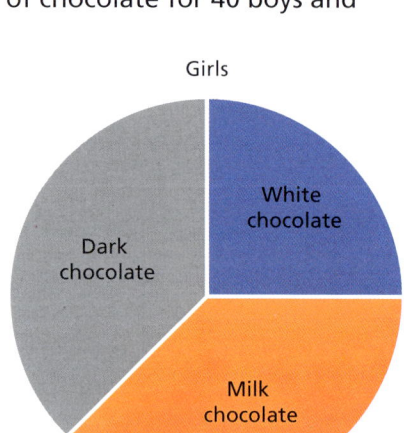

a) How many boys said that milk chocolate was their favourite?
b) How many more girls than boys said they liked white chocolate?
c) Which type of chocolate is favourite for equal numbers of boys and girls?

Think about

If you did not know the total number of boys and the total number of girls would you be able to answer part (c)?

5 The incomplete table and incomplete pie chart show information about what some people had for breakfast.

Breakfast	Frequency
Cereal	30
Toast	
Cooked breakfast	
Nothing	10

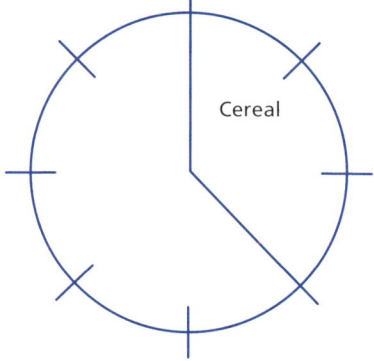

Equal numbers of people had toast and cooked breakfast.

a) Use the information provided and the pie chart to copy and complete the frequency table.
b) Use the information provided and the table to copy and complete the pie chart.

Tip

Remember to label your sectors.

6 **Vocabulary feature question**

Complete the statements using words in the box.

| frequencies   proportion   frequency |

In a pie chart, each .... of the circle is proportional to the .... that it represents. .... can be worked out if you know how many pieces of data there are in total.

End of chapter reflection

You should know that ...	You should be able to ...	Such as ...
Pictograms, bar charts and bar-line graphs show frequencies.	Construct and interpret these diagrams.	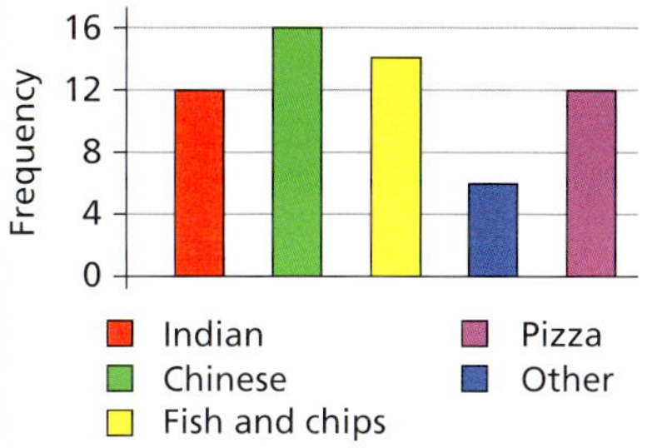 [Bar chart showing frequencies: Indian 12, Chinese 16, Fish and chips 14, Other 6, Pizza 12] Draw a pictogram to represent the data shown in this bar chart.
Pie charts show proportions.	Construct and interpret pie charts, including when the total amount is also given.	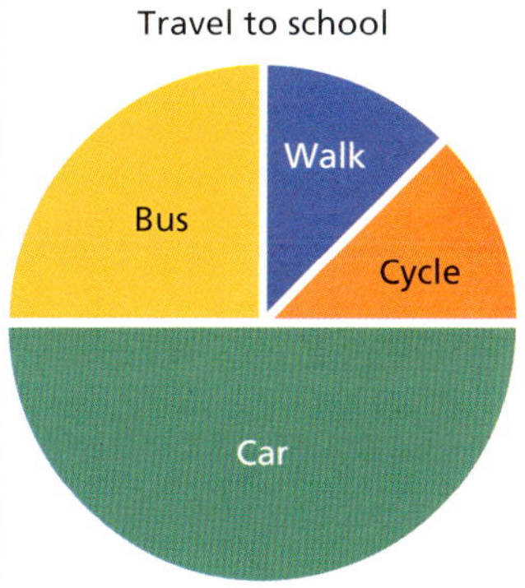 [Pie chart titled "Travel to school" with sections: Walk, Bus, Cycle, Car] This pie chart represents 32 students. How many students said they took the bus?

Unit 2C • Chapter 24

Probability 2

You will learn how to:
- Identify all the possible mutually exclusive outcomes of a single event.
- Use experimental data to estimate probabilities.
- Compare experimental and theoretical probabilities in simple contexts.

Starting point

Do you remember …?

- how to find a simple probability?
  For example, what is the probability of rolling a 4 on a fair six-sided dice?
- how to convert a fraction to a decimal or percentage?
  For example, what is $\frac{4}{5}$ as a percentage?

This will be helpful when …

you learn more about listing outcomes of events to find probabilities.
For example, two fair coins are tossed, what is the probability of getting heads on both coins?

Hook

The probability of something happening is used by insurance companies to determine the rate they charge for insurance.

Sanjay finds that insurance for a skiing holiday costs more than insurance for a beach holiday.
This table shows the travel insurance claims made against one travel company in 2012:

Type of claim	Percentage of claims
Medical expenses	56
Cancellations	34
Baggage and money	5
Other	5

What were the majority of claims made for?
What percentage of claims were for cancellations?

Identifying outcomes

Key terms

The possible **outcomes** of an **event** are the possible results when the event takes place. For example, there are 6 possible outcomes from rolling a six-sided dice. These are 1, 2, 3, 4, 5 or 6.

Two outcomes are **mutually exclusive** if they cannot happen at the same time. For example, you cannot roll a 4 and a 6 on a single roll of a six-sided dice, so rolling a 4 and rolling a 6 are **mutually exclusive.**

Worked example 1

Write all the possible mutually exclusive outcomes when the following events take place:

a) A coin is tossed

b) Spinning this spinner

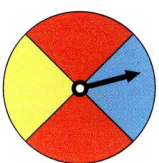

a) heads or tails	There are two sides to a coin; heads and tails. There are no other possible outcomes from tossing a coin.	
b) blue, red or yellow	There are three colours, so there are three possible outcomes.	

Exercise 1

1 List all the possible outcomes for rolling each of these numbered dice.

a) 　　b)

　　six-sided dice　　eight-sided dice

2 List all the possible outcomes for randomly selecting a ball from each bag.

a) 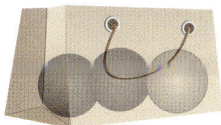　　b)

c) 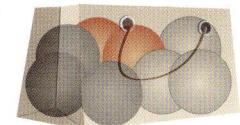　　d)

3 List all the possible outcomes for choosing a letter at random from each of these words.

a) M A T H S　　b) E V E N T

c) S P I N N E R　　d) P R O B A B I L I T Y

Chapter 24: Probability 2　　**211**

4 Are these pairs of outcomes mutually exclusive or not?
   a) Going to school and not going to school.
   b) Having toast for breakfast on a particular day and having cereal for breakfast on a particular day.
   c) A student picked at random from a class being a hockey player and a student picked at random from a class being a football player.

5 Are these pairs of outcomes of a single roll of a six-sided dice mutually exclusive or not?
   a) Rolling an even number on a six-sided dice
      Rolling an odd number on a six-sided dice
   b) Rolling an even number on a six-sided dice
      Rolling a multiple of 3 on a six-sided dice
   c) Rolling an odd number on a six-sided dice
      Rolling a factor of 10 on a six-sided dice

6 Sunita says,

"Rolling a prime number on a six-sided dice and rolling a square number on a six-sided dice are **not** mutually exclusive."

Is Sunita correct? Explain your answer.

7 You have an eight-sided dice.

Give pairs of outcomes that are:
   a) mutually exclusive.
   b) not mutually exclusive.

Try to list as many as you can for each part.

Estimating probabilities

Worked example 2

Ruth has a four-sided dice with sides labelled 1, 2, 3 or 4.

She has rolled the dice 20 times and wants to use the results to estimate the probability of rolling a 4.

Number on the dice	1	2	3	4
Frequency	7	8	2	3

What is the experimental probability Ruth will roll a 4 using this dice?

Estimated probability	Ruth rolled a 4 three times from 20 rolls of the dice.
$= \frac{\text{number of 4's rolled}}{\text{total number of rolls}}$ $= \frac{3}{7+8+2+3}$ $= \frac{3}{20}$	To estimate the probability you divide the number of 4's rolled by the total number of rolls. To find the total number of rolls you add all of the frequencies. As a decimal this is 0.15 and as a percentage it is 15%.

Exercise 2   1, 8

1 Marlene is spinning a spinner with three equal sectors. This is a record of the number of times that the spinner lands on red, yellow and blue.

Red	Yellow	Blue
2	5	3

Find an estimate for the probability of spinning:

a) red   b) yellow   c) blue

2 Noah's class are rolling six-sided dice. Find an estimate of the probability of each student rolling a 6 on their dice.

a) William

Number on dice	1	2	3	4	5	6
Frequency	3	1	7	3	4	2

b) Angelo

Number on dice	1	2	3	4	5	6
Frequency	11	6	9	9	11	4

c) Josef

Number on dice	1	2	3	4	5	6
Frequency	3	8	1	4	2	2

d) Ethan

Number on dice	1	2	3	4	5	6
Frequency	5	4	6	5	1	4

3 This is a record of how often Hildimar is on time for school and how often he is late over 30 days.

On time	Late
27	3

Estimate the probability that Hildimar will be late for school tomorrow.

4 Lakmi records the number of wins, draws and loses for his basketball team in one season.

Win	Draw	Lose
36	25	19

a) How many matches were played in total?
b) Based on these results estimate the probability of Pedro's team winning their next match.

5 Mrs Lopez travels to work by train. This is a record of how often the train she catches is on time, is early and is late.

On time	Early	Late
43	4	3

Chapter 24: Probability 2   **213**

Based on these results

a) Estimate the probability that the train will be on time.
b) Estimate the probability that the train will be early.
c) Estimate the probability that the train will be late.

6 Minoo has a restaurant. Customers can choose to have their meals with rice, with potato or with neither. These were the customer choices on one day.

Rice	Potato	Neither
29	13	1

Based on these choices estimate the probability that:

a) A customer will choose a meal with rice.
b) A customer will choose a meal with potato.
c) A customer will choose a meal with neither rice nor potato.

7 Traffic Watch is a company that surveys road traffic.

They record the traffic passing their camera between 9 a.m. and 5 p.m.

These are the results for Monday.

Car	Bicycle	Lorry
19	8	8

Based on these results find an estimate of the probability that:

a) The vehicle passing the camera will be a lorry.
b) The vehicle passing the camera will be a bicycle.
c) The vehicle passing the cameral will be a car.

8 Jacob's class are spinning spinners and recording their results.

Copy and complete the tables to show the estimated probability of spinning each colour using that spinner.

Give your estimated probabilities as fractions

a)

Colour	Red	Blue	Yellow	Green
Frequency	5	3	8	4
Estimated probability				

b)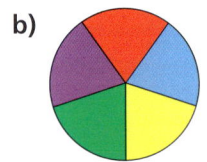

Colour	Red	Blue	Yellow	Green	Purple
Frequency	4	5	3	5	3
Estimated probability					

c)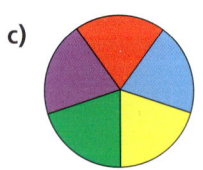

Colour	Red	Blue	Yellow	Green	Purple
Frequency	7	9	7	10	6
Estimated probability					

d)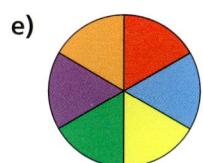

Colour	Red	Blue	Yellow	Green	Purple	Orange
Frequency	3	5	1	8	2	1
Estimated probability						

e)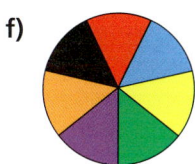

Colour	Red	Blue	Yellow	Green	Purple	Orange
Frequency	10	8	7	6	10	9
Estimated probability						

f)

Colour	Red	Blue	Yellow	Green	Purple	Orange	Black
Frequency	6	5	4	6	3	7	5
Estimated probability							

9 Using a six-sided dice roll the dice 10 times. Record the results in a spreadsheet and make a graph.

Roll the dice another 10 times. Record the results for all 20 rolls so far in a spreadsheet and make a new graph.

Keep adding the results from more rolls (more trials) and see what happens to the graphs you produce.

Comparing probabilities

Key term

The **theoretical probability** of an event is the number of ways an event can occur divided by all the possible outcomes.

$$P(\text{event}) = \frac{\text{Number of ways the event could occur}}{\text{Number of possible outcomes.}}$$

The probability of this spinner landing on yellow is $\frac{2}{5}$ because there are two out of five sections coloured yellow, and each section has an equal chance of being landed on as they are all the same size.

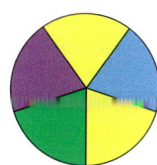

Worked example 3

Anna is going to roll a six-sided dice. She does not know whether or not it is fair.
Here are the results from rolling the dice 30 times:

Dice roll	1	2	3	4	5	6
Frequency	2	3	8	3	10	4

a) What is the theoretical probability of rolling each number on a six-sided dice?
b) What is the experimental probability that each number will be rolled on the dice?
c) Is the dice fair?

Chapter 24: Probability 2

a) P(1) = $\frac{1}{6}$
P(2) = $\frac{1}{6}$
P(3) = $\frac{1}{6}$
P(4) = $\frac{1}{6}$
P(5) = $\frac{1}{6}$
P(6) = $\frac{1}{6}$

The theoretical probability of rolling each number on a six-sided dice is the number of ways each number can occur over the number of possible outcomes.

b)

Roll	Experimental probability
1	$\frac{2}{30} = \frac{1}{15}$
2	$\frac{3}{30} = \frac{1}{10}$
3	$\frac{8}{30} = \frac{4}{15}$
4	$\frac{3}{30} = \frac{1}{10}$
5	$\frac{10}{30} = \frac{1}{3}$
6	$\frac{4}{30} = \frac{2}{15}$

To find the experimental probability you work out:

$$\frac{\text{Frequency of outcome}}{\text{Total number of trials}}$$

c) The probabilities are not similar so the dice is **not fair**.

You can see if the dice is fair by comparing the theoretical and experimental probabilities.

Discuss

How could Anna be more confident of her decision about whether the dice is fair?

Exercise 3

1 Charlie's results from rolling a four-sided dice are shown in the table.

	Charlie			
Number	1	2	3	4
Frequency	10	10	9	11

a) What is the theoretical probability that each number will be rolled?
b) What is the experimental probability that each number will be rolled?
c) Is Charlie's dice fair? Explain your answer.

Unit 2C: Handling data and geometry

2) Henry and Mason each roll a four-sided dice. Their results are shown in the tables.

Henry				
Number	1	2	3	4
Frequency	11	14	10	15

Mason				
Number	1	2	3	4
Frequency	33	17	28	22

a) How many times did they each roll their dice?
b) What is the theoretical probability that each number will be rolled on a four-sided dice?
c) What is the experimental probability that each number will be rolled for each dice?
d) Whose dice has results closer to those expected for theoretical probability? Whose dice is the fairest? Explain your answer.

3) Akong rolls a six-sided dice. His results are shown in the table.

Akong						
Number	1	2	3	4	5	6
Frequency	11	12	9	10	9	10

a) What is the theoretical probability that each number will be rolled?
b) What is the experimental probability that each number will be rolled?
c) Is Akong's dice fair? Explain your answer.

4) Abdo's results from rolling a six-sided dice are shown in the table.

Abdo						
Number	1	2	3	4	5	6
Frequency	10	7	7	11	10	15

a) What is the theoretical probability that each number will be rolled?
b) What is the experimental probability that each number will be rolled?
c) Is Abdo's dice fair? Explain your answer.

5) Talia and Favor's results from rolling a six-sided dice are shown in the tables.

Talia						
Number	1	2	3	4	5	6
Frequency	15	11	14	16	13	11

Favor						
Number	1	2	3	4	5	6
Frequency	20	19	11	15	11	4

a) What is the theoretical probability that each number will be rolled?
b) What is the experimental probability that each number will be rolled for each dice?
c) Whose dice is the fairest? Explain your answer.

6) Tariq spins a spinner with four equal sectors. His results are shown in the table.

Colour	Red	Blue	Green	Yellow
Frequency	17	20	13	30

Tariq says,
"The spinner is fair because the experimental probability for blue is equal to $\frac{1}{4}$".
Is Tariq correct? Explain your answer.

End of chapter reflection

You should know that …	You should be able to …	Such as …
An **outcome** is the possible result when an **event** takes place.	Identify all the possible mutually exclusive outcomes of a single event.	List all the possible outcomes of rolling a ten-sided dice.
Experimental Probability uses real experimental data P(event) = $\frac{\text{Number of times the event occurred}}{\text{Number of trials}}$	Use experimental data to estimate probabilities.	List the experimental probabilities of landing on each colour for this spinner from this table of results: 	Colour	red	blue	green
---	---	---	---
spins	12	16	12	
Theoretical probability requires every outcome to be mutually exclusive and equally likely. P(event) = $\frac{\text{Number of ways the event could occur}}{\text{Number of possible outcomes}}$	Compare experimental and theoretical probabilities in simple contexts.	These are Victoria's results when she rolled a four-sided dice. Is her dice a fair dice? Give a reason for your answer. | Number	1	2	3	4
---	---	---	---	---
Frequency	9	19	14	8	

3A

Unit 3A
Number and calculation

What's it all about?
- The order of operations
- Adding, subtracting, multiplying and dividing
- Working with percentages
- Working with ratios
- Direct proportion
- Comparing fractions

You will learn about:
- The order that calculations should be carried out in
- How to add, subtract, multiply and divide integers and decimals
- How to find a percentage of an amount
- How to make comparisons by using percentages
- Ratio notation, how to simplify ratios and how to divide in a ratio
- Working with direct proportion
- How to compare two fractions by using diagrams
- How to compare two fractions by converting to decimals

You will build your skills in:
- Arithmetic
- Comparing quantities
- Problem solving

Unit 3A • Chapter 25

Calculation

You will learn how to:
- Use the order of operations, including brackets, to work out simple calculations.
- Add and subtract integers and decimals, including numbers with different numbers of decimal places.
- Multiply and divide decimals with one and/or two places by single-digit numbers, for example, 13.7 × 8, 4.35 ÷ 5.
- Know that in any division where the dividend is not a multiple of the divisor there will be a remainder, for example, 157 ÷ 25 = 6 remainder 7. The remainder can be expressed as a fraction of the divisor, for example, $157 \div 25 = 6\frac{7}{25}$.

Starting point

Do you remember …?

- that multiplication and division should happen before addition and subtraction when you calculate?
  For example, calculate 7 + 3 × 4 in your head.
- how to add and subtract numbers mentally?
  For example, add 456 and 271 in your head.
- how to multiply and divide numbers mentally?
  For example, calculate 24 × 3 and 68 ÷ 4 in your head.
- how to add and subtract large numbers using a written method?
  For example, calculate 456 713 − 287 654.
- how to multiply a whole number by a single digit using a written method?
  For example, calculate 453 × 6.

This will be helpful when …

- you learn to calculate with decimals and percentages to solve problems with measures.
  For example, calculate 23% of 17.4 m.

Hook

Four Fours

| 4 | 4 | 4 | 4 |

How many of the numbers 1–20 can you make using only four 4s and the operations add, subtract, multiply and divide?

(You do not have to use all the 4s each time.)

Record your workings out, making sure your order of calculation is clear.
- Which numbers cannot be made? Why not?
- Are there any other numbers you can make beyond 20?
- What is the largest number that it is possible to make?
- Can you make a negative number?
- Can you make any decimals or fractions? For example, 0.5, 0.25, 0.2, $\frac{1}{3}$?

Order of operations

Key terms

The correct **order of operations** is the agreed order of calculating in mathematics.

The order is:
1. **Brackets**
2. **Indices** (powers and roots)
3. **Multiplication** and **Division**
4. **Addition** and **Subtraction**

Worked example 1

Calculate:

a) 2 + 3 × 5   b) 10 + 12 ÷ (7 − 3)

a) 2 + 3 × 5 2 + **3 × 5** = 2 + **15** = 17	When you calculate, you do multiplications and divisions BEFORE you do additions and subtractions. Therefore, you should calculate 3 × 5 first. Then you can calculate the addition.
b) 10 + 12 ÷ (7 − 3) 10 + 12 ÷ **(7 − 3)** = 10 + 12 ÷ **4** = 10 + **12 ÷ 4** = 10 + **3** = **10 + 3** = 13	You already know that you do multiplications and divisions BEFORE additions and subtractions. However, when there is a **bracket**, you calculate this first. Work out the bracket first. Next work out the division. Finally, work out the addition.

Did you know?

If there are brackets inside brackets, then you start from the innermost bracket out.

For example,

100 − (12 + (5 − 3)) = 100 − (12 + 2) = 100 − 14 = 86

Where there are two or more multiplications or divisions, the calculations should be carried out from left to right.

For example, 48 ÷ 8 ÷ 2 = 6 ÷ 2 = 3 because you calculate the 48 ÷ 8 first.

Where there are two or more additions and subtractions, the calculations are carried out from left to right.

For example, 36 − 17 + 5 = 19 + 5 = 24

Chapter 25: Calculation

Exercise 1

1 Calculate:
   a) 7 + 20 ÷ 4
   b) 24 − 5 × 2
   c) 6 + 9 ÷ 3 + 7
   d) 18 + 3 − 5
   e) 30 − 4 × 4 + 1
   f) 28 ÷ 4 × 3
   g) 24 ÷ 6 + 4 × 2
   h) (6 + 5) × 2
   i) 60 + (30 ÷ 5) × 2
   j) 15 × (8 − 6) + 5
   k) 56 ÷ (3 + 4) + 2
   l) 100 − (2 + 3 × 11)
   m) (6 + 5) × (3 + 8)
   n) (100 − 20) ÷ (2 + 8)
   o) $\frac{(12 + 4 \times 2)}{5}$
   p) (4 + 7 × (11 − 3)) ÷ 2

2 Li Jing is calculating 12 − 8 + 2.

She says, "I need to do the addition before the subtraction so the answer is 2 because 12 − 8 + 2 = 12 − 10 = 2".

Do you agree with Li Jing? Explain your answer.

3 By positioning a set of brackets in different places, how many different answers can you get to this calculation?

7 + 8 × 20 − 12 ÷ 2

How do you know you have got them all?

4 a) Use a scientific calculator to calculate 18 + 7 × 6 − 2.
   b) Use a basic calculator to calculate 18 + 7 × 6 − 2.
   c) Are your answers the same? Why or why not?

Addition and subtraction

Worked example 2

Calculate 13.8 + 7.56

13.8 + 7.56	Start by setting out your calculation in columns. Align the place values.	
1 3 . 8 + 7 . 5 6		
1 3 . 8 0 + 0 7 . 5 6	It's useful to fill any gaps with 0s to act as **placeholders**.	
1 3 . 8 0 + 0 7 . 5 6 6	Start adding from the column on the right. Add the hundredths.	

1 3 . 8 0
+ 0 7 . 5 6
          3 6
       1
	Now add the tenths.
	
	Because you end up with 13 tenths, you exchange ten of them for 1 unit and are left with only 3 tenths in the answer.	

1 3 . 8 0
+ 0 7 . 5 6
        1 . 3 6
   1 1
	You can now add the units. You have 3 and 7 and the extra 1 from the exchange – so 11 units altogether.
	
	Swap 10 units for 1 ten.	

1 3 . 8 0
+ 0 7 . 5 6
  2 1 . 3 6
   1 1
	Finally, you can add the tens.	

Worked example 3

Calculate 4562 – 3618

4562 – 3618 4 5 6 2 – 3 6 1 8	Start by setting out your calculation. Align the place values.	

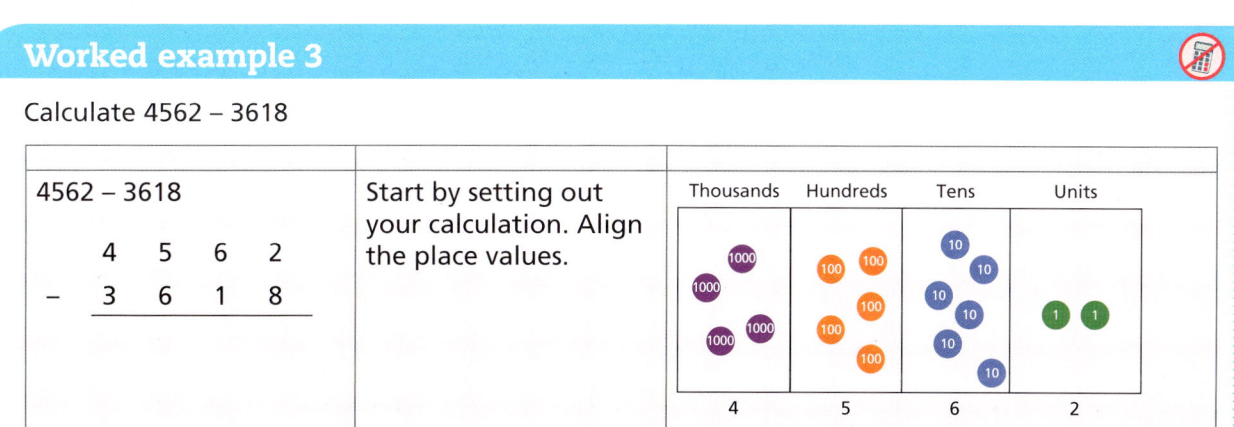

$\begin{array}{r} 4\ 5\ \overset{5}{\cancel{6}}{}^{1}2 \\ -\ 3\ 6\ 1\ 8 \\ \hline \end{array}$ $\begin{array}{r} 4\ 5\ \overset{5}{\cancel{6}}{}^{1}2 \\ -\ 3\ 6\ 1\ 8 \\ \hline 4 \end{array}$	**Now you can subtract the ones.** You don't have enough units to subtract 8, so you exchange 1 ten for 10 units leaving only 5 tens. You can now do the subtraction with 12 − 8 and remove 8 units.	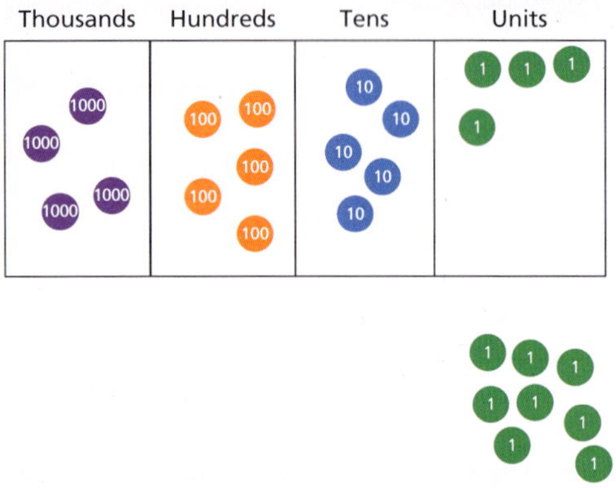
$\begin{array}{r} 4\ 5\ \overset{5}{\cancel{6}}{}^{1}2 \\ -\ 3\ 6\ 1\ 8 \\ \hline 4\ 4 \end{array}$	**Subtract the tens** by removing 1 ten from the remaining 5 tens.	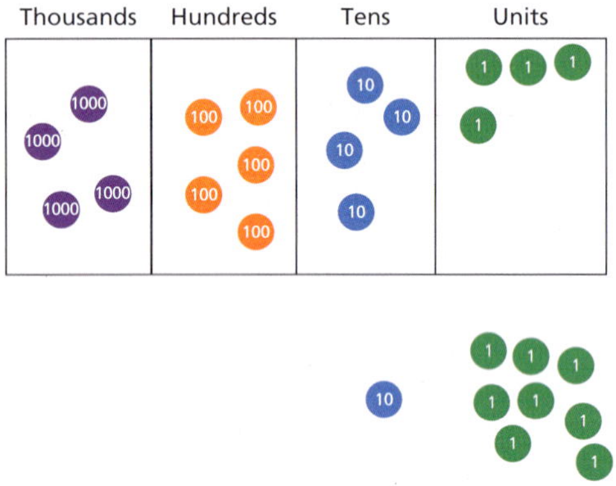
$\begin{array}{r} \overset{3}{\cancel{4}}{}^{1}5\ \overset{5}{\cancel{6}}{}^{1}2 \\ -\ 3\ 6\ 1\ 8 \\ \hline 4\ 4 \end{array}$ $\begin{array}{r} \overset{3}{\cancel{4}}{}^{1}5\ \overset{5}{\cancel{6}}{}^{1}2 \\ -\ 3\ 6\ 1\ 8 \\ \hline 9\ 4\ 4 \end{array}$	**Subtract the hundreds.** You need to subtract 6, but you only have 5. You exchange 1 thousand for 10 hundreds. You can now do the subtraction with 15 − 6, to leave 9 hundreds.	

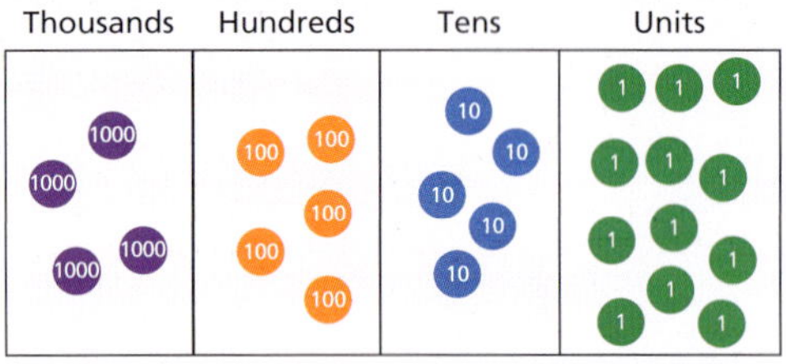

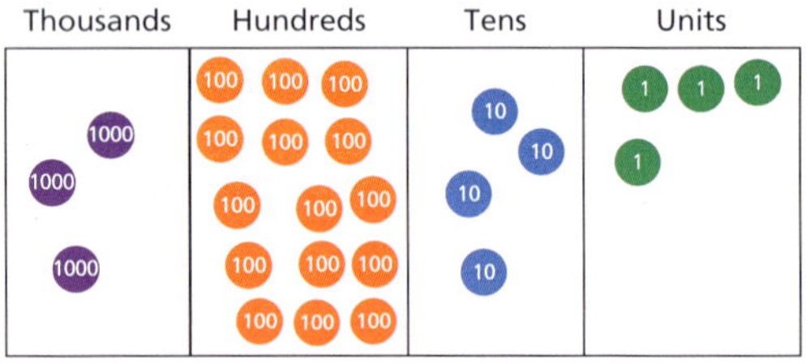

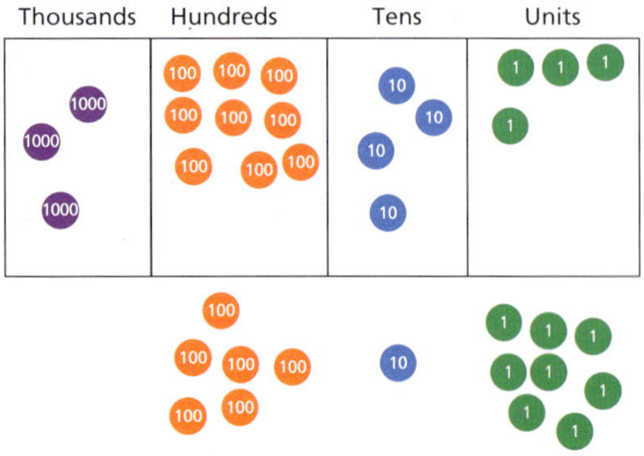

Unit 3A: Number and calculation

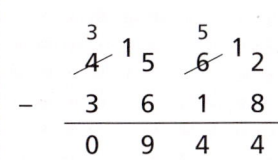

Finally you can subtract the thousands.

You have subtracted 3618 from 4562, which has left 944.

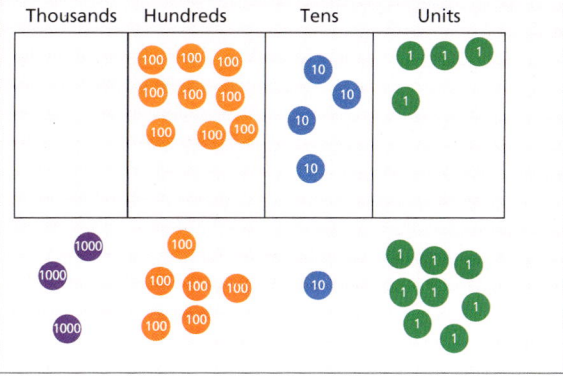

Exercise 2

1 Calculate these sums in your head first.

Check your mental calculation by using a written method.

a) 57 + 21   b) 53 + 28   c) 120 + 57   d) 143 + 28   e) 265 + 123

2 Use a written method to work these out.

a) 456 + 138   b) 389 + 715   c) 6714 + 1295   d) 13 416 + 6815

e) 367 + 2852   f) 7654 + 965   g) 4567 + 18 711   h) 38 755 + 72 219

3 Calculate these sums in your head first.

Check your mental calculation by using a written method.

a) 7.2 + 5.6   b) 5.6 + 8.7   c) 15.7 + 2.8

4 Use a written method to work these out.

a) 28.14 + 6.57   b) 2.059 + 3.65   c) 56.73 + 2.394

5 Calculate these differences in your head first.

Check your mental calculation by using a written method.

a) 46 – 21   b) 57 – 36

c) 73 – 49   d) 175 – 58

> **Tip**
>
> When using a written method, make sure you line up the decimal points so that you are adding digits with the same place value!

6 Use a written method to work these out.

a) 654 – 231   b) 6538 – 2126

c) 485 – 267   d) 917 – 268

e) 4372 – 2165   f) 8369 – 3581

g) 1672 – 958   h) 23 676 – 8589

7 Calculate these differences in your head first.

Check your mental calculation by using a written method.

a) 8.4 – 5.1   b) 6.73 – 2.52   c) 8.4 – 2.9   d) 13.5 – 6.7

8 Use a written method to work these out.

a) 35.61 – 19.48   b) 7.13 – 0.68   c) 5.2 – 3.61   d) 17.3 – 8.47

Chapter 25: Calculation

9 Imran is calculating 18.7 + 2.86.

Here is his working out:

```
    1   8 . 7
+   2 . 8   6
    4   7   3
    1   1
```

Imran says the answer is 47.3

Imran is wrong. Explain the error that Imran has made and correct it.

10 The difference between two numbers is 4.76.

One of the numbers is 8.9.

How many possibilities are there for the other number? Find them.

Multiplication and division

Worked example 4

Calculate: a) 42.6 × 7   b) 4.35 ÷ 3

a)	Set out your calculation. Align the place values.	42.6 × 7
$\begin{array}{r} 4\ 2\ .\ 6 \\ \times 7 \\ \hline \end{array}$		
$\begin{array}{r} 4\ 2\ .\ 6 \\ \times 7 \\ \hline .\ 2 \\ 4 \end{array}$	Start by multiplying the 6 tenths by 7 – this gives 42 tenths.	42 tenths
	42 tenths is the same as 4 ones and 2 tenths, so you record a 2 in the tenths column and an extra 4 ones at the bottom of the ones column.	

226   Unit 3A: Number and calculation

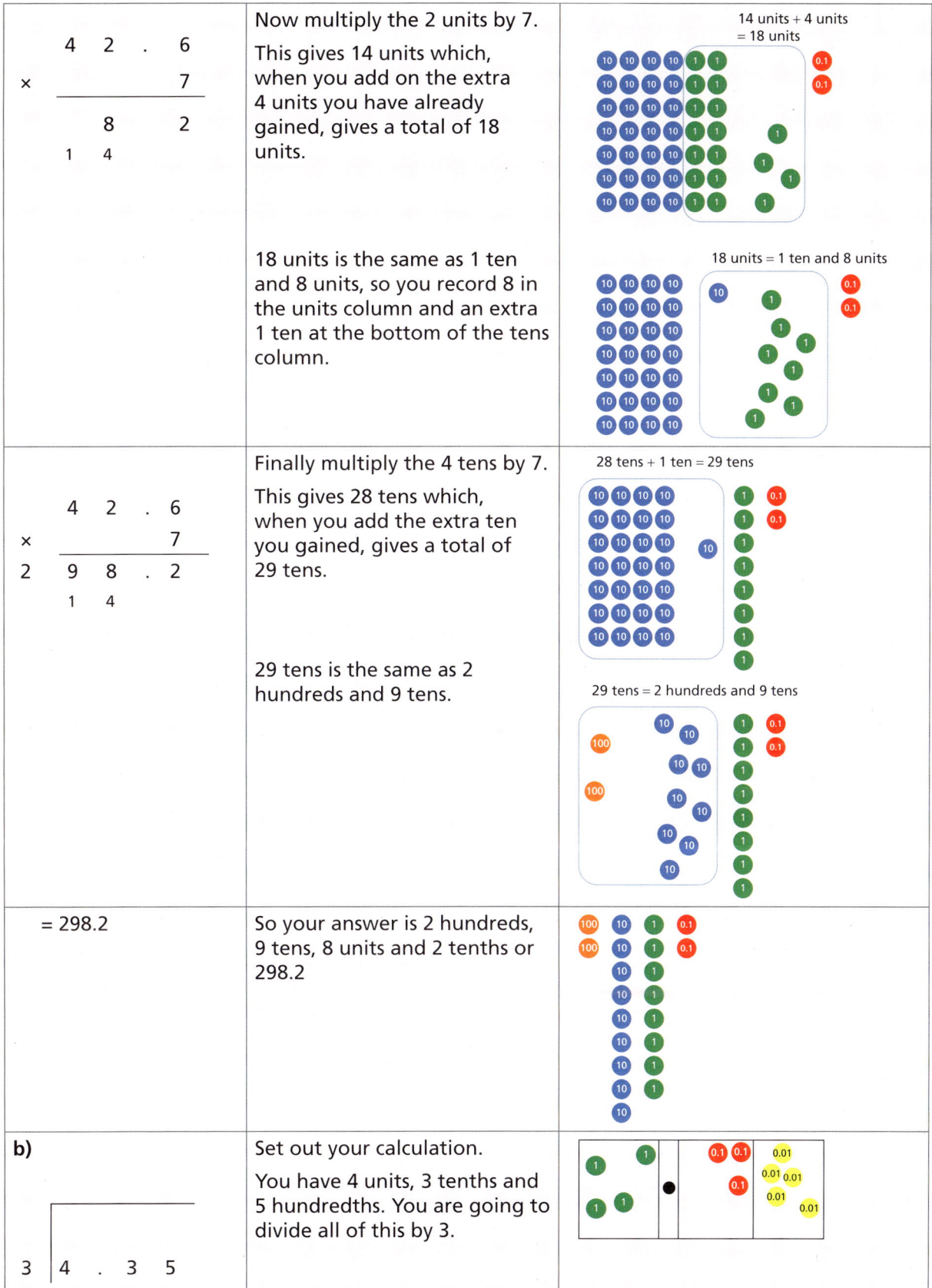

3)4 .¹3 5 with "1" above	Start by dividing or grouping the 4 units into 3s. You can make one group of three, with 1 unit remaining. You can exchange the remaining units for 10 tenths. You now have 13 tenths.	
1 . 4 3)4 .¹3 ¹5	You can now divide or group the tenths into 3s. You can make 4 groups with 1 tenth remaining. You exchange the tenth for 10 hundredths.	
1 . 4 5 3)4 .¹3 ¹5	Finally divide or group the hundredths into 3s. You can make exactly 5 groups.	
1.45	So your answer is 1 unit, 4 tenths and 5 hundredths or 1.45	

Exercise 3

1 Calculate mentally:
   a) 2.3 × 3   b) 5.1 × 5   c) 6.2 × 4   d) 3.5 × 4

2 Calculate using a written method:
   a) 4.2 × 3   b) 5.9 × 5   c) 17.2 × 6   d) 14.8 × 2
   e) 23.8 × 4   f) 24.6 × 9   g) 23.7 × 8   h) 15.3 × 7

3 Calculate using a written method:
   a) 3.12 × 3   b) 4.18 × 5   c) 9.23 × 6   d) 4.58 × 2
   e) 6.38 × 4   f) 4.65 × 9   g) 35.71 × 8   h) 28.27 × 7

4 Calculate mentally:
   a) 6.4 ÷ 2   b) 9.6 ÷ 3   c) 8.4 ÷ 4   d) 20.5 ÷ 5

5 Calculate using a written method:
   a) 8.7 ÷ 3   b) 5.2 ÷ 4   c) 13.2 ÷ 6   d) 37.5 ÷ 3
   e) 19.8 ÷ 9   f) 76.5 ÷ 5   g) 25.9 ÷ 7   h) 17.1 ÷ 9

6 Calculate using a written method:
   a) 7.82 ÷ 2   b) 9.24 ÷ 3   c) 5.32 ÷ 4   d) 7.14 ÷ 3
   e) 6.56 ÷ 8   f) 2.31 ÷ 7   g) 34.32 ÷ 6   h) 111.6 ÷ 9

7 Zoe has calculated 81.69 ÷ 7 using a written method.
   She has these digits in her answer: 1167
   Where should Zoe position the decimal point to give the correct answer?
   Explain how you know.

8 Calculate 5.38 × 6.
   Using your answer, what other related multiplication facts can you now write down?

> **Think about**
> How can you check whether your answer to a decimal multiplication is reasonable?
> For example, what would you estimate the answer to 8.39 × 7 to be?

Remainders

Worked example 5

Calculate 717 ÷ 5, leaving the **remainder** as a fraction.

Calculation	Explanation
5) 7 1 7	Set out the calculation.
1 5) 7 ²1 7	Then divide 7 into groups of 5. There is one group of 5, with 2 remaining.
1 4 5) 7 ²1 ¹7	Now divide 21 into groups of 5. There are 4 groups of 5, with 1 remaining.
1 4 3 r2 5) 7 ²1 ¹7	Finally divide 17 into groups of 5. There are 3 groups of 5 with 2 remaining.

Chapter 25: Calculation

$717 \div 5 = 143\frac{2}{5}$	You can express the remaining 2 as a fraction of the number you are dividing by – the **divisor**, 5. Therefore you write it as $\frac{2}{5}$.	Because $2 \div 5$ is $2/5$

Exercise 4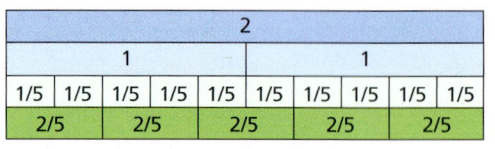

1 Calculate, expressing any remainder as a fraction of the divisor.

a) $823 \div 2$ b) $658 \div 3$ c) $457 \div 4$ d) $912 \div 5$
e) $842 \div 7$ f) $1013 \div 3$ g) $483 \div 8$ h) $1562 \div 12$

2 Seve is calculating $87 \div 12$

He writes $87 \div 12 = 7\frac{3}{87}$

Do you agree with Seve? Explain your answer.

3 What is the same and what is different about these three calculations?

$7185 \div 9$ $616 \div 3$ $4316 \div 6$

> **Discuss**
> How can you predict whether a division will leave a remainder? And how can you predict what that remainder will be?

4 Vocabulary feature question

Complete the sentences with the words from the box.

additions	multiplication or division	inside brackets	placeholders
multiplications	right	exact	remainder	left
divisor	order of operations	right	subtractions
divisions	zeroes	indices	left	addition or subtraction

When calculating in mathematics it is important to use the correct ....

First you should calculate operations that are .... Secondly, you should work out ....

Then you should calculate .... and .... before finally calculating .... and ....

If there is more than one ...., then you should calculate them from .... to ....

If there is more than one ...., then you should calculate them from .... to ....

Unit 3A: Number and calculation

When adding or subtracting decimals or numbers of different lengths, you can use .... as .... to keep your calculation aligned.

You can add, subtract and multiply any numbers; however, when you divide you do not always get an .... answer. In this case you have a ...., which you can express as a fraction of the ....

End of chapter reflection

You should know that …	You should be able to …	Such as …
The correct mathematical order of operations or calculations is 1. Brackets 2. Indices (powers or roots) 3. Multiplication and Division 4. Addition and Subtraction When there are multiple operations at the same level, it is correct to work through them from left to right.	Calculate in the correct order.	Calculate: (7 − 2) × 4 + 20 ÷ 2
	Add and subtract two whole numbers or decimals: • where the numbers are of the same size • where the numbers are of different sizes.	Calculate: a) 45.63 + 13.98 b) 6548 − 2167 c) 943 + 23 365 d) 15.6 − 4.39
	Multiply a decimal of 1 or 2 decimal places by a single-digit.	Calculate: 5.28 × 6
	Divide a decimal of one or two decimal places by a single digit.	Calculate: 5.61 ÷ 3
A remainder is the amount left over at the end of a division.	Predict when a division will result in a remainder.	Which of these calculations will not give an exact answer? 456 ÷ 4 712 ÷ 3 655 ÷ 5
A remainder can be expressed as a fraction of the original divisor.	Calculate the result of a division of whole numbers, leaving the remainder as a fraction of the divisor.	Calculate, leaving the remainder as a fraction 745 ÷ 9

Unit 3A • Chapter 26

Percentages

You will learn how to:
- Calculate simple percentages of quantities (whole number answers).
- Express a smaller quantity as a fraction or percentage of a larger one.
- Use percentages to represent and compare different quantities.

Starting point

Do you remember …?

- that a percentage tells you the number of parts in every 100?
- how to write these fractions as percentages: $\frac{1}{2}, \frac{1}{4}, \frac{1}{3}, \frac{1}{10}, \frac{1}{100}$?
- how to find simple percentages of a shape or a number?
  For example, find 25% of 160.

This will be helpful when …

you learn more about percentage increases and decreases.
For example, some shoes cost $60 and are reduced in a sale by 15%. What is the sale price?

Hook

You visit a shop to buy some biscuits.

One 200 g pack of biscuits usually costs $1.50.

There are four different offers on the biscuits …

| 50% extra free | 3 packs for the price of 2! | Save ¼ of the price! | 20% off |

- What is the price of each offer?
- Which is the best offer?
- Which is the worst offer?
- Are there any other things to consider when making your purchase?

232 Unit 3A: Number and calculation

Finding a percentage of an amount

Key terms

A **percentage**, notated using the % sign, represents a number of parts per 100.
For example, 15% means 15 out of every 100.
100% is called the **whole**.

Worked example 1

Find 15% of 240 g.

100% = 240 g	240 g is the whole amount so is 100%.	
240 ÷ 10 = 24 g 10% = 24 g	If you split 240 g into 10 equal pieces, each piece will have the value of 10% of the original amount.	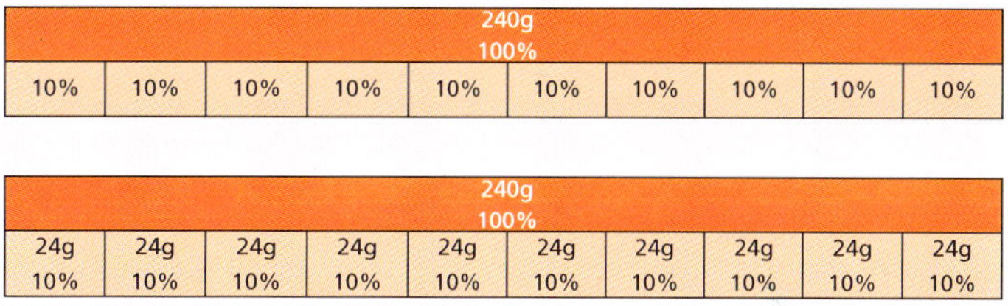
24 ÷ 2 = 12 g 5% = 12 g	You can find 15% by adding 10% and 5%. You need to start by finding 5%. You can find 5% by dividing 10% by 2.	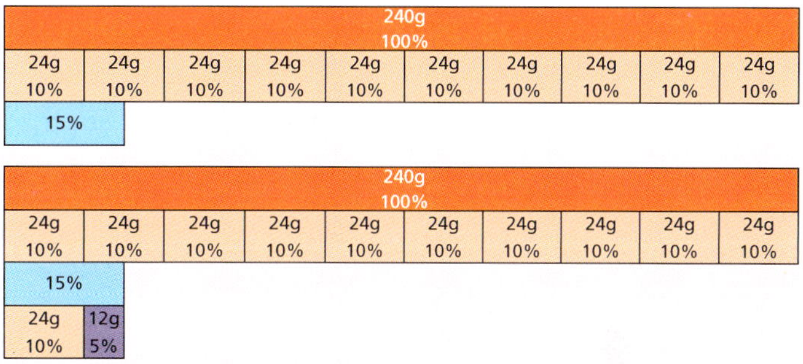
15% = 24 g + 12 g = 36 g	10% + 5% = 15%	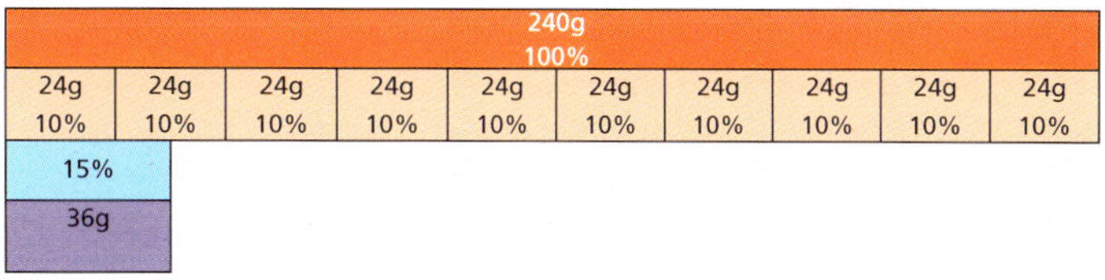

Worked example 2

Find 23% of $400.

100% = $400	$400 is the whole amount. This means $400 is 100%.	
$400 ÷ 10 = $40 10% = $40	If you split $400 into 10 equal pieces, each piece will have the value of 10% of the original amount.	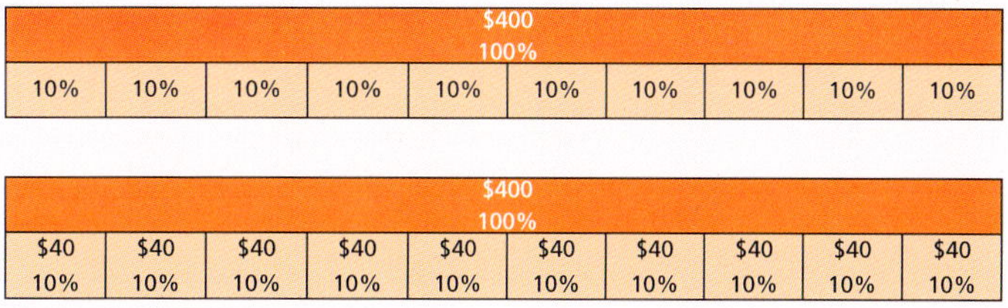

Chapter 26: Percentages 233

$40 ÷ 10 = $4 1% = $4	If you split 10% into 10 equal pieces, each piece will have the value of 1% of the original amount.	$40 / 10% split into ten 1% pieces $40 / 10% split into ten $4 / 1% pieces
23% = 2 × 10% + 3 × 1% = 2 × $40 + 3 × $4 = $92	You can make 23% with two lots of 10% and three lots of 1%. 2 × $40 + 3 × $4 = $92	23% shown as two $40 (10%) blocks plus three $4 (1%) blocks

Exercise 1

1 Find 10% of each of these quantities.
   a) 360   b) 900 km   c) 30 kg   d) $4000   e) 450 g
   f) 290 cm   g) 4250 ml   h) $14 000   i) 34 500 kg   j) 45 760 m

2 Find the given percentages of $160.
   a) 10%   b) 20%   c) 30%   d) 90%   e) 50%
   f) 5%   g) 15%   h) 35%   i) 55%   j) 95%

3 Find the given percentages of $7500.
   a) 10%   b) 20%   c) 30%   d) 90%   e) 50%
   f) 5%   g) 15%   h) 35%   i) 55%   j) 95%
   k) 1%   l) 2%   m) 3%   n) 23%   o) 91%

4 Calculate:
   a) 50% of 300   b) 40% of 600 kg
   c) 70% of 50 cm   d) 5% of 40 mm
   e) 15% of 20 tonnes   f) 25% of 140 miles
   g) 2% of 2300 g   h) 25% of 440 ml
   i) 11% of 5600 kg   j) 90% of 350 km
   k) 20% of $50   l) 16% of $250

5 Caleb is calculating 8% of 1400 kg.
He says, 'The answer is 1400 ÷ 8 = 175 kg'.
Caleb is wrong. Explain the error that Caleb has made and correct his answer.

6 How many ways can you show that 55% of 180 is 99?
Think about the different ways that you can show your calculation.

7 Use your calculator to find these percentages:
70% of 60% of $500
60% of 70% of $500
What do you notice?
Investigate for other percentages and other starting amounts.

> **Tip**
> You can use the % key on your calculator to type in a percentage or you can type the equivalent decimal.

Writing one amount as a percentage of another

Worked example 3

a) Express 75 g as a fraction of 175 g.
b) Express 65c as a percentage of $5.

a) You write the **part** required as the **numerator** of the fraction and the whole as the **denominator**. $\frac{75}{175}$	Here we are looking at a part of 75 g compared to a whole of 175 g.	
	You can divide both 175 and 75 by 25 to simplify the fraction.	
$\frac{75}{175} = \frac{75 \div 25}{175 \div 25} = \frac{3}{7}$		$\frac{3}{7}$
b)	Here you are looking at a part of 65c compared to a whole of $5.	
$5 = 500c	This comparison is quite difficult to make because one quantity is in dollars and the other in cents. Therefore, you need to convert them both to cents.	

$= \frac{65}{500}$	You can write these as a fraction as before, with 65 as the numerator and 500 as the denominator.	
$\frac{65}{500} = \frac{65 \div 5}{500 \div 5} = \frac{13}{100}$	A percentage is a comparison to 100, so you need to convert your fraction to one with a denominator of 100.	
$\frac{13}{100} = 13\%$	You can read a fraction with denominator 100 as a percentage.	

Exercise 2

1 Express the following masses as a fraction of 200 g, simplifying your answer wherever possible.
   a) 40 g   b) 20 g
   c) 75 g   d) 150 g
   e) 6 g   f) 2 g
   g) 9 g   h) 171 g
   i) 145 g   j) 160 g

2 Express the following lengths as a fraction of 60 cm, simplifying your answer wherever possible.
   a) 20 cm   b) 40 cm
   c) 50 cm   d) 45 cm
   e) 6 cm   f) 3 cm
   g) 25 cm   h) 33 cm
   i) 2 cm   j) 24 cm

3 Express, simplifying your answer where possible:
   a) 7 as a fraction of 20   b) 85 as a fraction of 90   c) 48 as a fraction of 72
   d) 14 as a fraction of 35   e) 16 as a fraction of 24   f) 96 as a fraction of 120
   g) 21 as a fraction of 49   h) 144 as a fraction of 360   i) 175 as a fraction of 625

4 Express the following capacities as a percentage of 50 ml.
   a) 23 ml   b) 16 ml   c) 49 ml   d) 2 ml   e) 6.5 ml   f) 10 ml

5 Express the following quantities as a percentage of 300.
   a) 30   b) 90   c) 240   d) 66   e) 213   f) 183

6 Express:
   a) 128 g as a percentage of 200 g
   b) 14 tonnes as a percentage of 25 tonnes
   c) 448 m as a percentage of 800 m
   d) 144 ml as a percentage of 1200 ml
   e) $17 as a percentage of $20
   f) $32 as a percentage of $40
   g) 54 seconds as a percentage of 60 seconds
   h) 36 cm as a percentage of 4 m
   i) 27 mm as a percentage of 5 cm
   j) 750 g as a percentage of 5 kg

7 Serena says that 75 mm is 10% of 750 cm.

Serena is wrong. Explain what Serena has done wrong and correct her answer.

8 Isra has 68 ml of liquid left in a container.

This is 4% of the total contents of the container.

How much liquid was there in the container originally?

Try to use a bar model to justify your answer.

> **Did you know?**
>
> In lots of countries and states there are taxes on sales of goods.
>
> These taxes are given in percentages.
>
> Shops and retailers need to work out the tax for each product and add it on to the cost.
>
> You might need to work them out in your head to see how much something will cost in total.
>
> For example, in the United Kingdom there is a 20% tax on most goods and services.

Comparing using percentages

Worked example 4

A company is testing a product.
In Trial A, the product was successful in 166 out of 200 tests.
In Trial B, the product was successful in 68 out of 80 tests.
In which trial was the product more successful?

166 out of 200 vs 68 out of 80	You cannot compare these trials easily because they are out of different amounts. Therefore, you need to convert each proportion to a percentage to help you compare.	
Trial A: 166 out of 200 $= \frac{166}{200}$ $= \frac{83}{100}$ $= 83\%$		

Chapter 26: Percentages

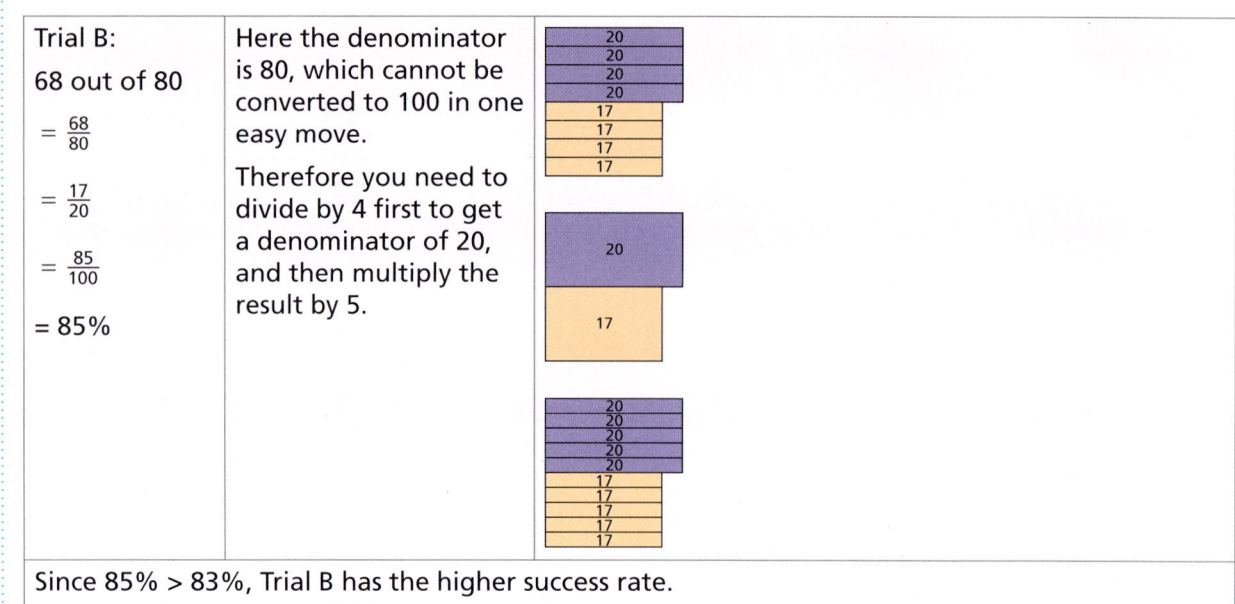

Trial B:
68 out of 80
$= \frac{68}{80}$
$= \frac{17}{20}$
$= \frac{85}{100}$
$= 85\%$

Here the denominator is 80, which cannot be converted to 100 in one easy move.

Therefore you need to divide by 4 first to get a denominator of 20, and then multiply the result by 5.

Since 85% > 83%, Trial B has the higher success rate.

Exercise 3

1. Convert these fractions to percentages and use this to state which is greater.
   a) $\frac{34}{50}$ and $\frac{67}{100}$
   b) $\frac{27}{50}$ and $\frac{14}{25}$
   c) $\frac{17}{25}$ and $\frac{7}{10}$

2. Convert these fractions to percentages and use this to state which is greater.
   a) $\frac{29}{50}$ and $\frac{11}{20}$
   b) $\frac{13}{20}$ and $\frac{7}{10}$
   c) $\frac{9}{20}$ and $\frac{11}{25}$

3. Two driving instructors are comparing their driving test pass rates.
   Driving instructor A has had 16 people pass out of 25 people who learned to drive with them.
   Driving instructor B has had 36 people pass out of 50 people who learned to drive with them.
   Which driving instructor has a higher percentage pass rate?

4. Convert these fractions to percentages and use this to state which is greater.
   a) $\frac{13}{20}$ and $\frac{31}{50}$
   b) $\frac{37}{50}$ and $\frac{225}{300}$
   c) $\frac{135}{500}$ and $\frac{104}{400}$

5. A cupcake recipe uses 140 g of butter out of ingredients totalling 400 g.
   Another recipe uses 90 g of butter out of ingredients totalling 250 g.
   Which recipe uses the higher percentage of butter?

6. In a sports competition, 7 out of 20 of the cycling team, 11 out of 25 of the athletics team and 14 of the 35 members of the swimming team won a race.
   Which sports team achieved the highest percentage of race wins?

Discuss
Can you have a percentage that is greater than 100%?
What would this mean?

Unit 3A: Number and calculation

7 Vocabulary feature question

Complete the sentences with words from the box.

| percentages | per | fraction | hundred | numerator | percentage |

A percentage represents the numbers of parts .... in a quantity.

You can compare quantities by writing them as .... of the whole.

A .... with a denominator of 100 can easily be converted to a percentage by reading

off the ...., which represents the .... of the whole you have.

End of chapter reflection

You should know that ...	You should be able to ...	Such as ...
A percentage represents the number of parts per hundred of the whole.	Find a percentage of an amount.	Find 15% of 720 m.
You can convert fractions to percentages by finding an equivalent fraction with denominator 100.	Express a quantity as a percentage of a larger quantity.	What is 28 g as a percentage of 35 g?
	Express a quantity as a percentage of a larger quantity with different units.	Write 420 kg as a percentage of 2 tonnes
	Compare two quantities using percentages to say which is larger.	Which is greater: 33 as a percentage of 75 or 162 as a percentage of 360

Unit 3A • Chapter 27

Ratio and proportion

You will learn how to:
- Use ratio notation, simplify ratios and divide a quantity into two parts in a given ratio.
- Recognise the relationship between ratio and proportion.
- Use direct proportion in context; solve simple problems involving ratio and direct proportion.

Starting point

Do you remember …?

- how to solve a scaling problem?

  For example, if 6 eggs cost $1.44, how much do 12 eggs cost? Or 3 eggs?
- how to write a proportion of a set of objects as a fraction?

  For example, what proportion of the letters in the word MATHEMATICS are vowels?

This will be helpful when …

you learn more about solving problems with ratios and proportions in real life such as scale drawing.

Hook

A hardware store has a special offer on cans of paint.

- Monique pays for 14 cans of paint. How many cans of paint does she get for free?
- Chen needs 12 cans of paint. How many cans of paint will he need to pay for using this offer?
- Write some of your own questions using this special offer.

Ratio

Key terms

A **ratio** compares the relative sizes of two quantities.

You write a ratio using a **colon** (:) between the two relative sizes of each quantity, in the order they appear in the text.

For example, if the ratio of boys to girls in a class is 2 : 3, this means that for every 2 boys there are 3 girls.

> **Think about**
>
> Where have you seen ratios in real life?

> **Did you know?**
>
> There are some ratios that are found in nature.
>
> The Golden Ratio, sometimes called phi or φ, can be found throughout the natural world and is often referred to as the Divine Proportion because it makes things seem so beautiful. The Mona Lisa is said to have a face in the Golden Ratio!

Key term

You can **simplify** a ratio by dividing the quantities it contains by a **common factor**.

For example, 20 : 50 can be simplified by dividing both sides by 10 (the highest common factor of 20 and 50) to give 2 : 5.

Worked example 1

Look at the diagram.

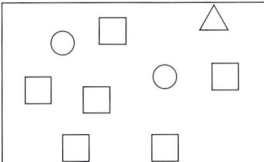

a) Write down the ratio of squares to triangles.

b) Write down the ratio of circles to squares. Give your ratio in its simplest form.

a) There are 6 squares and 1 triangle.

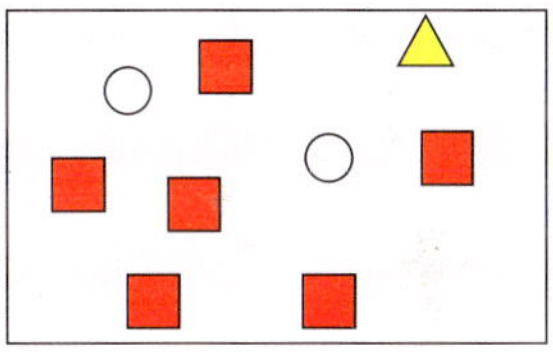

You write a **ratio** to compare two quantities in the order they appear in the text
squares : triangles
    6   :   1

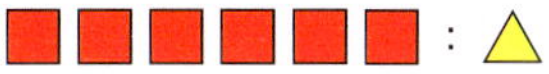

b) There are 2 circles and 6 squares.

You can write this ratio as
circles : squares
    2   :   6

However, you can **simplify** this ratio by dividing both numbers by a **common factor**, in this case 2, to get
circles : squares
    1   :   3

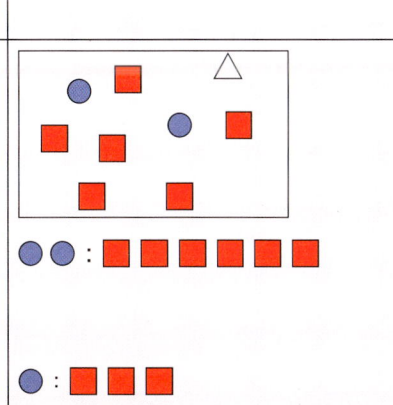

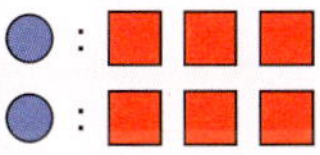

Chapter 27: Ratio and proportion

Exercise 1

1 Look at this diagram.

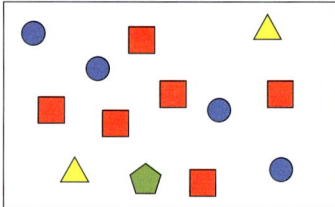

Write the following ratios, simplifying your answer where possible.

a) the ratio of squares to pentagons

c) the ratio of squares to circles

e) the ratio of triangles to squares

b) the ratio of triangles to pentagons

d) the ratio of circles to triangles

2 Simplify the following ratios where possible.

a) 6 : 4   b) 3 : 12   c) 30 : 40   d) 14 : 21

e) 15 : 20   f) 40 : 16   g) 9 : 24   h) 7 : 4

3 There are 15 girls and 9 boys in a class. Write down the ratio of girls to boys in its simplest form.

4 A farmer has 750 chickens and 150 cattle. Write down the ratio of chickens to cattle in its simplest form.

5 Here is a recipe for sponge cakes.

| 240 g flour |
| 200 g butter |
| 180 g sugar |
| 150 g whisked eggs |

a) Write down the ratio of flour to butter in its simplest form.

b) Write down the ratio of whisked eggs to sugar in its simplest form.

c) Write down the ratio of sugar to flour in its simplest form.

6 The ratio of blue marbles to black marbles is 1 : 3. There are 10 blue marbles. How many black marbles are there?

7 The ratio of boys to girls in a class is 5 : 4. There are 15 boys. How many girls are there?

8 The ratio of yellow sweets to green sweets in a pack is 2 : 3. There are 12 green sweets. How many yellow sweets are there?

9 There are 40 students on a school trip. The ratio of teachers to students is 1 : 5. How many teachers are there?

10 Melanie looks at this diagram.

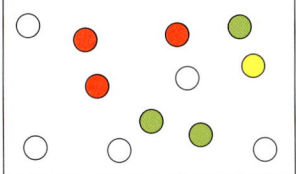

Melanie makes these statements:
- The ratio of red to green is 1 : 1
- The ratio of yellow to red is 3 : 1
- The ratio of red to not red is 3 : 12

Which of Melanie's statements are true and which are false?

Explain how you know.

11 There are 8 sweets in a bag. Some of them are red and some of them are yellow. How many possible different ratios of red to yellow sweets in the bag are there? Can you write these in their simplest form?

How do you know you have got them all?

Sharing in a ratio

Worked example 2

Divide 120 in the ratio 3 : 2

Divide 120 in the ratio 3 : 2.	You need to split 120 into two pieces with ratio 3 : 2.
3 + 2 = 5 120 ÷ 5 = 24	The ratio 3 : 2 contains 5 parts. So you need to divide 120 into 5 parts. Each part is worth 120 ÷ 5 = 24.
3 × 24 = 72 2 × 24 = 48 So the answer is 72 : 48	You need to group the parts into 3 : 2. 3 parts is worth 3 × 24 = 72 2 parts is worth 2 × 24 = 48

Chapter 27: Ratio and proportion

Exercise 2

1 Divide 60 in these ratios:
   a) 1 : 2   b) 11 : 1   c) 2 : 3   d) 1 : 3   e) 7 : 13   f) 3 : 7

2 Divide 105 in these ratios:
   a) 1 : 4   b) 6 : 1   c) 1 : 2   d) 3 : 2   e) 4 : 3   f) 20 : 1

3 A ribbon of length 65 cm is divided into two pieces in the ratio of 1 : 4. How long is each piece?

4 Two sisters divide 49 sweets in the ratio 3 : 4. How many do they each get?

5 Lily and Ezra share an inheritance of $25 000 in the ratio of 3 : 1. How much money do they each inherit?

6 Orange squash needs to be made using a ratio of 1 : 6 of concentrate to water. Susie wants to make 280 ml of squash. How much concentrate and water does she need?

7 Divide:
   a) $24 in the ratio 2 : 1
   b) 75 cm in the ratio 4 : 1
   c) 270 ml in the ratio 7 : 2
   d) $144 in the ratio 3 : 5
   e) 56 kg in the ratio 5 : 2
   f) $340 in the ratio 11 : 9
   g) 6 m in the ratio 3 : 2
   h) 3 hours in the ratio 1 : 8

> **Tip**
> Write the length in centimetres first.

8 Michael and Mo divide $12 870 in the ratio 3 : 2.

Michael says, "I should get $4290 and Mo should get $6435 because 12 870 ÷ 3 = 4290 and 12 870 ÷ 2 = 6435."

Do you agree with Michael? Explain your answer.

9 How can you check your answer to a question where you must divide in a given ratio?

Ratio and proportion

Key term

A **proportion** represents the size of a quantity relative to the whole.
It is usually expressed as a fraction.

Worked example 3

Gemma has a bag containing 17 sweets.
The **proportion** of red sweets in the bag is $\frac{5}{17}$.
The **proportion** of yellow sweets is $\frac{2}{17}$.
a) What is the ratio of red to yellow sweets?
The ratio of yellow sweets to green sweets is 1 : 2.
b) What is the proportion of green sweets in the bag?

a) The **proportion** of red sweets in the bag is $\frac{5}{17}$.

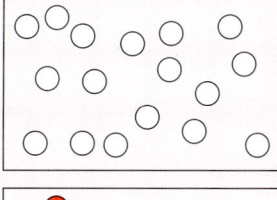

To find this ratio, represent the information in the question as a diagram.

Here are the sweets.

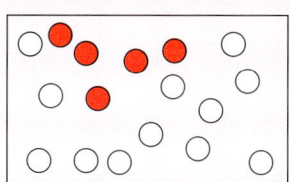

The **proportion** of red sweets is $\frac{5}{17}$.
This means 5 in every 17 sweets in the bag are red.

The **proportion** of yellow sweets is $\frac{2}{17}$

red : yellow

$\frac{5}{17} : \frac{2}{17}$
×17 ⤵ ⤵ ×17
5 : 2

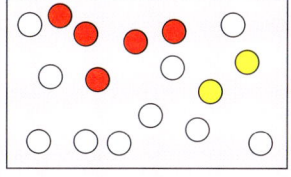

The proportion of yellow sweets is $\frac{2}{17}$.
This means 2 in every 17 sweets in the bag are yellow.

red : yellow
5 : 2

b) The ratio of yellow to green sweets is 1 : 2 so the proportion of green sweets in the bag

= $2 \times \frac{2}{17}$
= $\frac{4}{17}$

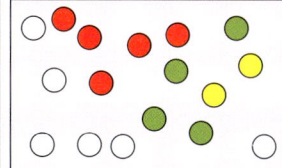

Since the ratio of yellow to green sweets is 1 : 2, for every yellow sweet there are 2 green sweets.

In every 17 sweets then, there are 2 × 2 = 4 green sweets.

So the proportion of green sweets = $\frac{4}{17}$.

Exercise 3

1 Alan and Bart share 15 marbles between them. Alan gets 7 and Bart gets 8.
   a) What is the ratio of Alan's marbles to Bart's marbles?
   b) What fraction of the marbles does Alan receive?
   c) What fraction of the marbles does Bart receive?

2 Charlotte and Deborah share 60 sweets. Charlotte gets 36 sweets.
   a) What is the ratio of Charlotte's sweets to Deborah's sweets?
   b) What fraction of the sweets does Charlotte receive? Give your fraction in its simplest form.
   c) What fraction of the sweets does Deborah receive? Give your fraction in its simplest form.

3 Fiona and Anders go on holiday. The holiday costs $750. Fiona pays $400.
   a) What proportion does Fiona pay? Write this proportion as a fraction in its simplest form.
   b) What proportion does Anders pay? Write this proportion as a fraction in its simplest form.
   c) What is the ratio of the amount Fiona pays to the amount Anders pays?

Chapter 27: Ratio and proportion

4 Blue and red paint is mixed to produce purple. The proportion of blue paint is $\frac{2}{5}$.
  a) What is the proportion of red paint? Write this proportion as a fraction.
  b) What is the ratio of blue to red paint?
  c) How much blue and red paint will be needed to make 20 litres of paint?

5 Mia and Hassan hire a car. Hassan pays $\frac{2}{3}$ of the bill.
  a) What proportion does Mia pay? Write this proportion as a fraction.
  b) What is the ratio of Mia's payment to Hassan's payment?
  c) If the cost of the hire car is $240, how much do they each pay?

6 In a cake recipe, 300 g of sugar is mixed with 800 g of flour.
  a) What proportion of the mix is sugar? Give your answer as a fraction in its simplest form.
  b) What proportion of the mix is flour? Give your answer as a fraction in its simplest form.
  c) Write the ratio of sugar to flour in its simplest form.

7 In a school there are 60 adults who represent $\frac{1}{10}$ of the school's population. The rest of the population are students.
  a) What proportion of the school's population is represented by the students?
  b) What is the ratio of adults to students?
  c) How many students are in the school?

8 Ali and Bill share some money. Ali receives $\frac{2}{5}$ of the money.
Bill says, "So Ali and I share the money in the ratio 2 : 5". Do you agree with Bill?
Explain your answer.

Direct proportion

Worked example 4

8 calculators cost $24. How much do 5 calculators cost?

8 calculators cost $24.	
Cost of 1 calculator = $24 ÷ 8 = $3. Therefore, cost of 5 calculators = $3 × 5 = $15	Share the $24 out equally to find the cost of each calculator. Now you can find the cost of 5 of these calculators by finding 5 lots of $3.

$24							
1 calculator	1 calculator	1 calculator	1 calculator	1 calculator	1 calculator	1 calculator	1 calculator

$24							
1 calculator	1 calculator	1 calculator	1 calculator	1 calculator	1 calculator	1 calculator	1 calculator
$3	$3	$3	$3	$3	$3	$3	$3

$24							
1 calculator	1 calculator	1 calculator	1 calculator	1 calculator	1 calculator	1 calculator	1 calculator
$3	$3	$3	$3	$3	$3	$3	$3
$15							

Exercise 4

1 5 tickets for the theatre cost $45. Calculate the cost of:
   a) 1 ticket   b) 3 tickets   c) 11 tickets

2 You need 240 g of flour to make 10 cupcakes. Calculate the amount of flour needed to make:
   a) 1 cupcake   b) 4 cupcakes   c) 13 cupcakes

3 Chris buys 7 pencils for 56 cents. Calculate the cost of:
   a) 2 pencils   b) 6 pencils   c) 10 pencils

4 A cleaner charges $72 for 6 hours of cleaning.
   a) How much does the cleaner charge for 2 hours of cleaning?
   b) How much does the cleaner charge for 9 hours of cleaning?

5 A 3 m ribbon costs $1.35. Calculate the cost of:
   a) a 2 m ribbon   b) a 12 m ribbon

6 1 foot is approximately equivalent to 30 cm.
   Calculate the approximate length of:
   a) 3 feet in cm   b) 8 feet in cm   c) 300 cm in feet   d) 90 cm in feet

7 There are 8 pints in 1 gallon.
   Calculate the number of:
   a) pints in 3 gallons   b) gallons in 40 pints

8 12 pens cost $18. Jasmine wants to find the cost of 15 pens. She says, "The cost will be $21, because you just add 3". Do you agree with Jasmine? Explain your answer.

9 18 cakes cost $12.96.
   Which other numbers of cakes are the easiest to find the cost of? Why?
   Find the cost of at least 5 different numbers of cakes.

10 **Vocabulary feature question**
   Complete the sentences with the key terms from the box.

   | ratio | dividing | part | simplify |
   | proportion | whole | multiplying | common factor |

   A .... compares two quantities directly to each other whereas a .... compares a single quantity to the ....

   You can .... both proportions and ratios by dividing by a ....

   You can use proportional reasoning to solve problems involving finding the value per item by .... or, if you know the value of one item, finding the value of more items by ....

End of chapter reflection

You should know that ...	You should be able to ...	Such as ...
A ratio compares two quantities directly.	Write a ratio to represent a situation.	a) An athlete has 4 gold, 11 silver and 3 bronze medals. Write the ratio of gold to silver medals.
	Simplify a ratio.	b) Simplify 14 : 56.
	Divide an amount in a given ratio.	c) Divide $150 in the ratio 4 : 1.
A proportion compares a quantity to the whole.	Write a proportion to represent a situation.	a) An athlete has 4 gold, 11 silver and 3 bronze medals. Write the proportion of silver medals.
	Work with both ratio and proportion in the same situation.	b) The proportion of boys in a class is $\frac{3}{7}$. What is the ratio of boys to girls in the class?
	Solve simple proportion problems.	c) If 5 apples cost 80 cents, how much do 9 apples cost?

Unit 3A • Chapter 28

Fractions and decimals

You will learn how to:
- Compare two fractions by using diagrams.
- Compare two fractions by using a calculator to convert the fractions to decimals, for example, $\frac{3}{5}$ and $\frac{13}{20}$.

Starting point

Do you remember …?

- how to convert from a fraction to a decimal by division?
  For example, convert $\frac{3}{8}$ to a decimal.

- the meaning of the symbols <, >, = ?
  For example, complete the gap by using the correct symbol from <, > and =   15…….23

This will also be helpful when …

- you learn more about converting between fractions, decimals and percentages.

Hook

Artem has a choice of two cakes.

Both cakes were the same size originally.

One of the cakes has $\frac{4}{5}$ left.

The other cake has $\frac{2}{3}$ left.

Artem wants to choose the cake with more left.

Which cake should he choose?

Artem draws the diagrams below to compare the amount of cake left.

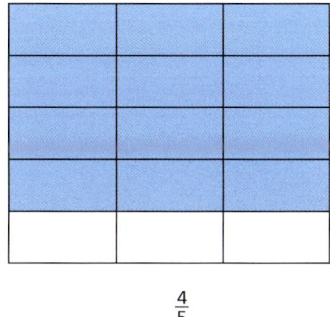

$\frac{4}{5}$ $\frac{2}{3}$

Artem chooses the cake with $\frac{4}{5}$ left.

Play this game with a partner.

Roll two dice. Write a fraction by putting the smaller number rolled as the numerator (top) of the fraction and the larger number as the denominator (bottom) of the fraction. If the two numbers are the same then roll again.

Make a second fraction by rolling the two dice again.

Compare the two fractions by drawing diagrams. Which is larger?

Chapter 28: Fractions and decimals   **249**

Comparing fractions using diagrams

Key terms

The **numer**ator is the number above the fraction line.
The **denominator** is the number below the fraction line.
< means less than
> means greater than

Did you know?

The Egyptians are the earliest known people to use fractions, but they wrote their fractions differently to how we do today.

Worked example 1

Compare $\frac{3}{4}$ and $\frac{5}{6}$ by using the fraction wall below.

Write a correct statement using <, > or =.

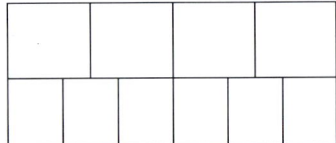

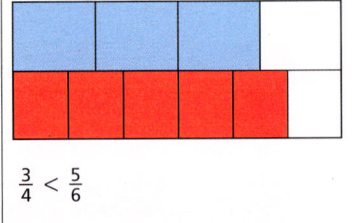 $\frac{3}{4} < \frac{5}{6}$ $\frac{5}{6} > \frac{3}{4}$	Shade in 3 of the 4 boxes in the top row to show $\frac{3}{4}$. Shade in 5 of the 6 boxes in the bottom row to show $\frac{5}{6}$. You can see that $\frac{3}{4}$ is less than $\frac{5}{6}$. You can also write that $\frac{5}{6}$ is greater than $\frac{3}{4}$.

Worked example 2

Compare $\frac{1}{3}$ and $\frac{2}{7}$ by drawing grids.
Use <, > or = to write your answer.

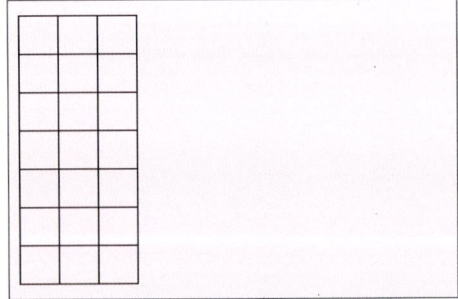	You need to choose a grid size that you could shade for either fraction. So you draw a 3 by 7 grid.

$\frac{1}{3}$ $\frac{2}{7}$		Draw one grid for each fraction and shade the squares to show the fractions.
$\frac{1}{3} > \frac{2}{7}$		More squares are shaded for $\frac{1}{3}$ than for $\frac{2}{7}$ so $\frac{1}{3}$ is greater than $\frac{2}{7}$.
$\frac{2}{7} < \frac{1}{3}$		You can also write $\frac{2}{7}$ is less than $\frac{1}{3}$.

> **Discuss**
> Is the fraction wall or the grid a better method for comparing fractions?
> Why is the method you have chosen better? Is that method always better?

Exercise 1

1 Use the fraction walls to find the larger fraction in each pair.

   a) $\frac{1}{4}$ or $\frac{3}{8}$ b) $\frac{3}{5}$ or $\frac{5}{8}$

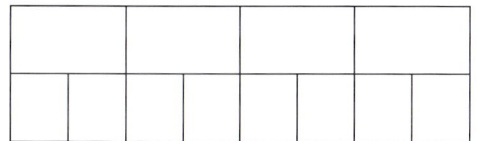 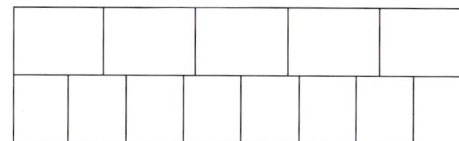

   c) $\frac{2}{3}$ or $\frac{3}{4}$ d) $\frac{3}{5}$ or $\frac{3}{4}$

 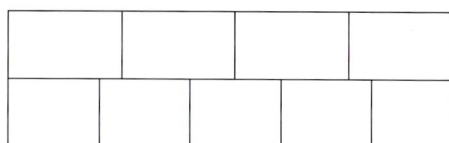

2 Use the fraction walls to compare the pairs of fractions. Write your comparison using <, > or =.

   a) $\frac{7}{10}$ and $\frac{5}{8}$ b) $\frac{1}{3}$ and $\frac{2}{5}$

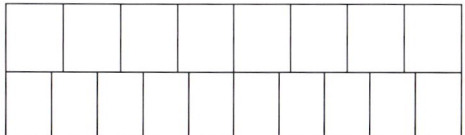 

   c) $\frac{5}{6}$ and $\frac{7}{9}$ d) $\frac{3}{8}$ and $\frac{6}{16}$

 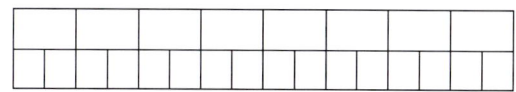

Chapter 28: Fractions and decimals

3 Use the diagrams to decide which of the two fractions is larger. The first diagrams have been shaded for you.

a) $\frac{3}{4}$ or $\frac{5}{8}$

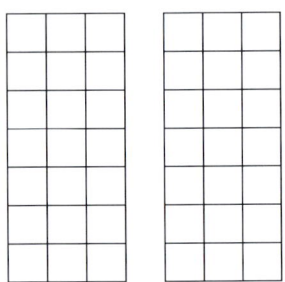

b) $\frac{1}{2}$ or $\frac{3}{5}$

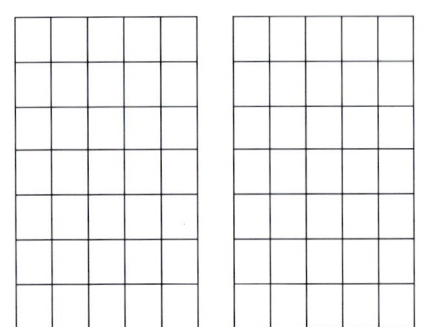

c) $\frac{3}{7}$ or $\frac{2}{3}$

d) $\frac{2}{5}$ or $\frac{3}{7}$

4 Use the diagrams to compare the fractions. Write your comparison using <, > or =.

a) $\frac{3}{4}$ and $\frac{7}{8}$

b) $\frac{2}{3}$ and $\frac{5}{7}$

c) $\frac{3}{5}$ and $\frac{4}{7}$

d) $\frac{5}{7}$ and $\frac{7}{9}$

5 Amandeep says, "$\frac{5}{6}$ is greater than $\frac{6}{7}$ because the numerator is bigger."
Is Amandeep correct? Include diagrams to explain your answer.

6 $\frac{2}{3}$ $\frac{3}{4}$ $\frac{5}{7}$

Put these three fractions in order from smallest to largest by:
a) drawing a fraction wall
b) drawing grids

252   Unit 3A: Number and calculation

Comparing fractions using decimals

Key terms

You can use the **fraction button** on your calculator to input fractions into your calculator.

 or

Your calculator will then convert the fraction to a decimal if you use the equals key or the s⇔d key

 or

Check the instructions for your calculator to make sure you can use the calculator to convert between fractions and decimals.

Did you know?

You can convert from a fraction to a decimal by working out a division.

For example,

$\frac{3}{4} = 3 \div 4 = 0.75$

Worked example 3

Here are two fractions:

$\frac{19}{25}$ $\frac{17}{20}$

a) Use a calculator to convert the fractions to decimals.
b) Use your decimals to decide which fraction has the greater value.

a) $\frac{19}{25} = 19 \div 25 = 0.76$ $\frac{17}{20} = 17 \div 20 = 0.85$	Divide the numerator of the fraction by the denominator to convert the fraction to a decimal.
b) $0.85 > 0.76$ $\frac{17}{20} > \frac{19}{25}$	Compare the two decimals to see which is larger. 0.85 is greater than 0.76 so $\frac{17}{20}$ is greater than $\frac{19}{25}$

Think about

How could you use this method if you did not have a calculator available?

Exercise 2

1. For each pair of fractions below convert the fractions to decimals and decide which fraction has the greater value.

    a) $\frac{4}{5}$ or $\frac{17}{20}$ b) $\frac{3}{20}$ or $\frac{4}{25}$ c) $\frac{7}{20}$ or $\frac{9}{25}$ d) $\frac{7}{8}$ or $\frac{43}{50}$

2. For each pair of fractions below convert the fractions to decimals and write a correct statement using <, > or =.

    a) $\frac{3}{5}$ or $\frac{5}{8}$ b) $\frac{7}{20}$ or $\frac{9}{25}$ c) $\frac{7}{16}$ or $\frac{11}{25}$ d) $\frac{7}{8}$ or $\frac{14}{16}$

3 Use a calculator to convert the fractions into decimals.

a) $\frac{5}{8}$ b) $\frac{19}{20}$

c) Draw a number line from 0 to 1. Mark each of the fractions with an arrow.

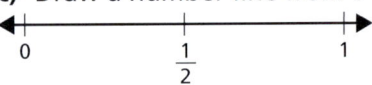

4 $\frac{3}{5}$ $\frac{30}{80}$ $\frac{13}{25}$ $\frac{26}{50}$ $\frac{21}{35}$ $\frac{6}{16}$ $\frac{9}{24}$ $\frac{9}{15}$

a) Convert these fractions to decimals. Use a calculator to help you.

b) Use your answers to group the fractions into equivalent fractions.

5 Dami says,

"$\frac{5}{8}$ and $\frac{17}{20}$ are equivalent because if you add 12 to 5 you get 17 and if you add 12 to 8 you get 20."

Is Dami correct? Explain your answer.

6 Sam recorded his test scores in maths over 7 weeks.

	Score	Out of
Week 1	6	10
Week 2	13	20
Week 3	19	25
Week 4	38	50
Week 5	8	10
Week 6	17	20
Week 7	23	25

a) Write a fraction for Sam's score each week.

b) Convert the fractions to decimals using your calculator.

c) Which was Sam's best score in maths?

d) Which was Sam's worst score in maths?

e) Can you say whether Sam is getting better or worse at maths from these results? Explain your answer.

7 **Vocabulary feature question**

Complete the sentences below by using the correct mathematical words.

The ………………… of a fraction is the number above the fraction line.

The ………………… of a fraction is the number below the fraction line.

………………… fractions and decimals are worth the same.

End of chapter reflection

You should know that ...	You should be able to ...	Such as ...
Fractions can be compared by using diagrams.	Compare two fractions by using diagrams.	Which is larger out of $\frac{3}{5}$ and $\frac{13}{20}$?
Fractions can be compared by converting to decimals.	Compare two fractions by converting to decimals.	Which is larger out of $\frac{5}{8}$ and $\frac{16}{25}$? Write a correct statement using these fractions and <, > or =.

Unit 3A: Number and calculation

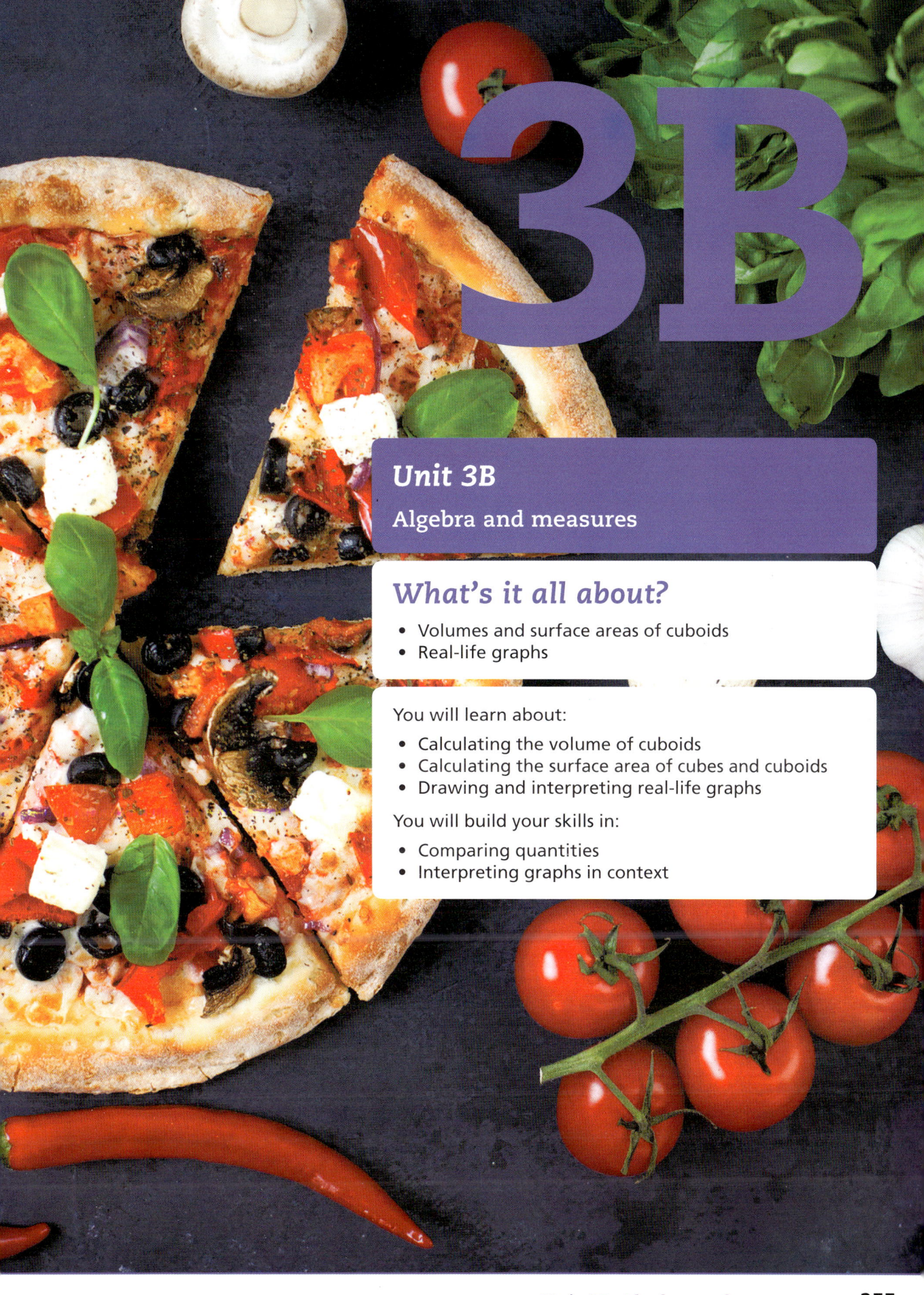

3B

Unit 3B
Algebra and measures

What's it all about?

- Volumes and surface areas of cuboids
- Real-life graphs

You will learn about:
- Calculating the volume of cuboids
- Calculating the surface area of cubes and cuboids
- Drawing and interpreting real-life graphs

You will build your skills in:
- Comparing quantities
- Interpreting graphs in context

Unit 3B • Chapter 29

You will learn how to:
- Derive and use the formula for the volume of a cuboid; calculate volumes of cuboids.
- Calculate the surface area of cubes and cuboids from their nets.

Volumes of cuboids

Starting point

Do you remember …?
- facts about cubes?
- how to find the area of a square and of a rectangle?

Hook

If you had 72 1-cm cubes and wanted to build bigger blocks with them, how many different blocks could you build?

The blocks must all have square or rectangular sides or faces.

You could start by making an 8 cm × 3 cm base.

This would use 24 cubes and could be the bottom layer.

You could then put two more layers on top of the bottom layer to make a block. This would use all 72 cubes.

What are the length, the width and the height of the block?

Can you combine these numbers to make 72?

Can you make other sizes of block with square or rectangular faces using all 72 small blocks?

Make a list of the length, width and heights of all the possible blocks that you can make.

Can you combine their measurements in the same way to get 72?

Volume of cuboids

Key terms

A **cuboid** is a three-dimensional shape with eight corners (or vertices) and six faces (or flat surfaces) which are all rectangles or squares.

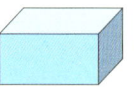

A **cube** is a special sort of cuboid with identical squares for all six faces. All its sides, or edges, are the same length.

The **volume** of a shape is how much space it occupies. This is often measured in cubic centimetres (centimetre cubes) which is written as cm^3. Other common measurements are cubic millimetres (mm^3) and cubic metres (m^3).

A volume does not have to be a whole number.

Unit 3B: Algebra and measures

Worked example 1

a) How many 1-cm cubes make up the shape shown on the right?
b) What is the volume of a container which is a cuboid with width 2 m, length 7 m and height 3 m?
c) How can you work out the volume of a cuboid if you know its length, its width and its height?

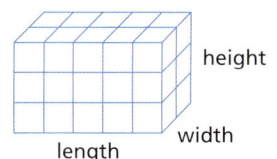

a) The base has 5 × 2 = 10 cubes. There are three layers so the total number of cubes is: 10 × 3 = 30 cubes	Start by finding the number of cubes in the base layer. There are three layers of cubes so you can multiply the number of cubes in one layer by 3 to find the total number of cubes.	There are 2 rows containing 5 cubes in the base layer. Number of cubes in the base layer = 5 × 2 = 10 Three layers: 10 + 10 + 10 = 30 cubes
b) The volume is: 2 × 7 × 3 = 42 m³	Find the number of cubes in the base layer. Multiply by the number of layers of cubes in the cuboid.	The number of metre cubes in the base layer is 2 × 7. You have 3 layers of 2 × 7 cubes. You can write this as: 2 × 7 × 3 = 42 m³
c) The volume is length × width × height	You can see from the examples above that the number of cubes to make up the base is found by multiplying length × width. To find the total number of cubes needed, multiply the number of cubes in the base by the height.	

Exercise 1

1 The following shapes are made up of centimetre cubes. Write down the length, width and height of each cuboid and work out its volume.

a) 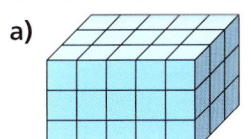 b) 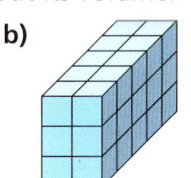 c) 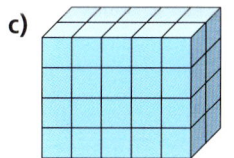 d)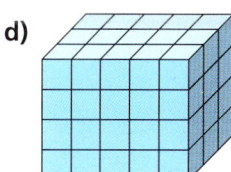

2 Find the volume of these cubes in cm³. The length of one side of the cube is given.
   a) 1 cm   b) 2 cm   c) 5 cm   d) 10 cm

3 A book is a cuboid 20 cm long, 13 cm wide and 3 cm thick. What is the volume of the book?

4 A cuboid has a square base of side 10 cm and is 8 cm high. What is its volume?

5 A large storage box is a cuboid 3 m long, 4 m wide and 2 m high. What is its volume?

6 A small cuboid is 5 mm long, 3 mm wide and 2 mm high. What is its volume?

Chapter 29: Volumes of cuboids

7 A cuboid is 5 mm long, 3 mm wide and 1 cm high. What is its volume in mm³?

8 A cuboid measures 10 cm long, 2.5 cm wide and 2 cm high. What is its volume?

> **Tip**
> Make sure your length, width and height are in the same units before multiplying.

9 Fill in the missing numbers in this table which gives the length, width, height and volume of some cuboids.

	Length (cm)	Width (cm)	Height (cm)	Volume (cm³)
a)	3	7	4	
b)	2	5	6	
c)	1	7	9	
d)	2	5	9	
e)	3	10	5	
f)	4	25	6	
g)	10	2	7	
h)	3	5		30
i)	4		6	72
j)		2	7	84

10 The first table gives the measurements of some cuboids. Match the measurements to the volumes in the second table and find the missing width and the missing volume.

Length	Width	Height
3 cm	8 cm	4 cm
2 m	?	3 m
6 cm	6 cm	3 cm
4.5 cm	2 cm	5 cm
4 cm	3.5 cm	3 cm
2.5 mm	8 mm	2 mm
7 cm	3 cm	5 cm

Volume
45 cm³
42 cm³
96 cm³
?
105 cm³
96 m³
108 cm³

11 A box is a cuboid measuring 10 cm long, 8 cm wide and 6 cm high. Some toy blocks are cubes of side 2 cm. What is the biggest number of the toy blocks that will fit into the box?

12 A cuboid has sides of 6 cm, 8 cm and 10 cm. It can be made using 480 cubes of side 1 cm. Samia has a set of cubes of side 2 cm. She says that she will need 240 of these to make the same cuboid. Is she right? Explain your answer.

13 Sebastian has 48 blocks. Each block is a cube with all its sides measuring 1 cm.

a) Sebastian says he can make 12 different cuboids which use all 48 blocks.

Is this statement true or false?

Sebastian has made a table with these headings to help him count the number of different cuboids.

Length	Width	Height

258   Unit 3B: Algebra and measures

Three of his rows are shown.

Length	Width	Height
6	2	12
1	1	48
12	6	2

b) i) Do all of these count as cuboids?

ii) Are all of these different cuboids?

c) How many different cuboids can be made from 48 cubes of side 1 cm?

14 Which of these statements is true?

"A cube is always a cuboid."

"A cuboid is always a cube."

Explain your answer.

Surface area of cubes and cuboids

Key terms

A **face** is one of the flat surfaces that makes up a three-dimensional shape. A face always has straight lines as its sides.

A **net** is a flat shape which can be folded to make a three-dimensional shape. The net of a cuboid could be folded to make the cuboid.

A solid can have more than one net. Here are two nets of the same cuboid, made up of the same six rectangles.

The **surface area** is the area of the outside of a three-dimensional shape. In the case of a cuboid the surface area is the total area of all six faces.

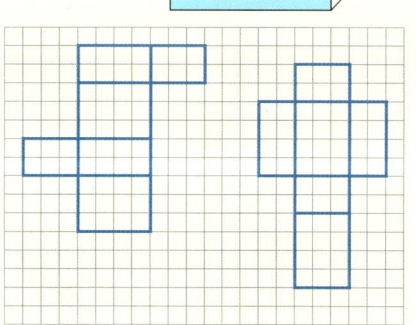

Did you know?

Not all combinations of the six rectangles is a net for the cuboid. This one is not a net for a cuboid as you could not fold it up to make a cuboid.

Can you see why?

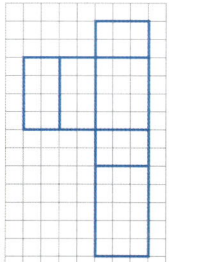

Chapter 29: Volumes of cuboids

Worked example 2

These two cuboids have the same volume which is 48 cm³.

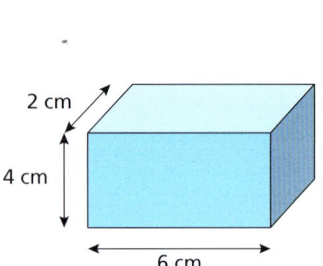
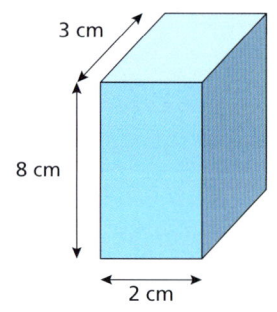

[Not to scale]

a) A net of the first cuboid is drawn for you on squared paper.
What is its surface area?

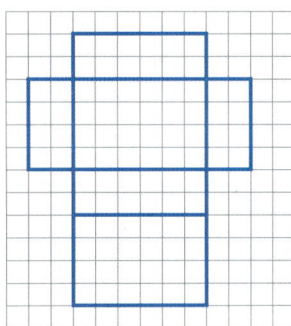

b) Draw a net of the second cuboid and calculate its surface area.

c) Do two cuboids with the same volume always have the same surface area?

a) Find the area of each face: 2 × 6 = 12 4 × 2 = 8 4 × 6 = 24 4 × 2 = 8 2 × 6 = 12 4 × 6 = 24 Surface area = 12 + 8 + 24 + 8 + 12 + 24 = 88 cm²	Put the measurements on the net. Check that you have three pairs of faces. Find the areas and add them up.	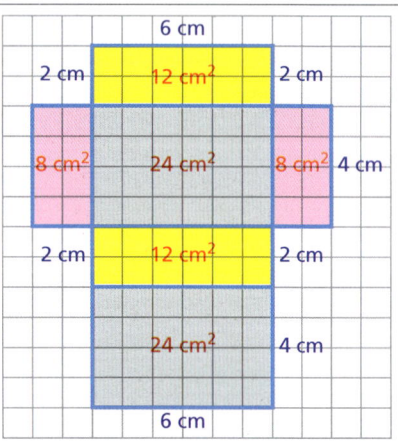 You have drawn the net using 1 square for 1 cm so you can find the area of each face by counting the number of squares. There are 88 squares altogether, so 88 cm².

b) Find the area of each face:	'Open up' the cuboid to find the six rectangles; this is the **net** of the cuboid.	
$3 \times 8 = 24$		
$3 \times 2 = 6$		
$2 \times 8 = 16$	Check that you have matching pairs of faces and that the shape would fold up to make a cuboid.	
$3 \times 8 = 24$		
$2 \times 8 = 16$		
$3 \times 2 = 6$		
Surface area	Then find the area by finding the areas of the individual rectangles and add them up.	
$= 24 + 6 + 16 + 24 + 16 + 6$		
$= 92 \text{ cm}^2$		
c) Two cuboids with the same volume do not have to have the same surface area.	In parts a) and b) you saw that the two cuboids of volume 48 cm^3 had two different surface areas – 88 cm^2 and 92 cm^2.	

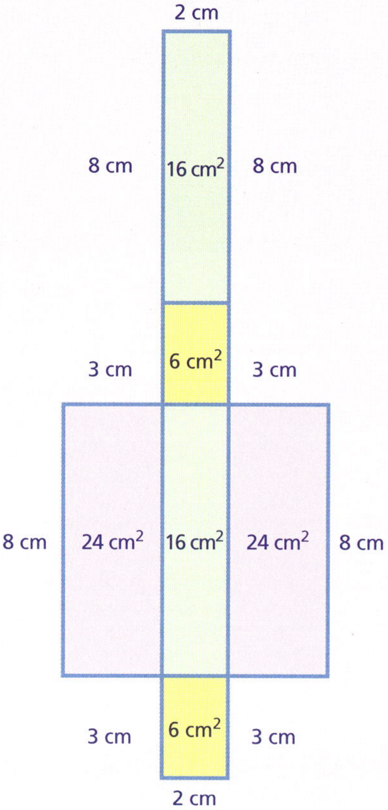

Exercise 2

1 These are nets of cuboids. Find the area of each one.

a)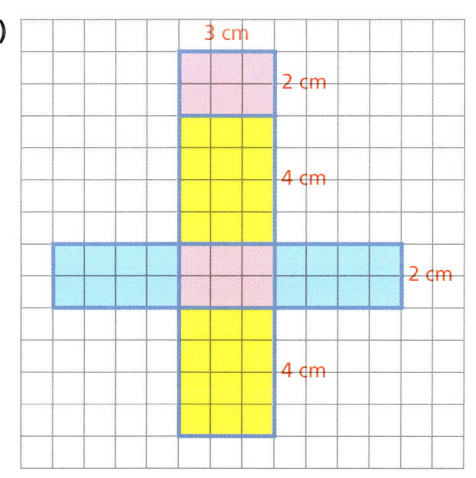

b)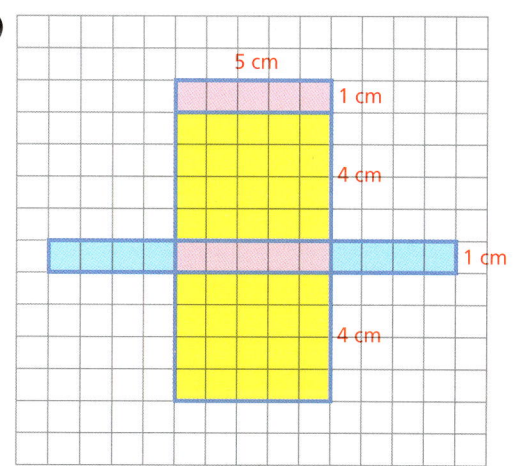

Chapter 29: Volumes of cuboids

c)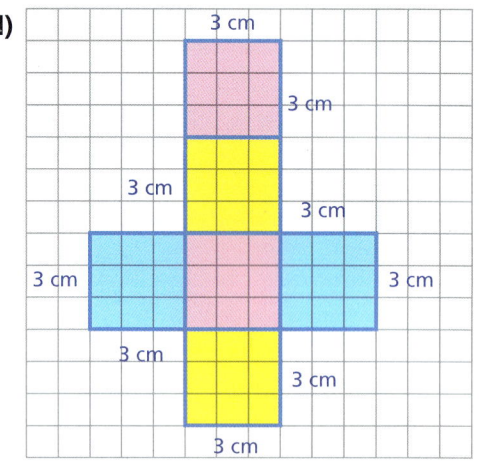

d)

2 For each cuboid:

  i) sketch the net and label its dimensions. Sketches do not have to be drawn to scale as long as they are labelled correctly.

  ii) calculate the surface area.

a)

b)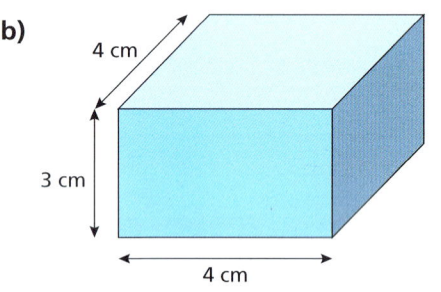

c)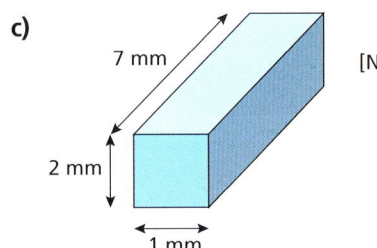

d)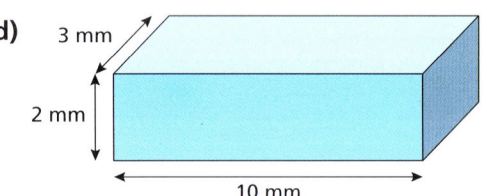

3 Which of these could be the nets of cubes and which could not? Explain your answer.

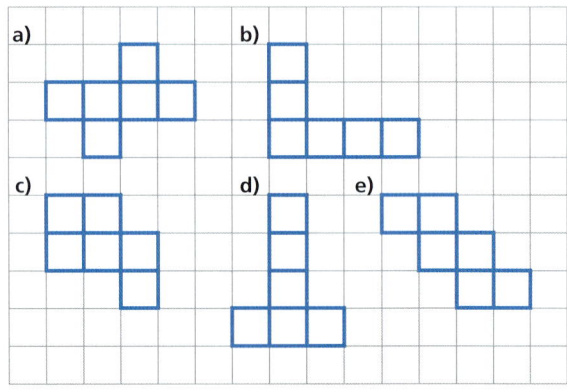

4 Draw the net and find the surface area of these cubes:

a)   b)   c)   d)

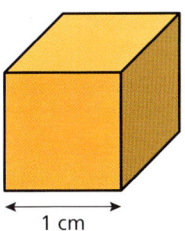 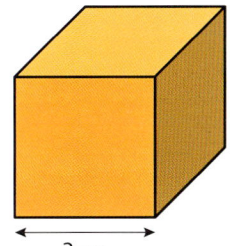 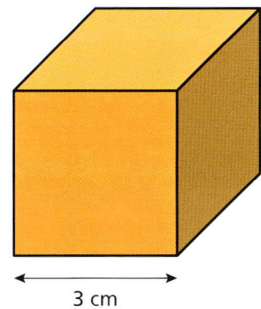 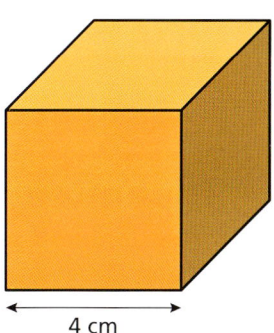

1 cm   2 cm   3 cm   4 cm

5 Dara has 18 cubes each of side 1 cm.

He says "the greatest possible surface area of a cuboid made from all 18 cubes is when the cuboid has measurements 1 cm, 1 cm and 18 cm."

Is this true? Explain your answer.

Think about

A cube has 11 different possible nets. How many can you draw? The nets must be different so if you cut them out you can't fit one exactly onto another.

These two nets are the same:

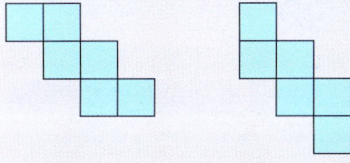

End of chapter reflection

You should know that …	You should be able to …	Such as …
A **volume** is measured in cubic units.	Decide which units are used for volume and which are not.	Which is a unit of volume, cm² or mm³?
The **formula** for the volume of a cuboid is: $V = l \times w \times h$	Use the formula to find the volume of a cuboid.	Find the volume of a cuboid with length 4 mm, width 10 mm and height 12 mm.
The **net** is what a 3-D shape looks like when opened out.	Draw the net of a cuboid from given dimensions.	Draw the net of a cuboid with length 3 cm, width 4 cm and height 5 cm.
Surface area is the area of the outside of a shape.	Either draw the net of the cuboid and work out its surface area from the net, or find the areas of the six faces of the cuboid and total them to find the total surface area.	Find the surface area of a cuboid with length 10 cm, width 5 cm and height 3.5 cm.

Unit 3B • Chapter 30
Graphs in real-life contexts

You will learn how to:
- Draw and interpret graphs in real-life contexts involving more than one stage, for example, travel graphs.

Starting point

Do you remember ...?
- how to read scales?
- how to read and plot coordinates on a graph?
- how to draw and interpret line graphs?
- the 24-hour clock?

This will be helpful when ...

you learn more about: finding distance, speed and acceleration from travel graphs and speed/time graphs.

Hook

Jana plots the height of water in her rainwater barrel during one day.

The diagram shows the height of the water in the barrel.

Jana only uses the water to fill the water bowls for her hens and uses the same amount of water each time.

She is the only one who takes water from the barrel.

She plots, on the diagram, the height of water every hour from 07:00 to 23:00, when she goes to bed.

How many times does Jana give water to the hens during this day?

Can you tell exactly when Jana gives water to the hens?

Can you say anything about what time Jana gets up?

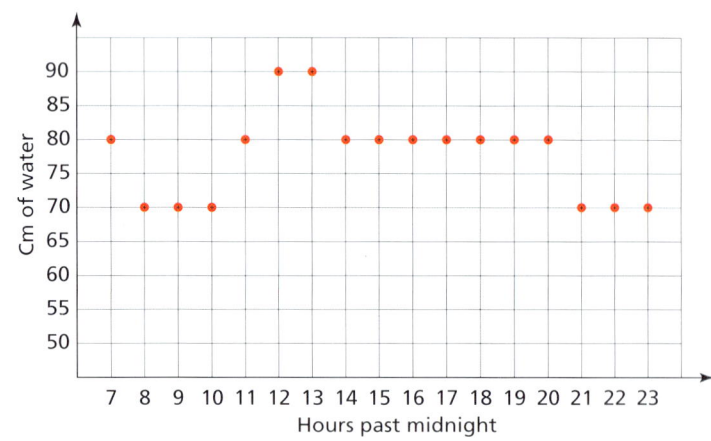

Discuss
What other information can you get from the diagram above?

Drawing and interpreting graphs

Key term

When you get information from a diagram or graph you are **interpreting** the graph.

264   Unit 3B: Algebra and measures

Worked example 1

Annie goes to the library to study. She cycles to the library from home, spends some time doing her homework at the library and then cycles home.

The graph represents her journey to the library, her time spent at the library and her journey home.

a) What time did she leave home?
b) How far from her home is the library?
c) How long did she spend in the library?
d) How long did it take her to cycle home?

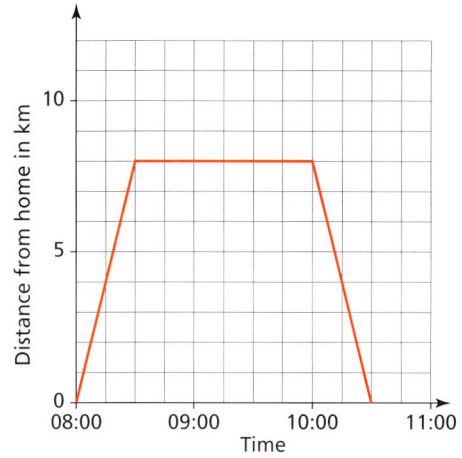

a) Annie starts to move away from home at 08:00 as this is when the graph line moves away from the horizontal axis.	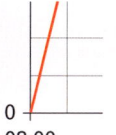
b) At 08:30 the graph line becomes horizontal showing that the distance Annie is from home is not changing so she has arrived at the library. This shows that the library is 8 km from her home.	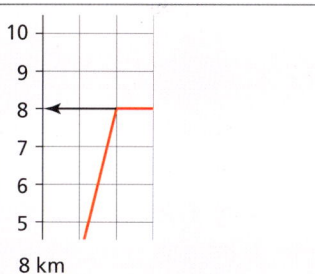 8 km
c) The graph line is horizontal between 08:30 and 10:00, which is 1 hour and 30 minutes spent in the library.	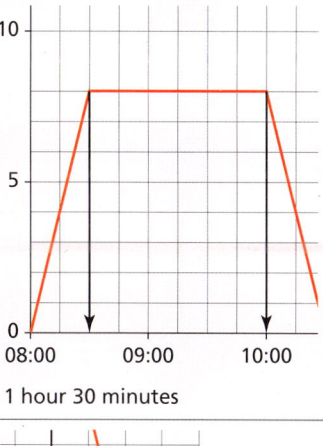 1 hour 30 minutes
d) She reaches home when the graph line reaches the horizontal axis. She leaves the library at 10:00 and arrives home at 10:30, a total time of 30 minutes.	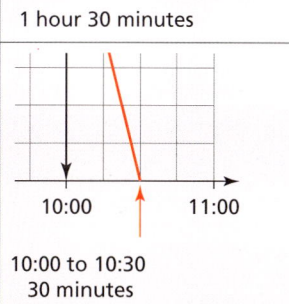 10:00 to 10:30 30 minutes

Chapter 30: Graphs in real-life contexts **265**

Tip

When reading a graph always look at the scales first and work out what each square represents. You can then check it by counting on. So if you look at this piece of a graph scale, there are 5 squares between 10 and 20. The gap between 10 and 20 is 10. 10 divided by 5 squares is 2. Count on from 10 to 20 in 2s for each square to check. The arrow points at 16.

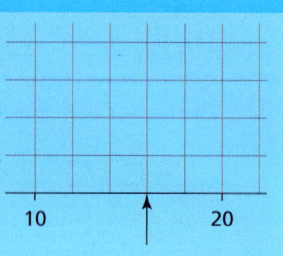

Key term

A graph which shows a journey in terms of distance and time is called a **travel graph**.

Exercise 1

1. The graph represents Paolo's journey as he cycles from home to the shop and back.

   State whether the following statements are true or false. If they are false then give the correct answer.

   a) Paolo leaves home at 13:00.
   b) Paolo spends 45 minutes at the shop.
   c) The shop is 7 km from his house.
   d) It takes him 1 hour to cycle to the shop and back.
   e) Complete these sentences.

   Paolo leaves home at ………… and arrives at the shop at ………… .

   He leaves the shop at ………… .

   He leaves home at ………… and arrives back to his home at ………… so he is away from home for a total of ………… hours.

2. Petra walks to the swimming pool from home. She then swims with her friends and walks home. The graph represents her journey.

   a) What time does Petra leave home?
   b) How far from her home is the swimming pool?
   c) How long does she spend at the swimming pool?
   d) How long does it take her to walk home?

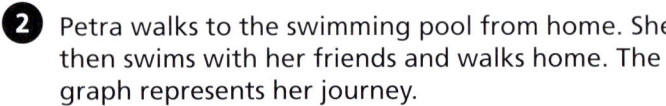

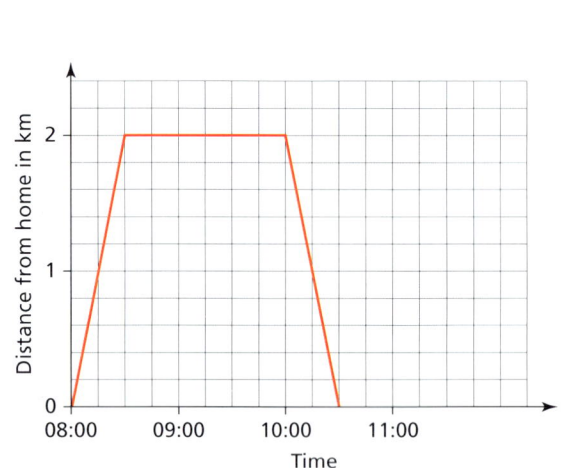

266   Unit 3B: Algebra and measures

3 Maya goes to the cinema with her friends. She walks from home to the cinema, watches the film and then walks home. The graph represents her journey.

   a) How far is the cinema from Maya's home?
   b) How long does it take her to walk to the cinema?
   c) How long did she spend at the cinema?
   d) How long was she away from home in total during her trip to the cinema and back?

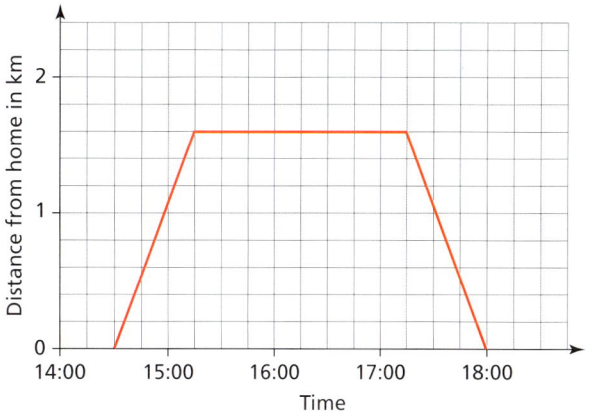

4 Carey is going skating. She cycles from home to the ice rink. On the way home she stops at the supermarket to buy some food for dinner. The graph represents her journey.

   a) What time did Carey leave home?
   b) How far from her home is the ice rink?
   c) How long did she spend at the ice rink?
   d) How far is the supermarket from her home?
   e) How long did she spend in the supermarket?
   f) How long did it take her to cycle from the supermarket to her home?

5 Peter is filling the bath. When the bathtub has enough water in it he gets into the bath. He washes, gets out of the bath and empties the bath. The graph shows the depth of the water in the bath during this time.

   a) What is the depth of water in the bath just before Peter gets in?
   b) What time does Peter get into his bath? How can you tell this from the graph?
   c) What is the depth of the water when Peter is in the bath?
   d) How long does Peter spend in the bath?
   e) How long does it take for the bath to empty?

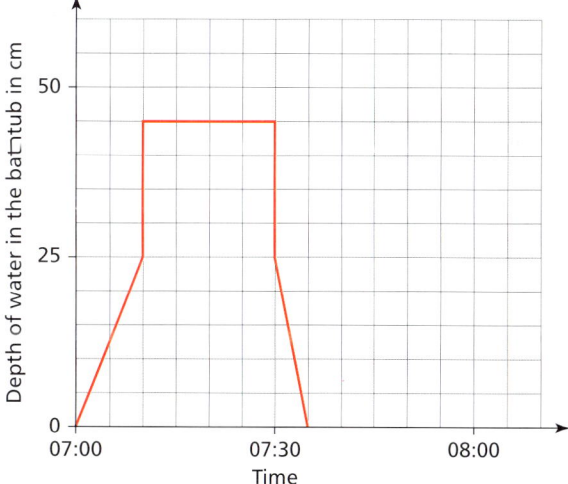

Chapter 30: Graphs in real-life contexts

6 The graph shows the temperatures in London on a day in June.

a) What was the temperature at 03:00?

b) What was the rise in temperature between 06:00 and 09:00?

c) What was the temperature at 12:00?

d) How much did the temperature rise between 12:00 and 15:00?

e) Did the temperature rise more quickly between 03:00 and 06:00 or between 06:00 and 09:00?

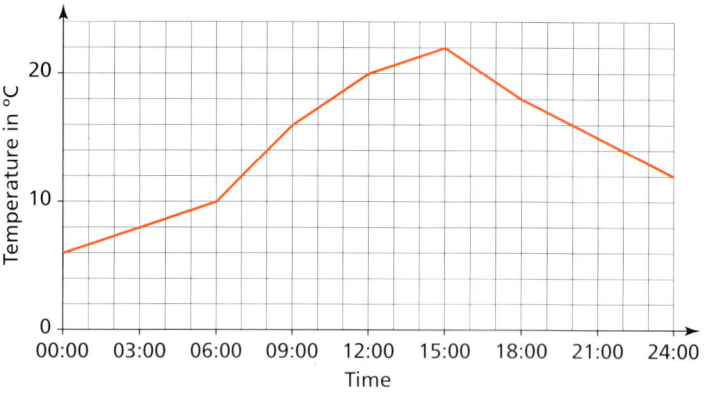

7 Adele leaves home at 08:00 to walk to school which is 2 km away. She takes 15 minutes to walk the first kilometre. She then stops to talk to her friend Jenna for 10 minutes. She then walks the rest of the way to school in another 15 minutes. Show her journey on a copy of the graph to the right.

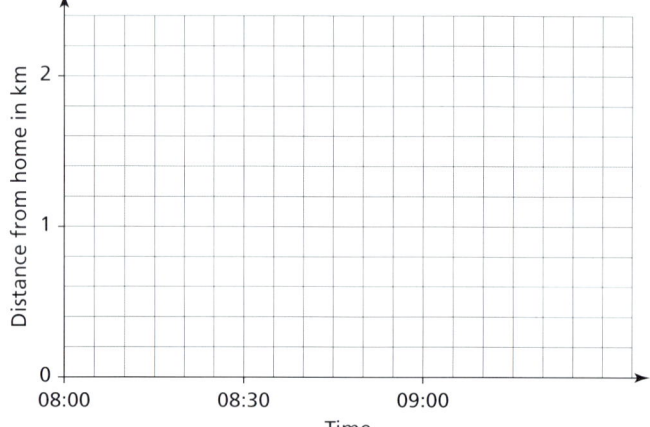

8 Shalissa leaves home at 15:00. She walks one kilometre to the cafe where she meets her friend Lauren. The walk takes 15 minutes. They stay in the cafe for 30 minutes. They then walk to the shopping centre, another kilometre away. The walk takes 15 minutes. They spend 2 hours at the shopping centre and then Susan immediately catches a bus home which is slowed by traffic and so it takes Susan 30 minutes to get home.

Draw a graph to show Susan's journey from home to the shopping centre and back. Choose an appropriate scale.

Did you know?

There are many different types of line graphs and you can find some of them on websites that forecast the weather.

Crete average temperatures

End of chapter reflection

You should know that …	You should be able to …	Such as …
You can draw and interpret graphs to represent real-life situations.	Draw and interpret graphs representing real-life situations.	Draw a travel graph to represent your journey to school.

Unit 3B: Algebra and measures

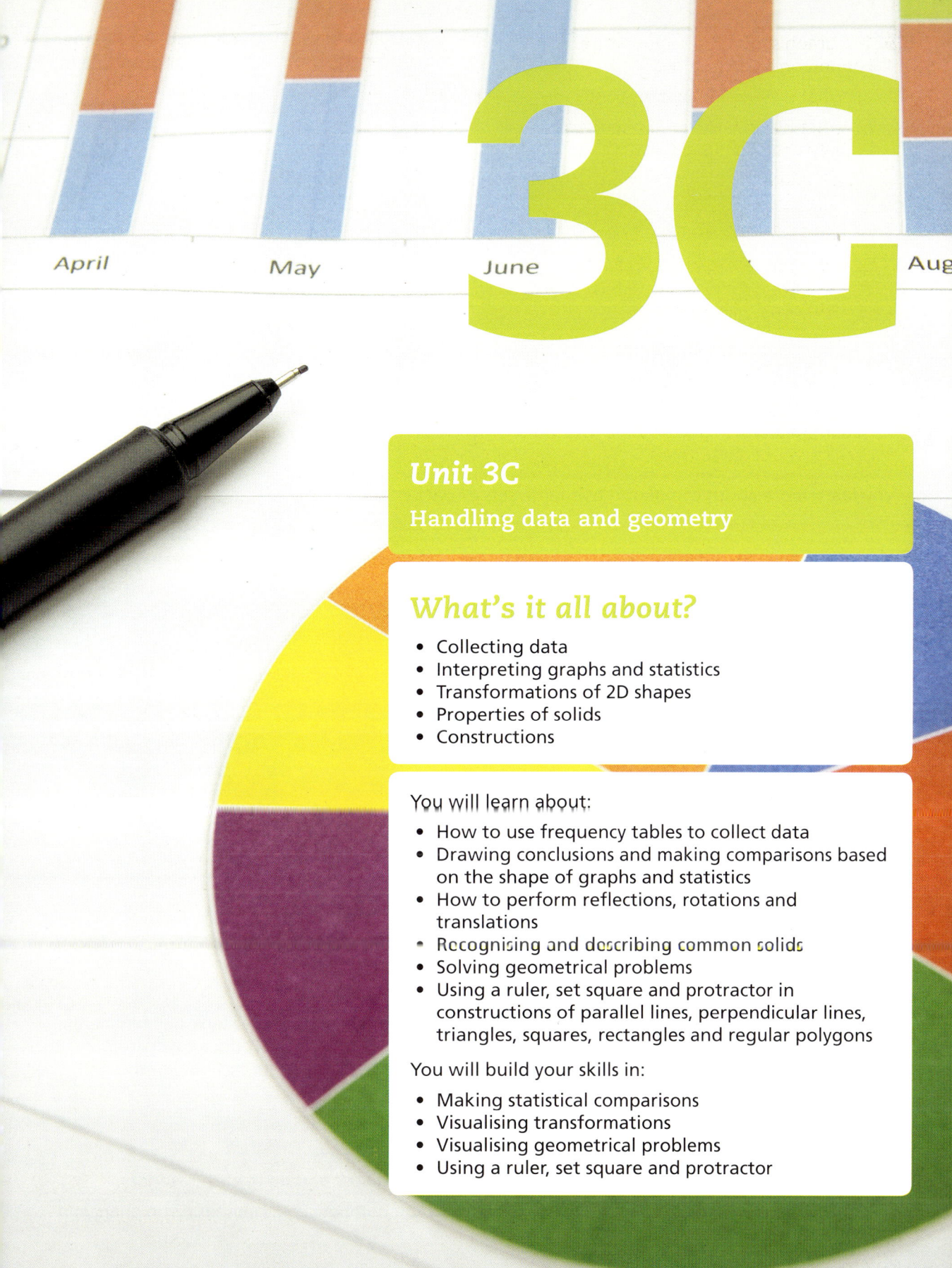

Unit 3C
Handling data and geometry

What's it all about?

- Collecting data
- Interpreting graphs and statistics
- Transformations of 2D shapes
- Properties of solids
- Constructions

You will learn about:

- How to use frequency tables to collect data
- Drawing conclusions and making comparisons based on the shape of graphs and statistics
- How to perform reflections, rotations and translations
- Recognising and describing common solids
- Solving geometrical problems
- Using a ruler, set square and protractor in constructions of parallel lines, perpendicular lines, triangles, squares, rectangles and regular polygons

You will build your skills in:

- Making statistical comparisons
- Visualising transformations
- Visualising geometrical problems
- Using a ruler, set square and protractor

Unit 3C • Chapter 31

Statistics

You will learn how to:
- Construct and use frequency tables to gather discrete data, grouped where appropriate in equal class intervals.
- Draw conclusions based on the shape of graphs and simple statistics.
- Compare two simple distributions using the range and the mode, median or mean.

Starting point

Do you remember …?
- how to construct a frequency table for a set of data?
- how to find the mode, median and range for a list of data or from a frequency table?
- how to draw and interpret charts and graphs like bar charts, pictograms, pie charts and bar-line graphs?

This will be helpful when …
you learn more about comparing two large sets of data.

Hook

A company makes snacks called GreatSnack.

The company conducts some market research to see whether people like their product.

They ask people which snack they prefer.

Here is a bar chart showing their results:

- How many people did they ask?
- Can you produce the frequency table that this bar chart comes from?
- The owners of Snackies and Snackeroo could complain about this chart – why?
- What other things could the owners of GreatSnack do to their bar chart to exaggerate their results?

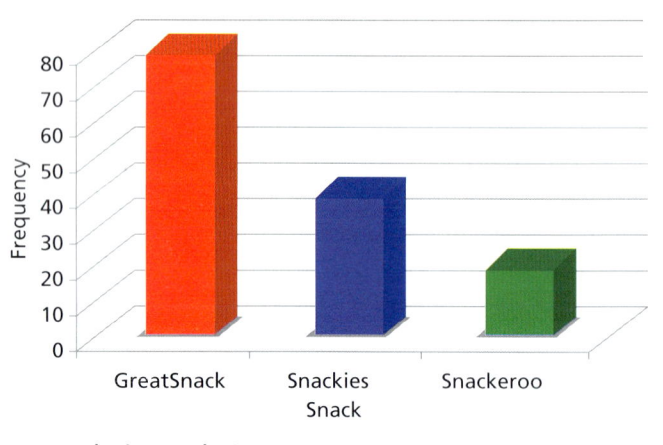

Did you know?
There are organisations that look out for the use of misleading graphs in product advertisements to make sure that people are not being misled.

Frequency tables

Key terms

A **frequency table** is a results table showing the number of pieces of data in each category.

The categories can be words (e.g. favourite colours), single numbers (e.g. number of brothers and sisters) or a range of numbers (e.g. ages).

You call each category a **class**.

Numeric data that can be counted is called **discrete data**. The values of data that is discrete are exact and separate.

When the table would be too big if each data value had its own row, you use a **grouped frequency table**. This is a frequency table where each class covers a range of values, for example, 7–9 or 2.0–2.5.

For example,

Age of visitor	Frequency
0–9	
10–19	
20–29	
30–39	
40–49	
50–59	

When data is **grouped**, the size of each **class** or category is called a **class interval**.

Class intervals are often equal but they do not have to be.

Think about

What is the problem with using the following groups for ages?

0–10   10–20   20–30   30 or above

Worked example 1

Here are the scores of 21 students who participated in a quiz:

27	35	24	33	16	43	49
11	24	37	48	30	56	42
15	54	39	42	29	35	45

Construct a **grouped frequency table** to represent this data.

Score	Tally	Frequency
10–19		
20–29		
30–39		
40–49		
50–59		

The data covers a spread from 11 to 56.

Therefore, you will need to group the data into equal class intervals, for example, 10–19.

You will use a **class interval** of 10 points.

Note that you could have used different intervals if you preferred.

Here is your frequency table.

Chapter 31: Statistics

Score	Tally	Frequency
10–19		
20–29	I	
30–39		
40–49		
50–59		

You now need to record each score as a tally mark in the correct place on the table.

The first score is 27.

You record this as a tally mark in the 20–29 class or category.

Score	Tally	Frequency
10–19	III	
20–29	IIII	
30–39	ℍ I	
40–49	ℍ I	
50–59	II	

Continue with the rest of the data, using a tally mark for each item and a strike through like this ℍ for every 5th in a row.

Score	Tally	Frequency
10–19	III	3
20–29	IIII	4
30–39	ℍ I	6
40–49	ℍ I	6
50–59	II	2
		21

Finally, find the total of each tally and record this in the frequency column.

As a check, add up the frequencies to make sure that you have recorded all 21.

3 + 4 + 6 + 6 + 2 = 21, so you have included all the data!

Exercise 1

1) Here are the ages of the children who visit a playgroup one morning:

| 3 | 3 | 4 | 2 | 0 | 0 | 1 | 3 | 2 | 2 |
| 2 | 3 | 4 | 1 | 1 | 2 | 0 | 3 | 2 | 2 |

Copy and complete the frequency table for this data.

Age	Tally	Frequency
0		
1		
2		
3		
4		
Total		

2) Here are the number of sales made by a shop each day for three weeks:

9	2	11	7	8	14	15
10	6	9	9	8	16	17
21	4	8	11	13	18	9

a) Copy and complete the frequency table.

Number of sales	Tally	Frequency
1–5		
6–10		
11–15		
16–20		
21–25		

b) On how many days did the shop make more than 15 sales?

c) How many sales did the shop make altogether?

3) Jenny is grouping some data about the number of books borrowed by university students over a month to produce a frequency table. She groups the data into equal class intervals. She has started her frequency table like this:

Number of books borrowed in one month	Tally	Frequency
0–4		
5–9		

a) Copy and complete Jenny's first column by producing equal class intervals.

Here is Jenny's data:

| 7 | 2 | 15 | 20 | 18 | 14 | 12 | 0 |
| 5 | 5 | 20 | 23 | 1 | 12 | 14 | 14 |

b) Copy and complete the frequency table using the data.

c) Work out the number of students who borrowed fewer than 10 library books in one month.

4 Petra is conducting a survey of the number of people who attend an art exhibition. She records the number of people each day for 24 days.

Here are her results:

| 75 | 54 | 89 | 61 | 59 | 75 | 74 | 81 | 86 | 79 | 90 | 59 |
| 60 | 66 | 68 | 71 | 70 | 65 | 73 | 75 | 82 | 80 | 63 | 72 |

Construct a grouped frequency table to represent this data.

5 Students in Adam's class build towers out of cubes. Adam records the number of cubes used in each person's tower. Here are his results:

154 132 126 143 129 144 137 129 151 119 125 138 125
149 139 136 133 144 147 158 137 136 111 129 134 143

Construct a grouped frequency table to represent this data. Make your class intervals equal.

6 Alisha is recording the number of pets owned by students in her class. She is planning to use the table below to help her collect her data.

Number of pets	Tally	Frequency
1–3		
4–6		
6–8		
9 or more		

Identify **two** problems with this table.

7 Clemence is finding out how much pocket money students get per week.

Here is her data:

$10	$14	$20	$10	$5	$0	$0
$50	$12.50	$24	$25	$20	$11	$15
$20	$5	$10	$10	$12	$15	$8

> **Tip**
> Use $0 to $4.99 as your first class interval.

Construct a grouped frequency table to represent this data.

8 How can you quickly work out the class intervals for your data if you know how many you want and the lowest and highest values?

> **Discuss**
> Do class intervals always have to be equal? When might it be useful to have class intervals that are not equal?

Unit 3C: Handling data and geometry

Drawing conclusions from graphs

Key term

A **conclusion** is a statement that you can make based on the data you have collected. A conclusion usually answers the original question you were investigating. You should use statistical language to express our conclusions.

Worked example 2

This pictogram shows the number of people who go to the gym on five days of the week:

Monday	🧍🧍🧍🧍🧍🧍🧍
Tuesday	🧍🧍🧍🧍🧍(half)
Wednesday	🧍🧍🧍🧍(half)
Thursday	🧍🧍🧍
Friday	🧍

Key: 🧍 represents 10 people

a) Work out the number of people who went to the gym on Monday.
b) Work out the mean number of people going to the gym on Tuesday and Wednesday.
c) Write a conclusion from the pictogram about when people go to the gym.

a) 10×7 $= 70$	Each stick person represents 10 people and there are 7 stick people in Monday's section. So, the number of people who went on Monday = $10 \times 7 = 70$	Monday: 🧍🧍🧍🧍🧍🧍🧍 10 10 10 10 10 10 10 70
b) Tuesday $10 \times 4.5 = 45$ Wednesday $10 \times 3.5 = 35$ Mean = $\dfrac{45 + 35}{2} = \dfrac{80}{2} = 40$	First, find the number of people who go to the gym on Tuesday. Next, find the number of people who go to the gym on Wednesday. Find the total number of people who go to the gym. You need to share these people out equally across the two days.	Tuesday: 🧍🧍🧍🧍🧍(half) 10 10 10 10 5 Wednesday: 🧍🧍🧍🧍(half) 10 10 10 5

Chapter 31: Statistics   275

c) The pictogram suggests that the number of people going to the gym decreases as the week goes on.

The pictogram shows the highest number of people go to the gym on Monday, then Tuesday and it keeps going down to Friday.

So fewer people go to the gym as it gets later in the week.

Monday	🯅🯅🯅🯅🯅🯅🯅🯅
Tuesday	🯅🯅🯅🯅🯅
Wednesday	🯅🯅🯅🯅
Thursday	🯅🯅🯅
Friday	🯅

Number of people reduces each day

Exercise 2   3–5

1 Here is a pictogram showing how students in a class travel to school:

Write two conclusions about how these students travel to school from the pictogram.

Walk	🯅🯅🯅
Car	🯅🯅🯅🯅🯅🯅
Bus	🯅🯅🯅🯅
Cycle	🯅🯅

Key: represents 2 students

2 Ali completed a survey to ask 40 students what their favourite subject was.

He drew this bar chart from his results:

a) Which subject was most students' favourite subject?

b) Ali says, "I conclude that Science was the subject chosen by fewest students as their favourite".

Do you agree with Ali? Explain your answer.

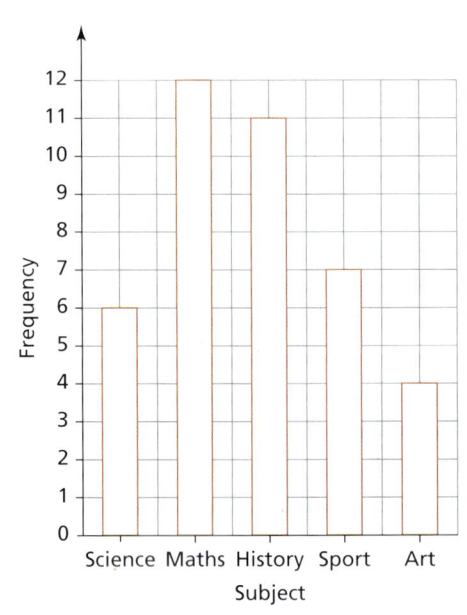

> **Did you know?**
>
> The bar chart was invented by William Playfair in the late 18th century – he also invented the line graph and, later on, the pie chart.

3 The bar-line graph shows the number of portions of fruit and vegetables eaten in one day for a group of children in a playgroup.

a) How many children have eaten no portions of fruit and vegetables?

b) Work out the total number of children who completed the survey.

c) Write the modal number of portions of fruit and vegetables eaten.

d) The World Health Organisation recommends that children eat at least 5 portions of fruit or vegetables daily. What proportion of the children surveyed were meeting this target? Give your answer as a fraction.

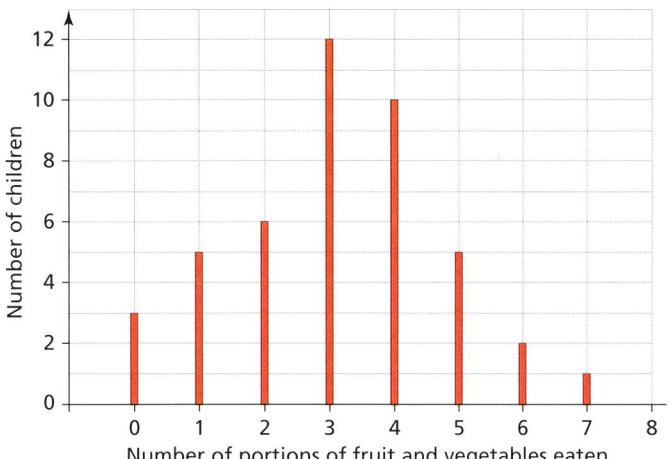

4 These bar charts show the number of pets owned by students in Class A and in Class B.

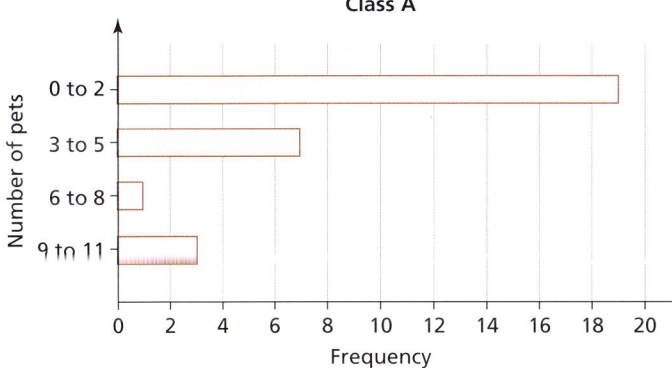

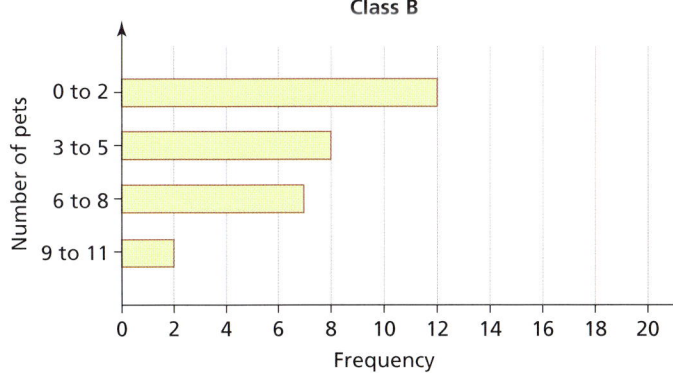

a) What is the modal class of number of pets in each class?

b) Which class has more pets? Explain your answer.

Chapter 31: Statistics

5. The dual bar chart shows the favourite colour of boys and of girls in Year 7.

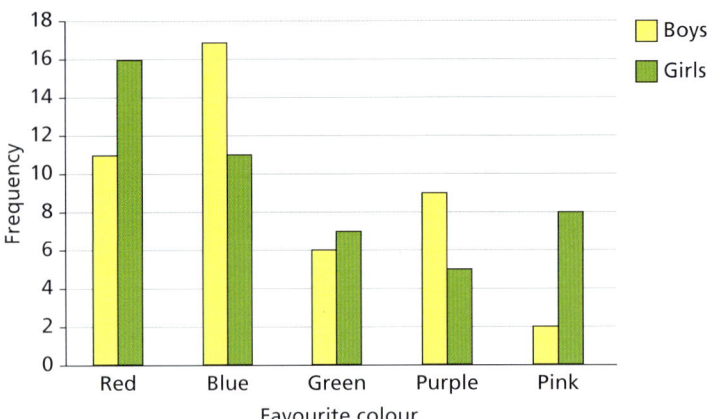

a) Copy and complete this sentence.

There were ………… more ………….. than ………….. in Year 7.

b) Write the colour that had the biggest difference in numbers of boys and girls that gave it as their favourite.

c) The school is planning to repaint the Year 7 social area using one of these colours. Use the dual bar chart to decide which colour they should use. Explain your answer.

6. The pie chart shows the different types of vehicle travelling along the road past a school in one day.

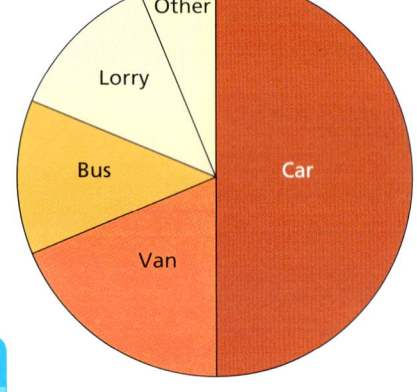

a) What proportion of the vehicles were cars?

b) A journalist says, "A quarter of the vehicles on the roads are buses or lorries".

Do you agree with the journalist? Explain your answer.

c) Marta says, "Half of the people who travel past the school are in a car".

Do you agree with Marta? Explain your answer.

> **Tip**
> Are there the same number of people in each vehicle?

d) Overall the pie chart represents 400 vehicles. Approximately how many lorries travelled along the road in one day?

7. These pie charts show the medals won by the same country at two Olympic Games.

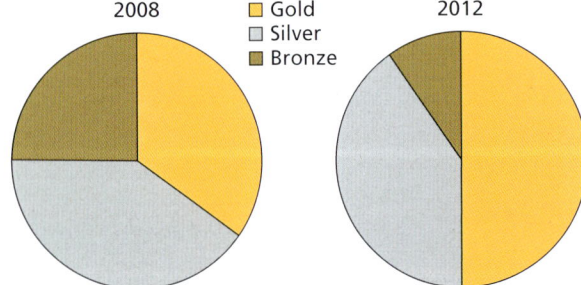

Vincent says, "The team did better in 2012 than in 2008 because they won more gold and silver medals".

Do you agree with Vincent? Explain your answer.

Unit 3C: Handling data and geometry

8 The table shows the number of people and the spending on public services in a city in 2004 and 2014.

	2004	2014
Number of people	1 850 000	2 240 000
Spending ($)	56 million	63 million

a) Enter this data into a spreadsheet and use it to produce charts showing the change in population and spending from 2004 to 2014.

b) Use your spreadsheet to calculate the spending on public services per person in each year.

c) Produce a chart to show the spending per person in 2004 and 2014.

d) Write a conclusion about spending on public services in 2004 and 2014.

Write a conclusion about the spending per person on public services in 2004 and 2014.

What do you notice about your two conclusions?

> **Tip**
> You can use a formula to calculate the spending per person. Remember to start your formula with =.

> **Think about**
> Does this explain examples from the media where headlines based on the same data seem to disagree?

Comparing sets of data using averages and the range

Key term

We say that data is more **consistent** if there is less variation in the values.

A higher range suggests that the data is less consistent while a lower range suggests that the data is more consistent.

> **Tip**
> Remember:
> Mean = $\frac{\text{sum of data}}{\text{number of pieces of data}}$
> Range = highest value − lowest value

Worked example 3

Lorena and Marius are both goalkeepers. Here are the number of goals that were scored against them in their last 10 games:

Lorena	0	0	4	0	3	0	2	0	0	5
Marius	1	0	2	1	2	1	1	2	1	2

Compare the performance of the two goalkeepers.

Lorena:

Mean
$= \frac{0+0+4+0+3+0+2+0+0+5}{10}$
$= \frac{14}{10}$
$= 1.4$

Marius:

Mean
$= \frac{1+0+2+1+2+1+1+2+1+2}{10}$
$= \frac{13}{10}$
$= 1.3$

Start by calculating the mean number of goals for each player.

Find the total number of goals that each goalkeeper let in and divide this by the number of games.

10 games

Total = 0+0+4+0+3+0+2+0+0+5
14 goals

| 1.4 | 1.4 | 1.4 | 1.4 | 1.4 | 1.4 | 1.4 | 1.4 | 1.4 | 1.4 |

10 games

Total = 1+0+2+1+2+1+1+2+1+2
13 goals

| 1.3 | 1.3 | 1.3 | 1.3 | 1.3 | 1.3 | 1.3 | 1.3 | 1.3 | 1.3 |

Chapter 31: Statistics

Lorena: Range = 5 − 0 = 5 Marius: Range = 2 − 0 = 2	Now calculate the range of the data. Lorena's highest number of goals was 5 and her lowest number of goals was 0. Marius's highest number of goals was 2 and his lowest number of goals was 0.	Lorena — Range = 5 Marius — Range = 2
So, in conclusion: Marius lets in slightly fewer goals than Lorena on average because Marius has a lower mean. Marius is more **consistent** than Lorena because Marius has a lower range.	Lorena and Marius are goalkeepers so they are aiming to reduce the number of goals they let in. Marius's mean score is 1.3 which is just lower than Lorena's at 1.4, so he lets fewer goals in on average. Marius's range is 2, which is much smaller than Lorena's, which is 5, so he is also more consistent.	**Tip** Remember to give your conclusion and a reason when making comparisons.

Exercise 3   1–4, 6–8

1 Billy is comparing the heights of the students in two classes.

Class A
Mean = 143 cm
Range = 52 cm

Class B
Mean = 140 cm
Range = 28 cm

Complete these statements.

a) On average, students in Class .... are taller than those in Class .... because the mean is higher.

b) The heights of students in Class .... are more consistent than those in Class .... because the range is lower.

2 Antonia is comparing the salaries of men and women in a company.

Men
Mean = $28 000
Range = $42 000

Women
Mean = $23 000
Range = $44 000

Tick the correct box to say whether each statement is true, false or you cannot tell. Give reasons for your answers.

	True	False	Cannot tell	Reason
On average, the salaries of women are higher than men.	☐	☐	☐	
The salaries for men are more consistent than those for women.	☐	☐	☐	
The highest paid employee is a woman.	☐	☐	☐	

3 Here is some information about the scores of two classes in a spelling test:

Class A
Mean score = 17
Range = 12

Class B
Mean Score = 16
Range = 5

Compare the performance of the two classes.

4 Here is some information about the ages of the teachers in two schools:

School X
Median age = 35
Range = 23

School Y
Median age = 44
Range = 39

Compare the ages of the teachers in the two schools.

5 Here are the scores of two diving teams in a competition.:

| Team 1 | 9 | 10 | 7 | 8 | 7 | 8 | 7 |
| Team 2 | 5 | 10 | 10 | 10 | 10 | 5 | 6 |

a) What is the mean score for each team?
b) What is the range of scores for each team?
c) Compare the performance of the two teams.

6 Two runners compete in a 100 m race.
Here are their performance statistics for a whole season:

Runner 1
Mean time = 10.7 seconds
Range of times = 1.2 seconds

Runner 2
Median time = 10.5 seconds
Range of times = 0.8 seconds

Megan says, "Runner 1 has done better because he has a higher average time than Runner 2".
Do you agree with Megan? Explain your answer.

7 Two football teams compare the number of goals they have scored this season.

Team A
Mean number of goals scored = 2.1
Range of goals scored = 3

Team B
Mean number of goals scored = 1.9
Range of goals scored = 5

Chapter 31: Statistics   281

Chen says, "Team B has done better because they have a higher range of goals than Team A". Do you agree with Chen?

Explain your answer.

8 Two basketball players' scoring statistics are shown below.

	Median score	Lowest score	Highest score
Player A	37	0	61
Player B	31	0	58

Compare the performance of the two players.

9 You can use the mean, median or mode to compare the average of two sets of data.

How can you decide which to use?

Give an example where you would use each type of average and explain why that is the most appropriate average to use in that case.

10 **Vocabulary feature question**

Match each key term on the left to its description on the right.

Complete the missing term and the missing description to produce eight matching pairs.

Key term	Description
Class	Data where each value is exact and separate
Grouped data	Data that has less variation (is closer together)
More consistent	The size of a group or category of data
Discrete data	A way to organise data into categories and say how many pieces of data are in each category
Mode	
Frequency table	A group or category of data
Mean	The most common item in a set of a data
	The difference between the highest and the lowest data value
Range	The middle piece of data when it is arranged in order
Median	Data that has been organised into classes
Modal class	The category with the highest frequency in a set of data

282   Unit 3C: Handling data and geometry

End of chapter reflection

You should know that …	You should be able to …	Such as …
A class is the name for a group or category of data. Discrete data can be grouped into classes. The class intervals or size of the classes for grouped data are often equal.	Construct and complete a frequency table, grouping the data as required.	Here is the number of flower stems sold in the last 20 sales at a flower shop: | 40	54	64	61	51
47	59	71	72	65
71	59	34	31	39
60	56	79	45	52	 Construct a grouped frequency table for this data.
When you have produced a chart or graph or average, you can draw a result or statement from it. You call this a conclusion.	Draw conclusions from charts and graphs.	Bryn investigated how many books students in his class read in a month. Here are his results: [Bar chart showing frequency of books read: 0 to 3: 5, 4 to 7: 7, 8 to 11: 11, 12 to 15: 6, 16 to 19: 4] Draw conclusions from Bryn's graph.
You can compare two sets of data by comparing their average values (mean, median or mode) and their spread (range). You say that the data is more consistent when it has a lower range and the values are closer together.	Compare two sets of data by comparing their average and their spread.	Two teams of runners completed a running relay. Here are their times in seconds: | Team 1	57.8	62.1	59.0	61.2
Team 2	57.0	59.8	59.7	62.4	 By finding the means and ranges, compare the performance of the two teams.

Chapter 31: Statistics

Unit 3C • Chapter 32

Transformations

You will learn how to:
- Transform 2D points and shapes by:
  - reflection in a given line
  - rotation about a given point
  - translation
- Know that shapes remain congruent after these transformations.

Starting point

Do you remember ...?

- the definition of vertex and vertices?
- how to reflect a shape in a mirror line?
- how to translate a shape left or right or up or down?
- how to rotate a shape about one of its vertices?

This will also be useful when ...

you learn more about combining transformations and enlarging shapes.

Hook

Take a piece of paper and draw a line on it.

Draw a point on the paper and label it A.

Now fold the paper flat along the fold line and use your pencil or pen to put a very small hole through the paper at A.

 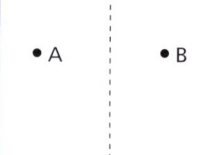

Now open the paper, which should have two small holes or marks in it, and label the second mark B.

Use your ruler to join A and B.

a) Are A and B the same distance from the fold line?

b) What angle does the line AB make with the fold line?

Try this with other points to see if the answers to (a) and (b) are always the same.

Key terms

A **reflection** is a mirroring or flipping of a shape. You usually state or draw the line in which the shape is reflected.

A **rotation** is the turning of a shape. You usually state the angle and direction of the rotation as well as the centre point around which the shape turns.

A **translation** is a movement of a shape. You usually state the size and direction of the movement horizontally (across) and vertically (up and down).

You call reflections, rotations and translations **transformations** because they transform or change one shape into another.

You call the shape you start with the **original** shape.

When you move this shape around you call the resulting shape an **image**.

> **Did you know?**
>
> You can find lots of examples of transformations in real life.
>
> For example, where can you see reflections, rotations and translations in this pattern?

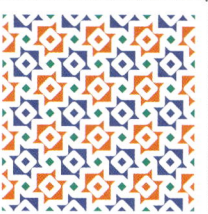

Worked example 1

Reflect each of these points in the lines shown.

a) 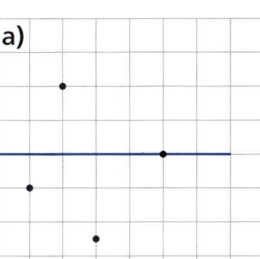   b) 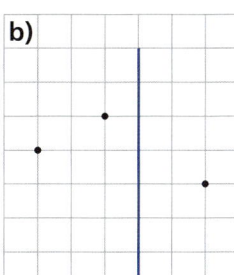   c)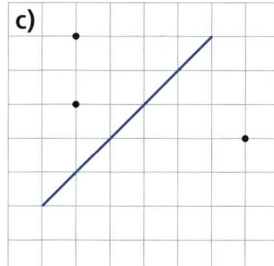

a) 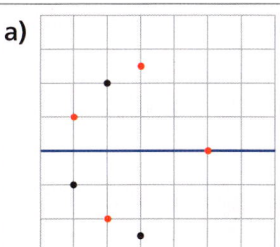	To reflect a point in a line you draw a line from the point perpendicular to the line. The point and its reflection are the same distance from the line. The reflection line behaves like a mirror. The point on the mirror line stays in the same place.	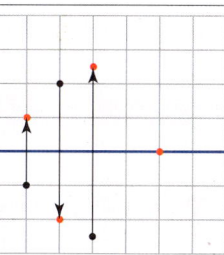
b) 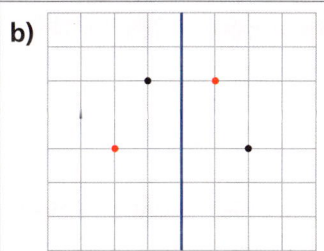	Draw a line from each point at right angles to the line and measure equal distances.	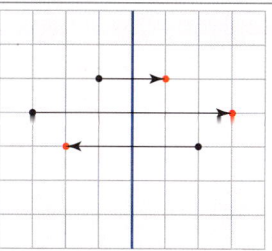
c) 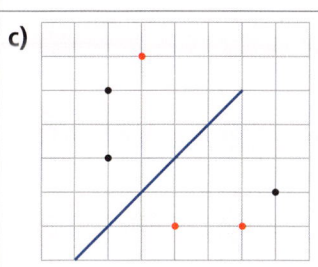	Draw a line from the point at right angles to the line and measure equal distances.	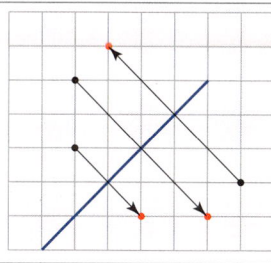

> **Tip**
>
> You could also do these reflections by folding along the reflection line.

Chapter 32: Transformations   285

Worked example 2

Transform the red triangle by reflecting it in the dotted line shown and draw the image.

a) 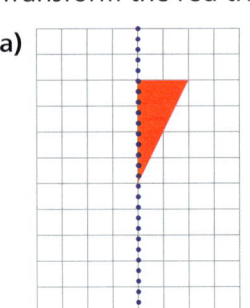 b) 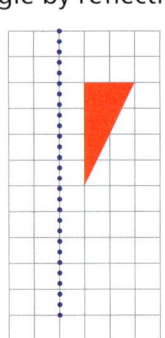 c) 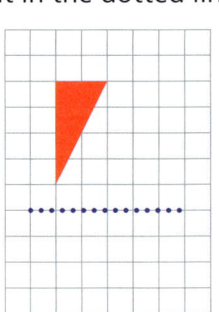 d)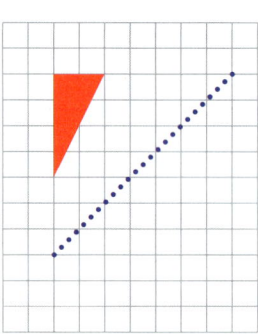

a)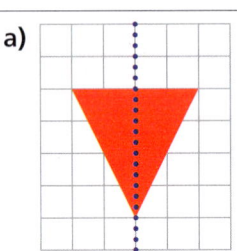

To reflect in a line: reflect each of the corners of the shape in the line and then join them up. Points on the line stay in the same place.

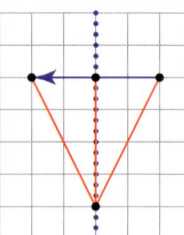

b)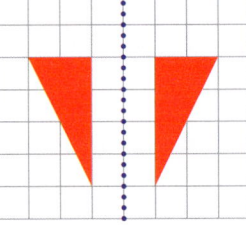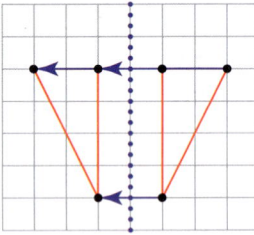

c)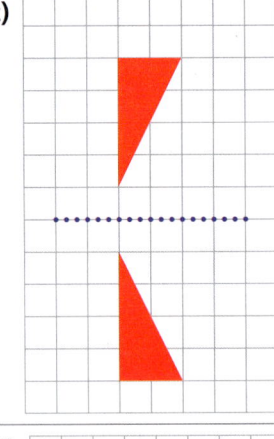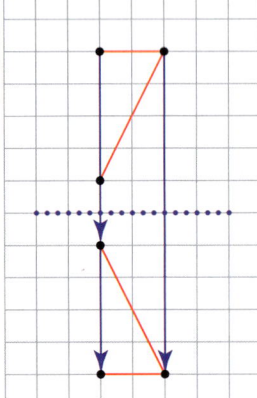

d)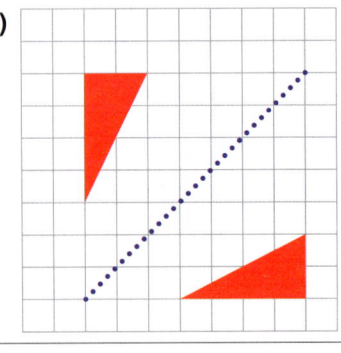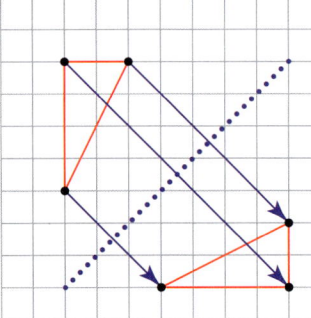

286   Unit 3C: Handling data and geometry

Worked example 3

Draw the image of the shape shown after rotating it about the dot through:
a) 90° anticlockwise
b) 180° anticlockwise

about the point shown.

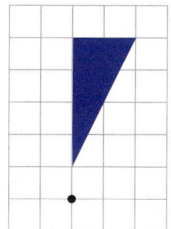

a) 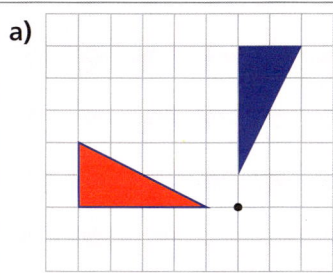	Put a piece of tracing paper over the diagram and draw the triangle. Hold the paper down using your pen or pencil point and turn the paper through 90° (a quarter turn).	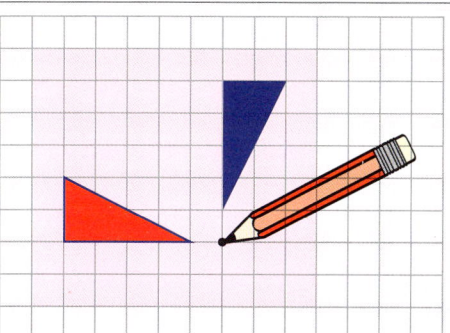
b) 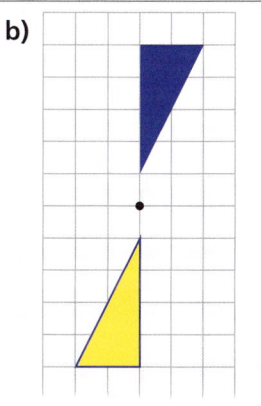	Use the tracing paper and pencil again but this time turn the paper through 180° (a half turn).	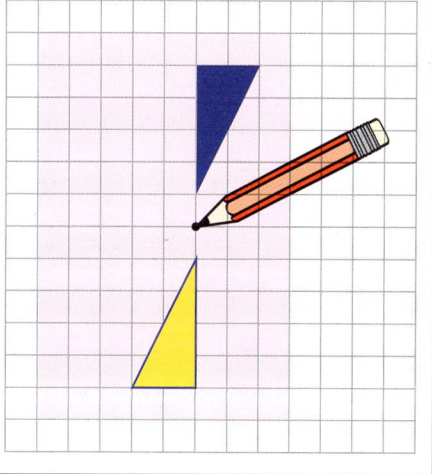

Worked example 4

Translate (move) the shape shown 3 squares to the right and 2 squares down.

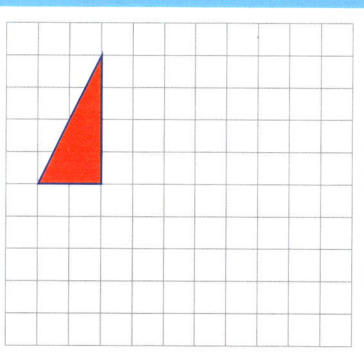

Chapter 32: Transformations   **287**

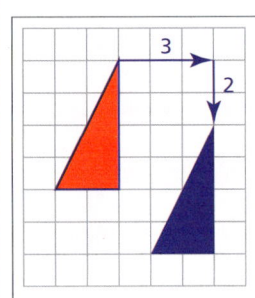

To translate the shape, move each of its vertices (corners) by the stated amount and then join the shape up. Two of these moves are shown in the diagram.

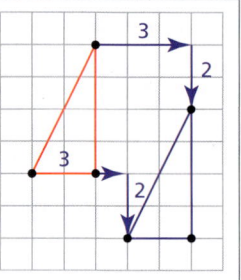

Key term
....

Two shapes are **congruent** if they are identical in both shape and size. The shapes you get by reflecting, rotating or translating a shape are congruent to the original shape.

Exercise 1

1 Reflect the shape in the mirror line which is shown by the dotted line.

a)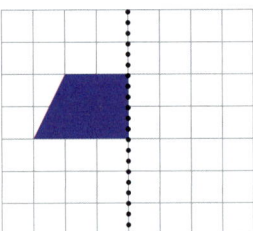

b)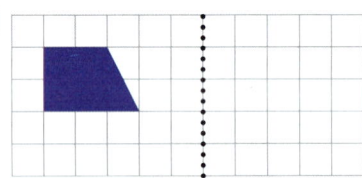

c)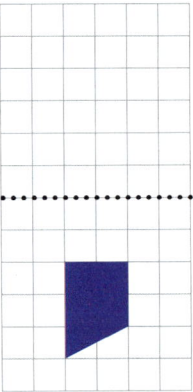

d)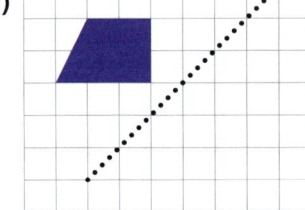

2 Rotate the shape anticlockwise about the dot by the angle shown.

a) 90°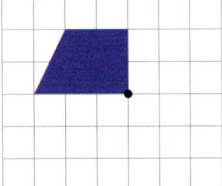

b) 180°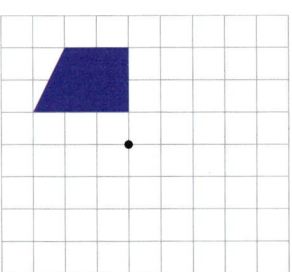

c) 270° 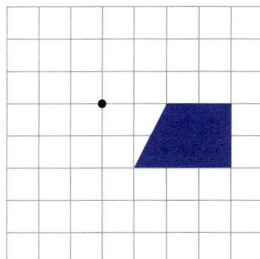   d) 90°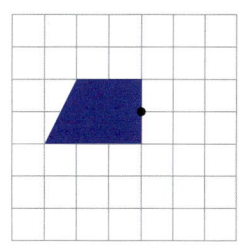

3 Draw shapes B, C and D if:

a) shape B is shape A translated 4 squares to the left

b) shape C is shape A translated 3 squares down

c) shape D is shape A translated 3 squares to the right and 2 squares down.

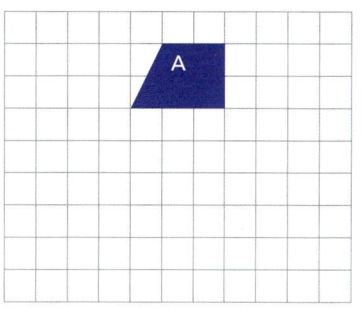

4 Which of these shapes is the odd one out? Explain your answer.

A: 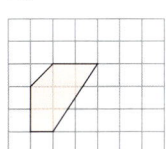   B: 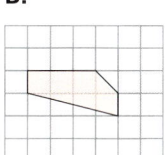   C: 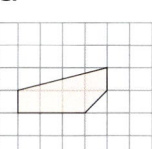   D: 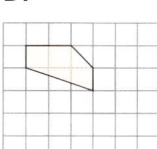   E: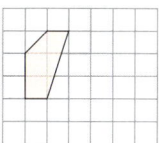

5 In each of these sets of shapes, which one is not congruent to the others? Explain your answer.

a) 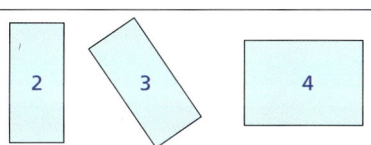   b)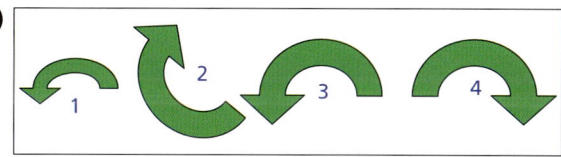

c) 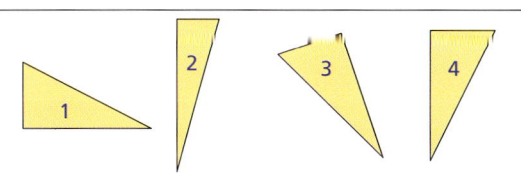   d)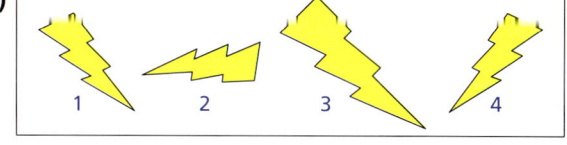

6 Here is a letter F shape.

Which of these shapes could be a reflection of this shape?

A: B: C:

7 Jadan draws a triangle and calls it A. He translates triangle A by 5 squares to the left and 4 squares up to get triangle B. He then translates triangle B by 3 squares to the right and 2 squares down to get triangle C. Mario says that you can get from triangle A to triangle C by moving A by 2 squares to the left and 2 squares up.

a) Is Mario correct?

b) How did Mario work this out without drawing any of the triangles?

Chapter 32: Transformations

End of chapter reflection

You should know that ...	You should be able to ...	Such as ...
Reflection is the process of mirroring or flipping a shape in a mirror line.	Reflect a shape in a drawn mirror line.	Reflect shape O in the line shown.
Rotation is the process of turning a shape around a **centre** point by a specified **angle** and **direction**.	Rotate a shape around a marked centre by a given angle and direction.	Rotate shape O 90° clockwise about the point shown.
Translation is the process of moving a shape horizontally and vertically a specified number of squares.	Translate a shape a given number of units horizontally and vertically.	Translate shape O 3 squares left and 2 squares down.
Congruent shapes have the same shape and size; they are produced by reflecting and/or rotating and/or translating the original shape.	Say whether shapes are congruent or not.	Which of these shapes are congruent? Explain your answer.

Unit 3C: Handling data and geometry

Unit 3C • Chapter 33

Geometrical reasoning and 3D shapes

You will learn how to:
- Recognise and describe common solids and some of their properties, for example, the number of faces, edges and vertices.
- Solve simple geometrical problems by using side and angle properties to identify equal lengths or calculate unknown angles, and explain reasoning.

Starting point

Do you remember …?

- the names and properties of two dimensional (2D) shapes such as isosceles triangles, parallelograms and regular pentagons?
- the names of common three dimensional (3D) shapes such as pyramids and cuboids?
- what faces, edges and vertices are?
- how to estimate the size of acute, obtuse and reflex angles?
- the rules about angles around a point, angles on a straight line, angles in a triangle, angles in a quadrilateral and vertically opposite angles?
- the marks you use to show equal lengths and parallel sides?

This will be helpful when …

you learn more about classifying shapes, producing models of 3D shapes and finding missing angles in parallel lines and larger polygons.

Hook

Here are some 3D shapes that you have met before:

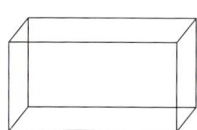 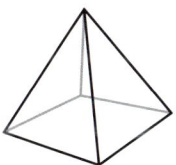 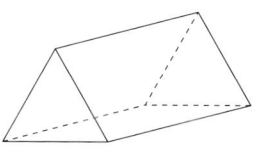

For each shape:

a) Count and record the number of faces (F), edges (E) and vertices (V).

b) Calculate the sum of the vertices and the faces (V + F).

You could copy and complete this table to help you:

Shape name	Number of faces, F	Number of edges, E	Number of vertices, V	V + F

- What do you notice about the sum of the vertices and the faces (V + F) compared to the number of edges (E)?
- Is this true for other 3D shapes? Investigate.

3D shapes

Key terms

3D shapes have **faces**, **edges** and **vertices**.

A surface can be flat or curved but a face is always flat with straight lines as sides and is usually part of a polygon. A sphere has a curved surface. A cube has 6 square faces.

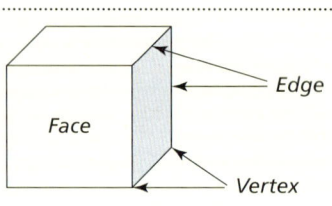

A **prism** is a 3D shape with the same **cross-section** all the way along its length.

We name a prism using the name of the shape on its cross-section. For example, triangular prism or octagonal prism.

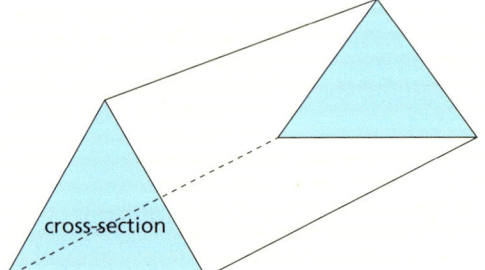 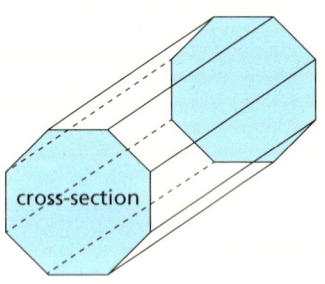

A **pyramid** is another special type of 3D shape.

Pyramids can have different shaped bases. The other faces of a pyramid are all triangles which meet at a single vertex.

For example, here is a pyramid with a base that is a hexagon.

We name a pyramid using the name of the shape on its base. For example, this is a hexagonal pyramid.

A pyramid with a triangle for a base is called a **tetrahedron**, which means four-faced shape, but you could call it a triangular pyramid.

Here are some 3D shapes that have curved surfaces.

| sphere | cone | cylinder | hemisphere |

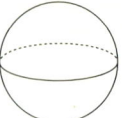 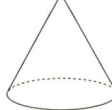  

Did you know?

Words such as semicircle and hemisphere which start with 'hemi', 'semi' or 'demi' usually refer to half of something. Which languages do you think these words come from? Check your answer online or in a dictionary.

Worked example 1

a) Name these solids.

i) 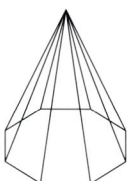   ii)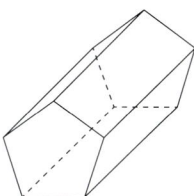

b) Describe the faces of a triangular prism.

c) State the number of vertices, edges and faces on a triangular prism.

a) i) This shape has an octagonal base. All of the other faces are triangles which meet at a single vertex. This is an octagonal pyramid. ii) This shape has a constant cross-section of a pentagon. So, this is a pentagonal prism.	✓ all faces are triangles except the base and these meet at a vertex → pyramid ✓ base is a octagon → octagonal pyramid ✓ constant cross-section connected by rectangular faces → prism ✓ cross-section is a pentagon → pentagonal prism
b) You need to start by sketching a triangular prism. Now you can identify the different faces.	A triangular prism has 5 faces; 2 triangular faces and 3 rectangular faces. 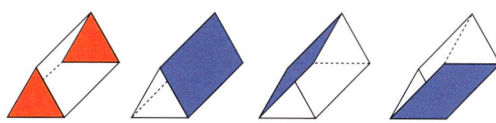
c) Look at your sketch of a triangular prism. Vertices: You can count the vertices shown by the red dots. There are 6 vertices. Edges: You can count the edges on the sketch of the triangular prism. There are 9 edges. Faces: You can count the faces on the sketch of the triangular prism. There are 5 faces.	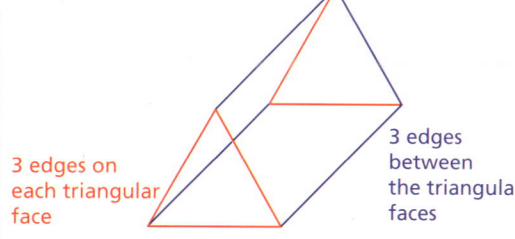 There are 6 vertices. 3 edges on each triangular face 3 edges between the triangular faces 9 edges in total. There are 5 faces; 2 triangular faces and 3 rectangular faces. 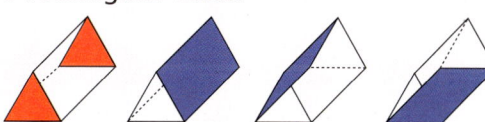

Chapter 33: Geometrical reasoning and 3D shapes

Exercise 1

1 Name each of these 3D shapes.

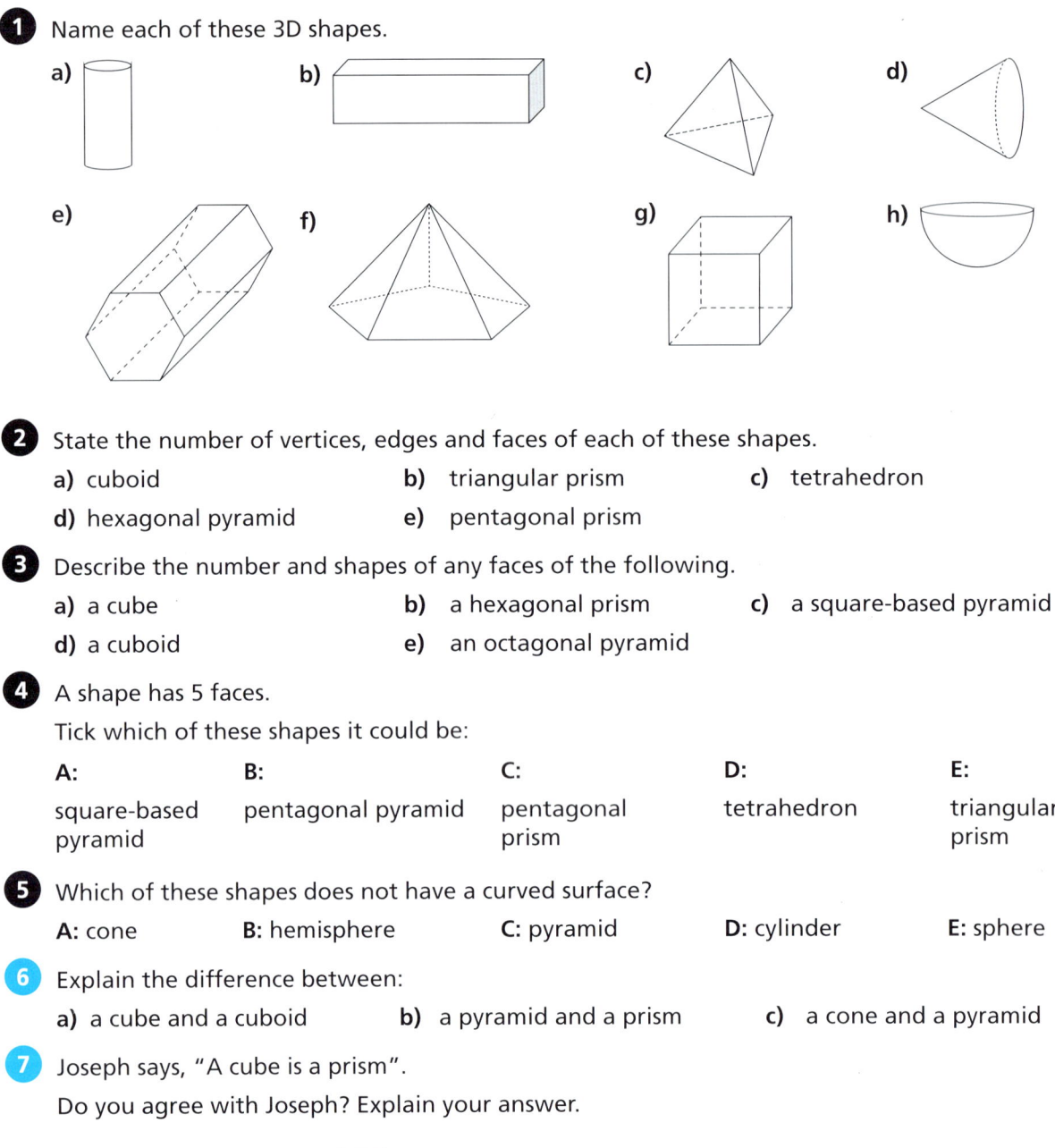

2 State the number of vertices, edges and faces of each of these shapes.
   a) cuboid
   b) triangular prism
   c) tetrahedron
   d) hexagonal pyramid
   e) pentagonal prism

3 Describe the number and shapes of any faces of the following.
   a) a cube
   b) a hexagonal prism
   c) a square-based pyramid
   d) a cuboid
   e) an octagonal pyramid

4 A shape has 5 faces.
   Tick which of these shapes it could be:

   A: square-based pyramid
   B: pentagonal pyramid
   C: pentagonal prism
   D: tetrahedron
   E: triangular prism

5 Which of these shapes does not have a curved surface?
   A: cone   B: hemisphere   C: pyramid   D: cylinder   E: sphere

6 Explain the difference between:
   a) a cube and a cuboid
   b) a pyramid and a prism
   c) a cone and a pyramid

7 Joseph says, "A cube is a prism".
   Do you agree with Joseph? Explain your answer.

Geometrical reasoning

Key facts

Remember:
- Angles in a triangle add up to 180°.
- Angles in a quadrilateral add up to 360°.
- An isosceles triangle has two equal angles and two equal length sides.
- Angles on a straight line add up to 180°.
- Angles around a point add up to 360°.
- Vertically opposite angles are equal.

Worked example 2

The diagram shows a parallelogram ABCD and a triangle CED.

Find:

a) the length of AB

b) ∠ADC

c) ∠DAB

Give reasons for your answers.

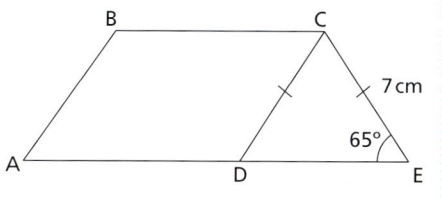

a) Triangle CDE is isosceles, so CD = CE = 7 cm	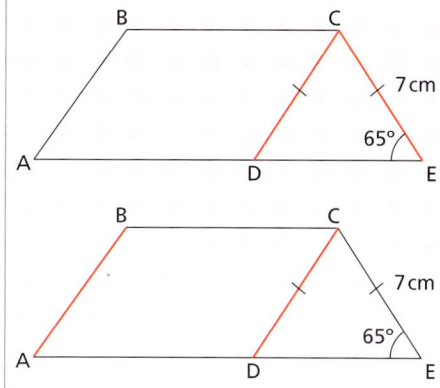
Since ABCD is a parallelogram and CD and BA are opposite sides, CD = AB = 7 cm	
b) Mark the angle you want to find, ∠ADC, on the diagram. Since triangle CDE is isosceles, ∠CDE = ∠CED = 65° ∠ADC lies on a straight line with ∠CDE. You know that angles on a straight line add up to 180° so, ∠ADC = 180° − ∠CDE = 180° − 65° = 115°	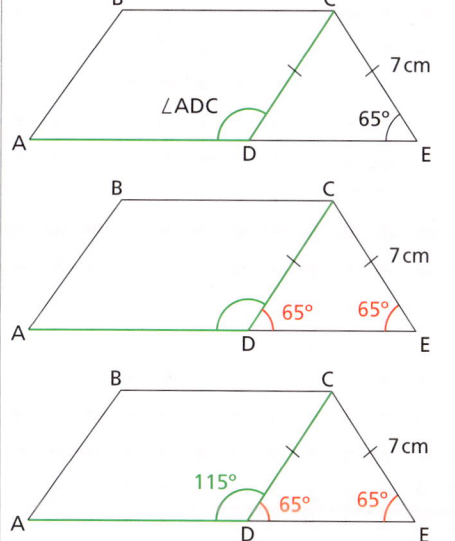
c) Mark ∠DAB on the diagram. ∠DAB is the angle formed by joining vertex D to vertex A to vertex B. ABCD is a parallelogram, so opposite angles are equal. So, ∠ABC = 115° And ∠DAB = ∠BCD A parallelogram is a quadrilateral so its angles sum to 360°.	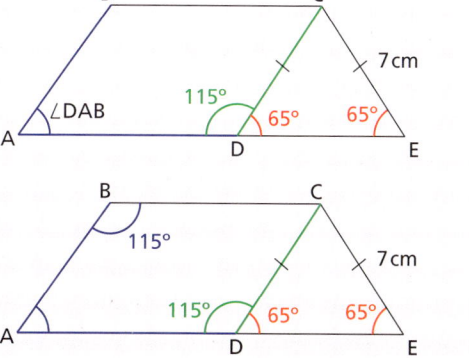

Chapter 33: Geometrical reasoning and 3D shapes   **295**

So

∠ABC + ∠BCD + ∠ADC + ∠DAB = 360°

which means that

∠DAB + ∠BCD
= 360° − 115° − 115°
= 130°

To find ∠DAB you can divide by 2 because ∠DAB and ∠BCD are equal.

∠DAB = $\frac{130°}{2}$ = 65°

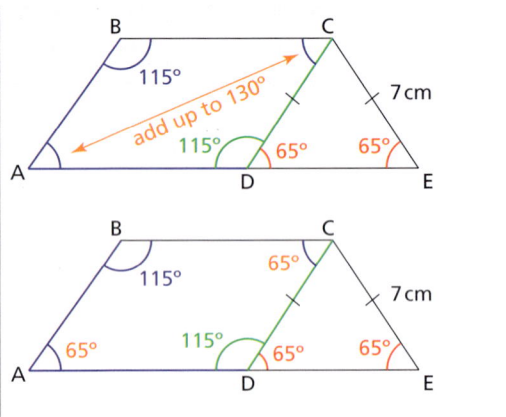

Exercise 2

1. Find the missing angles and lengths shown in each of these diagrams. Give reasons for your answers.

   a)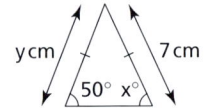

   b)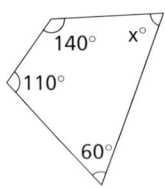

   c)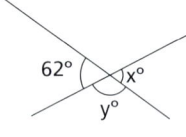

   d)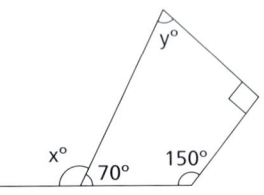

2. Michael is trying to find the size of angle *x*.

   He says, "The triangle is isosceles so 180° − 58° − 58° = 64°. Therefore, x° = 360° − 64° = 296°."

   Michael is wrong. Explain the error that Michael has made and correct his solution.

   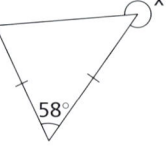

3. Which is the odd one out? Explain your answer.

   A: 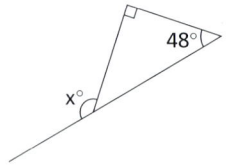   B: 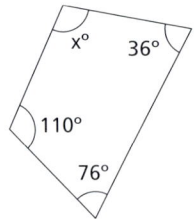   C: 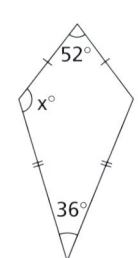   D: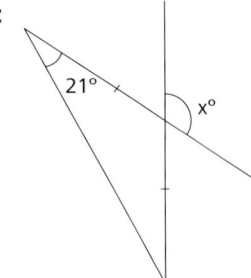

Unit 3C: Handling data and geometry

4. A rhombus has one angle of 126°. Find the sizes of the other three angles.

5. Find the missing angles and lengths marked with letters in each of these diagrams. Give reasons for your answers.

   a)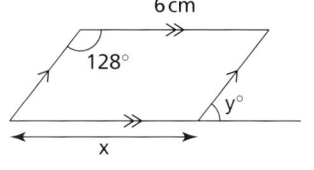
   b)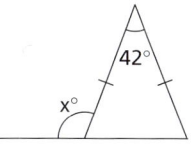
   c)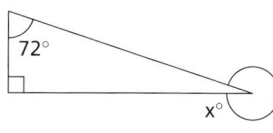
   d)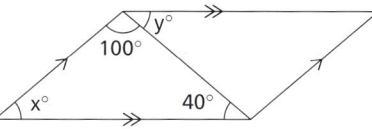
   e)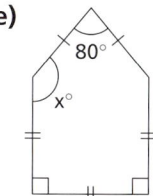

6. The shaded shapes in the diagram shown are an equilateral triangle and a square.

   Calculate angles *p* and *q*. Give reasons for your answer.

   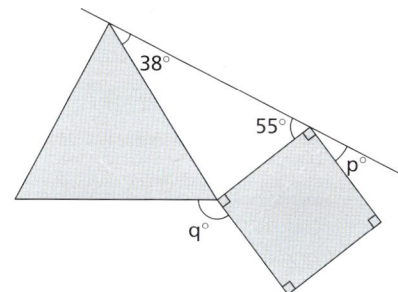

7. **Vocabulary feature question**

   Complete the sentences with the words in the box.

faces	section	edge	opposite
parallel	four	angles	tetrahedron
vertices	rhombus	isosceles	prism

   a) A line which joins two .... of a 3D shape is called an .... sides of a .... are .... and all its sides are the same length
   b) A .... is a shape with a constant cross-............... .
   c) A triangular pyramid is usually called a ...., it has .... faces.
   d) An .... triangle has two equal ....

   Chapter 33: Geometrical reasoning and 3D shapes   297

End of chapter reflection

You should know ...	You should be able to ...	Such as ...
• the names of some common solids. • what is meant by face, edge and vertex.	Name common 3D shapes. State the number of faces, vertices and edges of a 3D shape. Describe the faces of a 3D shape.	a) Name these 3D shapes: b) State the number of faces, vertices and edges of a pentagonal prism. c) Describe the faces of a square-based pyramid.
You can use geometrical rules to find missing sides or missing angles.	Calculate a missing angle in a diagram. Find the length of a missing side in a diagram, giving reasons for your answer.	ABC is an isosceles triangle with AB = AC. Find the value of angle x.

Unit 3C • Chapter 34

Construction

You will learn how to:
- Use a ruler, set square and protractor to:
  - measure and draw straight lines to the nearest millimetre, measure and draw acute, obtuse and reflex angles to the nearest degree
  - draw parallel and perpendicular lines, construct a triangle given two sides and the included angle (SAS) or two angles and the included side (ASA)
  - construct squares and rectangles and regular polygons, given a side and the internal angle.

Starting point

Do you remember…?

- how to use a ruler to measure and draw lines to the nearest centimetre and millimetre?
- how to use a protractor to measure an angle?
- how to recognise parallel and perpendicular lines?

This will also be helpful when…

you learn to solve problems about loci and bearings.

Hook

Seed of life

The seed of life is a pattern that can be created using a pair of compasses. This diagram shows a seed of life pattern.

> **Did you know?**
>
> The seed of life pattern has been found in the Temple of Osiris at Abydos, Egypt, and features in Italian art from the 13th century.

Construct a seed of life design.

- Open your pair of compasses to a size that you want to use for your diagram. You will need to keep them open to the same size for the whole drawing process.
- Use your pair of compasses to draw a circle.
- Mark a point on the circumference (outside edge) of your circle.
- Starting with the point of your compasses on the mark you have made, draw a circle.
- Move the point of your compasses to one of the points where your new circle crosses your original circle and draw another circle. Repeat this until you have gone all the way around the circumference of your circle.

You can find videos of this construction on the Internet.

There are other constructions that you might like to investigate. Try searching for Curves of Pursuit on the Internet.

Chapter 34: Construction

Measuring and constructing lines and angles

Key terms

Measure means to use equipment to find an accurate value for a feature of an object.

Construct means to draw accurately. You usually need to use equipment such as rulers and protractors to produce accurate drawings like this to ensure that you have accurate lengths and angles.

When an accurate drawing is not needed, you may be instructed to produce a **sketch**. A sketch is a rough drawing that is not to scale or accurate.

A **reflex** angle is one that is greater than 180°.

A **protractor** is a piece of equipment for measuring angles. It is marked in degrees from 0° to 180° in each direction.

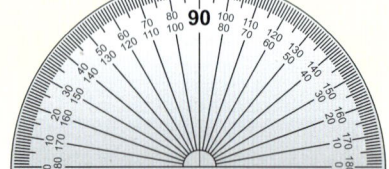

Worked example 1

a) **Measure**:
   i) the length of this line

   ii) the size of this angle (reflex)

   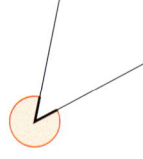

b) **Construct**:
   i) a line of length 78 mm
   ii) an angle of 125°

a) i) You need to line the ruler up alongside the line, with the 0 mark positioned at the very start of the line. You now read off the length of the line: in this case it is 2 marks past the 5, so the length of the line is 5.2 cm or 52 mm.	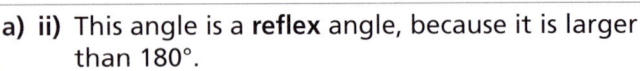
a) ii) This angle is a **reflex** angle, because it is larger than 180°. A **protractor** can only measure up to 180°. Therefore, measure the other (acute) part of the angle and use this to work out the angle you want.	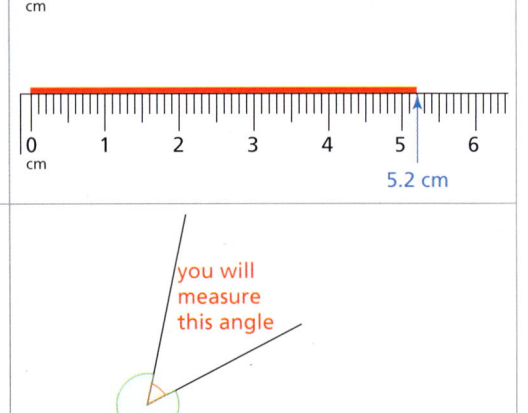

First, align the centre of the protractor at the centre of the angle, with a zero line lying along one line of the angle.

> **Tip**
> Make sure that you line up your protractor correctly and carefully or the angles that you measure will be inaccurate.

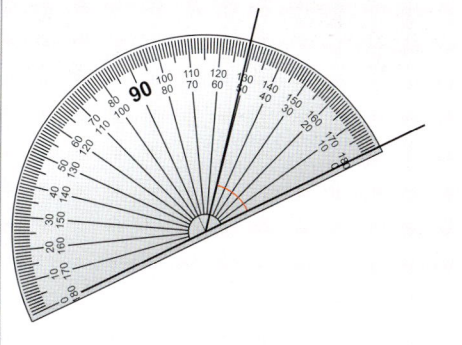

Reading from 0° round to the angle, you can see that this angle measures 51°.

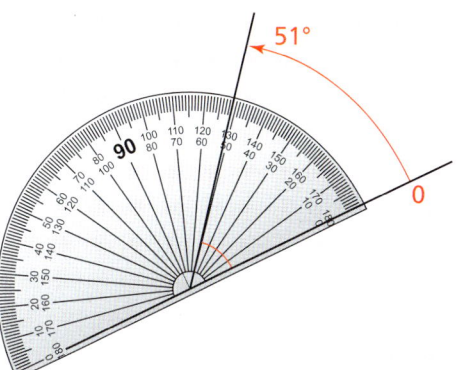

The reflex angle, which is a full turn less this red angle, measures 309°.

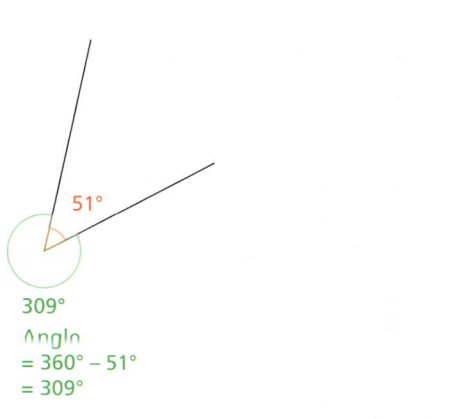

Angle
= 360° − 51°
= 309°

b) i) To draw a line of 78 mm, you need to position your ruler on the page.

You start drawing at 0 and continue until 8 marks past the 7 cm point.

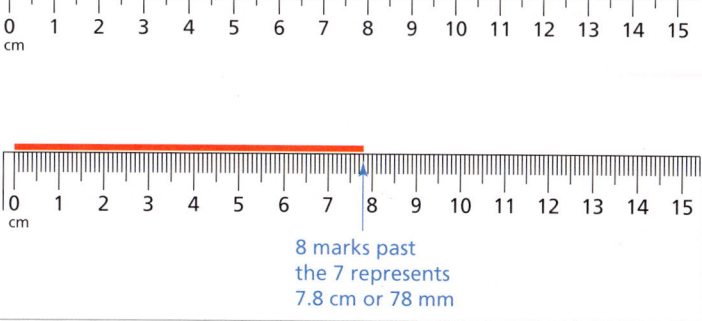

8 marks past the 7 represents 7.8 cm or 78 mm

Chapter 34: Construction   **301**

b) ii) To draw an angle of 125°, first draw a line on the page.

Then position the protractor so that that its centre is directly over one end of the line and the 0° line sits directly over the line you have drawn.

Now, reading round from 0° (on the inside this time) draw a mark at 125°.

Remove the protractor and connect the centre (end of the original line) to the mark you just made.

You now have an angle of 125° – you just need to label it.

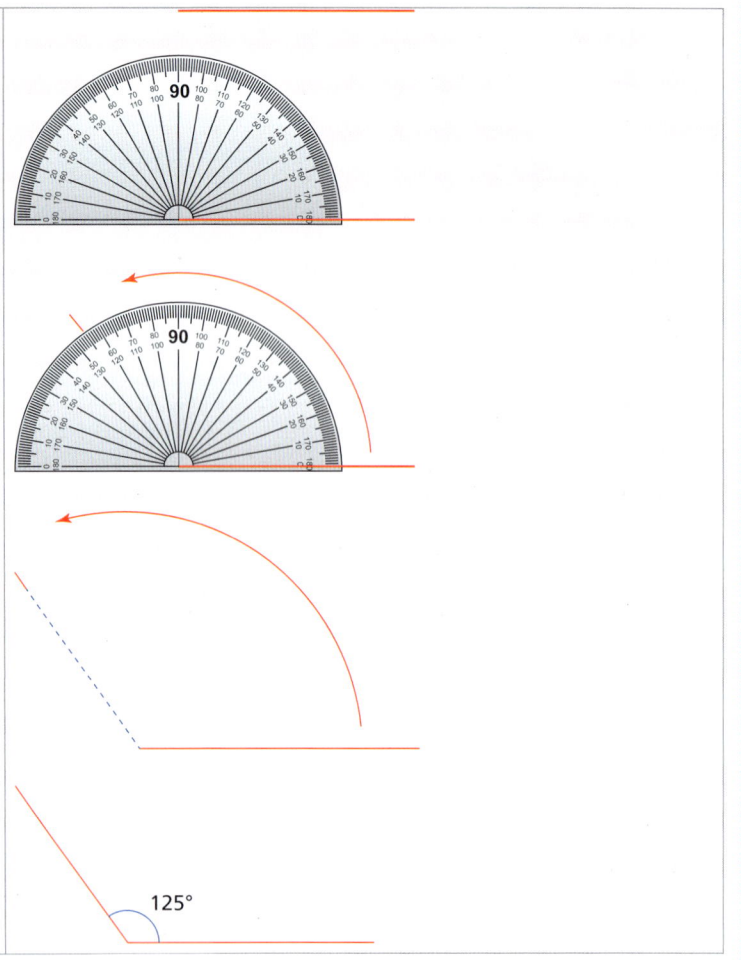

Exercise 1

1 Measure these lines to the nearest millimetre:

a) —————— b) \ c) \

2 Draw lines of length:

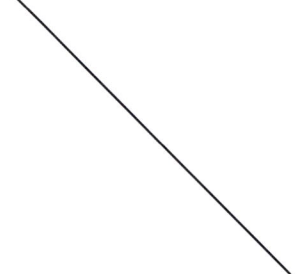

a) 5 cm   b) 5.9 cm   c) 74 mm   d) 123 mm

302   Unit 3C: Handling data and geometry

3 Measure these angles to the nearest degree:

a)

> **Tip**
> Check your answers are reasonable. For example, if the angle is acute then your answer should be less than 90°.

b)

c)

d)

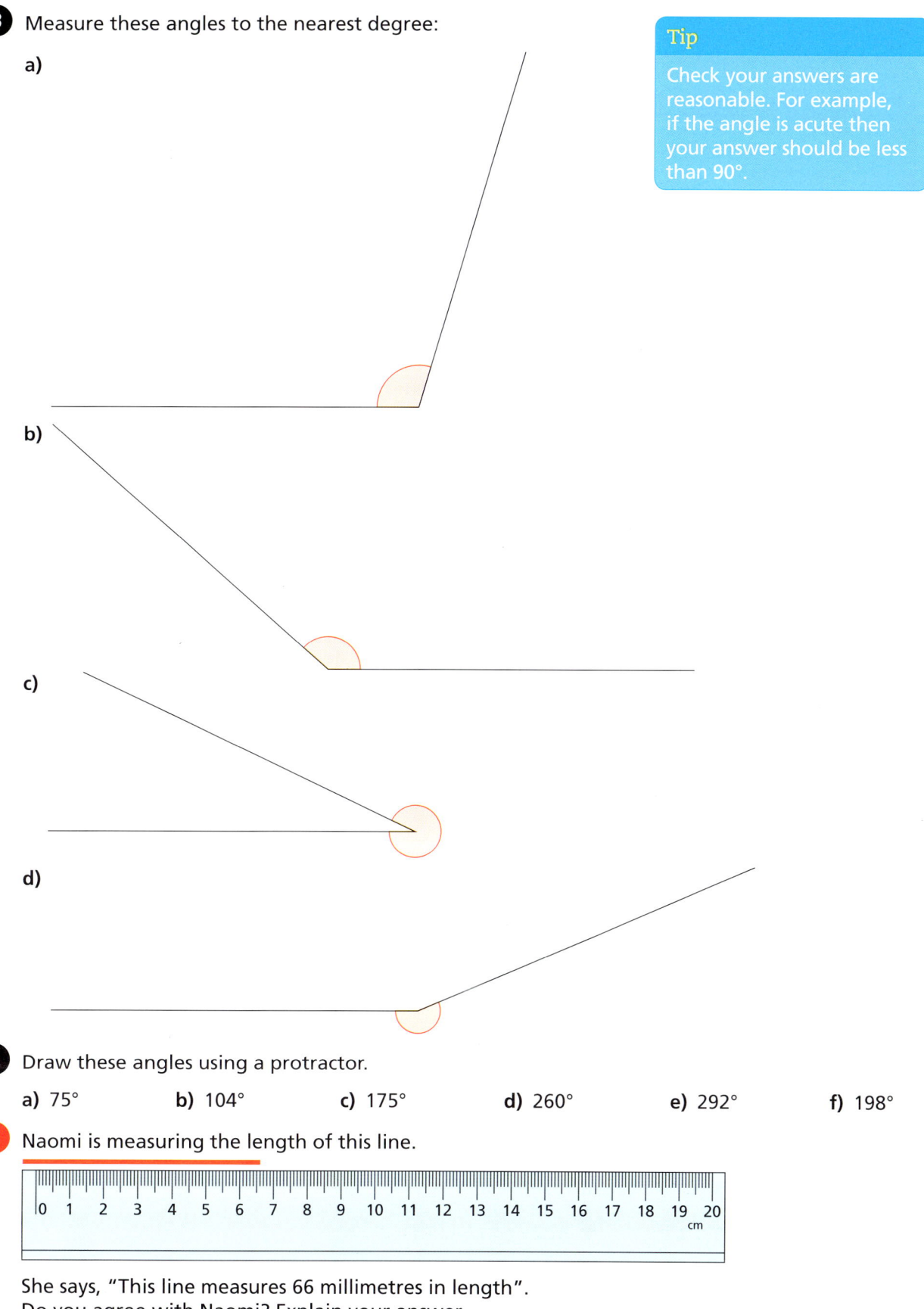

4 Draw these angles using a protractor.

a) 75°   b) 104°   c) 175°   d) 260°   e) 292°   f) 198°

5 Naomi is measuring the length of this line.

She says, "This line measures 66 millimetres in length".
Do you agree with Naomi? Explain your answer.

6 Max is measuring the size of this angle.

He says, "This angle measures 145°".

Max is wrong. Explain the error that he has made and correct his answer.

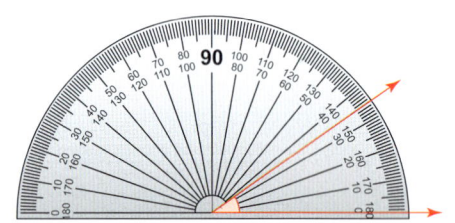

7 Here is an angle:

Juanita measures this angle using a protractor.

Which of these angles are definitely incorrect?

Explain your answer.

A: 49°   B: 131°   C: 229°

8 There are four angles that meet to form a straight line.

The second angle is double the size of the first angle.

The third angle is three times the size of the first angle.

The fourth angle is four times the size of the first angle.

Draw these four angles.

9 When measuring angles you could estimate the size of the angle first so that you can check your answer is reasonable. There are lots of games based on estimating angles available online. Search for angle estimation games on the Internet and try some of these games.

Construction of parallel and perpendicular lines and triangles

Worked example 2

Use a ruler and set square to construct:

a) a pair of perpendicular lines
b) a pair of parallel lines 4 cm apart

a) Begin by drawing a base line.

Put your set square on the base line as shown. The set square makes a 90° angle.

> **Tip**
>
> Your 90° angle does not have to be at the end of the base line – you could draw a perpendicular line part way along the base line.

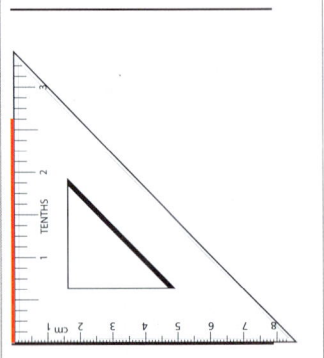

b) Begin by drawing a line. This will be one of your parallel lines.

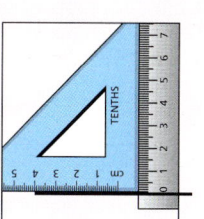

Put your set square on the line you have drawn.

Place your ruler against the set square with the 0 mark on the line you have drawn.

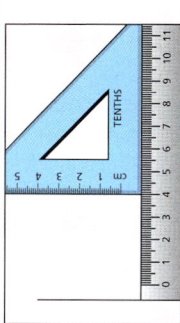

Hold your ruler still and slide the set square up the ruler to the 4 cm mark.

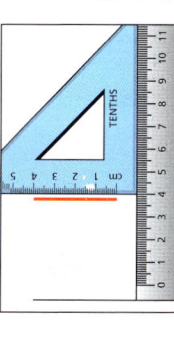

Draw along the base of the set square.

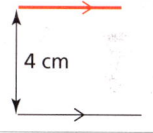

4 cm

> **Did you know?**
>
> Set squares are not only used to find 90° angles.
> Set squares are used by architects and engineers to create technical drawings.

Worked example 3

Construct:

a) this triangle

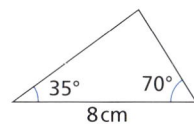

b) this triangle

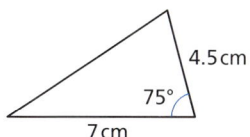

Chapter 34: Construction   **305**

a) Begin by drawing an 8 cm line as the base of the triangle using a ruler.

Now construct a 35° angle at the left-hand end of the line.

Now position the protractor on the right-hand end of the original base line.

Construct a 70° angle at the right-hand end of the base line.

Extend the new line as needed to cross the existing (green) line.

You now have your triangle.

b) Begin by drawing a 7 cm line as the base of the triangle using a ruler.

Position the protractor on the right-hand end of the base line. Align the 0° line so it is exactly over the base line.

Reading round from 0°, make a mark at 75°.

Remove the protractor and connect the right-hand end of the base to the mark you just made. Measure 4.5 along this line.

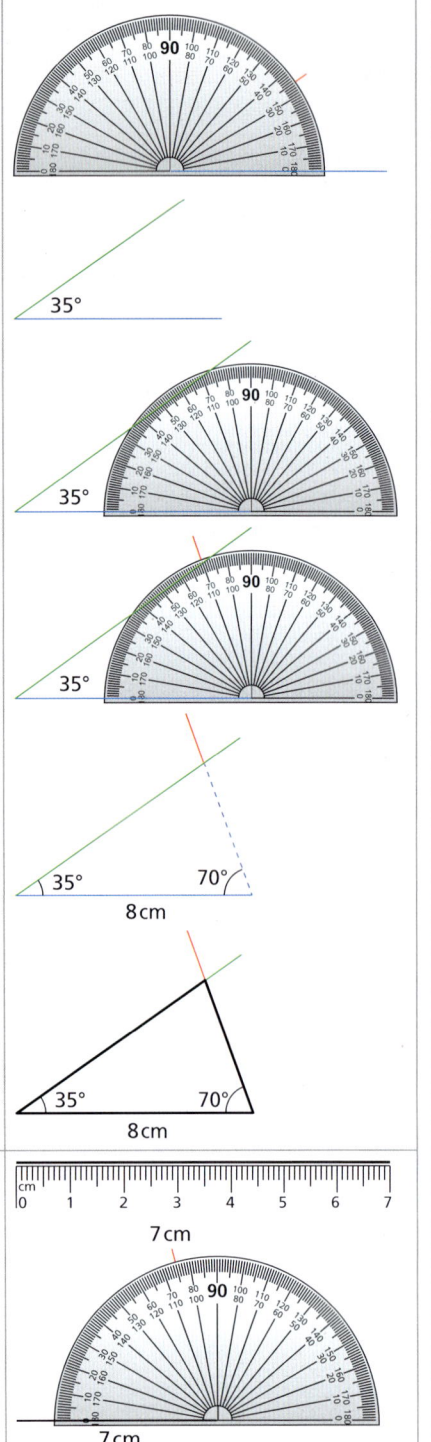

Join the ends of the 7 cm and 4.5 cm lines to make a triangle.

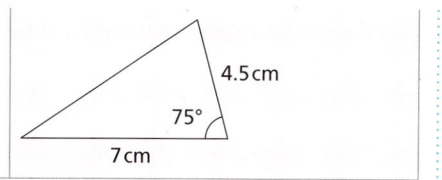

> **Discuss**
> True or False? To construct a triangle, you need to know the three angles.

Exercise 2

1 Using a ruler and a set square, construct:
   a) a pair of perpendicular lines.
   b) a pair of parallel lines 6 cm apart.
   c) a pair of parallel lines 3.5 cm apart.

> **Think about**
> Do lines that are perpendicular have to touch/cross?

2 Use a set square to draw a line that is perpendicular to AB and passes through point C.

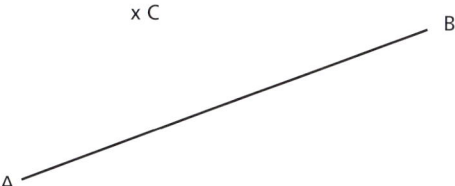

3 Using a ruler and protractor, construct these triangles:

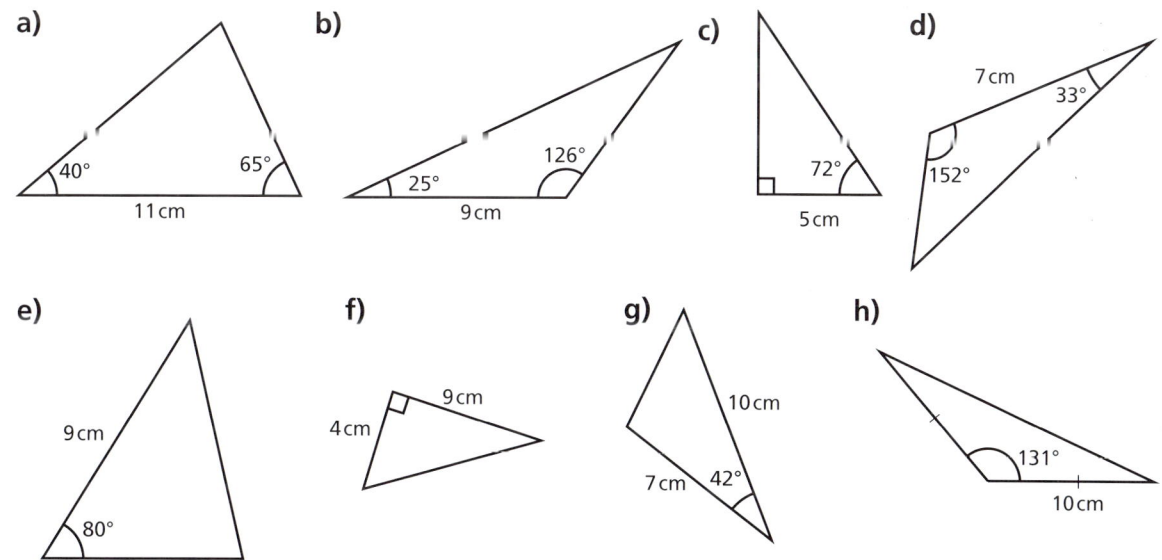

4 In triangle PQR, PQ = 60 mm, angle PQR = 48° and angle RPQ = 61°. Construct an accurate drawing of the triangle PQR.

5 Construct an isosceles triangle with base 4 cm and base angles 35°.

6 Construct an isosceles triangle with the base angles equal to twice the other angle.

Constructing squares, rectangles and simple polygons

Worked example 4

Use a ruler and set square to construct a square of side length 5 cm.

To construct a square you start by drawing the base, in this case using a line of 5 cm.

You now use your set square to produce a line that is perpendicular to the base and of 5 cm length.

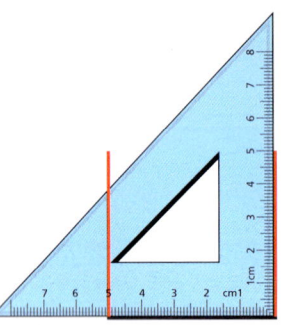

Put the set square at the other end of the base line. Draw another perpendicular line of length 5 cm.

Connect the ends of the vertical lines to complete the square.

> **Tip**
> You can check your square is accurate by measuring each side and checking that the angles are all right angles.

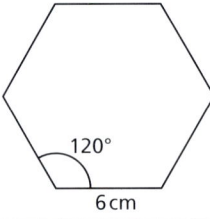

Worked example 5

Use a ruler and protractor to accurately draw the regular hexagon shown.

Use your ruler to draw a 6 cm line.

Position the protractor on the left-hand end of the base line. Align the 0° line so it is exactly over the base line.

Reading round from 0° make a mark at 120°.

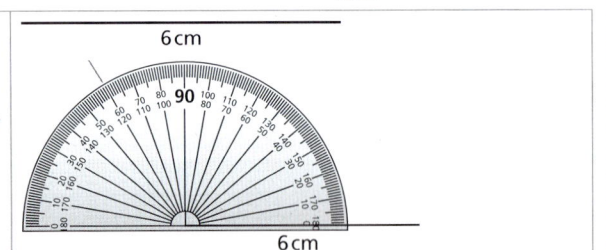

Remove the protractor and connect the left end of the base to the mark you just made. Make the line 6 cm long.

Position the protractor on the end of the new line. Measure a 120° angle.

Remove the protractor and connect the end of the second line to the mark you just made. Make the line 6 cm long.

Repeat the process of measuring angles and drawing lines until you have a hexagon.

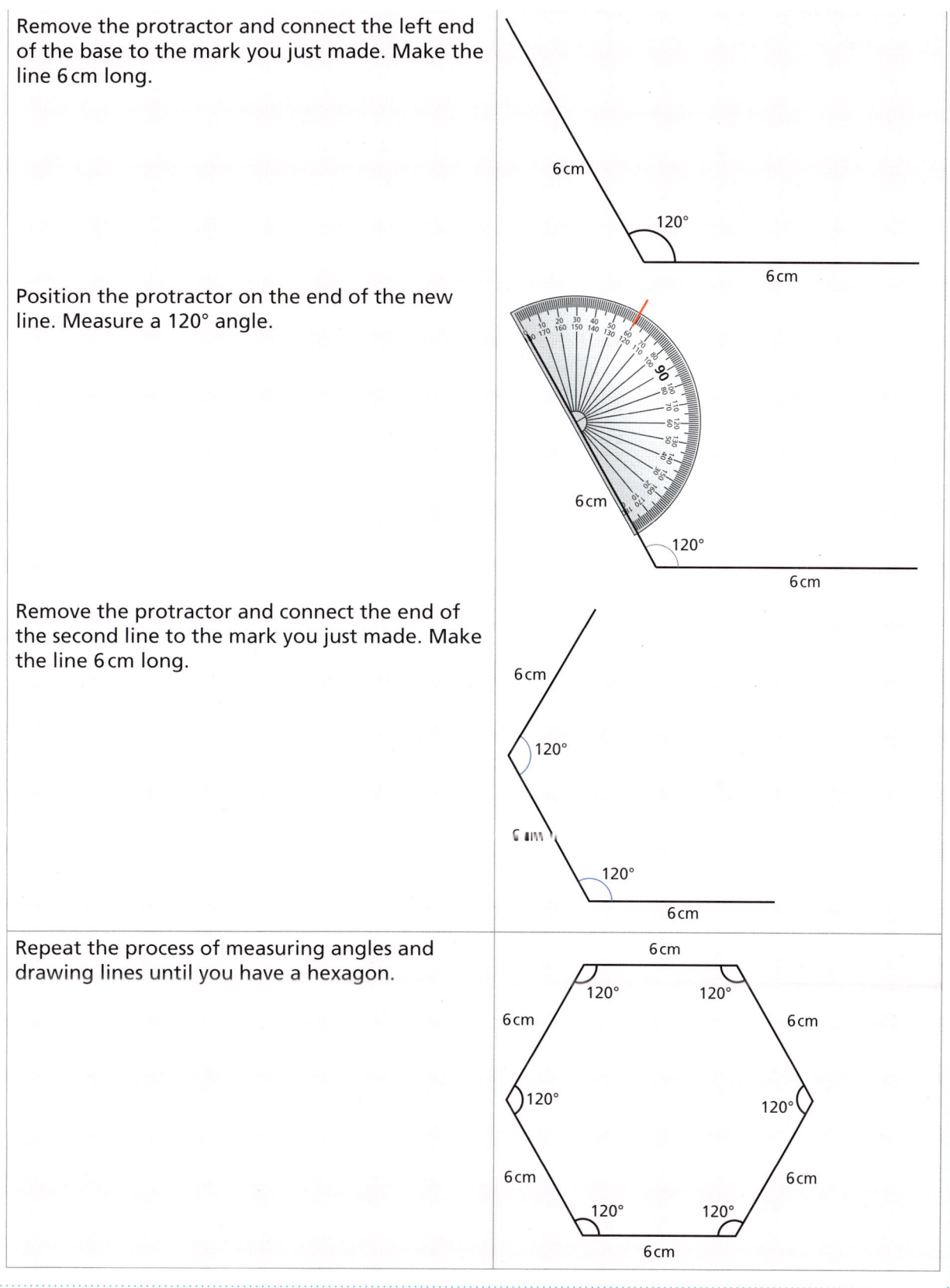

Chapter 34: Construction   **309**

Exercise 3

1 Use a ruler and set square to construct:
   a) a square with side length 7 cm
   b) a square with side length 4.5 cm

2 Use a ruler and set square to construct these rectangles.

a)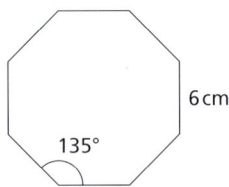
   3 cm / 7 cm

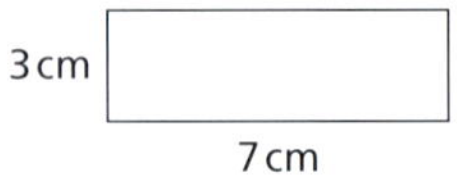

b) 4.5 cm / 1.5 cm

c) 19 mm / 2.5 cm

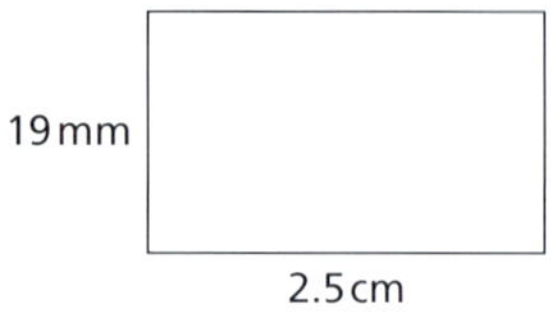

3 Construct a regular hexagon with side length 5 cm.

4 The diagram shows a regular octagon. Draw the octagon accurately.

6 cm, 135°

5 The diagram shows a regular decagon. Draw the decagon accurately.

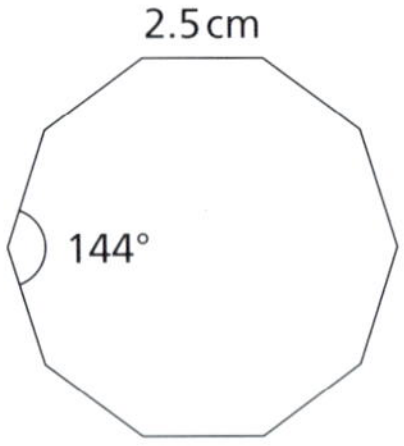

2.5 cm, 144°

6 Construct a regular polygon with a side length of 5 cm and interior angles of 108°.

7 Construct a regular polygon with a side length of 40 mm and interior angles of 140°.

8 Use a ruler and protractor to draw the trapezium below accurately:

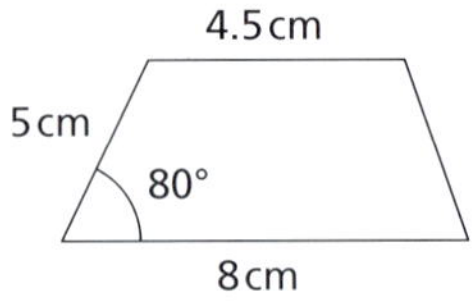

4.5 cm, 5 cm, 80°, 8 cm

> **Tip**
> Remember that a trapezium has a pair of parallel sides.

9 Write a set of instructions to explain how to construct an octagon with side length 5 cm.

10 Vocabulary feature question

Match each of the key terms below to one of the descriptions on the right.
Complete the missing key term and description to produce twelve matching pairs.

Key Term	Description
Measure	A polygon with all sides of equal length and all angles of equal size
Protractor	An angle that is greater than 180°
Regular	Use equipment to find an accurate value for a quantity
Ruler	Two lines (or planes) at right angles
	A piece of equipment for measuring lengths
Perpendicular	Draw a rough diagram, not necessarily accurate
Set Square	An angle that is greater than 90° but less than 180°
Sketch	A piece of equipment for measuring angles
Reflex	An angle that is less than 90°
Acute	
Parallel	Draw accurately using equipment
Obtuse	A piece of equipment for drawing perpendicular and parallel lines

End of chapter reflection

You should know that …	You should be able to …	Such as …
Measure means to find an accurate value for the size of a quantity. **Construct** means to produce an accurate drawing (using equipment).	Measure a line to the nearest mm.	Measure this line _____ Give your answer to the nearest mm.
A **protractor** measures angles from 0° to 180°. A **reflex angle** can be measured by finding the size of the smaller angle and subtracting from 360°.	Measure an angle to the nearest degree.	a) Measure this reflex angle.
	Draw an angle to within one degree.	b) Draw an angle of size 57°. c) Draw an angle of size 143°.
	Construct a triangle given a sketch of it or information about its sides and angles.	Triangle *ABC* has side *AB* = 4.5 cm, angle *ABC* = 65° and side *BC* = 3.5 cm Make an accurate drawing of triangle *ABC*.

Chapter 34: Construction 311

You should know that …	You should be able to …	Such as …
A **set square** is used to produce parallel and perpendicular lines.	Construct sets of parallel and perpendicular lines using a set square.	a) Draw a pair of perpendicular lines. b) Draw a pair of parallel lines 5 cm apart.
A **ruler** and a **set square** can be used to construct a rectangle.	Construct a rectangle.	Construct a rectangle with length 6 cm and width 4.7 cm.
A **ruler** and a **protractor** can be used to construct a regular polygon.	Construct a regular polygon, given a side length and the interior angle.	Construct a regular polygon with side length 4.5 cm and interior angle 120°.